American History
a visual encyclopedia

THE BOSTON TEA PARTY was celebrated by the Patriots as a brilliant protest. Patriot leader John Adams called it "the grandest event … since the controversy with the British began!"

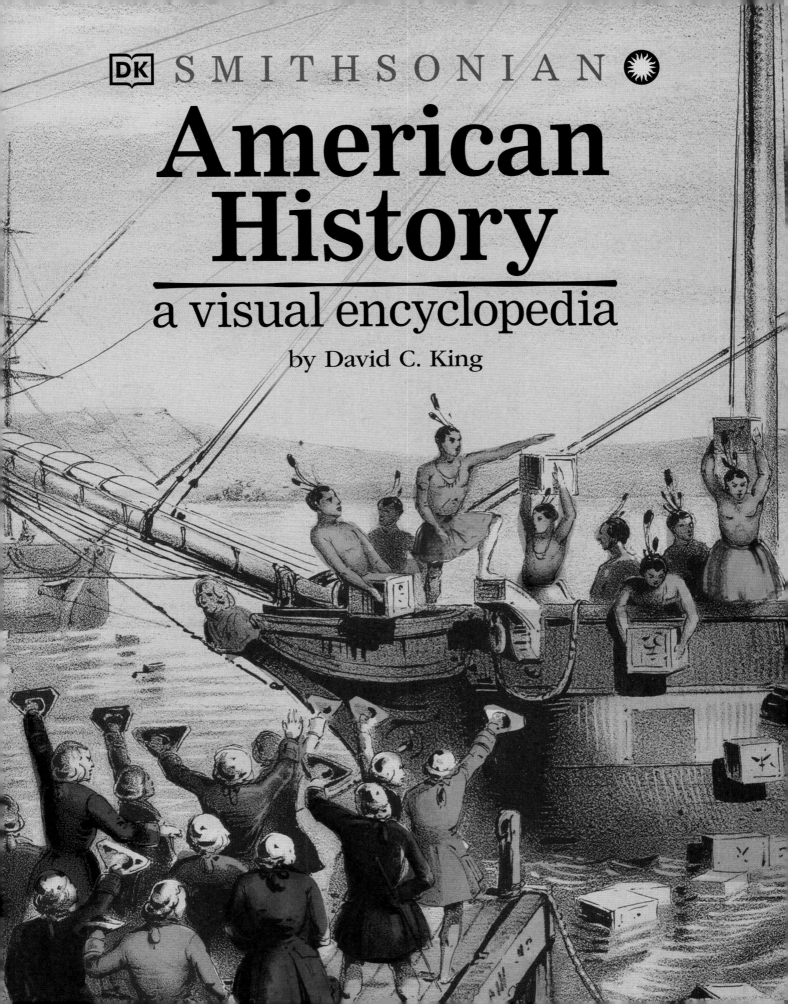

DK SMITHSONIAN

American History

a visual encyclopedia

by David C. King

THIRD EDITION

DK Delhi
Senior Editor Shatarupa Chaudhuri
Senior Art Editor Pallavi Narain
Assistant Editor Bipasha Roy
Assistant Art Editor Sifat Fatima
Picture Researcher Rituraj Singh
Jacket Designer Tanya Mehrotra
Jackets Editorial Coordinator Priyanka Sharma
DTP Designers Jaypal Singh Chauhan, Nityanand Kumar, Rakesh Kumar
Managing Editor Kingshuk Ghoshal
Managing Art Editor Govind Mittal

DK London
Project Editor Sarah MacLeod
Art Editor Kit Lane
US Editor Megan Douglass
US Executive Editor Lori Cates Hand
Jacket Designer Surabhi Wadhwa-Gandhi
Jacket Editor Emma Dawson
Jacket Design Development Manager Sophia MTT
Producer, Pre-production Jacqueline Street-Elkayam
Senior Producer Mary Slater
Managing Editor Francesca Baines
Managing Art Editor Philip Letsu
Publisher Andrew Macintyre
Associate Publishing Director Liz Wheeler
Art Director Karen Self
Design Director Phil Ormerod
Publishing Director Jonathan Metcalf
Consultants Philip Baselice, Peter N. Stearns
Additional text for third edition Shannon Reed
Additional text for second edition on pp263–283 Andrew Moran

FIRST EDITION
Managing Editor Beth Sutinis
Senior Art Editors Mandy Earey, Susan St. Louis
Art Editor Megan Clayton
Assistant Editor Madeline Farbman
Publisher Chuck Lang
Creative Director Tina Vaughan
Editorial Director Valerie Buckingham
Photo Editor Amy Pastan
Additional Picture Research Jo Walton
Cartography David Roberts, Simon Mumford, Iorwerth Watkins

For Roundtable Press, Inc.
Directors Julie Merberg, Marsha Melnick
Editors John Glenn, Meredith Wolf Schizer
Production Editor Sara Newberry
Design/Production Steven Rosen
Copyeditor William Meyers

This American Edition, 2019
First American Edition, 2003
Published in the United States by DK Publishing
1450 Broadway, Suite 801, New York, NY 10018

Copyright © 2003, 2014, 2019 Dorling Kindersley Limited
DK, a Division of Penguin Random House LLC
21 22 23 14 13 12 11
012–314194–June/2019

A catalog record for this book is available from the Library of Congress.
ISBN 978-1-4654-8366-9 (Paperback)
ISBN 978-1-4654-8367-6 (ALB)

DK books are available at special discounts when purchased in bulk for sales promotions, premiums, fund-raising, or educational use. For details, contact: DK Publishing Special Markets, 1450 Broadway, Suite 801, New York, NY 10018
SpecialSales@dk.com

Printed and bound in UAE

For the curious
www.dk.com

MIX
Paper from responsible sources
FSC™ C018179

This book was made with Forest Stewardship Council ™ certified paper – one small step in DK's commitment to a sustainable future. For more information go to www.dk.com/our-green-pledge

Smithsonian

Established in 1846, the Smithsonian—the world's largest museum and research complex—includes 19 museums and galleries and the National Zoological Park. The total number of artifacts, works of art, and specimens in the Smithsonian's collection is estimated at 156 million. The Smithsonian is a renowned research center, dedicated to public education; national service; and scholarship in the arts, sciences, and history.

Contents

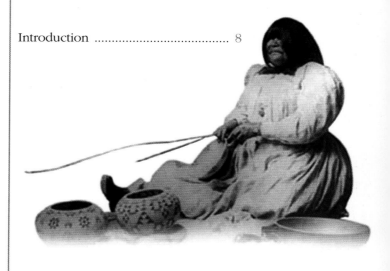

Introduction

BASKETS woven by the women of the tribes of the Far West were some of the most durable and decorative baskets in all of North America.

History is the story of people. *American History: A Visual Encyclopedia* tells the tale of the men and women who have had a part in creating, shaping, or changing the United States of America—from the time before there was a USA, when American Indians first encountered European explorers, to the struggles our leaders face today in keeping a large, dynamic nation secure in changing times.

The parents of today's children may remember their history education as being long on dates, places, and war, and short on good stories and excitement. Those of us lucky enough to have had teachers who engaged their students in the narrative of history grasp that the value of knowing the precise date of an event by heart pales in comparison to understanding why it happened and the impact it had.

Studying the past shows us how ideas evolve from one time to another, how people have solved problems presented to them, how conflict can escalate, and how it is resolved.

In learning about the past, we have a unique opportunity to glimpse what our ancestors experienced and imagine how those experiences have had an effect on how we live our lives now.

Creating a resource that invites this kind of investigation was the object of this illustrated survey of American history. Simply, children should have compelling words and pictures available to them as they undertake the journey of educating themselves about the story of their nation.

Solid silver sheriff's badge c. 1880

EMANUEL LEUTZE'S PAINTING depicting General George Washington leading troops across the frozen Delaware River to attack the British at Trenton is an idealized view of a great moment in American history. Washington is shown standing, which would have been dangerous, since it would have unbalanced the boat. Plus, the painting shows the wrong kind of boat and a flag that had not yet been created.

Since most students won't read this book from start to finish, it became a goal of its creation to make every page inviting, so that a quest to find out the date of the Louisiana Purchase might become an adventure in learning about the flip-flopping fortunes of European nations vying for power in the New World.

A PUBLIC SERVICE POSTER tells citizens about their rights under the Social Security Act, which passed through Congress as part of FDR's New Deal.

This encyclopedia is organized chronologically into chapters that cover commonly understood eras in American history, from the time of the American Indian to the present. Within the chapters, individual two-page spreads discuss specific topics or periods in history, and explain how they are connected. Structuring the book in this way helps the reader link events, draw conclusions, and, we hope, ask more questions.

With an understanding of recurring themes in history, children can apply what they have learned to information they will gather in the future, perhaps about events that will someday be

FLAPPERS was the nickname given to young women of the Jazz Age who lived independent lives.

counted as history. It is in developing analytical skills and learning to think critically that lasting education happens.

The unique look of *American History: A Visual Encyclopedia* presents photography, painting, period commercial art, portraiture, and innovative maps in a way that shows as much as it tells about a subject. The images don't play a bit part to the text's starring role in this book. The information in these pictures is too rich to favor one medium over another, and so the words and images have been considered together to bring this wealth to the page—and to the eye of the reader.

It is a rare thing when a book hearty with educational content—real brain food—such as this one can keep a child's interest. This volume gives parents and educators an opportunity to engage a young mind in the fascinating story of discovery, challenge, democracy, struggle, and prosperity that is told in these pages about the American people and the nation they built.

BUTTONS advertise the 1971 March on Washington protesting the war in Vietnam.

MALCOLM X, shown here speaking to passersby on the streets of New York in 1963, strove to educate the public about injustices done to black people in America.

AMERICAN INDIANS trade furs with English explorer Henry Hudson on board his ship. Indians, as Christopher Columbus mistakenly called the people who lived in the New World, had developed complex, diverse cultures throughout North and South America. These cultures were disrupted by the Europeans' arrival. As explorers arrived to claim land, the two groups grew wary of each other. Some Europeans, such as Hudson, were friendly with the Indians. Many of the better relationships were based on the fur trade.

c. 1000
Leif Eriksson is the first European to set foot in North America

1400s
Portugal and other nations search for new ocean trade routes

Aug. 3, 1492
Columbus sails west from Spain for Asia

Oct. 12, 1492
Columbus lands in West Indies

1493
Line of Demarcation established

1494
Spain and Portugal sign the Treaty of Tordesillas

1519–1521
Hernando Cortés conquers the Aztec empire

1524
Giovanni da Verrazano maps New York Bay, claims land for France; Franciscan friars arrive in the New World

1534–1542
Jacques Cartier explores the Gulf of St. Lawrence and the St. Lawrence River

1532
Francisco Pizarro conquers the Inca empire

| 1000 | 1100 | 1400 | 1500 | 1510 | 1520 | 1530 |

c. 1400
Navajo, Apache, and other native tribes move into the Southwest from the North

1488
Bartholomeu Dias sails around the Cape of Good Hope

1497
Vasco da Gama sails east, around Africa, to India; John Cabot explores the coastline of Newfoundland

1513
Ponce de León claims Florida for Spain

Sept. 6, 1522
Magellan's crew completes voyage around the world

1534
Founding of New France

TWO WORLDS MEET

1000–1607

The first Europeans traveled to North America in about 1000 CE, when Leif Eriksson and his Viking crew discovered a land they called Vinland, after the grapes that grew there. The Vikings eventually abandoned their settlements in eastern Canada and returned to their homes in Greenland. No more Europeans arrived for nearly 500 years. In 1492, Christopher Columbus sailed west from Spain, searching for a new trade route to China and the Spice Islands, where he could buy the spices and silks Europeans desired. Instead of Asia, he landed on the outer edges of the vast landmass of North and South America. Soon, other European explorers headed west in search of glory and riches. Native peoples had lived on these continents for centuries, and the Europeans' arrival completely changed their way of life. Within a century, European countries were planning permanent colonies on North America's Atlantic coast.

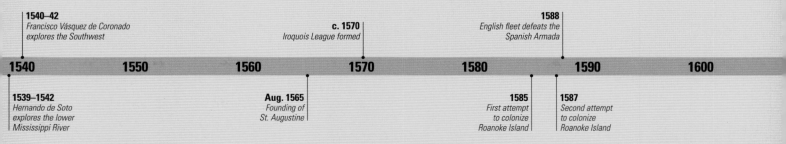

1540–42
Francisco Vásquez de Coronado
explores the Southwest

c. 1570
Iroquois League formed

1588
English fleet defeats the
Spanish Armada

| 1540 | 1550 | 1560 | 1570 | 1580 | 1590 | 1600 |

1539–1542
Hernando de Soto
explores the lower
Mississippi River

Aug. 1565
Founding of
St. Augustine

1585
First attempt
to colonize
Roanoke Island

1587
Second attempt
to colonize
Roanoke Island

The First Americans

At the time of their first contact with Europeans, millions of American Indians—the first inhabitants of North America—lived throughout the continent in hundreds of social groups called tribes. They spoke more than 1,000 different languages and dialects. In each geographical region, American Indians made the most of their environment to survive—and thrive.

1000–1607

Culture Areas

Although each American Indian tribe had its own unique customs and beliefs, the geography of their tribal homelands—whether baking-hot desert, dense forest, grassy plain, or fertile river valley—meant that tribes living near each other shared similar ways of life. This is why anthropologists who study native North Americans have divided the tribes into culture areas, as shown on the map.

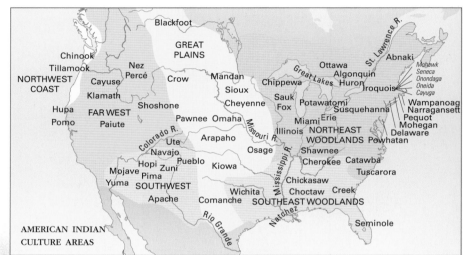

AMERICAN INDIAN CULTURE AREAS

Blackfoot
GREAT PLAINS
Chinook
Tillamook
NORTHWEST COAST
Nez Percé
Cayuse
Klamath
Crow
Mandan
Sioux
Cheyenne
Chippewa
Great Lakes
Ottawa
Algonquin
Huron
St. Lawrence R.
Abnaki
Mohawk
Seneca
Onondaga
Oneida
Cayuga
Iroquois
Hupa
Pomo
FAR WEST
Paiute
Shoshone
Pawnee
Omaha
Colorado R.
Ute
Navajo
Hopi
Zuni
Mojave
Pima
Yuma
SOUTHWEST
Apache
Pueblo
Arapaho
Kiowa
Osage
Missouri R.
Mississippi R.
Comanche
Wichita
Natchez
Sauk
Fox
Potawatomi
Miami
Illinois
Erie
Susquehanna
NORTHEAST WOODLANDS
Shawnee
Cherokee
Chickasaw
Choctaw
SOUTHEAST WOODLANDS
Creek
Catawba
Tuscarora
Wampanoag
Narragansett
Pequot
Mohegan
Delaware
Powhatan
Seminole
Rio Grande

SOME NORTHEASTERN TRIBESPEOPLE lived in longhouses, sturdy, wood-framed structures built for several families. The dense forests in the area provided plenty of wood for houses and stockades.

THE LEAGUE OF THE IROQUOIS

The five tribes of the Iroquois—the Seneca, Cayuga, Mohawk, Oneida, and Onondaga—were frequently at war, battling one another, as well as the Algonquins. According to legend, a Mohawk leader named Hiawatha proposed a treaty of unity among the Iroquois tribes. This union, or league, not only ended the fighting but also helped the Iroquois become powerful and strong, which became especially important in their later dealings with European settlers. Women played an important part in the way the new league was organized—and ruled. A "fireside," made up of a woman and her children, was the smallest tribal unit. Several firesides together made up a clan; all the clans in a tribe made up the nation. Women picked men to represent the clan, and they named the 50 chiefs, or sachems, who made up the ruling council.

Northeast Woodlands

Most natives of this culture area, made up of New England and the lands surrounding the Great Lakes, lived by both hunting and farming. The tribes of this region were split into two groups by their language. The Algonquian-language tribes included the Huron, the Narragansett, and the Powhatan of Virginia. The Iroquois group, a powerful union of tribes based in what is now New York, included the Mohawk, Oneida, and Seneca.

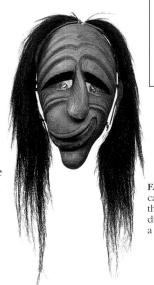

FALSE FACE MASKS like this one were carved from the wood of a living tree; the masks' features were inspired by dreams. The False Face Society was a group of powerful Iroquois healers.

GEORGE CATLIN'S PAINTINGS from the early 1800s captured tribal life before the full impact of European settlement was understood. This painting shows how horses, brought to the New World by Spanish explorers, made it much easier for American Indians to hunt buffalo, a major source of food and leather.

Southeast Woodlands

Most of the tribes who lived around the Gulf of Mexico spoke the Muskogean family of languages. Some tribes—such as the Creek, Choctaw, and Seminole—farmed, but all relied on hunting and the gathering of wild foods. To obtain what they could not grow, kill, or catch, they traded with other tribes, sometimes traveling as far as the Great Lakes region.

A CREEK TRIBAL COUNCIL HOUSE was made of mud walls and a roof of tree trunks with birch bark "shingles." There was only one door and no windows, to ensure that the council meetings were private.

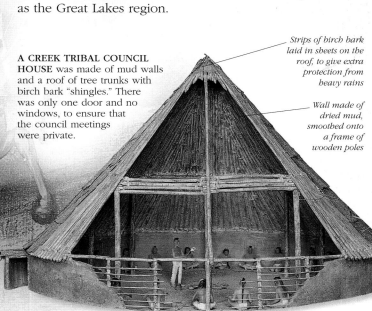

Strips of birch bark laid in sheets on the roof, to give extra protection from heavy rains

Wall made of dried mud, smoothed onto a frame of wooden poles

Small entrance leading into windowless council house

15

Southwest

The rocky mesas and desert plains of the Southwest made a beautiful, but dry, home. Because there were few trees to use for building, the Pueblo tribes who lived there (including the Hopi, Zuni, and Acoma) built villages of stone or of a sun-dried mixture of mud and water called adobe. The kiva—an underground room for special ceremonies—was the center of town life. Tribespeople grew corn, beans, squash, and cotton, using irrigation to bring water to the desert. Their pottery and weaving were among the finest in North America. Other tribes, including the Navajo and Apache, moved to the region from the north around 1400.

THIS ZUNI POT is decorated with images of white-tailed deer.

NAVAJO SERAPES like this one featured intricate geometric designs. The Navajo originally learned weaving techniques from the Pueblos in the late 1600s, shortly after Spanish settlers introduced sheep to the Southwest.

A GROUP OF PLAINS CHILDREN wave blankets and bang spears to force a herd of buffalo to stampede over a cliff, where men wait with bows and arrows to finish them off.

Great Plains

The tribes of the Great Plains lived in an area west of the Mississippi River, from Canada to present-day Texas—the Sioux and Cheyenne in the north, the Comanche in the south, and the Pawnee and Arapaho in between. Everything they needed to survive, from food to clothing and shelter, came from the huge herds of buffalo that roamed the grasslands of the central plains. The entire tribe took part in the hunt—a noisy group of children drove a herd over a cliff, where the men moved in for the kill with spears or bows and arrows; the women followed with knives and scrapers to butcher the beasts for meat, saving select bones and sinews to shape into tools or weapons. Buffalo hides were used to make clothing as well as the coverings of portable tent-like dwellings called tepees.

Far West

The Great Basin, a vast desert located between the Rocky Mountains and the Sierra Nevada, was home to the Shoshone, Ute, and other tribes. There were few crops or large game animals, but the people survived by roaming the basin in small bands, gathering wild food and small animals, such as rabbits, squirrels, and snakes. The women wove some of the most durable and decorative baskets in all of North America—perfect for people on the move. Across the mountains in California, the Hupa, Pomo, Chumash, and other tribes also made baskets, which they used to gather acorns and other food.

BASKETS woven with willow and sedge root were used to carry and store objects.

Northwest Coast

The tribes of the Pacific Coast lived among towering trees and great fishing waters. The people here—Tlingit, Kwakiutl, Chinook, and others—didn't farm. Instead, they lived off large game animals, like deer and caribou, and fished in streams full of spawning salmon. They used the abundant trees to build large, wood-plank houses; carve totem poles showing the symbols of the family, from ancestors to guardian animal spirits; and make wooden canoes sturdy enough for hunting whales. Their cloth and blankets were made of pounded bark, which they decorated beautifully.

A TLINGIT FIGHTING KNIFE, with an iron blade and an intricately carved ivory handle inlaid with bits of shell, was tied to the wrist with a leather strap.

EACH RING ON THIS CARVED WOODEN HAT represents one potlatch—a lavish feast in which the host gave away hundreds of gifts. A man who wore a hat with many rings would be given great respect in Tlingit society.

TOTEM POLE VILLAGES like this one included carved totems recording family history and each family's relationship to powerful animal spirits.

1000–1607

Exploration and Conquest

In the 1400s, Europeans in search of new trade routes began a great age of sea exploration Improved ship designs and better instruments helped captains sail far from their home shores. Portugal led the way, its ships sailing east to reach Asia. Christopher Columbus, daring to sail west for Asia, instead found the Americas, where Spain would eventually conquer two empires.

TERRIFYING TALES of sea monsters, such as the serpent in this later engraving, kept many would-be explorers from sailing far from land.

Portugal's Pioneering Voyages

In the mid-1400s, Portugal led the rest of Europe in its search for sea routes to Asia and other, unknown lands. Portugal's Prince Henry founded a navigation school, where captains and crew learned how to sail ships expertly and plot voyages with the latest equipment.

Henry sent expeditions down the African coast, trading for gold, ivory, and slaves.

In 1488, Portuguese explorer Bartholomeu Dias sailed all the way around the southern tip of Africa, called the Cape of Good Hope, before his terrified crew—fearing sea monsters, or worse—forced him to turn back. Ten years later, Vasco da Gama rounded the Cape, crossed the Indian Ocean to India, and returned with a ship full of valuables. Portugal later set up trading posts in India, China, and the East Indies, bringing back silk, tea, ivory, gold, and spices to sell in Europe.

THE MARINER'S ASTROLABE
was an invention of the Portuguese, modified from an Islamic navigating tool of the Mediterranean. It measured the altitude of stars in the night sky to help calculate a ship's distance from the equator.

THE PORTUGUESE CARAVEL,
seen in this model, combined both triangular and square sails, enabling ships to sail into the wind as well as with the wind. The caravel's innovative design helped Portugal rule the waves in the 1400s.

The Voyages of Columbus

Italian sea captain Christopher Columbus believed he could find a shorter, safer passage to the trading centers of Asia by sailing west, instead of using da Gama's eastern route. Columbus persuaded Spain's Queen Isabella and King Ferdinand to pay for an expedition; in 1492, he set out with 90 crew and three ships—the *Niña*, the *Pinta*, and the *Santa Maria*—on his first voyage across the Atlantic.

After more than two perilous months at sea, a lookout spotted land—what would later be named the Caribbean Islands. Columbus was so sure he had reached the Indies that he called the islanders he met there "Indians."

Columbus made three more voyages. Although he never reached Asia, he did pave the way for later European settlement of the Americas.

Spain's Conquests

Many Spanish adventurers followed Columbus's route west, hungry for gold, silver, and land. These soldiers, known as *conquistadores*, or conquerors, eventually took over two mighty empires, finding treasures far greater than Columbus had envisioned.

In 1519, the Spanish soldier Hernando Cortés led the conquest of the Aztecs in Mexico. After looting valuable items made of gold, silver, and precious stones and loading them onto Spanish ships, Cortés destroyed the Aztec capital city, and—after a fierce fight—wiped out its people, too.

In the Andes Mountains of South America, conquistador Francisco Pizarro seized the Inca empire in 1532. After plundering the cities, Pizarro enslaved the natives to work in gold and silver mines. Ships laden with treasure sailed back to Spain, making its empire the envy of all of Europe.

COLUMBUS AND HIS CREW claim new lands for Spain, where he was hailed as a hero.

DIVIDING THE WORLD

To prevent disputes over land claims between Spain and Portugal, the two countries signed the Treaty of Tordesillas in 1494, which was approved by Pope Julius II in 1506. The treaty set up an imaginary north-south line through the Atlantic Ocean; Spain had the right to claim lands west of the line, and Portugal could claim lands to the east. Brazil became a Portuguese colony in 1500 because it was east of the line, while Spain claimed the rest of South America.

Exploring the New World

For more than a century after Columbus's voyages, European adventurers continued to explore North America, still looking for a quick route to Asia. In 1497, Italian John Cabot explored the east coast for England, paving the way for English settlements there. Another Italian, Giovanni da Verrazano, mapped what became New York Bay and claimed land for France, who paid for the trip. French explorer Jacques Cartier made three journeys into the Gulf of St. Lawrence and up the St. Lawrence River, marking Canada as a future French colony.

The Northwest Passage

Explorers were convinced that a faster route to Asia was still to be found; they had little idea that such a huge continent was in the way. The quest for a sea route around the top of North America, which was called the Northwest Passage, was a big priority for explorers such as France's Jolliet and Marquette, who sailed all the way down the Mississippi River searching for a way to the Pacific Ocean.

MAJOR EXPLORATIONS
OF NORTH AMERICA

Cabot 1498
Ponce de León 1508–1521
Cortés 1519–1521
Verrazano 1524
Cartier 1534–1542
De Soto 1539–1542
Coronado 1540–1542
Champlain 1603–1635
Hudson 1610
Jolliet/Marquette 1673
La Salle 1682

CASTILLO DE SAN MARCOS was built by the Spanish in the late 1600s to defend their settlement at St. Augustine, Florida. The natural cement they used, called *coquina*, was so strong that the fort withstood a 30-day bombardment by ships from the English colony of Georgia in 1740.

French and Dutch Settlements

In the early 1600s, the first European colonies—which were settlements far away from, but still tied to, a home country—in North America were founded. Between 1603 and 1635, Frenchman Samuel de Champlain made 11 voyages to North America, mostly to the St. Lawrence River valley. In 1609, he founded a trading post at Québec—the first town of the French colony, New France. In that same year, English navigator Henry Hudson sailed up the river that bears his name, claiming the surrounding lands for the people who paid for his voyage, the Dutch. The Hudson River valley soon became the Dutch colony of New Netherland. French explorer René-Robert Cavelier de La Salle built a chain of fur-trading posts along the Great Lakes and the Mississippi, completing them in 1682. He claimed the land for France and named it Louisiana, to honor his king, Louis XIV.

HENRY HUDSON TRADES FURS with American Indians in this later painting. Some Indian tribes traded furs for guns, beads, and rum.

ENGLAND *V.* SPAIN

Spain's greatest rival in the 1500s was England. Under the rule of Queen Elizabeth I, England was rapidly becoming richer—and bolder. Some of Elizabeth's sea captains, led by John Hawkins and Francis Drake, began running down Spanish treasure ships and seizing their cargo for England. These "sea dogs" infuriated Spain's King Philip II. In 1588, he sent the Armada—a huge invasion fleet of 130 ships—to conquer England. The fleet was crushed by a combination of English sailing skill, cannon fire from the shore, and a fierce storm. The defeat of the Armada marked the beginning of Spain's decline as a great European power.

Spain's Explorations

Tales of treasure and adventure told by returning *conquistadores* led other Spanish explorers to strike out for the New World. Juan Ponce de León was fascinated by Indian legends of a "fountain of youth;" in 1513, he sailed from Puerto Rico to search for it on a peninsula he named Florida, meaning "Land of the Flowers." The fountain was never found, but in 1565, Spain built a settlement at St. Augustine, which became the oldest permanent European settlement in the United States.

Francisco Vásquez de Coronado was also inspired by Indian tales of "seven cities of gold." From 1540 to 1542, his expedition looked for the cities throughout the Southwest, but Coronado didn't find gold—only "monstrous beasts," which were probably buffalo. Another Spaniard, Hernando de Soto, spent the same years exploring the Southeast and the lower Mississippi River valley.

THE FIRST THANKSGIVING was a feast shared by the Pilgrims in New England and the Wampanoag Indians native to the area. Together, they enjoyed the harvest that the Indians had taught the Pilgrims to grow. Conditions in the New World were harsh for Europeans, who were largely unprepared for life in a different climate.

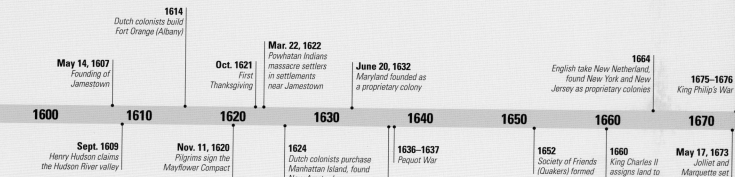

1614
Dutch colonists build Fort Orange (Albany)

Mar. 22, 1622
Powhatan Indians massacre settlers in settlements near Jamestown

May 14, 1607
Founding of Jamestown

Oct. 1621
First Thanksgiving

June 20, 1632
Maryland founded as a proprietary colony

1664
English take New Netherland, found New York and New Jersey as proprietary colonies

1675–1676
King Philip's War

| 1600 | 1610 | 1620 | 1630 | 1640 | 1650 | 1660 | 1670 |

Sept. 1609
Henry Hudson claims the Hudson River valley

Nov. 11, 1620
Pilgrims sign the Mayflower Compact

1624
Dutch colonists purchase Manhattan Island, found New Amsterdam

1636–1637
Pequot War

1652
Society of Friends (Quakers) formed

1660
King Charles II assigns land to proprietors to be sold or leased to colonists

May 17, 1673
Jolliet and Marquette set out to explore the Mississippi River

Dec. 1620
Pilgrims found Plymouth

1636
Anne Hutchinson and Roger Williams found Rhode Island

COLONIAL AMERICA
1607–1763

By the early 1600s, Europeans had established colonies along the waterways of North America. These settlements struggled to survive their first winter but soon prospered. Settlers came to the New World for religious freedom or economic opportunity, or to acquire great fortune for the "mother country." Many felt a moral duty to spread Christianity; some Europeans used this cause to justify enslaving American Indians and seizing their land.

European nations with claims to North America often feuded over land. Following the French and Indian War of 1756, when colonial soldiers helped Britain defeat France, Britain established dominance in the New World.

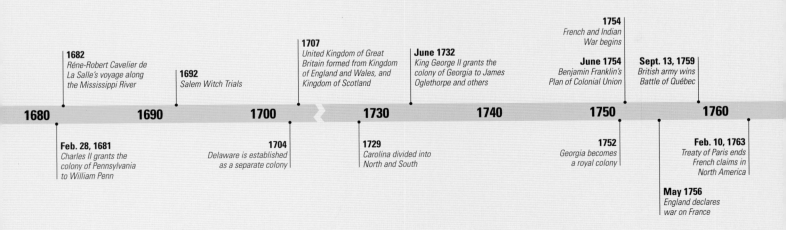

1682
Réne-Robert Cavelier de La Salle's voyage along the Mississippi River

1692
Salem Witch Trials

1707
United Kingdom of Great Britain formed from Kingdom of England and Wales, and Kingdom of Scotland

June 1732
King George II grants the colony of Georgia to James Oglethorpe and others

1754
French and Indian War begins

June 1754
Benjamin Franklin's Plan of Colonial Union

Sept. 13, 1759
British army wins Battle of Québec

1680 **1690** **1700** **1730** **1740** **1750** **1760**

Feb. 28, 1681
Charles II grants the colony of Pennsylvania to William Penn

1704
Delaware is established as a separate colony

1729
Carolina divided into North and South

1752
Georgia becomes a royal colony

Feb. 10, 1763
Treaty of Paris ends French claims in North America

May 1756
England declares war on France

The Atlantic Colonies

While some European explorers searched for cities of gold or a Northwest Passage to Asia, others saw the continent's real riches: fertile soil for farming, waters swarming with fish, and American Indian tribes eager to trade. The French, Dutch, and Swedes established colonies in the North, while the English settled the southern region they named Virginia. After a difficult start, the English colonies grew and developed faster than the colonies of other European countries.

England Secures a Foothold

In the early 1580s, British explorer Sir Humphrey Gilbert suggested that England establish colonies in North America. Gilbert tried, but his entire expedition was lost at sea. Attempts to start a colony on Roanoke Island failed in 1585, and again in 1587.

Finally, in 1607, three ships landed 105 men and boys—mostly wealthy "gentlemen" who came to find adventure and riches—on the coast of Virginia. They called their settlement Jamestown, to honor King James. But they built in a swampy area where malaria and starvation combined to kill 73 in one year.

Nevertheless, Jamestown survived—largely because a soldier and explorer named Captain John Smith took charge. He persuaded the powerful Powhatan Indian tribe to give them food and teach them how to grow corn and to fish. Smith told the colonists, "He that will not work shall not eat."

The Mystery of Roanoke

In 1587, a group of 130 English men, women, and children started a colony on Roanoke Island off the coast of Virginia. As soon as the colonists were settled, their governor, John White, went back to England for supplies. When he returned three years later, White found the island deserted, but saw no signs of a struggle. The only clue was the word Croatoan carved on a post. White thought this meant the colonists had moved to nearby Croatoan Island; but no trace of the settlers was found there—or anywhere else. Their fate remains a mystery, though legend holds that they were killed or sold to another tribe by the Powhatan Indians.

THE VIRGINIA COMPANY of London used pamphlets describing the wonders of their New World colony to attract new settlers.

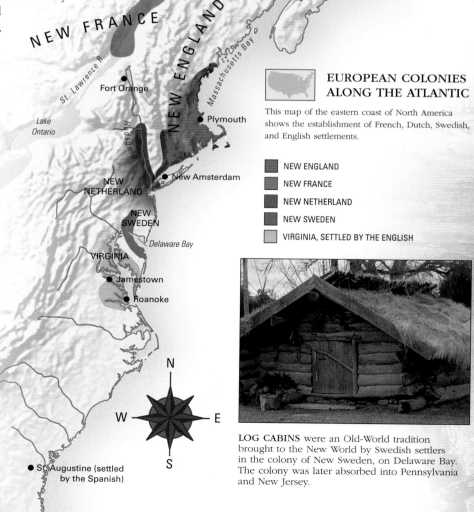

EUROPEAN COLONIES ALONG THE ATLANTIC

This map of the eastern coast of North America shows the establishment of French, Dutch, Swedish, and English settlements.

- NEW ENGLAND
- NEW FRANCE
- NEW NETHERLAND
- NEW SWEDEN
- VIRGINIA, SETTLED BY THE ENGLISH

LOG CABINS were an Old-World tradition brought to the New World by Swedish settlers in the colony of New Sweden, on Delaware Bay. The colony was later absorbed into Pennsylvania and New Jersey.

French and Dutch Colonies

New France, now known as Canada, was founded in 1534 by French adventurer Samuel de Champlain. It attracted several thousand fur trappers and traders, who hunted the beavers that brought such high prices in Europe. Called *coureurs de bois*, "forest runners," the French colonists got along well with the neighboring Algonquian tribes and often took Indian brides.

Dutch colonists settled in the fertile Hudson River valley, establishing a network of trading posts, towns, farms, and forts. They built Fort Orange—now Albany, New York—in 1614, and later purchased part of Manhattan Island from the Indians. There, in 1624, they established New Amsterdam, today's city of New York.

THE FORT protecting the English settlement of Jamestown, seen in a later artist's painting, was built in the summer of 1607.

THE STORY OF POCAHONTAS

Captain John Smith claimed that in 1607, he was captured by the Powhatans and was about to be executed by having his head bashed in with stones, when the chief's 11-year-old daughter Pocahontas rushed forward, placed her head on Smith's, and convinced his captors to spare his life.

While Smith's rescue story may be more legend than fact, we do know that Pocahontas spent a good deal of time with the Jamestown settlers. In 1614, she married one, John Rolfe, who took her to visit England. She died in 1617 on the return voyage to Virginia.

POCAHONTAS intervening to save Smith's life, as per the legend

1607–1763

The Gulf Coast and the West

American Indians had lived in the southern and western parts of North America since around 11,000 BCE In the late 1500s, Spanish and French began settling there; the Europeans then brought African slaves to the region. These diverse groups traded furs, used the Gulf of Mexico for fishing and shipping, and took advantage of the long, warm growing season to farm this fertile area.

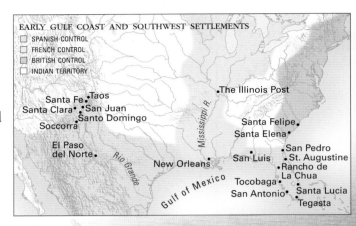

EARLY GULF COAST AND SOUTHWEST SETTLEMENTS
- ☐ SPANISH CONTROL
- ☐ FRENCH CONTROL
- ☐ BRITISH CONTROL
- ☐ INDIAN TERRITORY

Spain Establishes Claims

The Spanish came to the New World searching for gold and treasures, as well as a trade route to China. In the first half of the 1500s, Spain established claims in the South and West of America when explorers Francisco Vázquez de Coronado, Hernando de Soto, and Álvar Núñez Cabeza de Vaca became the first Europeans to explore these areas (see pp. 20–21). Starting in the late 1500s, Catholic Spanish clergy arrived and built missions in an effort to convert the Indians to Christianity. These missions were supported by farming communities and military forts, giving Spain a solid presence in the West. Eventually, Spain's colonial territories stretched across the South, from the Gulf of Mexico to the Pacific coast.

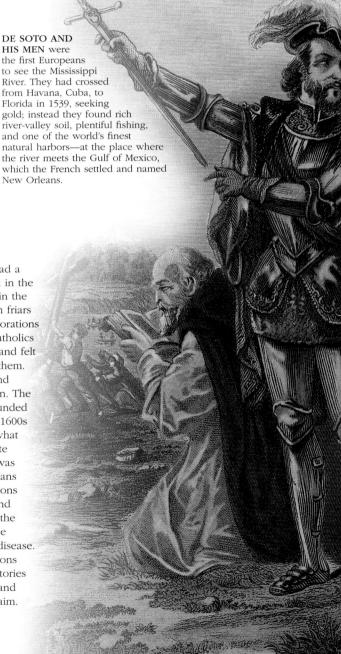

DE SOTO AND HIS MEN were the first Europeans to see the Mississippi River. They had crossed from Havana, Cuba, to Florida in 1539, seeking gold; instead they found rich river-valley soil, plentiful fishing, and one of the world's finest natural harbors—at the place where the river meets the Gulf of Mexico, which the French settled and named New Orleans.

MISSION SAN LUIS DE APALACHEE, in what is now Tallahassee, was the western outpost of the Florida mission system from 1656 to 1704. The settlement was home to 1,400 Apalachee Indians, various Spanish military personnel, officials of the Roman Catholic Church, farmers, and ranchers. The mission was prosperous, given the good soil, but conflicts with Creek Indians and the British forced it to be abandoned in the summer of 1704.

Spanish Missions and the Catholic Church

The Roman Catholic Church had a large role in Spain's expansion in the Americas. Having first arrived in the New World in 1524, Franciscan friars accompanied most of the explorations to expand Spanish territory. Catholics saw Indians as unsaved souls and felt a moral obligation to convert them. This resulted in both forced and peaceful attempts at conversion. The first Spanish missions were founded in the 1500s in Florida; in the 1600s missions were established in what is now New Mexico; by the late 1700s, the coast of California was dotted with missions. The Indians who were taken into the missions were forced to settle nearby and work the farms that sustained the missions; many of these people suffered from hard labor and disease. Guarded by soldiers, the missions protected Spain's colonial territories from the French and English, and others who might try to lay claim.

SHUFFLING EMPIRES

During the 1700s and 1800s, the major powers of Europe and then the newly formed United States of America struggled with each other for control of North America. The following chart details some of the major occurrences in the early years of empire building.

DATE	EVENT	NATIONS INVOLVED	OUTCOME
1763	Treaty of Paris	France, England, Spain	Having lost the French and Indian War, France divides its territory between England and Spain.
1795	Treaty of San Lorenzo	United States, Spain	The Mississippi River becomes the border between the U.S. and the Spanish colonies. Spain agrees to leave the port of New Orleans open for American trade.
1800	Treaty of San Ildefonso	Spain, France	Spain gives the Louisiana Territory to France on the condition that they not sell it or give it to an English-speaking nation, i.e., Great Britain or the United States.
1802	Violation of Treaty of San Lorenzo	Spain, United States	Spain violates the Treaty of San Lorenzo by closing New Orleans to American trade. The Spanish reopen the port later, but, as a result, the U.S. pushes harder to buy Louisiana from the French.
1803	Louisiana Purchase	France, United States	France violates the Treaty of San Ildefonso and sells the Louisiana Territory to the United States.
1819	Adams-Onis Treaty	Spain, United States	The United States acquires Florida from Spain. Spain gains full control of Texas.

French Louisiana

French explorers were among the first Europeans to enter central and western America, as they followed the profitable fur trade across the continent. Unlike Spain, France was more interested in developing new trade routes than in the glory of acquiring land, though it was certainly a goal to create a barrier to stop the English from spreading their colonial empire westward. Eventually, French claims included Acadia in Canada, the Great Lakes area, the Gulf Coast, and the Mississippi River valley, whose base was New Orleans. This thriving community was settled equally by Europeans, American Indians, and Africans, who intermingled to become the Creole people. Their influences in Louisiana culture include Mardi Gras parades, zydeco music, and foods such as gumbo.

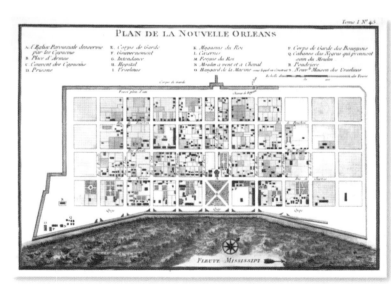

THIS MAP OF THE CITY OF NEW ORLEANS from 1744, during the French colonial period, shows the city was planned on a European-modeled grid system with large central plazas.

French Relations with the Indians

Unlike other Colonial powers, the French did not enslave American Indians or take over all of their land. The French fur trade relied on Indians' interest in exchanging furs for manufactured goods such as iron tools, wool blankets, and firearms. Also, the French Jesuits who established missions treated Indians more kindly than did the Spanish friars and did not use them as farm laborers. This level of friendship was not true for all tribes, however. For instance, conflict with the Natchez Indians led the French to destroy the entire tribe.

England's Colonies

The first English colonies in New England were started by Puritans, a religious sect seeking the freedom to worship as they chose. Their large numbers and hard work led to prosperity, and the English rulers recognized the colonies' economic potential; by 1650, England had established a dominant position in the New World.

The Pilgrims at Plymouth

In 1620, a ship called the *Mayflower,* bearing 101 passengers—half of whom were Pilgrims, a religious sect of Puritans seeking to break ties with the Church of England—was blown off course. Since the ship didn't land in Virginia where it was supposed to, and its landing site at Plymouth in New England wasn't governed by Virginia law, the settlers decided to make their own laws. The resulting agreement, the Mayflower Compact, established the important idea that there is a contract—or compact—between government and the people.

SQUANTO AND THE FIRST THANKSGIVING

Imagine their surprise when the Pilgrims met an Indian who spoke English. Squanto had been captured by slave traders, but he escaped and returned to New England. He was among those who helped the Pilgrims survive. In 1621, the Pilgrims invited more than 90 Indian guests to a feast to give thanks.

THE FIRST THANKSGIVING, as depicted by a later artist

A Struggle for Survival

After establishing their settlement of Plymouth, the Pilgrims suffered—and starved—through their first winter. In the spring, friendly Wampanoag Indians showed the surviving Pilgrims how to grow corn, beans, squash, and pumpkins—foods that didn't exist in Europe.

In 1630, Plymouth drew more than 1,000 new settlers, who arrived with supplies and farm animals. The settlers formed Massachusetts Bay Colony. By 1640, 20,000 more colonists had followed their lead.

THE *MAYFLOWER,* shown in this modern replica, measured only 90 feet long—the same distance between home plate and first base in baseball!

ENGLAND'S THIRTEEN COLONIES

NEW ENGLAND
THE MIDDLE COLONIES
THE SOUTH

MAINE (governed by Massachusetts)

NEW FRANCE

Lake Ontario

NEW HAMPSHIRE

Salem
Boston
Plymouth

MASSACHUSETTS

NEW YORK

RHODE ISLAND
CONNECTICUT

Lake Erie

New York

PENNSYLVANIA

NEW JERSEY
Philadelphia

Baltimore

DELAWARE
MARYLAND

VIRGINIA
Jamestown

Appalachian Mountains

NORTH CAROLINA

ATLANTIC OCEAN

SOUTH CAROLINA

Charleston

GEORGIA

FLORIDA

N
W   E
S

The First Indian Wars

As the New England colonies expanded, tensions grew with American Indian tribes angered by the loss of their hunting grounds. In 1635, the Pequot tribe fought the settlers in the Connecticut River Valley before being trapped and killed by a colonial army.

The Pequot War was followed by 40 years of peace until King Philip's War in 1675. A Wampanoag chief named Metacomet, also called King Philip, united several tribes and spread terror and bloodshed throughout New England. In one deadly year, more than 600 colonists and 3,000 Indians—including King Philip—were killed and a dozen towns destroyed. This conflict ended American Indians' resistance to the colonies east of the Hudson River.

KING PHILIP, as Paul Revere drew him many years later

1607–1763

New England Grows

The Puritans came to New England to worship according to their own beliefs, but they were not tolerant of other religions. Dissenters—those who disagreed with Puritan teachings—were banished, or sent away. Two banished dissenters, Anne Hutchinson and Roger Williams, started the colony of Rhode Island in 1636, and granted freedom to all religions.

New England continued to grow as others sought their freedom. In 1636, a minister named Thomas Hooker led his congregation west to the Connecticut River valley. Soon 15 towns stretched along the river, forming the colony of Connecticut. Several hundred hardy colonists followed the river north into the woods of New Hampshire and Maine. New Hampshire became an English colony in 1679, but Maine stayed part of Massachusetts until 1820.

ANNE HUTCHINSON during the trial that led to her banishment

Mercantilism and the Crown of England

By the early 1600s, European rulers had realized that they could increase their nations' wealth, power, and status by establishing colonies. Each colony provided valuable raw materials, such as cotton and timber, to the mother country; in turn, the colonists bought the mother country's manufactured goods. Colonies could also take some of the mother country's poor—and its criminals. The idea that having colonies makes good business sense is known as mercantilism.

In 1660, King Charles II wanted to expand England's empire. He created colonies by giving land to one or more proprietors, who could then lease or sell the land to colonists. The proprietors could also appoint a governor, who shared power with representatives elected by male property owners in the colony.

PAPER MONEY like this twenty-shilling note was issued partly because silver and gold for coins were scarce.

Colonies for the King's Friends

In 1664, King Charles II granted a large area of colonial land to his brother James, the Duke of York. It did not matter to the king or duke that the land included New Netherland, which had been colonized by the Dutch in the early 1600s; they were both eager to get rid of the Dutch and secure English dominance of the New World once and for all.

James, an admiral of the English fleet, sent three warships into New Amsterdam harbor and ordered the city to surrender. The Dutch administrator Peter Stuyvesant was furious, but the Dutch people, who were unhappy with the lack of opportunities under his harsh rule, welcomed the change. New Netherland became New York. To make his colony easier to govern, James gave the area now known as New Jersey to two of his friends, establishing yet another proprietary colony.

PETER STUYVESANT, the peg-legged ruler of New Netherland, surrendered the Dutch colony to the Duke of York in 1664, and an era of English rule began.

VIRGINIA'S INDIAN WARS

In 1622, the Powhatan Indians, disturbed by the increasing takeover of their lands in the colony of Virginia, turned to warfare, killing more than 300 settlers near Jamestown— about one-third of the entire colony. An uneasy peace was established, but in 1624, King James I decided the best way to avoid future conflicts was to make Virginia a royal colony, and appoint its governor himself.

CHIEF POWHATAN, as depicted by Captain John Smith in 1607

William Penn's Holy Experiment

To pay off a debt, Charles II presented a proprietary colony to William Penn, who named it Pennsylvania. (The Duke of York, who was also indebted to the Penn family, added "the lower counties," which became the colony of Delaware.) Penn was a member of a religious sect called the Society of Friends, or Quakers, which was formed in 1652. The Quakers were persecuted in England and often jailed for their beliefs, which conflicted with the teachings of the Church of England. In creating a charter, or set of rules, for his colony, Penn granted freedom of religion to all. He also insisted on treaties of friendship with all Indian tribes, and unlike other colonial governors, he paid them for land. The colony prospered, and by 1750, the city Penn had planned, Philadelphia, became the largest, most modern city in the English colonies.

DEFINITION

*A **treaty** is an official agreement between two or more sides of a political issue.*

WILLIAM PENN signs a treaty with the native peoples of Pennsylvania.

Oglethorpe's Ideals

In 1729, the colony of Carolina was divided into North and South; in 1732, England's 13th colony was established in neighboring Georgia. King George II granted Georgia to English humanitarian James Oglethorpe. Oglethorpe hoped to populate his colony with English debtors, who were kept in prison until someone paid off their loans. He set strict rules for Georgia's new settlers: every family had to have mulberry trees for silkworms, to establish a silk industry; there would be no slavery; no family could own more than 500 acres of land; and drinking rum was prohibited.

The realities of life in the New World made enforcing these rules impossible. The climate was too hot for silkworms, so the trees were a useless expense. Landowners, seeing the prosperity of plantations in other colonies, soon insisted on owning slaves and larger plots of land. By 1750, families could own slaves and hold up to 2,000 acres of land. Two years later, Georgia became a royal colony.

Tomochichi, a tribal leader

James Oglethorpe

OGLETHORPE, shown meeting a tribal leader, worked to establish friendly relations with Georgia's Indian tribes.

Colonial Life

From the mid-1600s to the mid-1700s, as the colonies grew, the inhabitants of each region developed unique lifestyles. In part, the differences arose from how people responded to the environmental conditions of their region, as was true of the American Indians before them.

New England

Long winters and thin, rocky soil made farming in the New England colonies—Vermont, New Hampshire, Massachusetts, Rhode Island, and Connecticut—a challenge. Some farm families specialized in dairy products, since the land was better for grazing. In the early 1700s, young people started to move from the countryside to coastal towns. Many became apprentices, learning a craft or trade to meet the growing demand for carpenters, cobblers, dressmakers, hatters, and other skilled workers.

Philadelphia harbor in the 1730s

BENJAMIN FRANKLIN, 1706–1790

AN AMERICAN ORIGINAL

No achievement seemed out of reach for versatile, Boston-born Benjamin Franklin. As a printer and writer, he gained fame and enough fortune to "retire" at age 40. The innovations he helped bring to his home city, Philadelphia, included streetlights, a hospital, paid police and fire departments, and a lending library. He founded a school in Philadelphia, which became the University of Pennsylvania. Franklin also served the colonies as postmaster and foreign ambassador, and he helped draft the Declaration of Independence. Plus, he was world-famous as a scientist and inventor, making key discoveries about electricity and inventing both the Franklin stove and bifocal glasses.

COLONIAL NEW ENGLANDERS turned to the sea for careers in fishing, whaling, shipbuilding, and commercial trade. By 1750, fishing and shipbuilding alone employed more than 10,000 people in New England—a large percentage of the working population. Harbors like Philadelphia's were filled with ships, and the shady streets of seaports like Boston, Salem, and Providence were lined with stately mansions owned by merchants and ship captains.

HOW COLONIAL CITIES GREW

The booming sea trade helped Northern harbor cities grow at a faster pace than southern cities like Charleston, where trading ships sailed along rivers, directly to plantation docks.

	1690	1710	1730	1760
Boston	7,000	9,000	13,000	15,600
New York	3,900	5,700	8,600	18,000
Philadelphia	4,000	6,500	11,500	23,750
Charleston	1,100	3,000	4,500	8,000

SLAVES on a South Carolina plantation haul freshly cut indigo plants used to make dye.

The Middle Colonies

The mild climate and good soil of the Middle Colonies—New York, New Jersey, Pennsylvania, and Delaware—were ideal for large, efficient farms, many owned by German immigrants. These "bread colonies" produced enough grain to feed the growing colonial towns, and to be sold in other countries. As in New England, the Middle Colonies had bustling port cities, such as Philadelphia and New York, where growing wealth could be seen in the elegant homes, churches, and public buildings.

THE "COMMON ROOM" was the most important room in a colonial home. As this replica shows, it was part kitchen and part workroom, so that busy homemakers could do several jobs at once.

The South

Although 80 percent of the people in the five Southern colonies lived on small family farms, the region's economic, political, and social life was dominated by the plantations. Each of these enormous land holdings, often covering several thousand acres, was like a self-sufficient village with its own blacksmith's shop, pottery kiln, chapel or small church, and tutor for the owner's children. The plantations relied on cash crops—tobacco in Maryland and Virginia, rice and indigo in the Carolinas and Georgia. For cheap workers, they depended on slave labor. The plantation owners, much like the nobility in Europe, held important government positions and served as officers in the militia.

THE INDIGO PLANT was a mainstay of the southern economy in the 1700s because of the dye made from its leaves. Indigo became valuable due to the innovations of 17-year-old Eliza Lucas of South Carolina who developed a deep blue dye that became wildly popular.

INDENTURED SERVANTS

Many poor Europeans paid for their passage to America by becoming indentured servants. They signed a document called the indenture, which committed them to work for the person who paid their passage for a period of time—usually seven years. Indentured servants could be severely punished for breaking their contracts. At the end of the agreed-upon time period, they received land or money to help them start their lives in freedom.

Slavery Emerges

As colonial farms and industries thrived, the need for workers grew. Slavery had existed around the world throughout history; in the 1600s, Europeans introduced it to the New World to provide cheap labor. Wrenched from their homes in faraway Africa, slaves were shipped to the Americas, then sold and traded like property. The slave trade expanded rapidly in the 1700s as the South's plantation economy grew.

A Slave's Journey Begins

While ships waited off the western coast of Africa, Muslim slave traders emerged from the interior, bringing dozens of prisoners in chains. These terrified men, women, and children had been captured in tribal wars or kidnapped from their homes in Benin, Ashanti, and other kingdoms in what is now Nigeria. The English or colonial captains of the slave ships often bought one or two hundred slaves, paying for them with rum, salted codfish, muskets, and "African iron"—iron bars used as money.

TO BE SOLD on board the Ship *Bance-Island*, on tuesday the 6th of *May* next, at *Ashley-Ferry*; a choice cargo of about 250 fine healthy NEGROES, just arrived from the Windward & Rice Coast. —The utmost care has already been taken, and shall be continued, to keep them free from the least danger of being infected with the SMALL-POX, no boat having been on board, and all other communication with people from *Charles-Town* prevented. *Austin, Laurens, & Appleby.*

N. B. Full one Half of the above Negroes have had the SMALL-POX in their own Country.

SLAVE AUCTIONS were usually held after the slaves had been trained—or "seasoned"—in the British West Indies for a few weeks. As this advertisement suggests, prospective buyers were very cautious about smallpox; an epidemic could wipe out an entire village.

AMERICA

NEW ENGLAND

Rum, Guns, and Iron

Sugar, Molasses, and Slaves

ATLANTIC

WEST INDIES

CARIBBEAN SEA

Store Room

Store Room

CHAINED-UP SLAVES TRAVELED IN HOLDS like this one after they were captured and sold. During the horror of the Atlantic crossing—called the middle passage—an estimated 25 percent did not survive, including those who leaped into the sea.

SLAVE COLLARS like this one ensured that slaves were kept in check during the long sea voyage from Africa. These metal bands fit tightly around the neck and were chained to other slaves' collars. Leg irons also helped secure the ship owner's "investment."

The Spread of Slavery

The first Africans brought to the colonies seem to have been treated much like indentured servants, and some eventually received their freedom. As the need for workers increased, especially on huge Southern plantations, more and more Africans were imported.

In New England and the Middle Colonies, there were far fewer slaves. Most were household servants, while others worked alongside their owners in trades or in the fields. These slaves were usually treated fairly, but they were always aware that they were not free.

Enslaved for Life—by Law

As slave numbers grew, so did the anxieties of many white colonists. In the tobacco-growing colonies of Maryland and Virginia, for example, Africans made up less than 10 percent of the population in 1690, but by 1719, they were 25 percent of the population, and grew to 40 percent by 1750. White colonists feared being outnumbered and overpowered, and, as a result, between 1700 and 1750, every colony passed laws saying that Africans were to be slaves for life—except for a few exceptions—and were to be treated as property. To ease white fears even more, laws called "slave codes" were enacted. These prevented large numbers of slaves from gathering in one place, or from traveling without a permit.

TRIANGULAR TRADE

Ships established several "triangular trade" routes, so that colonists could exchange goods rather than money for slaves and avoid English customs taxes. Goods from the colonies were traded for slaves in Africa; then ships sailed to the West Indies, where most of the slaves were exchanged for molasses and sugar. Any remaining slaves were sold at ports in America; the molasses was used to make more rum.

▬ ▬ ▬ Rum, Guns, and Iron Route

▬ ▬ ▬ Sugar, Molasses, and Slaves Route

▬ ▬ ▬ Slaves Route

PHILLIS WHEATLEY, 1753–1784

Brought to Boston as an eight-year-old slave in 1761, Phillis was bought by the Wheatley family to serve in their house. The Wheatleys saw how bright she was, and gave her an education. Phillis became a writer; when she was 20, a book of her poetry made her famous. The Wheatleys gave her both her freedom and their name, and her achievement as the first slave to publish a book inspired free blacks for many years.

1607–1763

Daily Life for Slaves

The day-to-day lives of slaves varied widely. On plantations, household slaves had less strenuous work, and often fared much better than the field hands. Field slaves worked in "gangs" for long, exhausting hours, while an overseer (sometimes another slave) kept them moving—often with his whip. Some slaves were trained in trades or crafts and often worked in towns, building houses and working at other jobs.

Plantation slaves were usually housed in small, basic cabins. Families lived together, prepared their own meals, tended private gardens, and made their own clothing. While some owners treated their slaves with kindness, many owners seemed to enjoy cruel treatment of the slaves in their power, often using physical punishment to enforce rules.

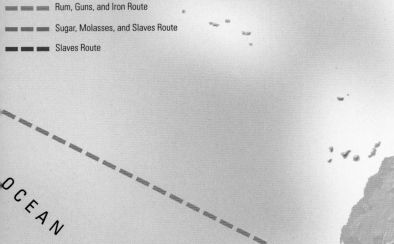

OCEAN

Slaves

ARROWS SHOW one of the triangle-shaped colonial slave trade routes. Other routes ran from the colonies to Europe, then to the West Indies and back to New England.

AFRICA

GOLD COAST

MIXING CULTURES

Many slaves managed to hold on to the customs of their homelands—songs, dances, ceremonies, and beliefs. They found ways to incorporate their traditions into the customs of colonial America. A great many slaves became Christians, for example, and they combined Bible stories, church hymns, and their own African rhythms and song styles to produce gospel music.

A Clash of Empires

The Old World's superpowers, France and England, often clashed. Their ultimate struggle began in the New World in 1755, when the French, looking to extend their territory, met English colonists moving west. On one side of the fight were the English and their colonists, and on the other side were the French and their Indian allies. The series of battles they fought was called the French and Indian War. Britain won in 1759; now they had control of the colonies.

MAJOR BATTLES OF THE FRENCH AND INDIAN WAR

- BRITISH TOWN
- FRENCH TOWN
- BRITISH FORT
- FRENCH FORT
- BRITISH LINE OF ATTACK
- FRENCH LINE OF ATTACK
- BRITISH VICTORY
- FRENCH VICTORY

NEW FRANCE

Sept. 13, 1759 — Québec

MAINE

Sept. 8, 1760 — Montreal

July 31, 1759

Crown Point

Lake Champlain

Ft. Ticonderoga — July 8, 1758 — 1759

NEW HAMPSHIRE

Aug. 27, 1758 — Ft. Frontenac

1756 — 1755

Ft. William Henry

Boston

Ft. Oswego

Aug. 4, 1756

Albany — MASSACHUSETTS

RHODE ISLAND

1759 — NEW YORK

CONNECTICUT

Lake Ontario

Ft. Niagara — July 25, 1759

Hudson R.

Lake Erie

New York

NEW JERSEY

PENNSYLVANIA

Philadelphia

Ft. Duquesne — Ft. Necessity

July 9, 1755 — 1754

ATLANTIC OCEAN

Nov. 25, 1758

MARYLAND — DELAWARE

VIRGINIA

St. Lawrence R.

ALBANY PLAN OF UNION

In 1754, before war with France was declared, delegates from seven British colonies met in Albany, New York, to consider ways of defending themselves. Benjamin Franklin presented a daring plan—the creation of a colonial "union" that could tax citizens in order to pay for a unified army. The delegates adopted the plan, but none of the colonies approved it; they did not want to give too much power to a central authority.

The French and Indian War Begins

In the 1750s, the French expanded their fur-trading empire south into the Ohio River valley, building forts for protection. At the same time, English colonists were crossing the Appalachian Mountains to settle in the region. The French encouraged their Algonquin Indian allies (see p. 15) to raid the English settlements, spreading terror along the frontier. When a Virginia militia, or army, led by 22-year-old George Washington was sent to protect English settlers in 1754, they were driven out by the French.

Gulf of St. Lawrence

July 26, 1758

Louisbourg

Halifax

1607–1763

The War Rages On

In 1754, Britain sent General Edward Braddock, Colonel Washington, and 2,500 British troops to the Ohio frontier to confront the French. A force of Frenchmen and Indians, fighting from the cover of trees and ravines, caught the soldiers in a deadly crossfire, killing or wounding more than half the British soldiers and mortally wounding Braddock. Fighting raged along the frontier for nearly a year, with the French pushing back every attack. In 1756, England formally declared war on France.

IN HONOR OF THE YOUNG BRITISH KING, GEORGE III, statues were erected in dozens of towns in America in celebration of Britain's amazing victory over France.

A Stunning Victory

This clash between England and France was part of the first global war; battles were also fought in Europe, India, Africa, and the Caribbean. In 1757, William Pitt became the leader of Parliament, and Britain's fortunes changed. Pitt wanted to focus Britain's military might on North America. With help from the colonial militia and the Iroquois tribes (see p. 15), the British attacked Fort Niagara and Lake Champlain, and sent an invasion force up to Québec. The plan worked; the British won. The Treaty of Paris in 1763 ended all French claims in North America. Canada became a British colony, and the huge French territory of Louisiana was given to Spain as thanks for its support. Britain was now the world's most powerful empire, and its colonists were proud to be part of it.

PONTIAC'S REBELLION was led by Chief Pontiac of the Ottawa Indians in May 1763. American Indians resented English control of their land and resolved to win it back by attacking English forts. The rebellion failed, but it made the English recognize the Indians' claim to North American lands.

FIGHTING NORTH AMERICAN–STYLE

When George Washington entered the wilderness with Braddock's troops, he was furious to see the army march out in the open, and in perfect rows. Washington explained that the Indians fought from behind the cover of trees and boulders, not in formation, but Braddock did not listen. His reluctance to adapt fighting styles led to a tragic British defeat. Washington himself escaped uninjured, although he had two horses shot out from under him.

MUSKETS like this one were the standard weapon for those fighting on both sides in the French and Indian War. Twenty-four separate steps were needed to load them.

stock (butt)

trigger

flint

pan

barrel

ramrod

muzzle

MEMBERS OF THE CONTINENTAL CONGRESS, like many Americans, were angered by British rule. They met to draft a document that stated their right and intention to form a new, independent government. On July 4, 1776, the Declaration of Independence was approved and signed by America's leaders, including John Adams and Thomas Jefferson. The creation of the document was an inspiration to the Americans who would fight the British for their freedom.

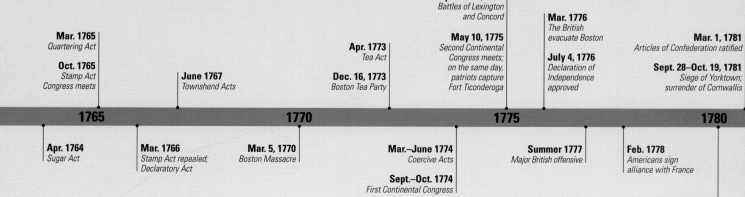

Apr. 18–19, 1775
Battles of Lexington and Concord

Mar. 1765
Quartering Act

Oct. 1765
Stamp Act Congress meets

June 1767
Townshend Acts

Apr. 1773
Tea Act

Dec. 16, 1773
Boston Tea Party

May 10, 1775
Second Continental Congress meets; on the same day, patriots capture Fort Ticonderoga

Mar. 1776
The British evacuate Boston

July 4, 1776
Declaration of Independence approved

Mar. 1, 1781
Articles of Confederation ratified

Sept. 28–Oct. 19, 1781
Siege of Yorktown; surrender of Cornwallis

1765   **1770**   **1775**   **1780**

Apr. 1764
Sugar Act

Mar. 1766
Stamp Act repealed; Declaratory Act

Mar. 5, 1770
Boston Massacre

Mar.–June 1774
Coercive Acts

Sept.–Oct. 1774
First Continental Congress

Summer 1777
Major British offensive

Feb. 1778
Americans sign alliance with France

May 12, 1780
Battle of Charleston

CREATING A NEW NATION

1763–1800

The cordial relationship between Great Britain and the American colonies soured shortly after the French and Indian War. The English king needed to raise money to pay for the war and offset the cost of protecting and governing Britain's huge empire. The decision to tax colonists was met at first with peaceful protests. But when Britain tried to punish Massachusetts for rebelling, the 13 colonies united and formed a Continental Congress of delegates from each of the colonies. The first shots of the American Revolution were fired in 1775, and the United States Congress approved the country's Declaration of Independence one year later. The colonists won the war and their independence, and, in 1787, created the U.S. Constitution to establish the nation's democratic structure.

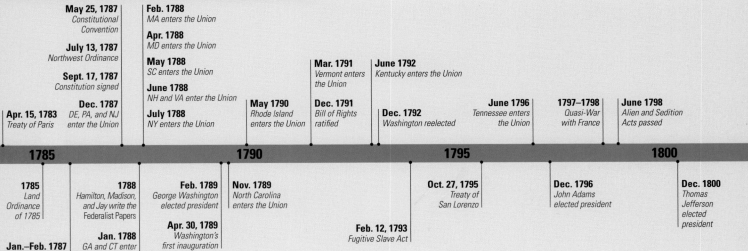

May 25, 1787
Constitutional Convention

July 13, 1787
Northwest Ordinance

Sept. 17, 1787
Constitution signed

Dec. 1787
DE, PA, and NJ enter the Union

Apr. 15, 1783
Treaty of Paris

Feb. 1788
MA enters the Union

Apr. 1788
MD enters the Union

May 1788
SC enters the Union

June 1788
NH and VA enter the Union

July 1788
NY enters the Union

May 1790
Rhode Island enters the Union

Mar. 1791
Vermont enters the Union

Dec. 1791
Bill of Rights ratified

June 1792
Kentucky enters the Union

Dec. 1792
Washington reelected

June 1796
Tennessee enters the Union

1797–1798
Quasi-War with France

June 1798
Alien and Sedition Acts passed

1785 · **1790** · **1795** · **1800**

1785
Land Ordinance of 1785

1788
Hamilton, Madison, and Jay write the Federalist Papers

Jan. 1788
GA and CT enter the Union

Jan.–Feb. 1787
Shays's Rebellion

Feb. 1789
George Washington elected president

Apr. 30, 1789
Washington's first inauguration

Nov. 1789
North Carolina enters the Union

Feb. 12, 1793
Fugitive Slave Act

Oct. 27, 1795
Treaty of San Lorenzo

Dec. 1796
John Adams elected president

Dec. 1800
Thomas Jefferson elected president

Road to Rebellion

Great Britain won the French and Indian War against France and her Indian allies, leaving the English with a huge debt and a larger empire to defend and govern in North America. Parliament—the British governing body—and King George III insisted that the colonies help pay off the debt. After all, colonies existed solely to benefit the mother country under the mercantile system of colonizing lands for their wealth. Almost everything the British tried angered the colonists and pushed them toward open revolt.

WHO'S WHO IN THE REVOLUTION

Patriots:	Name used by colonists for those who supported revolting against the British
Rebels:	Derogatory name given to Patriots by the British
Yankees/ Yanks:	Derogatory name given to all colonists, even those who didn't support the rebellion
Continentals:	Soldiers in the colonial army
Tory/Tories or Loyalists:	Colonists loyal to Britain
Regulars, Redcoats, or Lobsterbacks:	Names used for British soldiers

LIBERTY POLES were raised in many towns and decorated with pennants and ribbons to declare the American love of liberty. They were the kind of protest Patriots liked—a symbolic image that made a memorable statement.

Taxation without Representation

What upset the colonists about a tax such as the 1765 Stamp Act was that it was imposed on them without their consent. Their assemblies could not vote on the tax, and they had no representatives in Parliament. "No taxation without representation" became their rallying cry.

A large minority, known as Patriots, formed the Sons of Liberty and the Daughters of Liberty. These organizations asked colonial merchants not to trade with the British, and the Daughters of Liberty boycotted British goods.

A Stamp Act Congress with delegates from nine colonies met in New York in October 1765. It sent a petition urging Parliament to repeal the tax. One delegate stated what many were feeling: "There ought to be no New Englanders, no New Yorkers ... but all of us Americans." Parliament repealed the stamp tax but immediately passed a Declaratory Act, which said that only Parliament had the authority to make laws for the colonies.

BRITISH ACTS OF PARLIAMENT

These taxes and acts were imposed upon the colonists by Parliament:

1764 Sugar Act	Taxed foreign imports such as sugar, wine, and cloth
1765 Stamp Act	Required printed items be on special, stamped paper
1765 Quartering Act	Required colonists to provide housing for 10,000 British troops
1766 Declaratory Act	Said Parliament could make laws for the colonies on all matters
1767 Townshend Acts	Taxed colonial imports, including paper, glass, lead, paint, and tea
1773 Tea Act	Required colonists to buy tea only from Britain's East India Company
1774 Coercive Acts	A group of acts designed to punish Patriots for the Boston Tea Party; also included the Québec Act, which extended the boundaries of Canada south to the Ohio River, plus a new Quartering Act, forcing colonists to house more British soldiers

DEFINITION

*A **boycott** is a refusal to buy from or deal with another person, company, or nation.*

MARCH 5, 1770

The Boston Massacre

In 1765, Parliament passed the Quartering Act, requiring the colonies to provide housing for 10,000 British soldiers. A year later, two regiments of Redcoats, as British soldiers were sometimes called because of their uniforms, arrived in Boston. The people maintained an uneasy peace with the Redcoats until March 5, 1770, when an unruly mob taunted some soldiers. The soldiers opened fire, killing three Bostonians; two more later died of their wounds. Calm followed for the next two years, but the basic conflict had not been resolved.

Samuel Adams, one of the most radical Patriots, began calling the incident the Boston Massacre. For several years, Patriots cited this incident as an example of British brutality.

What Really Happened?

In Paul Revere's view of the Boston Massacre, British Captain Thomas Preston seems to be ordering a mass shooting of innocent-looking Patriots, including women. In fact, the first shot was fired by accident, leading most of the other soldiers to fire, too. The mob wasn't completely innocent, either—they had been pelting the Redcoats with rocks and snowballs.

SAMUEL ADAMS, 1722–1803

Samuel Adams was often called the "Firebrand of the American Revolution." A few months after the Boston Massacre, Adams called for "Committees of Correspondence" in every colony. By 1774, these committees were exchanging news and ideas, which helped build a sense of national unity.

1763–1800

PAUL REVERE'S ENGRAVING OF THE BOSTON MASSACRE was a widely circulated piece of Patriot propaganda.

From Protest to War

I n 1773, Americans learned that they would now be required to purchase all their tea from Britain's East India Company. Angry Patriots in every port refused to accept the tea. They saw the Tea Act as the first step in controlling colonial business. In Boston, Sons of Liberty, dressed as Mohawk warriors, dumped 342 chests of tea into Boston harbor. The British acted to punish the colonists for this Boston Tea Party, so the Patriots responded by calling a Continental Congress, resorting to armed resistance, and finally creating a Continental Army.

SPRING–FALL 1774

The "Intolerable Acts"

Parliament and King George III, outraged by the Boston Tea Party, passed the Coercive Acts during the spring of 1774. The laws closed the port of Boston, took away most self-government rights in Massachusetts, and sent a military governor to take control. In September 1774, 50 delegates from 12 colonies met in Philadelphia at the First Continental Congress to decide what to do about these "Intolerable Acts." They demanded that the laws be repealed and insisted on having a voice in all tax measures. They also agreed to meet again the following spring. Parliament rejected the delegates' demands and the king declared the colonies to be in a state of rebellion.

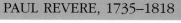

PAUL REVERE, 1735–1818

THE FAMOUS RIDE:
FACT AND LEGEND

D uring the night of April 18–19, 1775, Patriots Paul Revere and William Dawes rode from Boston toward Concord to warn Massachusetts towns that British Redcoats were advancing. Neither Revere nor Dawes actually made it all the way to Concord; they were stopped by British officers. It was a young doctor named Samuel Prescott riding with them who carried the warning to Concord. Little attention was paid to Revere's ride until, some 80 years later, American poet Henry Wadsworth Longfellow wrote "Paul Revere's Ride."

MINUTEMEN became a symbol of the Patriots' willingness to fight for their rights. They got their name because they could get dressed, grab their rifles, and be out the door in a minute.

SPRING 1775

The Outbreak of War

Shortly before dawn on April 19, 1775, as church bells and signal cannons sounded the alarm of the approaching British Redcoats, Minutemen, so called because they could be ready at a moment's notice, arrived from every direction. The British fired on one band of Minutemen on Lexington's village green, killing eight, then marched on to Concord, where they had planned to capture Patriot weapons and two Patriot leaders— Sam Adams and John Hancock. The Minutemen clashed with the Redcoats at a bridge in Concord, then harassed them on their long march back to Boston.

When the Second Continental Congress met on May 10, 1775, it voted to create a Continental Army out of the militiamen who camped outside Boston. George Washington was chosen to command. By the time he met up with his men, Patriots had already fought the Battle of Bunker Hill.

Also on May 10, 1775, a band of Patriots from Connecticut captured Fort Ticonderoga, a strong British fort on Lake Champlain in New York state. The British hadn't heard that war had begun, so the assault mounted by Ethan Allen and his Green Mountain Boys was a surprise. Allen shared command of the fort with militia officer Benedict Arnold.

RIFLES *V.* MUSKETS

The inside of a rifle barrel had grooves, or "rifles," carved in it, which spun the bullet as it left the barrel, making it accurate up to 400 yards. A musket ball was accurate for only 50 yards. Using the rifle gave the Americans a tremendous advantage. However, a rifle required more time to load and could not hold a bayonet. When facing a massed Redcoat charge with fixed bayonets, a rifle was a handicap.

rifle grooves

bullet

A Rifled Gun Barrel

barrel

butt

ramrod

cock to hold flint

frizzen struck by flint to produce sparks

sling

British Brown Bess Musket

socket fitted over muzzle of musket

blade of bayonet

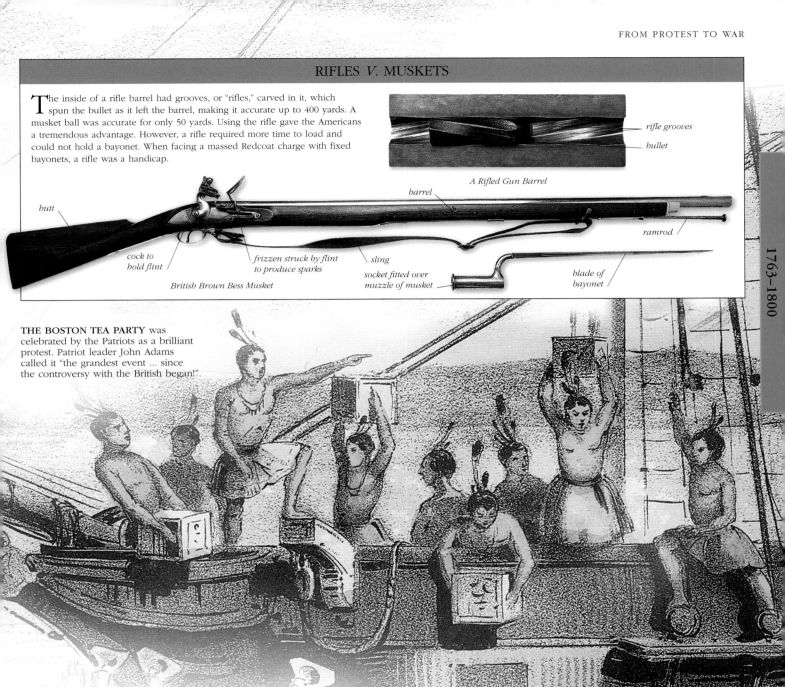

THE BOSTON TEA PARTY was celebrated by the Patriots as a brilliant protest. Patriot leader John Adams called it "the grandest event ... since the controversy with the British began!"

JUNE 17, 1775

Morale Victory at Bunker Hill

On the morning of June 17, 1775, 2,400 British troops were ferried across the bay to Charlestown in Massachusetts and marched up the steep slope of Breed's Hill against 1,600 Patriot militiamen. The Patriots had dug trenches overnight and piled up logs and rocks in front, creating chest-high "breastworks," but the British were confident that the untrained militia would be no match for their battle-hardened regulars. After British warships in the harbor stopped their artillery bombardment, the Redcoats approached, only to be driven back down the hill by musket fire. The British attacked a second time, with the same result, but on the third assault the Americans ran out of ammunition. The British took both Breed's Hill and Bunker Hill, but at a great cost—nearly half their force—while the Patriots achieved a great victory in morale by proving they could stand up to professional soldiers in the world's mightiest army.

Bunker Hill 1775 by Trumbull

US Bicentennial IOc

Stamp depicting the Battle of Bunker Hill

Declaring Independence

In July 1775, Washington began organizing roughly 15,000 militiamen camped outside Boston into the Continental Army. During the training, he sent two forces to invade Canada before the British could attack New York by way of Lake Champlain and the Hudson River.

One invasion force went north from Fort Ticonderoga; the other struggled through the Maine wilderness, nearly dying of starvation. The Americans attacked Québec during a driving snowstorm on the night of December 31, 1775. The attack fell apart and the invasion attempt ended.

Far to the south, Patriots in every colony debated the drastic step of declaring independence from Britain. They knew that, to the British, this would be treason.

THE SPY IN BOSTON

The British commander in Boston, General Thomas Gage, knew there was a spy in his inner circle, because there was no other way to explain how the Patriots knew about every move he planned. The fortifying of Breed's Hill the night before the British sent troops there was clearly the result of spying. Gage never discovered who the spy was, but there is considerable evidence that it was his wife, Margaret. She was American by birth and was related to a Patriot leader in New York. When Gage was recalled to England late in 1775, he and his wife separated and never reconciled.

The British Evacuation of Boston

The British remained in Boston for nearly a year after the Battle of Bunker Hill, trapped by Washington's Continental Army and several thousand militia. Over that same winter of 1775–1776, Patriots hauled cannon, captured at Fort Ticonderoga, across Massachusetts. When Washington's troops placed the cannon on the heights overlooking Boston, the British commander knew his army could not remain in the city. In mid-March 1776, as Patriots wept and cheered, the British evacuated Boston and set sail for Canada. Washington knew the British would be back.

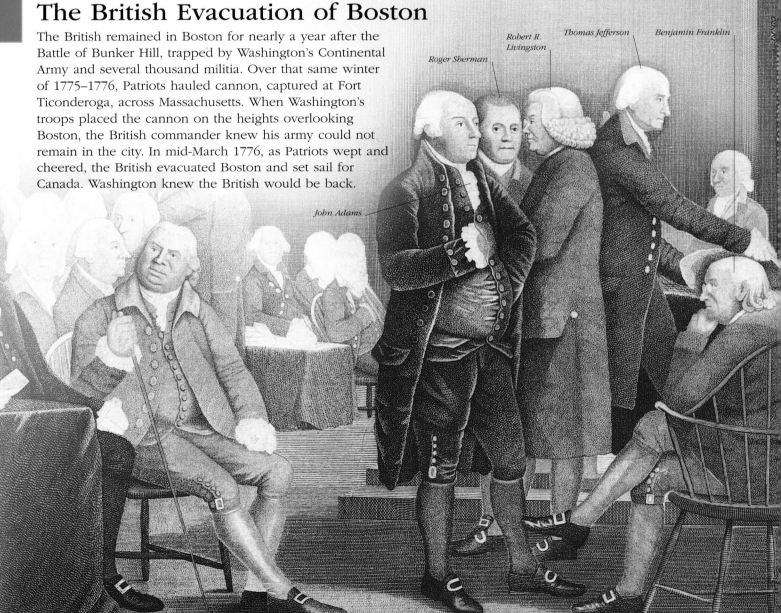

THE SIGNING of the Declaration of Independence

Roger Sherman

Robert R. Livingston

Thomas Jefferson

Benjamin Franklin

John Adams

The Decision to Declare Independence

By spring of 1776, the Americans had been at war for a year. A growing number were convinced that they were fighting to be permanently free of Britain's rule, and that the time had come to issue a declaration of independence. In January, Thomas Paine had published *Common Sense*, which helped many colonists decide to press for independence. In June, the Continental Congress named a committee of five to draft a declaration.

The committee chose Thomas Jefferson to write the draft. The Continental Congress then debated the document, striking out a long passage in which Jefferson blamed the king for making slavery possible. On the evening of July 4, 1776, the Continental Congress approved the Declaration of Independence. In the following weeks, public readings of the document were greeted with cheers and celebrations in towns across the land.

The Philosophy Behind the Declaration

Thomas Jefferson drew on the ideas of great political thinkers, including England's John Locke. In 1688, Locke wrote that government is a contract, or compact, between the government and the people; if the government did not live up to that contract, the people had the right to change the government or create a new one.

1763–1800

John Hancock

JEFFERSON'S DRAFT OF THE DECLARATION OF INDEPENDENCE as a bold statement of a people's right to create their own government. The men who signed the document knew they were risking everything, but they willingly added their names.

THOMAS JEFFERSON, 1743–1826

The primary author of the Declaration of Independence was one of the most brilliant and versatile of the nation's founders. While best known as a political leader and writer, Jefferson's curiosity carried him into many different roles: farmer, lawyer, scientist, inventor, architect, linguist, amateur musician, and founder of the Library of Congress.

His career in government was also varied—diplomat, delegate to Congress, and governor of Virginia. After the government of the United States was established, he served as secretary of state, vice president, and served two terms as president, from 1801–1809. In spite of his achievements, Jefferson was tormented throughout his life by his failure to find a solution to the contradiction of slavery existing in a free society. Fearing financial ruin he freed only a few of his own slaves.

Jefferson and his old friend—and former adversary—John Adams both died on July 4, 1826, the 50th anniversary of the Declaration of Independence!

Dark Days of War

After declaring independence, the former colonies—now the 13 American states—faced months of hardship and defeat. Through those dark days, a solid core of dedicated Patriots and the leadership of General George Washington kept hope alive.

DECEMBER 25, 1776–JANUARY 3, 1777

Striking Back at Trenton and Princeton

While Congress debated the Declaration of Independence, a huge British invasion force had entered New York harbor. The British and their auxiliary German soldiers, called Hessians, smashed through Washington's Continental Army and militia to conquer New York. After New York fell, Washington was forced to retreat across New Jersey into Pennsylvania with the remnants of his army.

On Christmas night, 1776, Washington's men suddenly struck back. They crossed the half-frozen Delaware River and, at dawn, captured a surprised Hessian garrison at Trenton, New Jersey. A week later, the Continentals won another stunning victory at Princeton over General William Howe's Redcoats. The two triumphs could not have come at a better time for boosting Patriot morale.

BENEDICT ARNOLD, 1741–1801

Benedict Arnold was an outstanding general. At Saratoga, he showed enormous courage leading the charge that broke through Burgoyne's lines. But he was a vain and sensitive man, who felt that he had been badly treated by Congress and the army. In April 1779, Arnold persuaded Washington to put him in charge of West Point, the fort on the lower Hudson. Once there, he arranged to sell the fort to the British. The plot was discovered; Arnold escaped and was made a general by the British, but they never trusted him, even after he moved his family to England.

PAPERS INTENDED FOR BENEDICT ARNOLD detailing the sale of West Point to the British are found in a fellow traitor's boot.

CROSSING THE DELAWARE
Washington's decision to cross the Delaware River at night in small boats was a daring maneuver that has been the scene of many paintings. Usually, as in this painting by Emanuel Leutze, Washington is shown standing, which would have been dangerous, since it would have unbalanced the boat and possibly tipped it over. Leutze's painting also shows the wrong kind of boat and a flag that had not yet been created. Still, the artist captured the drama and suspense of the event.

General George Washington

SUMMER 1777

The British Strategy

In the summer of 1777, the British launched another large-scale attack, this time coming south from Canada. General John Burgoyne led the main force down the corridor between Lake Champlain and the Hudson River to Albany. There he planned to meet up with General Howe coming north from New York City, while a third force crossed New York State from the east. If the British succeeded in this plan to join their armies, New England would be isolated and the "rebellion" would be stopped.

Turning Point for the Americans

But the plan ran into massive Patriot resistance. The army crossing New York was stopped at Fort Stanwix, so it retreated to Canada. At the same time, General Howe set out to capture Philadelphia, confident that Burgoyne would have an easy victory at Albany.

More than 10,000 militiamen arrived to join a division of Continentals near Albany. These Americans, led by General Horatio Gates, won a tremendous victory at the Battle of Saratoga in October. Burgoyne surrendered 6,000 men, including many officers.

The Battle of Saratoga marked a turning point in the war. The French, now convinced that the Americans could win, formed an alliance with them. Troops and ships would come later; but desperately needed supplies were sent immediately. Victory now seemed possible, but the Americans still faced four years of war.

MAJOR BATTLES OF THE AMERICAN REVOLUTION

▲ AMERICAN VICTORY

● BRITISH VICTORY

This map of Revolutionary battles shows the borders between the states. The states' western borders hadn't been established yet, so they have not been shown.

THE HANGING OF NATHAN HALE

In the autumn of 1776, a 21-year-old schoolteacher named Nathan Hale volunteered to be a spy to investigate British troop strength in New York City. Hale was discovered by the British and taken prisoner. Since he was not in uniform, he didn't need to be considered a prisoner of war—so he was hanged. Hale's last words, recorded by a bystander, served as an inspiring motto for Patriots: "I regret that I have but one life to give for my country."

The Road to Yorktown

After the victory at Saratoga, the Continental Army suffered through starvation, exposure, and illness during a nightmarish winter in Valley Forge, Pennsylvania. The one bright spot was that a German volunteer, Baron Friedrich von Steuben, drilled the men relentlessly. By spring, the army was a tough fighting force. In battles in New Jersey and New York, Washington was able to lead his troops to victory. In the South, however, it was more difficult. Patriot bands and a few Continental regiments under Nathanael Greene struggled against a British invasion. After a few key victories, though, the British army was trapped on the coast of Virginia, waiting for help from the navy. It didn't come in time, and the British were forced to surrender.

BARON VON STEUBEN was one of the European military officers who led American troops during the war.

1763–1800

Britain's Southern Strategy

In mid-1778, General Henry Clinton took command of British forces. His strategy included launching invasions of the South from the British base in New York. The British knew that in the South they would be welcomed by Loyalists—those who remained loyal to Great Britain and the king. Clinton led an invasion of Georgia in December 1778, captured Savannah, and put a new royal governor in power. Early in 1780, Clinton struck again, attacking Charleston, South Carolina, and handing the Americans their worst defeat of the entire war. Clinton returned to New York, leaving General Charles Cornwallis in charge of the South, where the British controlled much of Georgia and South Carolina.

Hit-and-Run Tactics Win Out

Patriot guerrilla bands were experts at hit-and-run fighting— using rocks and trees as cover while shooting, rather than marching into battle in straight rows like the British army did. Under the command of Washington's best general, Nathanael Greene, Continental and local militia forces, with the help of the bands of Patriots, struck at the British forces and Loyalists again and again in battles in the South. Several times Greene lost to Cornwallis, but the Americans did enough damage to Cornwallis's army that he had to retreat into Virginia.

Benjamin Lincoln, Washington's second-in-command

OCTOBER 19, 1781

Finale at Yorktown

By late summer, 1781, Cornwallis's army was stationed at Yorktown on the Virginia coast, where the British fleet could come to their rescue. However, Clinton underestimated George Washington, who seized a unique opportunity. With his Continental Army and a 5,000-man French force, Washington raced south from outside New York. With perfect timing, a French fleet drove off the British warships, while American and French soldiers closed the trap on Yorktown.

After three weeks of being battered by artillery, Cornwallis surrendered on October 19, 1781. The Americans had won their independence.

MARIE-JOSEPH-PAUL-YVES-ROCH-GILBERT DU MOTIER DE LAFAYETTE
One of the most popular European military officers to serve in the Patriot cause was the Marquis de Lafayette, a wealthy French nobleman. He became a favorite of Washington and his men, and was a brilliant general. In 1826, a half-century later, Lafayette returned to the United States to a hero's welcome.

1763-1800

THE SURRENDER OF CORNWALLIS
John Trumbull's painting shows the British surrender at Yorktown. Cornwallis claimed to be too ill to attend the ceremony, so he sent his second-in-command to hand over his sword. Washington wouldn't accept it, though, and directed that it be given to his own second-in-command.

General George Washington

The Confederation Era

The Declaration of Independence in 1776 transformed the colonies into 13 independent states. Each former colony started to write a state constitution. Never before had people written out exactly what powers government would—and would not—have. Although only adult white males who owned property could vote, these governments were the most democratic ever achieved by a large society.

The Continental Congress did not have the same kind of power; in fact, it could barely function because it had so little authority. For example, the states could levy taxes to raise money, but Congress could not. Soon the States were arguing over a variety of problems.

Currency from Massachusetts

Currency from the Continental Congress

Currency from New Jersey

ALL THE STATES printed their own money; without a standard form of currency, trade between the states was nearly impossible.

1763–1800

DANIEL BOONE, 1734–1820

OPENING THE WEST

Even before the Revolution, Daniel Boone and other pioneers blazed trails and led pioneers into the western wilderness. In 1775, Boone joined several Indian trails together to create the Wilderness Road. Thousands of pioneers used this road to cross the Cumberland Gap into what is now Kentucky. Boone eventually moved west to Missouri, where he continued to hunt and explore the wilds well into his eighties.

DEFINITION

*A **confederation** is an alliance of independent states.*

THE TREATY OF PARIS AND BEYOND

The Revolutionary War had ended after six hard years, and it took two more years to finish a formal peace treaty. The British were in no rush to satisfy the Americans, and they hoped delay would persuade the states to pay Loyalists for the property they had lost when they fled the country. In the final Treaty of Paris, ratified by The Continental Congress on April 15, 1783, the British recognized the independence of the United States of America. The nation's boundaries would stretch from the Atlantic Ocean to the Mississippi River, and from the Great Lakes south to Florida.

As part of the treaty, the British agreed to move all their forces out of America. However, they were slow to carry out this provision. The issue of British troops on America's northwest frontier poisoned relations between the two countries and would eventually contribute to the War of 1812.

The Treaty of Paris, with the signatures of John Adams, Benjamin Franklin, and John Jay

Forming State and National Governments

In creating state constitutions, the government was divided into three branches: a legislature to make laws; an executive branch to enforce the laws and manage the government; and a judiciary to interpret the laws. This "separation of powers" was intended to prevent any one branch from becoming too powerful. In addition, each constitution began with a "bill of rights"—a statement of freedoms individuals held that the government could not take away.

A Weak National Government Is Formed

The Second Continental Congress, which met in 1775 and guided America through the war, didn't have much authority; it couldn't demand that the states comply with its decisions.

When it was time to create a central government, the Congress couldn't agree on how much power it should have. The leaders in most states guarded their independence and did not want a strong national government. The document they finally came up with was called the Articles of Confederation. In 1781, after 18 months of debate, the Articles were ratified, or approved.

The document created a single branch of government—the Congress—which had a hard time enforcing trade regulations between the states and with other nations, deciding which states held claims to land in the West, and many other issues.

Dividing Western Lands

The young American nation gained a huge land area south of the Great Lakes and between the Ohio River in the east and the Mississippi River, which was called the Northwest Territory. One achievement of the Confederation era was coming up with a way these and other new lands would become part of the nation.

The Land Ordinance of 1785 divided new lands into townships and then into sections, which would be sold to settlers—except for five sections, which were set aside for the national government and for maintaining public schools.

Then, in 1787, Congress passed the Northwest Ordinance to regulate how new states would be created out of the Northwest Territory.

Creating New States

Congress would first appoint a governor to a new territory. When 5,000 white adult males were living in that territory, those people could elect a legislature and send a delegate to Congress. Then, when the population reached 60,000 white adult male voters, the territory could become a state.

However, the new state could not allow slavery, and the governments would "forever be encouraged to support public education."

IN SHAYS'S REBELLION, desperate farmers who couldn't pay their taxes took over a courthouse so their farms wouldn't be seized by the government.

Shays's Rebellion

Even in good economic times, farmers usually had only a little bit of extra goods to trade or sell after they had provided for their families— they rarely had much actual money. So farm families had trouble paying their taxes. Many, like Captain Daniel Shays of Massachusetts, had been paid for serving in the army, but the paper money was worthless because the government had no wealth which would give it value. In January 1787, Shays and about 1,000 other farmers seized weapons from the Springfield Armory and closed courts so their property could not be sold off. Shays's Rebellion was easily put down, but it convinced many that a stronger government was needed to address the country's problems.

The Constitution

In May 1787, 55 delegates from the 13 states met at Philadelphia's State House. It was a gathering of uniquely gifted men, including George Washington, who served as chairman. Instead of trying to adjust the weak Articles of Confederation, they started anew to frame a completely new form of government—the United States Constitution.

The Division of Powers

The framers of the Constitution, as the delegates were called, created a federal government with three branches: the legislative branch was the Congress, made up of the Senate—with two senators coming from each state—and the House of Representatives—whose numbers were based on each state's population; the executive branch was composed of the president and the executive departments, such as the Cabinet; and the judicial branch was the Supreme Court and other federal courts. Through an innovative system of checks and balances, any two branches could prevent the third from gaining too much power.

Another great achievement was in dividing power between the states and the national government. This sharing of power is called federalism. The Constitution gave certain delegated powers to the national government; other powers were reserved solely for the states; and some "concurrent powers," such as taxation and road building, were shared.

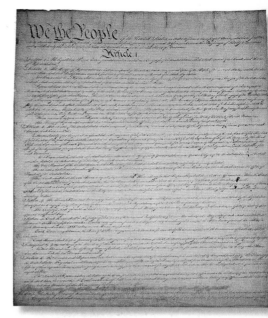

The Constitution of the United States of America

POWER SHARING IN THE GOVERNMENT

POWERS DELEGATED TO THE FEDERAL GOVERNMENT:	POWERS SHARED (HELD CONCURRENTLY) BY THE FEDERAL AND STATE GOVERNMENTS:	POWERS RESERVED FOR STATE GOVERNMENTS:
Maintain an army and a navy; Admit new states; Establish a post office; Coin money; Declare war; Regulate foreign and interstate commerce; Make laws necessary and proper for carrying out delegated powers	Maintain law and order; Establish courts; Charter banks; Borrow money; Levy taxes; Build roads; Protect the people's health and safety	Establish schools; Conduct elections; Establish local governments; Charter and regulate corporations; Regulate business within the state; Regulate marriages; Assume other powers not given to the national government or prohibited to the states

HOW THE FEDERAL GOVERNMENT IS ORGANIZED

FEDERAL GOVERNMENT

EXECUTIVE BRANCH	JUDICIAL BRANCH	LEGISLATIVE BRANCH
The President; the Cabinet; other departments	Supreme Court; other federal courts	House of Representatives; Senate

The Debate Over Ratification

Beginning in the fall of 1787, state conventions were held to ratify, or approve, the Constitution, with nine states' approval needed for the Constitution to go into effect. Several states ratified quickly, but usually after a vigorous debate, because many people feared that the new government would have too much power. In Massachusetts, ratification won by a narrow margin only after delegates promised that they would vote to amend, or change, the Constitution by adding a bill of rights—the first ten amendments to the Constitution.

Slavery Compromises

One long-simmering issue remained unresolved: the question of slavery. Compromises were made throughout the Constitution in order to keep the South from splitting off, including counting each slave as three-fifths of a person, so that slave-holding states would have larger population counts and therefore a larger number of congressmen in the House of Representatives.

THE BILL OF RIGHTS

When the new Congress met in 1789, James Madison proposed several amendments to the Constitution. As well as being inspired by the Virginia Declaration of Rights created by anti-Federalist George Mason, the amendments included proposals from state representatives. Congress approved the ten amendments to the Constitution, which were named the Bill of Rights.

The first four amendments listed the individual rights of Americans, such as freedom of speech, freedom of the press, and freedom of religion. The next four were protections of people who were arrested. The ninth amendment stated that other rights of the people were also protected even though they weren't listed, and the tenth said that powers not given to the government belonged to the states or to the people.

Federalism v. States' Rights

In June 1788, the Constitution officially went into effect. But four states, including Virginia and New York, had not ratified yet, and the new government could not succeed without their support.

The debate between those who supported the Constitution, called "Federalists," and their opponents, "Anti-Federalists"—those who supported the rights of the states over the federal government—was long and spirited. The final victory for ratification, in late June 1788, was very close. By the spring of 1790, all thirteen states had approved the Constitution.

1763–1800

George Washington

James Madison

Benjamin Franklin

Alexander Hamilton

THE FRAMERS OF THE CONSTITUTION met from May to September, 1787. Despite the heat, doors and windows were kept shut, so no one else could listen to the deliberations and influence the delegates. Sand was even spread over the cobblestone streets to muffle sound. When the delegates were done, they had created one of history's great documents—a framework that has served the nation for more than two centuries and has been a model for other governments around the world.

The Federalist Years

George Washington, the most revered man in America, was everyone's choice to be president of the new nation. The electors chosen by the state legislatures unanimously voted him into office. Washington served two terms, beginning in 1788, and he was followed by his vice president, John Adams, who served one term beginning in 1796. These 12 years became known as the "Federalist Years."

Interpreting the Constitution

During this time, some government leaders, such as Alexander Hamilton of New York, believed in a loose interpretation of the Constitution, which broadly defined the role of the government and would enable the expansion of federal power (see p. 53).

Thomas Jefferson, Washington's secretary of state, opposed this view. Jefferson wanted a strict interpretation, which would give the government only those powers that were clearly stated in the document.

The Federalist Papers

When it first met, the New York State convention had an Anti-Federalist majority. During the spring of 1788, however, three leading Federalists—Alexander Hamilton, James Madison, and John Jay—wrote a series of essays supporting the Constitution's strong central government. These were published in New York newspapers and were also collected in a book entitled *The Federalist*.

JOHN ADAMS was one of the great political thinkers among the founders of the United States government. Although never popular outside of New England, he served the nation well as its second president.

ALEXANDER HAMILTON is often credited with saving the United States from the huge debt it got into to pay for the Revolutionary War.

When John Adams took office in March 1797, Washington was relieved that he could finally leave public life. In his farewell address in September 1796, he left the American people with two warnings: to be careful of the "continual mischiefs" of party politics, and to "steer clear of permanent alliances with any portion of the foreign world."

THE QUASI-WAR WITH FRANCE AND THE ALIEN AND SEDITION ACTS

In 1797, conflict erupted when French ships interfered with American ships trading around the world and three American diplomats were offered bribes. Federalists in the government were eager to go to war.

The conflict, which neither France nor President John Adams wanted, was soon over, but Federalists had used it as an excuse to silence Republican opponents: they created the Alien and Sedition Acts. The Alien Act said the president could deport foreigners who were "dangerous to the peace or safety" of the country. Even worse, the Sedition Act was a danger to basic freedoms, making it a crime to say, write, or publish anything "false, scandalous, and malicious" about the government. The restoration of peace ended the crisis, but the incident demonstrated the importance of protecting freedom of speech.

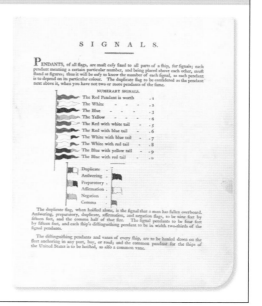

Truxtun's signal flags, 1797, with instructions and explanations, ordered for the United States Fleet.

The Election of 1800

The framers had feared that if political parties, or factions, began to form in the government, they could lead to differences of opinion that would make it hard to come to agreement on issues. Just as they predicted, by 1800, political parties were taking shape in the United States. In the fourth presidential election, Federalist John Adams lost to Thomas Jefferson and his Anti-Federalist, or Republican, party. Many feared that the election would lead to chaos, but the transition was smooth, and the nation began a new century.

A Tie for the Presidency

In the first elections under the Constitution, the person receiving the most electoral votes was made president and the person with the second-most votes vice president. Political party politics complicated that situation, though, because electors now voted for a single party "ticket" with candidates for president and vice president from the same party. In 1800, Jefferson—a presidential candidate—and Aaron Burr—his vice-presidential candidate—each received 73 electoral votes.

The House of Representatives was supposed to settle electoral ties. It took nearly 40 separate votes in the House before they named Jefferson. The Twelfth Amendment, passed in 1804, solved this problem for future elections by establishing separate votes for president and vice president.

WHERE TO PUT THE NATION'S CAPITAL?
One of the issues facing the new government was where to locate the nation's capital, or the "Federal City," as it was first called. A site on the Potomac River was selected because it was neither in the North nor the South; John Adams became the first president to reside in the "President's House," which was later named the White House.

THE TRAIL OF TEARS was the path taken by Cherokee Indians on the march from their home in Georgia to the "Indian Territory" in Oklahoma. They were forced off their land by President Jackson's Indian Removal Act, and many died from the harsh conditions on the journey. To fulfill their dreams of westward expansion, Americans tried to remove all other groups from the land. The government continued to clash with American Indians, and fought two wars to remove Britain and Mexico from American land and affairs.

Mar. 1803
Ohio enters the Union

Apr. 30, 1803
Louisiana Purchase

Oct. 1802
Spain closes New Orleans to American trade

Dec. 1804
Jefferson reelected

Dec. 1808
James Madison elected president

Apr. 1812
Louisiana enters the Union

June 18, 1812
United States declares war against Great Britain

Dec. 1812
Madison reelected

Aug. 24, 1814
British burn Washington, D.C.

Sept. 13, 1814
Bombardment of Fort McHenry; "Star-Spangled Banner" written

Dec. 24, 1814
Treaty of Ghent ends the War of 1812

1820
Missouri Compromise; Maine separates from Massachusetts

Mar. 1820
Maine enters the Union

Dec. 6, 1820
Monroe reelected

Aug. 1821
Missouri enters the Union

Oct. 26, 1825
Erie Canal opens

Dec. 1823
Monroe Doctrine

1800	1805	1810	1815	1820	1825

Dec. 1800
Thomas Jefferson elected president

May 1804–Sept. 1806
Lewis and Clark expedition

1807
Aaron Burr tried for treason; first successful steamboat built

Mar. 1807
Foreign slave trade abolished

Nov. 7, 1811
Battle of Tippecanoe

Jan. 8, 1815
Battle of New Orleans

Dec. 1816
James Monroe elected president; Indiana enters the Union

Dec. 1817
Mississippi enters the Union

Dec. 1818
Illinois enters the Union

Feb. 22, 1819
U.S. acquires Florida from Spain (Adams-Onis Treaty)

Dec. 1819
Alabama enters the Union

Dec. 1824
John Quincy Adams elected president

AMERICA GROWS

1800–1850

A flood of settlers moved westward across the Appalachian Mountain barrier in the early 19th century in pursuit of America's "Manifest Destiny." New roads, canals, and railroads were built, allowing Americans to travel farther and transport goods and belongings faster. The invention of the cotton gin made cotton such a profitable crop that it soon dominated the South's economy. Plantations—and slavery—spread west in search of more land. To make room for land-hungry settlers, President Jackson approved the forcible removal of eastern Indian tribes to "Indian Territories" beyond the Mississippi. Expansionist fever peaked in the 1840s, when the United States annexed Texas and defeated Mexico, extending its borders to the Pacific.

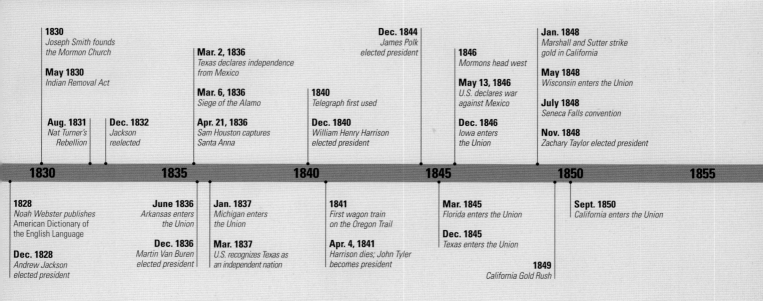

1830
Joseph Smith founds the Mormon Church

May 1830
Indian Removal Act

Aug. 1831
Nat Turner's Rebellion

Dec. 1832
Jackson reelected

Mar. 2, 1836
Texas declares independence from Mexico

Mar. 6, 1836
Siege of the Alamo

Apr. 21, 1836
Sam Houston captures Santa Anna

1840
Telegraph first used

Dec. 1840
William Henry Harrison elected president

Dec. 1844
James Polk elected president

1846
Mormons head west

May 13, 1846
U.S. declares war against Mexico

Dec. 1846
Iowa enters the Union

Jan. 1848
Marshall and Sutter strike gold in California

May 1848
Wisconsin enters the Union

July 1848
Seneca Falls convention

Nov. 1848
Zachary Taylor elected president

1830   **1835**   **1840**   **1845**   **1850**   **1855**

1828
Noah Webster publishes American Dictionary of the English Language

Dec. 1828
Andrew Jackson elected president

June 1836
Arkansas enters the Union

Dec. 1836
Martin Van Buren elected president

Jan. 1837
Michigan enters the Union

Mar. 1837
U.S. recognizes Texas as an independent nation

1841
First wagon train on the Oregon Trail

Apr. 4, 1841
Harrison dies; John Tyler becomes president

Mar. 1845
Florida enters the Union

Dec. 1845
Texas enters the Union

1849
California Gold Rush

Sept. 1850
California enters the Union

Jefferson and the West

Like many Americans, third president Thomas Jefferson saw the future of America in the West. Kentucky and Tennessee had become states in 1792 and 1796, respectively; Ohio joined the Union in 1803; and new territories were being formed in the Northwest. In 1803, Jefferson persuaded Congress to fund an expedition to explore the land from the Mississippi River to the Pacific Ocean and bring back as much information about the land, people, plants, and animals as possible. Before the expedition left, the United States had the chance to purchase the uncharted Louisiana territory from France. The Louisiana Purchase doubled the land area of the growing nation.

JEFFERSON CALLED THE LOUISIANA PURCHASE "a widespread field for the blessings of freedom and equal laws."

SOLDIERS FIRE A SALUTE as the American flag is raised in New Orleans, the major port on the Gulf of Mexico, to commemorate the purchase of the Louisiana territory.

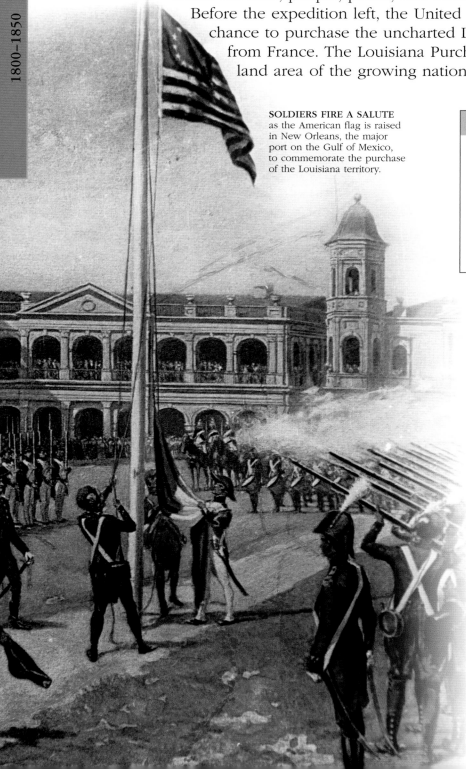

TOUSSAINT LOUVERTURE, 1743–1803

Napoleon, emperor of France, planned to base an empire in North America after establishing a naval base on the island of Hispaniola in the Caribbean Sea. His plans were ruined by Toussaint Louverture, who led a revolution of slaves and free blacks there. Louverture was captured, but his followers kept the revolution alive, frustrating Napoleon's plans. Napoleon lost interest in Louisiana and sold it to the United States.

NOVEMBER 1803

The Louisiana Purchase

Buying the Louisiana territory raised a constitutional issue for President Jefferson, since the document said nothing about purchasing new lands. Jefferson decided that keeping France from controlling the Mississippi River was too important, though, to turn down the opportunity. So the purchase was judged necessary and the Senate readily approved it in 1803. Congress paid France about $15 million for the land.

The Louisiana Purchase doubled the land area of the nation, adding 800,000 square miles and more than 200,000 people—primarily American Indians, Spanish, and French.

New Orleans

As settlers poured into the Midwest, farm families needed markets for their farm products. Shipping goods east over the Appalachians was difficult, but floating them on rafts down the Mississippi River to New Orleans, where they could be shipped to the East or foreign markets was cheap and easy. New Orleans played a key role in the decision to purchase Louisiana.

AARON BURR, 1756–1836

Aaron Burr was a brilliant, erratic man with great personal charm—and huge ambition. He served as vice president during Jefferson's first term, but the president considered him a dangerous schemer and replaced him for the 1804 election. Burr ran for governor of New York instead, but lost. He blamed the defeat on vicious newspaper attacks Alexander Hamilton had written. When Hamilton refused to apologize, Burr challenged him to a duel with pistols and fatally wounded him. With a warrant out for his arrest, Burr, still vice president, fled west. He was arrested and put on trial for treason in 1807. He was acquitted due to lack of evidence, but he spent the rest of his life in obscurity.

Burr and Hamilton's duel

MAY 1804–SEPTEMBER 1806

The Lewis and Clark Expedition

In May 1804, two army officers—Meriwether Lewis and William Clark—set out from St. Louis on a historic expedition. Thomas Jefferson sent Lewis and Clark to explore the huge, unmapped wilderness west of the Mississippi, and instructed them to report back with their findings. The 45-member expedition party was led in part by a 17-year-old Shoshone Indian named Sacagawea, who was their guide and interpreter. She played a vital role in helping the expedition travel peacefully. After 28 months, Lewis and Clark returned to St. Louis—when many thought they were dead—bringing with them detailed journals and crates of plant, animal, and rock specimens.

 THE ROUTE OF LEWIS AND CLARK

⬅ ST. LOUIS TO THE PACIFIC OCEAN

➡ RETURN TRIP

The Louis and Clark expedition sailed and rowed up the Missouri River, spent the winter in a Mandan village, then continued on horseback over the Rocky Mountains. The round-trip journey crossed a total of about 8,000 miles of rugged western terrain.

SACAGAWEA is credited with helping Lewis and Clark avoid armed conflict with Indian tribes. Her husband and infant son traveled with her.

The War of 1812

In the early 1800s, the United States tried to steer a neutral course between Great Britain and France, as they battled each other in the Napoleonic Wars in Europe and around the world. However, both warring nations repeatedly trampled on America's rights, making neutrality difficult. Finally, after calling for "free trade and sailors' rights," America declared war on the British. Not everyone agreed with the decision to go to war. Nonetheless it gave the young nation a renewed sense of pride.

MAJOR BATTLES OF THE WAR OF 1812

BATTLE	LOCATION	DATE	VICTOR
Battle of Lake Erie	Ohio	Sept. 10, 1813	U.S.
Leading American figure involved: Captain Oliver H. Perry			
Battle of the Thames	Canada	Oct. 5, 1813	U.S.
Leading American figure involved: General William Henry Harrison			
Burning of Washington	Washington, D.C.	Aug. 24, 1814	British
Leading American figure involved: Dolley Madison			
Battle of Lake Champlain	New York	Sept. 11, 1814	U.S.
Leading American figure involved: Captain Thomas Macdonough			
Fort McHenry	Maryland	Sept. 13, 1814	U.S.
Leading American figure involved: Francis Scott Key			
Battle of New Orleans	Louisiana	Jan. 8, 1815	U.S.
Leading American figure involved: General Andrew Jackson			

"Free Trade and Sailors' Rights"

During the Napoleonic Wars, both the British and the French harassed American ships, but the British were the worst offenders. British warships repeatedly stopped American ships, seized sailors, and "impressed" them into service in the Royal Navy. Outraged Americans began to demand war with the rallying cry, "Free trade and sailors' rights."

Trade or War?

Although the Northeastern seafaring areas were most affected by these events, the "war hawks" who wanted a military solution came mostly from the South and West. Seafarers needed peace with their trading partners in order to keep trading, while the hawks saw war as a chance to stop the British from encouraging Indian raids on the frontier. They thought Canada could even be taken in victory from Great Britain.

Presidents Jefferson and Madison tried economic policies such as embargoes to make Britain and France change their ways. They didn't work.

DEFINITION

*An **embargo** is a ban on trade with another nation.*

THIS AMERICAN FLAG, c. 1795, with 15 stars, represented the 13 original colonies, now states, plus the new states of Vermont (1791) and Kentucky (1792). Now hanging in the Smithsonian Institution in Washington, D.C., the flag survived the British bombardment of Fort McHenry and inspired the lyrics of "The Star-Spangled Banner."

TECUMSEH AND THE INDIAN ALLIANCE

Tecumseh, a powerful Shawnee chief, made a strong alliance of the tribes along the western American frontier in what is now Michigan and Indiana. In November 1811, the governor of the Indiana Territory, William Henry Harrison, launched an attack on warriors led by Tecumseh's brother. The fierce Battle of Tippecanoe was a draw. However, it was discovered that some of Tecumseh's warriors had used British weapons, adding to the demand for war. After war was declared, General Harrison led a force into Canada, where he defeated the British and Indians at the Battle of the Thames. Tecumseh was killed there. Without his leadership, his confederacy quickly collapsed.

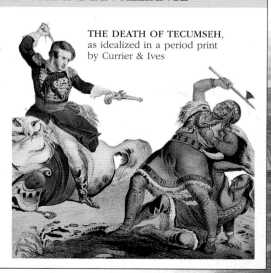

THE DEATH OF TECUMSEH, as idealized in a period print by Currier & Ives

JUNE 1812–SEPTEMBER 1814

Mr. Madison's War

On June 1, 1812, President James Madison asked Congress to declare war against Britain. With a navy of only 16 ships and a 7,000-man army, the United States was in no position to fight. "War hawks" were eager to conquer Canada, however, and organized an invasion. The mission failed.

James Madison, fourth President of the United States

When, in 1814, Napoleon was defeated in Europe, battle-hardened British troops became available to send to America. One regiment sailed up the Chesapeake River in August, defeated the militia, and marched into Washington. As First Lady Dolley Madison fled with a portrait of George Washington, the British torched the White House, the Capitol, and other buildings, then moved on to Fort McHenry.

WINTER 1814–1815

Peace and the Battle of New Orleans

The British, weary after many years of war with France, wanted peace, and the American government had no more funds for waging war. Negotiators, meeting in Belgium, signed the Treaty of Ghent on Christmas Eve, 1814. However, the most important event of the war happened *after* the signing.

On January 8, 1815, unaware that the war was over, General Andrew Jackson led his militia and army against a powerful British invasion force at New Orleans. Jackson's men were victorious, forcing the British to retreat or surrender.

Until that moment, the War of 1812 had been an embarrassment for America. It had failed to accomplish what the war hawks had wanted, and the burning of Washington had made the nation look helpless. The Battle of New Orleans made Americans feel as if they had won the war. A surge of national pride swept over the country. Albert Gallatin, one of the American peace commissioners, said that the war made Americans "feel and act more like a nation."

THE BRITISH BOMBARDED FORT MCHENRY in Baltimore, Maryland, after having burned Washington, D.C. While arranging an exchange of prisoners onboard a nearby British warship, Baltimore lawyer Francis Scott Key witnessed the fort's defense. He was inspired to write "The Star-Spangled Banner," which would become the United States' national anthem in 1931.

1800–1850

Shaping a New Nation

The United States emerged from the War of 1812 with a stronger sense of national unity. It was further strengthened by the growth of American industry, advances in transportation, and the development of a uniquely American literature and language. This new confidence found political voice in the Monroe Doctrine, which warned Europe to stay out of the affairs of the Americas. But tension rose between the North and the South over the issue of whether to allow slavery in new states.

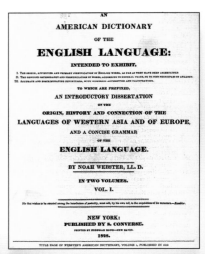

THE TITLE PAGE of *Webster's American Dictionary of the English Language*

The Industrial Revolution Begins

The development of American industry was greatly influenced by the innovations of England's industrial revolution. Manufacturing was transformed through mass production: the slow process of making things by hand in homes or craft shops gave way to the mass production of cheap factory goods. Water power was used to run machines that spun cotton into thread. The same basic system was then used to make clocks, furniture, farm tools, and other items.

The beginnings of this industrial system affected regions in different ways. The Northeast was becoming the center of manufacturing. In the new regions of the West, farmers shipped grain and meat products to cities in the East and in Europe; in turn, they were buying more goods, such as clothing and furniture, from Northeastern mills. The South supplied cotton to the mills, while becoming dependent on factory-made goods. The South was also becoming more dependent on slave labor, which threatened the nation's unity.

BEFORE ELI WHITNEY INVENTED THE COTTON GIN in 1792, cotton had not been a good cash crop, because separating out the sticky seeds was a time-consuming task. The gin made cleaning the seeds out of cotton 50 times faster, which made growing cotton profitable. To supply the Northern mills with cotton, plantation owners in the Deep South began planting more of it. More slave labor was then needed to work the land, and so slave trading and ownership increased in the South.

The Growth of American Literature and Language

Several American figures contributed to the growing sense of an American language and literature separate from British styles. Noah Webster devoted his life to making the English language in America distinct from the language as it was spoken and used in Great Britain. In 1828, he published *Webster's American Dictionary of the English Language*. It was the largest dictionary ever published and established America as culturally independent from Great Britain.

First American Fiction

The two most famous stories of Washington Irving (1783–1859)— "The Legend of Sleepy Hollow" and "Rip Van Winkle" (both published between 1819 and 1820)—helped make him the first American to earn his living by writing, and the first to gain world fame.

Also in the 1820s, James Fenimore Cooper wrote *The Last of the Mohicans*, one of his *Leatherstocking* series of popular novels about life in frontier America.

An illustration from a Cooper novel about the frontier

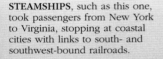

STEAMSHIPS, such as this one, took passengers from New York to Virginia, stopping at coastal cities with links to south- and southwest-bound railroads.

Modes of Transportation

Many states had started an extensive program of road building, and soon hundreds of roads knit together towns and regions. Also, by the 1830s, 3,000 miles of canals were built. The Erie Canal was the most remarkable; it connected Lake Erie with the Hudson River—a distance of 362 miles. The cost of shipping Midwestern-grown grain from Buffalo to New York City dropped from $100 a ton to $10. Then, in 1807, Robert Fulton revolutionized water travel with his paddle-wheel boat powered by steam, which chugged up the Hudson River—*against* the current.

SLAVERY AND THE MISSOURI COMPROMISE

By 1804, every state north of Delaware had abolished slavery. In 1818, however, the issue of slavery flared up when Missouri asked to be admitted to the Union as a state with legal slavery. Northerners were bitterly opposed. The Missouri Compromise of 1820 said Missouri could enter the Union as a "slave state" if Maine entered as a "free state." This allowed the South to keep its power balance in the Senate. Congress voted in favor of the measure as the only way to avoid a crisis between North and South. It would be the first of many nonresolutions.

1820–1850 The Age of Reform

From the 1820s to the 1850s, Americans engaged in a variety of reforms, confident that they could improve society. Their desire to make change in part grew out of the Puritanical emphasis on moral law in religion and culture. The Puritans were a religious sect of Christians who believed in a stricter interpretation of the Protestant religion than existed in England in the 1600s. Their ideas were unpopular in Europe, so they came to America to escape persecution. The age of reform carried on the Puritans' tradition of societal improvement, which, it was hoped, would extend to government.

1800–1850

ANDREW JACKSON, 1761–1845

People refer to the 1830s as the period of "Jacksonian Democracy," but these terms refer more to the spirit of reform that swept Jackson into office than to any democratic reforms that he created. Jackson's own ideas of democracy were limited. He was, for example, a slave owner, and he designed the Indian Removal Policy. The American people embraced him in large part because he was a self-made man who, like many of them, had settled in the frontier West.

Women Reformers

In the early 1800s, women could not vote. In most states they could not sue in court, run a business, or own property; and, if they worked, they could not keep their own wages. Because of these inequalities, women such as Elizabeth Cady Stanton, Lucretia Mott, and Susan B. Anthony protested a society which made them almost completely dependent on men. Some women were individual pioneers. Elizabeth Blackwell finished first in her medical-school class and became the nation's first female doctor. Emma Hart Willard created educational opportunities by starting the first high school for girls. Still other women combined women's causes with health-care issues. One of these was Dorothea Dix, who toured the country emphasizing the inhumane treatment of the mentally ill.

Dorothea Dix

Organizing at Seneca Falls

In 1848, Stanton and Mott spearheaded the first organized movement for women's rights. The men and women who gathered at the convention in Seneca Falls, New York, presented and signed a "Declaration of Sentiments," which was based on the Declaration of Independence and called for full citizenship rights for women. The group was criticized and mocked for this radical position. Stanton, Susan B. Anthony, and other women then went on public speaking tours to win support for their ideas. Progress toward greater equality was painfully slow, however. Winning the right to vote, for example, would require nearly a century of struggle. The 19th amendment to the Constitution, stating that no citizen could be denied the right to vote on account of her sex, wouldn't be passed until 1920 (see p. 120).

BLACK LEADERS OF THE MOVEMENT TO ABOLISH SLAVERY

Sojourner Truth, a former slave, was a dramatic speaker for both abolition (see p. 76) and women's rights. Harriet Tubman became the most famous "conductor" on the Underground Railroad—a network of blacks and whites who helped hide and transport slaves so they could escape to freedom in the North or Canada. "Moses," as Tubman was known, conducted more than 300 blacks to freedom.

Frederick Douglass traveled throughout the North urging action to end slavery. The *North Star,* his newspaper, carried that same message in print.

SOJOURNER TRUTH's Pentecostal religion inspired her reform work.

FREDERICK DOUGLASS, a former slave, advised President Lincoln on black Americans' struggles.

ELIZABETH CADY STANTON speaks at the Seneca Falls Convention. Stanton continued to fight for suffrage and more freedom for women in all areas of life.

METHODIST CAMP MEETINGS helped spread the ideas of the reform era, as well as the word of God.

UTOPIAN SOCIETIES

During the age of reform, some idealistic people tried to create small, perfect societies—utopias. New England literary figures started two of the most famous communities—Brook Farm and Fruitlands. Both eventually ran into debt and failed. John Humphrey Noyes was more successful with his Oneida community in New York. At Oneida, outstanding silver products were crafted, providing the society with a solid economic foundation.

Religious Reformation

The Christian ideals that helped create the reforms of the early 1800s brought about direct change in religion, too. A number of Protestant ministers organized revivals and camp meetings in order to reawaken people's Christian faith. Preaching with great fervor, the revivalists remained popular throughout the 19th century.

Brand-new religious movements were also started. In rural New York, for example, Joseph Smith, convinced that he had received the revealed word of God, founded a faith known as the Church of Jesus Christ of Latter-Day Saints, whose followers were called Mormons.

Blazing Trails

Even after the Lewis and Clark expedition from 1804 to 1806 (see p. 59), the American people knew very little about the western half of the continent. Then, from roughly 1820 to 1850, settlers in search of farmland and adventurers in search of gold pried open that wild, mysterious land. Texas, Oregon, and California, especially, became an irresistible lure for more and more people.

Oregon Fever

Tales of Oregon as a "pioneer's paradise" filled Easterners with curiosity. Between 1841 and 1845, more than 5,000 "overlanders" took part in the Oregon fever and trekked across the continent on the Oregon Trail, a difficult wagon-train journey of 2,000 miles that took four to six months.

Beavers

The first Americans to explore the far West went in search of beaver pelts, which fetched high prices back east and were used to make tall beaver hats for fashionable gentlemen. The pelts were a valuable frontier commodity and could be traded for either supplies or money. When the beavers were "trapped out" and Europeans turned to silk top hats, the trappers pushed farther west to Oregon.

Beaver trap

The California Trail

In the mid-1820s, a party of trappers, led by legendary mountain man Jedediah Smith, followed beaver streams through the imposing Sierra Nevada mountains into California. They were the first white men to find a route through the mountains into the "land of perennial spring." In 1841, two traders who had joined the first wagon train to Oregon, left the others in present-day Idaho. They headed south, picked up Smith's trail, and made it into California. During the 1840s and 1850s, more than 200,000 farmers and gold seekers would follow in their footsteps in one of the greatest mass migrations in U.S. history.

Texas—The Lone Star Republic

In the 1820s, Moses Austin, followed by his son Stephen, gained permission from the Mexican government to settle 300 American families in the state of Coahuila, soon to be known as Texas. Thousands more settlers were granted permission and followed. By 1830, they outnumbered Mexicans in the region four to one.

In 1835, the dictator of Mexico, General Santa Anna, moved an army into Texas to establish military control. About 100 Texans defended their settlements at the Alamo. On March 6, 1836, surrounded by 5,000 troops, they were all killed. Other conflicts followed. The Texans, inspired by the rallying cry "Remember the Alamo!" overwhelmed the Mexicans and captured Santa Anna. In September, the Republic of Texas was formed, with Sam Houston as president. The Lone Star Republic would remain independent until 1845, when it was annexed (see p. 68) by the United States.

TRAILS TO THE FAR WEST

- Oregon Trail, about 2,170 miles
- Mormon Trail, about 1,500 miles
- California Trail, about 550 miles
- The Trail of Tears, over 1,000 miles
- ☼ Sites mined for gold

The trails on this map represent the most famous—and in the case of the Trail of Tears, most infamous—routes used for traveling west.

OREGON TERRITORY

- Oregon city

PACIFIC OCEAN

SIERRA NEVADA MOUNTAINS

- Soda Springs   South Pass
- Donner Pass
- *Great Salt Lake*
- ☼ Carson City   • Salt Lake City
- Sacramento •
- ☼ Jenny Lind
- ☼ Bear Valley
- San Francisco

CALIFORNIA   Santa Fe

Colorado R.

- • San Diego

Removal of the Eastern Indians

In 1830, President Jackson and Congress responded to the demands of land-hungry Americans by passing the Indian Removal Act. Throughout the 1830s, tribe after tribe was forced to give up its lands and move to Indian Territory beyond the Mississippi River in what is now Oklahoma.

The removal policy seemed particularly cruel for the Five Civilized Tribes. These five—the Cherokee, Creek, Choctaw, Chickasaw, and Seminole (see p. 15)—had adopted white men's ways, living in settled communities, and building schools and churches. When the Cherokee were forced off their Georgia lands, about one-quarter died on the journey, which the Cherokee named the Trail of Tears.

1800–1850

THIS PAINTING OF THE TRAIL OF TEARS depicts the suffering of the Cherokee on their forced journey to Oklahoma. Four thousand Cherokee died of cold, hunger, or disease as a result of displacement.

THE MORMONS

Joseph Smith's Mormon Church, now under the leadership of Brigham Young, joined the westward movement in 1846. The Mormons' society was governed by the church. They were persecuted, in part because they practiced polygamy, meaning that husbands could have more than one wife. They encountered violence wherever they settled, and Joseph Smith and his brother were killed in fights.

After a year of travel and hardship, about 15,000 Mormons reached the Great Salt Lake. Using complex irrigation systems, they transformed the desert valley into a green and fertile farmland.

THE MORMONS INVENTED THE ROADOMETER to measure how far they had traveled.

GREAT PLAINS

Missouri R.

• Nauvoo

• St. Joseph

• Kansas City   St. Louis •

Mississippi R.

GEORGIA

INDIAN TERRITORY

ATLANTIC OCEAN

TEXAS

Rio Grande

• The Alamo

THE SIEGE OF THE ALAMO left more than 100 Texans and 600 Mexicans dead, among them frontiersman Davy Crockett and Texan hero James Bowie, inventor of the Bowie knife.

MEXICO

Manifest Destiny

By the 1840s, many Americans had become convinced that the nation was meant to expand all the way across the continent to the Pacific Coast. Congressmen and newspaper editors began referring to this expansion as America's Manifest Destiny. Americans focused their attention on annexing Texas—which caused conflict with Mexico—and Oregon. Further westward settlement was sparked by the discovery of gold in California.

Texas and Oregon

President James K. Polk was one of the nation's most aggressive expansionists. He had hoped to annex Texas himself, but outgoing president John Tyler and Congress beat him to it just before he took office in March 1845.

Polk turned his attention to Oregon, where American settlers had set up their own government. To avoid war with America, the British, who had held joint occupation of Oregon since 1818, agreed that the U.S. border with Canada, Great Britain's last North American possession, should extend along the 49th parallel to the Pacific, releasing Oregon to be a U.S. territory.

WESTWARD EXPANSION was an idea romanticized by some Americans, such as the creator of this print. The woman represents "American Progress" leading settlers toward land and success. The print shows the stagecoaches once used to transport mail and passengers, the railroads that replaced them, and the "prairie schooner" wagons in which pioneers traveled with their belongings. The open landscape was originally home to Indians and the buffalo they hunted, but settlers had arrived to farm the land.

DEFINITION
*When a country increases the area under its control by incorporating new land, it has **annexed** that new land.*

War with Mexico

When President Polk entered office in 1845, he faced the ongoing dispute between the United States and Mexico over where to draw the Texas-Mexico border. The April 1846 clash between American and Mexican troops in the disputed territory moved President Polk to ask Congress to declare war. The declaration passed, largely because Southerners in Congress wanted to extend slavery into the conquered territories and preserve the balance of power between pro- and anti-slave forces. Mexican forces lost many soldiers but surrendered only after much negotiation, and the Treaty of Guadalupe Hidalgo was signed on February 2, 1848, establishing the Texas-Mexico border, and giving the United States New Mexico and California. In exchange, the United States paid Mexico $15 million. The territory that the United States acquired from the war with Mexico provided land for settlers and contained valuable resources such as gold.

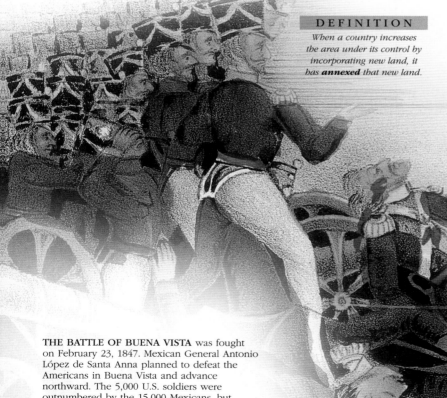

THE BATTLE OF BUENA VISTA was fought on February 23, 1847. Mexican General Antonio López de Santa Anna planned to defeat the Americans in Buena Vista and advance northward. The 5,000 U.S. soldiers were outnumbered by the 15,000 Mexicans, but they held their ground and the Mexican troops retreated. The battle gave the U.S. control of Northern Mexico.

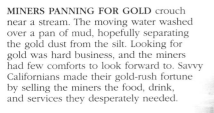

MINERS PANNING FOR GOLD crouch near a stream. The moving water washed over a pan of mud, hopefully separating the gold dust from the silt. Looking for gold was hard business, and the miners had few comforts to look forward to. Savvy Californians made their gold-rush fortune by selling the miners the food, drink, and services they desperately needed.

1800–1850

The Gold Rush

In January 1848, James W. Marshall was working at John Sutter's sawmill in northern California when he found some rocks that turned out to be gold nuggets. Marshall and Sutter tried to keep it secret, but word leaked out, starting the most famous gold rush in history. Throughout 1849, thousands of "Forty-Niners" flooded into San Francisco and dozens of boom towns in the Sierra Nevada mountains. Few prospectors found fortunes, but so many people came to try that California collected a large enough population to apply for statehood. Since California's constitution did not allow slavery, its entry into the Union would tip the pro- and anti-slavery balance in the Senate. The Gold Rush brought back the issue of slavery, which had remained relatively quiet in national politics since the Compromise of 1820 (see p. 63).

DEFINITION

*A mining strike of gold or silver led to a rush and, in a matter of days, a **boom town** would be built. When a mine "played out," a town might be abandoned. Many **ghost towns** can still be seen in the West.*

WHEN A MINER STRUCK GOLD, he would take it to be appraised. The gold would be molded into an ingot, like the one above, and stamped with its weight, purity, and the appraiser's mark.

THE BATTLE OF GETTYSBURG lasted three days and left thousands of soldiers dead. It was a crucial Civil War victory for the North, who had kept the Confederate South from advancing into Pennsylvania.

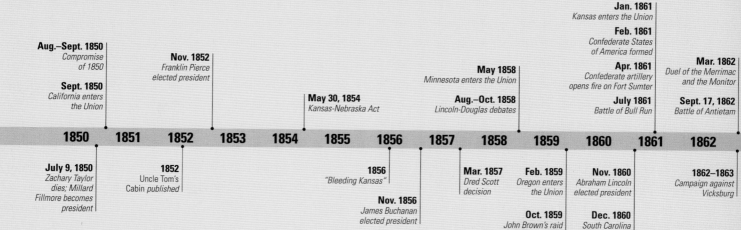

Aug.–Sept. 1850
Compromise of 1850

Sept. 1850
California enters the Union

Nov. 1852
Franklin Pierce elected president

May 30, 1854
Kansas-Nebraska Act

May 1858
Minnesota enters the Union

Aug.–Oct. 1858
Lincoln-Douglas debates

Jan. 1861
Kansas enters the Union

Feb. 1861
Confederate States of America formed

Apr. 1861
Confederate artillery opens fire on Fort Sumter

July 1861
Battle of Bull Run

Mar. 1862
Duel of the Merrimac and the Monitor

Sept. 17, 1862
Battle of Antietam

1850	1851	1852	1853	1854	1855	1856	1857	1858	1859	1860	1861	1862

July 9, 1850
Zachary Taylor dies; Millard Fillmore becomes president

1852
Uncle Tom's Cabin published

1856
"Bleeding Kansas"

Nov. 1856
James Buchanan elected president

Mar. 1857
Dred Scott decision

Feb. 1859
Oregon enters the Union

Oct. 1859
John Brown's raid on Harpers Ferry

Nov. 1860
Abraham Lincoln elected president

Dec. 1860
South Carolina secedes

1862–1863
Campaign against Vicksburg

THE UNION SHATTERED

1850–1876

"In *your* hands … and not in mine is the momentous issue of civil war." With those words of warning to the leaders of the South, President Abraham Lincoln took the oath of office in 1861. Southerners insisted that slavery be allowed in new territories in the West; Lincoln and the Republican Party, while promising not to limit slavery where it existed, were firmly opposed to any extension. Eleven states, feeling they had been denied the right to make such decisions for themselves, refused to accept Lincoln's presidency and seceded from the Union. In April 1861, America plunged into the Civil War. After four years of grim fighting, the North's victory restored the Union; four million slaves were freed. A decade of rebuilding followed—a time of uncertainty and struggle known as Reconstruction.

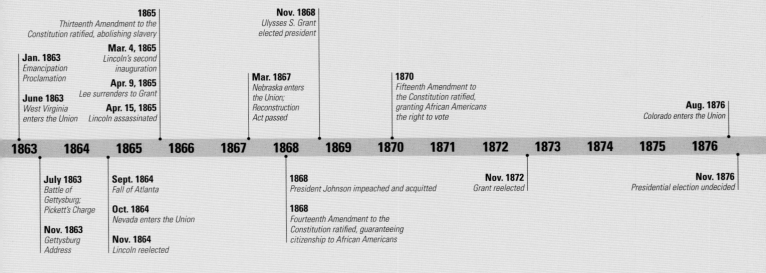

1865
Thirteenth Amendment to the Constitution ratified, abolishing slavery

Nov. 1868
Ulysses S. Grant elected president

Jan. 1863
Emancipation Proclamation

Mar. 4, 1865
Lincoln's second inauguration

June 1863
West Virginia enters the Union

Apr. 9, 1865
Lee surrenders to Grant

Apr. 15, 1865
Lincoln assassinated

Mar. 1867
Nebraska enters the Union; Reconstruction Act passed

1870
Fifteenth Amendment to the Constitution ratified, granting African Americans the right to vote

Aug. 1876
Colorado enters the Union

1863 | **1864** | **1865** | **1866** | **1867** | **1868** | **1869** | **1870** | **1871** | **1872** | **1873** | **1874** | **1875** | **1876**

July 1863
Battle of Gettysburg; Pickett's Charge

Sept. 1864
Fall of Atlanta

1868
President Johnson impeached and acquitted

Nov. 1872
Grant reelected

Nov. 1876
Presidential election undecided

Oct. 1864
Nevada enters the Union

Nov. 1863
Gettysburg Address

Nov. 1864
Lincoln reelected

1868
Fourteenth Amendment to the Constitution ratified, guaranteeing citizenship to African Americans

North and South Drift Apart

From the 1820s to the 1850s, industry developed at a fast pace in the North, while the South relied on farming its plantations. Cash crops had long been profitable there due to the use of slave labor, which many Northerners opposed. Southerners depended on the North for manufactured goods, and Northern factories depended on raw goods produced in the South. As the territories west of the Mississippi River joined the nation as new states, the issue of whether to allow slavery erupted nationally, both North and South fighting for control of the decision.

DEFINITION

Cash crops are grown for sale at market, rather than personal use.

PETER COOPER, 1791–1883

Peter Cooper was an inventor, industrialist, and philanthropist who believed that the wealthy have a duty to help society. Before the age of 30, Cooper made his fortune with a glue factory. About 1828, he built an ironworks in Baltimore and began a second career in the iron industry. During his life, Cooper produced many inventions, including a steam-powered locomotive and flavored gelatin, and he supported the development of the new telegraph network. He also helped to secure public education and improve sanitation in New York City. In 1859, he founded the Cooper Union, a university that gives all its students a free education.

The Industrial North

By 1860, the North's 75,000 mills and factories produced 85 percent of the country's manufactured goods, such as farm tools, furniture, and clothing. Of the 30,000 miles of railroad track connecting cities and factory towns east of the Mississippi, two-thirds of that mileage was in the North. Controlling the means of shipping allowed Northern industries to sell manufactured goods to the newly settled West. In return, Midwestern farms shipped grain, meat, and the raw materials needed for industry to the East.

Mills and Railroads

The North's industry started with a handful of cotton mills on the banks of rivers. Francis Cabot Lowell's mill on the Merrimack River in Massachusetts grew into the "mile of mills on the Merrimack" where cotton and wool were spun into thread to make cloth. Other mills turned out everything from boots and bottles to watches and wrenches. Then America steamed into the railroad age, adding swift transportation to the industrial revolution.

TOM THUMB, a steam-powered locomotive built by Peter Cooper, was raced against a horse-drawn railroad car in 1830. The horse won, but the event heralded a new age of railroads.

CHANGES FOR NORTHERN WORKERS

Some of the first mill owners felt a sense of fatherly responsibility for their workers, many of whom were young women who left their farming families to earn wages. In Lowell, Massachusetts, the "Lowell Girls" lived in clean boarding houses, continued their schooling, and published their own literary magazine, the *Lowell Offering*.

These working conditions changed after 1840. Company owners wanted to increase production, so they hired managers to run their growing businesses; and the managers cut wages. Due to political turmoil in Germany and a potato famine in Ireland, immigrants came to America in large numbers. The newcomers were willing to work for less than others, which kept wages low. Workers who tried to strike or to organize into groups—called unions—to negotiate pay and working conditions were simply fired.

AT FIRST, THE MILLS on the Merrimack River provided jobs for women wanting a life off the farm.

The Plantation South

Large plantations had dominated the economic, political, and social life of the South for more than a century. Most Southern farmers—about 70 percent—owned no slaves, but they supported and looked up to the region's planting class—categorized as those who owned at least 20 slaves. These wealthiest "gentlemen farmers" were the leaders of Southern society.

King Cotton!

Before the invention of the cotton gin (see p. 62), it was hard to produce the large amount of cotton needed to make a profit. Once the gin was in use, though, it was easier to do. Cotton production grew quickly as new land was planted along the Gulf of Mexico; plantations then bought more and more slaves to plant and harvest the cotton. By 1820, two-thirds of America's exports consisted of bales of cotton. Southerners boasted: "Cotton is king."

BALES OF COTTON on the dock at Union Wharf, in Charleston, South Carolina, wait to be loaded onto ships.

FALSE FREEDOM

By the end of the 1700s, laws had freed the slaves in most Northern states. After that, about 250,000 free blacks lived in the North; another 250,000, mostly enslaved, lived in the South. Southern slaves became free by escaping to the North, buying their own freedom, or being freed by their masters. Some African Americans descended from indentured servants or freed slaves were free since birth. Free blacks flocked to Northern cities, finding employment in factories and the shipping industry. Northern blacks usually lived in segregated communities (see p. 212) apart from whites and formed their own churches, schools, and businesses. Racial discrimination was widespread in the North; creating separate places to live together gave blacks protection and support. The vast majority of free blacks were poor, but some had skilled professions and earned enough to purchase homes and land.

1800s Southern Plantation Life

Plantations were farms that produced a large amount of a single cash crop, such as cotton, tobacco, or sugar. In Southern society, plantation owners held the power, while black slaves were owned as property and worked for the owner and his family. Southerners justified their way of life by saying that great civilizations such as ancient Greece and Rome had been built on systems of slave labor, and that unlike Northern factory owners, slave owners cared for their slaves for life.

SLAVES' CABINS were usually small, cramped, and dark. Many had no windows.

In the Plantation House

The master of the plantation lived in a big house with his wife and family, and some house slaves. Although not all plantation owners were rich, many could afford to furnish their houses luxuriously. The white family ate well, dining on the livestock they owned and the vegetables that were grown for them.

In Slaves' Quarters

A family of slaves would live together in one or two rooms, in a wood building with a dirt floor. They owned little furniture; a bed could be made out of planks and a mattress stuffed with corn husks. Slaves ate mostly corn, with small amounts of other foods such as molasses, fish, or bacon. Many slaves kept small vegetable gardens.

THE PLANTATION HOUSE at Boone Hall Plantation in South Carolina

On the Plantation Grounds

The big house was surrounded by the outbuildings needed to run a plantation, such as storage buildings, slave quarters, blacksmith's shop, ice house, smokehouse, laundry, dairy, and cotton gin (see p. 62). The kitchen was kept close by, but was also an outbuilding so the main house would not get overheated.

CHILDREN AND THEIR NURSE relax on the Poydras Plantation. The original owner of this sugarcane plantation, Julien Poydras, was a prominent Louisiana statesman and poet. As the wealthiest Southerners, plantation owners held the most social and political power. They and their families enjoyed the privileges of an upper-class life.

Field Work v. House Work

Labor on the plantation was divided between house slaves and field slaves. House slaves performed domestic work such as cooking, cleaning, and child care. They received better food and clothing and interacted with the family, but they were always on call.

Field work was extremely exhausting, requiring long hours of hard, physical labor. However, at the end of the day, field slaves could retire to the slave quarters with their families. At any moment, slaves could be sold and taken away from their families. This happened more often to field slaves, who were seen as more replaceable than domestic slaves.

PICKING COTTON was a back-breaking job. Slaves worked from sunup to sundown to pick the required amount. Planting, tending, and harvesting cotton required a huge expenditure of human labor, so the Southern economy became increasingly dependent on slavery.

NAT TURNER, 1800–1831

Nat Turner was born a slave on a Virginia plantation. He was a devout Christian, and he preached his visions of freedom to other slaves. In 1831, Turner led a group of slaves in a rebellion against local white landowners. Fifty-five whites were killed, including Turner's master, Joseph Travis, and Travis's family. A militia caught the gang and hanged about 15 slaves. Both pro- and anti-slavery forces saw Turner's Rebellion as a reason to fight for their causes. This and other uprisings led state leaders to toughen their Slave Codes, laws that prohibited educating slaves and restricted their movement from place to place.

Nat Turner

A SLAVE HUNTER found Nat Turner two months after his rebellion ended. Turner was tried and hanged.

African Culture in America

Legislation in the South forbade slaves from learning to read or write, so they continued the African oral storytelling tradition that passed knowledge down through generations. Slaves also stayed connected to their African roots by gathering together for entertainment. They sang songs and performed dances descended from West African rituals. An African diet relied on fresh fruits and vegetables; in America, slaves cooked new vegetables such as collard greens and kale. Eventually, such dishes showed up on their masters' tables as well.

Religion and Faith

Southern whites encouraged slaves to adopt Christianity, hoping that it would make them easier to control. Although plantation owners provided church buildings and hired preachers, slaves often preferred to worship in private. Slaves identified with the story of Moses, and so strongly with Jesus's sacrifice that Christianity became a call to freedom. Especially in South America and the Caribbean, Christianity mingled with slaves' ancestral African beliefs, creating a distinct form of worship.

THE BANJO, an adaptation of an African lyre, was a common instrument in slave quarters. Singing songs reinforced slaves' sense of community and tied their lives in America to their ancestors' in Africa.

The Gathering Storm

Beginning about 1850, tension between North and South reached the boiling point over the issue of slavery. Most Northerners saw slavery as incompatible with a free society, while Southerners felt that their right to decide their own way of life was being attacked. The fight now centered on whether to allow slavery to expand into new territories with large enough populations to become states. Both North and South wanted the territories to follow their lead in deciding whether the nation would continue to have legal slavery.

Compromising on Slavery

In 1850, California was to be admitted into the Union as a state. Since the Missouri Compromise of 1820 (see p. 63), there had been an equal number of states where slavery was legal—slave states—and states where slavery was illegal—free states. Henry Clay, the Speaker of the House, wanted to maintain this balance to avoid conflict. He thought if California entered as a free state, then anti-slavers should compromise and allow the people who lived in such territories as Utah and New Mexico to vote on whether or not to allow slavery.

Clay's compromise was debated in the Senate for seven months. Senator John C. Calhoun of South Carolina was so ill that a friend read his speech declaring that the compromise would snap "the cords that bind us," forcing South Carolina to leave the Union. When Massachusetts Senator Daniel Webster gave a thundering speech of approval, the Compromise of 1850 passed.

JOHN BROWN, 1800–1859

On October 16, 1859, a wild-eyed abolitionist named John Brown led a small band of men in a raid on a federal arsenal at Harpers Ferry, West Virginia. Brown, who had fought against pro-slavers in Kansas a few years earlier, planned to use the arsenal's weapons to arm a great slave rebellion. The raid was quickly stopped by the army and militia under Colonel Robert E. Lee. Brown and six others were tried, convicted, and executed. Many Northerners, while horrified by the violence, considered Brown a martyr to the cause of freedom. Southerners were worried because they feared the event was a sign that abolitionists were taking control of the North.

DANIEL WEBSTER'S stirring speech demanding the preservation of the Union at all costs led to the signing of the Compromise of 1850.

UNCLE TOM'S CABIN

The events triggered by the fugitive slave laws inspired Harriet Beecher Stowe, a white woman from Connecticut, to write the novel *Uncle Tom's Cabin*. Published in 1852, the book sold 300,000 copies in a few months. Southerners complained that the book presented an unrealistic view of slavery; Northern readers were deeply moved by the suffering Stowe depicted.

THE SLAVE OVERSEER, Simon Legree, whips Uncle Tom in an illustration from *Uncle Tom's Cabin*.

The Fugitive Slave Laws

The Fugitive Slave Act of 1793 said that escaped slaves must be returned to their masters in the South. In many places in the North the law wasn't enforced because of local personal-liberty laws or the anti-slavery ideals of the residents. However, part of the Compromise of 1850 gave slaveowners more power to go after escaped slaves and levied big penalties on those who interfered with their capture. This new law made the cruelty of slavery vivid to many Northerners. In 1852, the people of Syracuse, New York, were outraged when an escaped slave, Jerry McHenry, was seized by U.S. Marshals and led through the streets in chains. Abolitionist ministers broke McHenry out of jail and led him to safety through the Underground Railroad—a network of abolitionists who hid slaves and guided them to freedom in the North. But often, escaped slaves could not be helped, and were recaptured.

DEFINITION

*An **abolitionist** was someone who wanted slavery abolished: made illegal.*

The Kansas-Nebraska Act

In 1854, Senator Stephen A. Douglas proposed that the residents of the territories of Kansas and Nebraska vote yes or no to decide whether to have slavery when they became states. People who didn't live in Kansas or Nebraska but who were for slavery moved to the territories just long enough to vote. This swayed the vote and the pro-slave forces won. Defying the result, angry "free-soilers" moved to the town of Lawrence, Kansas, to establish a government without slavery. Violence erupted in Lawrence in 1856. "Bleeding Kansas" claimed more than 200 lives before the U.S. Army established order.

DEFINITION

Free-soilers *were those who believed that slavery should not be allowed in new territories.*

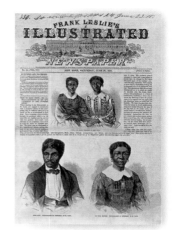

DRED SCOTT and his family, pictured in a newspaper article about the case

The Dred Scott Case

In 1857, Northerners who opposed slavery received another shock when the Supreme Court ruled against a slave named Dred Scott who was suing for his freedom. Scott's owners had brought him with them from the South to a Northern free state to live. The Court declared that it did not matter whether Scott lived in a slave state or a free state, because slaves were property and owners could take their property wherever they pleased.

Most Southerners were happy with the ruling, which meant that slavery could be extended into any territory, whether voters approved of it or not.

1850–1876

LINCOLN DEBATING DOUGLAS in Illinois became a matter of nationwide interest.

Stephen A. Douglas

Abraham Lincoln

The Lincoln-Douglas Debates

In 1858, Abraham Lincoln emerged as the leading figure in the Republican Party following a series of seven debates with Stephen A. Douglas, the Democratic senator from Illinois. The debates were part of a Senate race in which Lincoln was running against the popular incumbent. They debated the issue of slavery in the territories. The short, stout Douglas, known as the "little giant," and Lincoln, a tall, bony frontier lawyer, attracted huge crowds and nationwide newspaper attention. Both men opposed slavery, but Lincoln insisted that there should be no expansion of slavery in the territories. Douglas proposed a theory called "popular sovereignty," which relied on a vote of the people in each territory. Douglas won reelection, but Lincoln had appealed to a wide range of voters across the country.

The Union Dissolved

The survival of America as one unified nation was in doubt when Abraham Lincoln won the 1860 presidential election. Southerners had warned that they would not remain in the Union with a president who did not support their position on slavery. Lincoln's election led seven states to secede and form a new country, the Confederate States of America. Four more followed in 1861. When Southern artillery fired on Fort Sumter, a military fort in South Carolina controlled by the U.S. Army, the North and South were at war.

A CAMPAIGN POSTER promotes Lincoln and his vice presidential candidate, Hannibal Hamlin.

NOVEMBER 1860

The 1860 Election

Early in 1860, the two major political parties held their conventions to choose presidential candidates. The Democratic party was split. Democrats in the North chose Stephen Douglas, who supported letting the territories decide themselves whether to allow slavery. Democrats in the South chose pro-slavery candidate John C. Breckinridge. Republicans were confident of victory since the Democrats did not support a single candidate. They chose Abraham Lincoln. Republicans didn't focus on slavery only, though; they called for a railroad to be built that would cross the whole continent, and for a homestead law to make it easy for settlers to buy land. This appealed to voters in the West. Even with the Democratic vote split in two, it was a close election. Lincoln was elected president.

DECEMBER 1860–MARCH 1861

Secession

Most Northerners, Lincoln included, did not think the South would carry out its threat to leave the nation. On December 20, a South Carolina convention voted unanimously to secede. By February, Mississippi, Florida, Alabama, Georgia, Louisiana, and Texas had followed. By the time Lincoln took the oath of office in March 1861, delegates from these seven states had met in Montgomery, Alabama, to form the Confederate States of America, with Jefferson Davis as president. They adopted a constitution protecting slavery and chose a flag with seven stars on a blue field and three red and white bars.

DEFINITION

*An act of **secession** is formal withdrawal from an alliance or political organization.*

The Border States

There were 15 slave states in the nation, and eight of them lay between the North and the seven states of the Deep South that initially formed the Confederacy. In Virginia, the six western counties voted to remain loyal to the Union; they formed a new state—West Virginia—and entered the Union in 1863. Of the four border states that remained in the Union, only Delaware did so with a unanimous vote. Maryland, Kentucky, and Missouri were so deeply divided that federal troops were needed to keep order. In Kentucky and Missouri, open warfare broke out.

AMERICA AFTER SECESSION

In 1863, America divided into two separate nations.

- CONFEDERATE BORDER STATES
- UNION BORDER STATES
- CONFEDERATE STATES
- UNION STATES
- TERRITORIES NOT YET STATES

IN THE SPRING OF 1861, officers requested supplies and more men for Fort Sumter, a Federally controlled fort in the harbor of Charleston, South Carolina. President Lincoln sent food and supplies only. Confederate leaders decided that it was an act of war. They ordered the Federals to surrender, and when they refused, Confederate cannons opened fire. Confederate troops fired 3,341 shells at the fort over the course of 34 hours. It was April 12, 1861. The next day, their own ammunition exhausted, the Federals took down the U.S. flag and withdrew, as the Confederates occupied the fort. During the bombardment, a horse was the only fatality, but the armed conflict was enough to start the Civil War.

WHO'S WHO IN THE CIVIL WAR

The two regions of America involved in the Civil War were known by many names and nicknames, as were the people who fought for both sides. This table will help keep them straight.

THE NORTH

The United States of America (official name)
Union (adjective and noun)
Yankees, or Yanks (nicknames)
Federals (of the federal, or national, government)
The Blue (the color of their uniforms)
Free states (where slavery was illegal)

THE SOUTH

The Confederate States of America (official name)
Confederacy (noun)
Confederate (adjective)
Rebels, or Rebs (nicknames)
The Gray (the color of their uniforms)
Slave states (where slavery was legal)

1860s A People Divided

After the outbreak of war at Fort Sumter, every American had to make a choice between loyalty to the nation and loyalty to his or her state or region. Entire states were wrenched apart by this conflict, and so were towns, villages, and families. People often called it the "Brother's War," because major battles often included family members fighting against each other.

UNION CAPTAIN GEORGE A. CUSTER
(right) poses with his West Point classmate, captured Confederate officer J. B. Washington. More often than not, officers in the Civil War fought against their friends.

Jefferson Davis

Jefferson Davis had served as congressman, senator, and secretary of war in the U.S. government. After the 1860 presidential election, he hoped Southerners would accept Lincoln as their leader. But when his own state of Mississippi joined six others in forming the Confederacy and chose him as president, Davis felt obligated to serve.

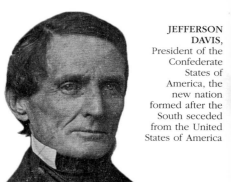

JEFFERSON DAVIS, President of the Confederate States of America, the new nation formed after the South seceded from the United States of America

Abraham Lincoln

Born in a log cabin in Kentucky in 1809, raised in poverty, and almost entirely self-educated, Abraham Lincoln became a successful lawyer in Springfield, Illinois, where he married Mary Todd. Lincoln came to the presidency with little experience—a few years in the Illinois legislature and one term in Congress. But he had a remarkable gift for helping people see the war as a test of popular government, "of the people, by the people, and for the people" (Gettysburg Address).

After his assassination in 1865 (see p. 88), Lincoln came to be seen as a leader of nearly mythic proportions—a towering, legendary figure who had saved democracy and freed the slaves.

Lincoln's Conflicts in the War

Although the majority of Northerners were determined not to let the South destroy the nation by breaking it in two, some urged Lincoln to allow the South to leave the Union without a fight, to avoid a war.

At the same time, abolitionists (see p. 76) were furious that Lincoln would not free the slaves. But Lincoln said the Constitution did not give him the authority to end slavery. He finally issued the Emancipation Proclamation in January 1863 (see p. 82), because he felt it was necessary to win the war. He wanted to stop the Confederacy from forcing slaves to join their army. He also hoped it would improve Northern morale and convince Great Britain that by aiding the South it would be supporting slavery.

First Ladies

The conflict of loyalties was particularly hard on families, including both presidential families. Varina Davis, wife of Confederate president Jefferson Davis, had several close relatives in the Union armies. The three brothers of Kentucky-born American First Lady Mary Todd Lincoln fought in the Confederate army. All three were killed.

Varina Davis

Mary Todd Lincoln

THE LAST GENTLEMEN'S WAR

On every battlefield there were gestures of kindness and compassion on both sides. A soldier might take a last letter home for a dying enemy soldier; men often called across enemy lines to ask about friends or relatives; at night, when opposing sides were camped near each other, the troops often swapped goods, such as coffee for tobacco.

A PATRIOTIC ENVELOPE used in the Confederate South

Military Officers

Civil War officers had been educated at a handful of military academies, including West Point, the Virginia Military Institute, and the Citadel. As a result of their common backgrounds, leaders from both sides sought to uphold ideals of self-reliance and civic responsibility.

Robert E. Lee

Regarded as the best officer in the U.S. Army, Lee symbolized the conflict faced by many. Lee had mixed feelings about slavery. Though he never publicly spoke against it, he considered it a "moral and political evil", but also felt it was a necessary lesson to civilize the slaves. He opposed secession, however, and so President Lincoln offered him command of the Union armies in 1861. But when Virginia joined the Confederacy, Lee turned down the offer and accepted a commission in the Confederate army. He said, "I cannot raise my hand against my birthplace, my home, my children."

Confederate General Robert E. Lee as a young man

Ulysses S. Grant

Union General Ulysses S. Grant as photographed by Mathew Brady

Virtually unknown when the war began, Grant rose to become the Union's best general and supreme commander of the Union armies. In a crisis, he was the man the soldiers wanted to lead them. Lee, his Confederate counterpart, seemed like the clever, elusive fox, while Grant appeared to be the slow, plodding bloodhound.

William Tecumseh Sherman

Sherman was the head of a military school in Louisiana when the Civil War began. Ohio-born, Sherman rejected the South's offer of a command and enlisted in the Union army. Early in the war, he suffered from severe depression, considering himself a failure. Sherman went on to become a relentless leader, and was Grant's most trusted general.

William Tecumseh Sherman

"Stonewall" Jackson

Thomas "Stonewall" Jackson

One of Virginia's outstanding officers and a deeply religious man, Jackson proved to be a courageous battlefield leader. In the first battle of the war, an officer declared, "There is Jackson, standing like a stone wall!" The nickname stuck. Jackson's skillful use of speed and surprise fit perfectly with General Lee's strategies.

Triumphs of the Confederacy

From 1861 to 1863, the Confederate army in the East repeatedly stopped the Union's efforts to capture Richmond, capital of the Confederate States of America. The Rebels held off the Yankees in the West, too, where they controlled the Mississippi River. Confident from these victories, the Southerners invaded Pennsylvania, and came close to winning their independence at Gettysburg.

MAJOR BATTLES OF THE CIVIL WAR

★ Union victory
★ Confederate victory
▢ Union states
▢ Confederate states
···· Union sea blockade 1861–1862
-- Union sea blockade 1863–1865
— Slave owning was legal south of the red border

THE EMANCIPATION PROCLAMATION

Lincoln personally opposed slavery, but he insisted that the Civil War was being fought to preserve the Union, not abolish slavery. The Emancipation Proclamation, issued in January 1863, was Lincoln's official declaration of freedom, or emancipation, for slaves in the Confederacy. It was meant to satisfy abolitionists (see p. 76) who pressured Lincoln to make ending slavery a goal of the war. It was also a strategic move to help the North win the war—the South had an advantage, since the Confederates could force slaves to help the war effort.

Ultimately, the document was more a symbolic than an actual end to slavery, since the Union could not force the rebellious Southern states to free slaves, and it did not pertain to slaves in border states loyal to the Union, such as Maryland and Kentucky. The Thirteenth Amendment to the Constitution freed the remaining slaves.

JULY 1861–MAY 1863

The Road to Richmond

The war's first battle took place just 20 miles from Washington, D.C., on July 20, 1861. A huge Union army advanced toward the Confederate capital at Richmond and collided with a smaller Confederate force at Bull Run, a small river near Manassas Junction, Virginia. The inexperienced Union troops panicked and fled back to Washington. The Battle of Bull Run was an embarrassment for the North.

Nearly a year later, the North's Army of the Potomac launched a second campaign for Richmond. General Robert E. Lee was by then in command of the South's defenses and led his Army of Northern Virginia to a series of brilliant victories, forcing the North to retreat yet again.

Lee relied on boldness and surprise, usually sending one corps under General Thomas "Stonewall" Jackson around the side, or flank, of the enemy, in a "flanking maneuver." Meanwhile, Lincoln was still looking for a strong leader who could win battles.

DECEMBER 1862–JUNE 1863

Time of Decision

By early 1863, many Northerners had come to feel that further fighting was useless, since the North had made no headway.

A Union general, Ulysses S. Grant, had emerged from obscurity in 1862 to capture Forts Henry and Donelson in Tennessee and Kentucky—the North's first victories. But Grant's army was driven back in December 1862, when he tried to take Vicksburg.

Many Southerners faced 1863 with great confidence. "There never was an army like this," Lee boasted of his tough troops. In June 1863, Lee led his army in an invasion of Pennsylvania. If he could win a victory on Northern soil it might convince Northerners that they could not defeat the South.

Map labels:
OHIO
Indianapolis
Cincinnati
ILLINOIS
INDIANA
KENTUCKY
Lexington
St. Louis
Booneville — June 17, 1861
Perryville — Oct. 8, 1862
MISSOURI
Fort Donelson — Feb. 16, 1862
Springfield
Fort Henry — Feb. 6, 1862
Nashville — Dec. 15–16, 1864
Knoxv — Nov. 23–2
Wilson's Creek — Aug. 10, 1861
Murfreesboro — Dec. 31, 1862–Jan. 2, 1863
Chattanooga — Nov. 25, 1863
TENNESSEE
Memphis — June 5, 1862
Shiloh (Pittsburg Landing) — April 6–7, 1862
Chickamauga — Sept. 19–20, 1863
Kenn
ARKANSAS
ALABAMA
Atlanta — Sept. 2, 1864
MISSISSIPPI
GEORGIA
Vicksburg — May 19–July 4, 1863
Montgomery
TEXAS
LOUISIANA
Port Hudson — May 27–July 8, 1863
Mobile — April 12, 1865
Pensacola
Tallahassee
Baton Rouge — May 12, 1862
Sabine
New Orleans
Mobile Bay — Aug. 5, 1864
Galveston
GULF OF MEXICO

Lake Ontario

NEW YORK

NEW JERSEY

PENNSYLVANIA

Antietam (Sharpsburg) Sept. 17, 1862

● Philadelphia

Gettysburg July 1–3, 1863

● Baltimore

Chancellorsville May 1–4, 1863

MARYLAND

The Wilderness May 5–7, 1863

DELAWARE

Bull Run July 21, 1861; Aug. 29–30, 1862

Fredericksburg Dec. 13, 1862

Spotsylvania Court House May 8–12, 1864

Staunton June 8–9, 1862

Cold Harbor June 3, 1864

Richmond ●

Appomattox Court House April 9, 1865

● Norfolk

● Columbia

NORTH CAROLINA

untain

SOUTH CAROLINA

Fort Sumter April 12–14, 1861

ATLANTIC OCEAN

● Jacksonville

ustee 20, 1864

● St. Augustine

FLORIDA

JULY 1–3, 1863

The Battle of Gettysburg

On July 1, 1863, some of Lee's men ran into part of the Union army on the edge of Gettysburg, Pennsylvania, launching the most dramatic battle of the war. For the first two days, the Confederates had more men and pushed the Union troops south of the town, where they clung to high ground. Late on each day, the Rebels seemed about to smash through the Yankees' line, but additional Union troops arrived just in time to keep the South from advancing into Pennsylvania.

1850–1876

JULY 3, 1863

Pickett's Charge

Lee felt that one more attack at Gettysburg would give the South the victory they needed. Late on the third day of battle, Confederates, led by General George Pickett, marched toward the Union army in formation. They walked straight into the Union's cannon and musketfire; many men were killed, and huge gaps were made in their lines. They closed the gaps and fired back. Then, calling the "rebel yell," they charged.

A few Rebels made it to the top of the ridge where the Union line was barely holding on after two days of brutal fighting. Just then, Union reinforcements arrived. The Confederates were defeated. The great attack known as "Pickett's Charge" was over, and so was the South's invasion of the North.

AFTER THE CARNAGE AT GETTYSBURG, in which he lost 28,000 Confederate troops, a dispirited General Lee offered his resignation to Jefferson Davis, who refused to accept it.

LINCOLN'S GETTYSBURG ADDRESS

In November 1863, President Lincoln delivered his most famous speech at the dedication of the Gettysburg battlefield cemetery. The speech was so short that half the people there were not aware he had given it. Only later, when people read the speech reprinted in newspapers, did they see it as an eloquent statement of the meaning of the war and as a reaffirmation of America's great experiment in democracy. (Read the text on p. 303.)

LINCOLN WROTE THE SPEECH on White House stationery during the train ride to Gettysburg.

Executive Mansion.

Washington, ___ 186

Four score and seven years ago our fathers brought forth, upon this continent, a new nation, conceived in liberty, and dedicated to the proposition that "all men are created equal."

Now we are engaged in a great civil war, testing whether that nation, or any nation so conceived, and so dedicated, can long endure. We are met on a great battle field of that war. We have come to dedicate a portion of it, as a final resting place for those who died here that the nation might live. This we may, in all propriety do. But, in a larger sense, we can not dedicate—we can not consecrate—we can not hallow, this ground— The brave men, living and dead, who struggled here, have hallowed it, far above our poor power to add or detract. The world will little note, nor long remember what we say here; while it can never forget what they did here.

It is rather for us, the living, to stand here,

JULY 4, 1863

After Gettysburg

The next day, July 4, 1863, Lee led his battered troops back to Virginia. The wagon train carrying the South's wounded stretched an agonizingly long 14 miles.

Nine hundred miles away, Grant's Union army had begun a siege of Vicksburg in mid-May, trapping 30,000 Southern troops in a ring of artillery. After six weeks, with both soldiers and civilian townspeople close to starvation, Confederate general John C. Pemberton surrendered the city and his army to Grant—on the Fourth of July. The defeats at Gettysburg and Vicksburg were too great a loss for the South to recover from. It was close to the end for the Confederacy.

1860s The First Modern War

Americans had last seen war on their own soil in the War of 1812, but the Civil War was to be unlike any war previously fought. The world's first modern war brought new means of transportation and communication, which helped manage huge armies; new weapons had greater killing power; and civilians were involved as never before.

Battle Becomes Efficient

For most people, the greatest shock of modern warfare was the destructive power of its weapons. Traditionally, at the start of a battle, armies would advance toward one another in straight lines along a half-mile front line, stopping on orders to fire, then charging the last few yards with bayonets. Such tactics were used because muskets took time to load and were only accurate at a short range. The newer weapons could be loaded much more rapidly, but they were also more accurate, and the new bullets they used were deadlier.

As a defense against the new weapons, Confederate general Robert E. Lee had his troops dig networks of protective trenches. Others followed his lead.

THE UNION'S EYE IN THE SKY

Professor Thaddeus Lowe made history by using a hot-air balloon to soar above Confederate lines and report troop positions, often using a telegraph. Named chief of the Union's Aeronautics Corps, Lowe developed a small fleet of balloons. Although not a major factor in any battle, the balloons paved the way for the zeppelins, airplanes, and helicopters that would be crucial in future wars.

ONE OF LOWE'S BALLOONS prepares for a mission.

MODEL 1857 CANNONS fired so-called canister rounds—exploding tin cans filled with heavy lead slugs and sawdust.

Transportation and Communication Advances

Railroads had expanded by the 1860s, making it possible to move men and supplies much more quickly than by horse and wagon.

The telegraph, which first appeared in 1840, made instant communication possible across great distances. Cutting off supply routes and lines of communication, intercepting messages, and breaking codes—all became new elements of war.

Battlefield Medicine

Medical advances lagged behind weapons advances. For example, a field hospital near Richmond performed 400 amputations and about 250 of those patients died, most of infection or blood loss. Surgeons wore dirty, bloody coats and kept surgical needles dangling from their buttonholes—they had no understanding that they were spreading deadly germs every time they touched something. Ironically, at the same time, Joseph Lister in Scotland was proving that antiseptics prevented the spread of disease, and Dr. Louis Pasteur in France was confirming that disease was caused by germs. The death toll of the Civil War might have been reduced by one-third to one-half if those discoveries had come five years earlier.

ETHER—one of the only painkillers available—was delivered to the patient through an inhaler.

The Concept of Total War

During the Civil War, military leaders were beginning to move toward the concept of total war—the idea that the whole society was involved in waging war, not just the armies in the field. A large percentage of the agricultural and industrial output of the time was used for war production, and both sides tried to destroy the crops, warehouses, and railroads of the enemy. The Union leaders, for example, used the North's sea-power advantage to blockade the South's seaports. This interfered with the South's economy, since it could no longer ship cotton to other countries in trade for food, clothing, or weaponry.

REPORTING THE WAR

Photography was in its pioneering stage during the Civil War. Mathew Brady, a New York portrait photographer, and his assistants took pictures of the Union armies in every campaign. They were the first to chronicle a war in this way.

People at home read about the war in newspapers. Never before had reporters followed armies into battle and recorded the details of the action.

In addition, a number of artists, including Winslow Homer, made detailed sketches of battle scenes, which were made into engravings in newspaper offices to illustrate the news stories.

SELLING NEWSPAPERS FROM A CART near the front

THE *MERRIMAC* AND THE *MONITOR* fought the Duel of the Ironclads on March 9, 1862. Confederates fitted a captured Union ship with iron plates, cannons, and a battering ram in the hope that it could destroy the Union's regular ships and end the North's blockade of the South's seaports. The strange-looking vessel, the *Merrimac*, chugged into the Chesapeake Bay on March 8, 1862, and promptly sank three Union ships. The Union answered with its own ironclad—the *Monitor*, another odd-looking vessel with history's first revolving gun turret. In the most famous sea battle of the war, the ships clanged cannon shells off each other's iron plates for five hours without doing much damage. The duel ended in a draw. The blockade remained.

The South Surrenders

After the battles of Gettysburg and Vicksburg, the nature of the war changed. In March 1864, President Lincoln gave Grant the rank of Lieutenant General, and with it the command of all Union forces. Grant began a massive assault on the South. The better resources of the North gradually wore down the South until Lee was forced to surrender.

SUMMER 1863

The North Pulls Ahead

At the end of the summer of 1863, Lee led his ragged troops back to Virginia to defend Richmond against the next assault by Union troops. It was his only option—the South no longer had the resources to go on the offensive.

The industrial power of the North now began to tip the balance. Union armies were larger and better equipped than ever, while the South had few reserves to draw on. The one slim hope of the Confederacy was to keep fighting until Northerners grew tired of war, forcing Lincoln to seek peace.

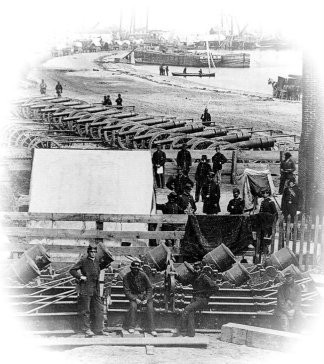

A STOCKED UNION SUPPLY DEPOT in City Point, Virginia, shows how the North was well equipped for the war.

AFRICAN AMERICANS IN THE WAR

Although Northern blacks had been eager to join in the war effort from the start, Lincoln resisted, not wanting to anger the slave states still in the Union. Lincoln issued the Emancipation Proclamation in 1863 (see p. 82), which freed, or emancipated, slaves in the Confederate states. After that, African Americans enlisted in large numbers. They served in segregated units with white officers in charge. The all-black 54th Massachusetts regiment was one of the first to see action and showed its heroism in the attack on Fort Wagner near Charleston, South Carolina.

Also, General Benjamin F. Butler established a refugee camp for escaped slaves. He paid them to work on roads and bridges, and trained volunteers as soldiers.

"MAKE WAY FOR LIBERTY": An image of blacks fighting in the Civil War.

"HE DIED FOR ME": A black soldier dies for the Union cause.

General George A. Custer

General Robert E. Lee

SUMMER 1864

Total War

General Grant's plan to end the war was to put constant pressure on Lee and not give him time for clever maneuvers. Grant and his generals led assaults against Lee's smaller army, and there were horrible losses on both sides. The critical Northern press called him "Butcher Grant." Lee's losses weren't as bad, but his army was depleted and there were no replacements.

Grant Changes Tactics

Grant decided to bypass Richmond and attack Petersburg, Virginia, the South's important rail center. Meanwhile, General Sherman overcame stiff Confederate resistance to capture and burn Atlanta in September 1864. That victory boosted morale in the North and helped Lincoln win reelection in November.

Atlanta was the beginning of the campaign known as "Sherman's March to the Sea," during which he burned down both civilian and military property up to Savannah to "make Georgia howl." He intended to disrupt the South's economy and make Confederate civilians realize that they were losing.

LEE SURRENDERED TO GRANT in the town of Appomattox Court House, Virginia. Grant's terms were generous—Confederate soldiers were allowed to keep their side arms, horses, and personal possessions, and they would be allowed to return to their homes unopposed.

THE HUMAN TOLL OF THE CIVIL WAR

More Americans died in the Civil War than in all other American wars from the Revolutionary War through the Korean War. Most of them died not from battlefield injuries but from the disease that followed.

THE BLOODIEST ...	PLACE AND DATE	CASUALTIES
DAY	Antietam September 17, 1862	17,000 wounded; 6,000 dead
BATTLE	Gettysburg July 1–3, 1863	51,000 dead (23,000 Union; 28,000 Confederate)
AMERICAN WAR	Civil War 1861–1865	Over 600,000 dead

APRIL 1865

Surrender at Appomattox

By April 1865, Lee's army was down to about 25,000 half-starved men. The Confederates tried one more breakout but were easily pushed back. On April 7, Grant sent a letter to Lee inviting him to surrender. On April 9, Robert E. Lee met with Ulysses S. Grant to discuss the terms of surrender. Then, on April 26, General Joseph E. Johnston surrendered to General Sherman in North Carolina, ending the war.

General Philip H. Sheridan

General George G. Meade

General Ulysses S. Grant

The Reconstruction Years

In April 1865, President Lincoln was shot and killed. Americans were shocked and grief-stricken. Congress demanded harsh terms as part of the rebuilding of the defeated South, which had been all but destroyed during the war. Newly freed slaves were now citizens and enjoyed a first taste of political participation, although their future was uncertain.

Lincoln's Assassination

On the night of April 14, 1865, just five days after Lee's surrender at Appomattox, President Abraham Lincoln was assassinated while attending a play at Ford's Theater in Washington, D.C. The assassin, actor John Wilkes Booth,

A DYING LINCOLN is attended by his eldest son Robert (far left); the Surgeon General; his youngest son Tad; his wife Mary Todd Lincoln; and actress Clara Harris (far right), who was with the Lincolns at Ford's Theater.

thought he was striking a blow for the Confederacy. Booth was tracked down and killed. Several co-conspirators were arrested, convicted, and executed as well.

A WANTED POSTER for John H. Surrat, John Wilkes Booth, and David C. Harold offers rewards for the capture of Booth and the conspirators who were thought to have helped him kill the president.

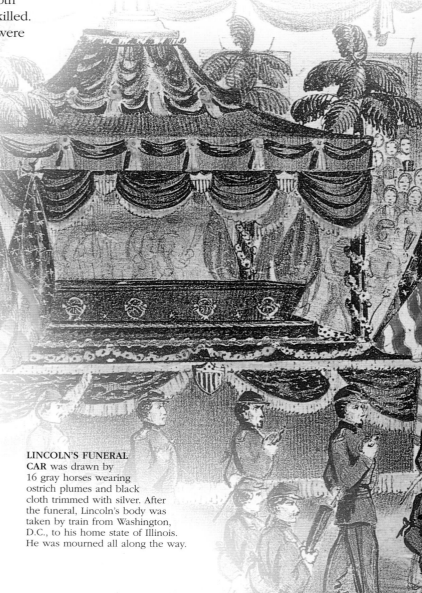

LINCOLN'S FUNERAL CAR was drawn by 16 gray horses wearing ostrich plumes and black cloth trimmed with silver. After the funeral, Lincoln's body was taken by train from Washington, D.C., to his home state of Illinois. He was mourned all along the way.

THE HANGING of Booth's co-conspirators was a public event.

Reconstruction Becomes Radical

Six weeks before his death, President Lincoln urged Americans to "bind up the nation's wounds" in his second inaugural address. He wanted to make it easy for the defeated South to rejoin the United States and he wanted government to help the former slaves adjust to their new lives.

Lincoln's successor, President Andrew Johnson, had also hoped for a lenient policy, but he struggled with Congress as a plan was formed. The Republican Congress, who wanted harsher terms for the South, won and the South was divided into five military districts, with a Northern army officer overseeing the creation of new state governments. Many former Confederates were upset by this plan because they felt the military occupation was humiliating for the South.

President Johnson Is Impeached

President Andrew Johnson decided to challenge the power of Congress to carry out the plan for Reconstruction. One branch of Congress, the House of Representatives, responded by voting to impeach him—placing him on trial before the Senate. Removal of the president failed by a single vote.

"SCALAWAGS" AND "CARPETBAGGERS"

Southern whites, especially former Confederate soldiers, disliked "scalawags"—a negative term they applied to any Southern white who voted Republican or worked for the Freedmen's Bureau founded to help former slaves. They were even more hostile toward "carpetbaggers"—the thousands of Northerners who went South to help with Reconstruction. Many suspected that they only came to exploit economic opportunities and fill their luggage, or carpetbags, with Southern money.

A CARPETBAG— popular luggage of the day made of rug and leather—was carried by Northerners who went South after the war. It gave them their name.

African American Reconstruction

Former slaves, now called *freedmen*, faced an uncertain future. The Thirteenth Amendment, ending slavery, had been passed late in the war and was ratified in 1865. The Fourteenth Amendment, ratified in 1868, guaranteed citizenship to African Americans and the Fifteenth, ratified in 1870, protected their right to vote. These Constitutional amendments ensured that state governments could not limit or remove those rights. Still, free blacks had few skills, no land or money, and most could not read or write. Some used their knowledge of farming to become tenant farmers—paying a landowner in cash or crops to use his land. Others without money became sharecroppers and borrowed money for food, tools, and other needs, then repaid the land owner with a share of the crop. Sharecropping created a permanent cycle of debt and poverty.

The "Freedmen's Bureau," a government agency, was formed to help freedmen and poor whites. The Bureau encouraged blacks to vote and helped elect some blacks to office. It also opened more than 4,000 schools.

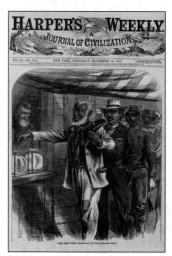

A *HARPER'S WEEKLY* COVER pictures African Americans voting for the first time.

The White Backlash

Many Southern whites were bitter about the rights Reconstruction gave to blacks; they wanted to restore "white supremacy." Some joined secret societies such as the Ku Klux Klan, which spread terror. KKK members dressed in hooded robes, set fire to barns and homes, and murdered black people and sympathetic whites.

Because of this intimidation, which existed in the North, too, black participation in elections declined for the rest of the century.

America's Centennial

In 1876, Americans were ready for a fresh start. They had been through years of political corruption and the problems of Reconstruction. The celebration of the nation's 100th birthday was marked by a special exposition which helped create a new sense of hope for the future.

DEFINITION

Corruption occurs when people ignore official duty in order to satisfy selfish or greedy desires.

Scandals in Government

Civil War hero Ulysses S. Grant was elected to the presidency in 1868. He had been an outstanding general, but as president he made poor decisions and placed too much trust in his friends. The result was that scandals tainted his time in office, though he was not accused of being personally involved in them.

For example, government-authorized construction companies were created by officials of the Central Pacific and Union Pacific railroads to build the nation's first transcontinental railroad (see p. 94). The work cost about $44 million, but the officials charged $94 million, pocketing the rest. When the scandal was exposed, it turned out that Grant's vice president, Schuyler Colfax, and several senators had accepted large bribes as part of the deal.

ULYSSES S. GRANT, 1822–1885

A few years after leaving the presidency, Grant found himself penniless; trusted friends had led him into an investment scheme. He did not want to leave his wife, Julia, and his family destitute, so he set to work writing his memoirs. Grant knew he was in a race against time—he was dying of throat cancer caused by years of heavy cigar smoking.

The famous author Mark Twain (see p. 110), who was a friend of Grant's, encouraged him and then had the book published. Grant finished just four days before he died on July 19, 1885. The memoirs, which are still regarded as one of the nation's best military histories, earned a substantial fortune.

Corruption at the Local Level

Corruption was also widespread in state and local governments. In New York State, two of America's biggest scoundrels—Jay Gould and "Jubilee Jim" Fisk—arrived in Albany in 1868 with two suitcases full of money, which they used to bribe legislators to get approval for a phony railroad stock scheme. And, in New York City, William Marcy "Boss" Tweed, the leader of Tammany Hall, a fraternal organization that controlled local politics, bilked the city treasury out of millions until he was exposed with the help of Thomas Nast's cartoons.

THOMAS NAST, 1840–1902

Thomas Nast was a 20-year-old German immigrant when the Civil War began. He first became famous as an artist for Harper's Weekly with a drawing called "Emancipation," which showed what life might be like for freed slaves. But Nast is most remembered for his later work. From the mid-1860s to the 1880s, Nast drew editorial cartoons to attack political corruption. He also created the elephant symbol for the Republican Party and the Democrats' donkey. And it was Nast's drawings of Santa Claus as the jolly, red-suited figure handing out gifts from his sleigh that gave the world the modern image we know today.

SANTA CLAUS about to go down a chimney in a drawing by Nast

THE CORLISS STEAM ENGINE, towering 45 feet above the exhibits in Machinery Hall, represented for many the beginning of the Industrial Age and America's place as its leader.

Reconstruction Ends

In the 1876 presidential election, both candidates—Democrat Samuel J. Tilden and Republican Rutherford B. Hayes—promised reform after the years of corruption. Tilden won the popular vote and had 184 electoral votes to Hayes's 165, but 20 electoral votes were in dispute. Tilden needed one more vote for a majority of 185. Congress set up a committee to decide who would get the disputed votes. They awarded all 20 to Hayes, giving him the presidency.

Rutherford B. Hayes

Democrats called it a "stolen election," but their complaints stopped when President Hayes ended Reconstruction by removing the last federal troops from the former Confederate states of Florida, Louisiana, and South Carolina.

1850–1876

RESTORING THE UNION

The Reconstruction Act of 1867 set terms for the Confederate states to rejoin the Union, including adopting constitutions to allow all adult males to vote.

	READMITTED TO THE UNION	RECONSTRUCTION GOVERNMENT ENDS
Tennessee	1866	1869
Alabama	1868	1874
Arkansas	1868	1874
Florida	1868	1877
Louisiana	1868	1877
North Carolina	1868	1870
South Carolina	1868	1877
Georgia	1870	1871
Mississippi	1870	1875
Texas	1870	1873
Virginia	1870	1870

The Centennial Exposition

The United States celebrated the 100th anniversary of the Declaration of Independence with a grand exposition in Philadelphia. Eight million visitors toured thousands of displays of American technical, agricultural, and social achievements, which showed the world that the United States was an industrial power. The exhibits filled Americans with renewed confidence in their future.

The star of the Expo was the giant Corliss steam engine, which silently produced enough power to run every machine in Machinery Hall. Another hint of the future was the "speaking telegraph," later known as the telephone, invented by Alexander Graham Bell (see p. 109). When the device was demonstrated to the Emperor of Brazil, he exclaimed, "Good Lord! It talks!"

91

A FAMILY OF SETTLERS poses in front of their sod house on the Nebraska prairie. Homesteaders, who worked hard to make a living off their land, were just some of the Americans who moved out west to settle the frontier. Cowboys and railroad workers found plenty of work, but American Indians—the original residents of these lands—had to fight to defend their way of life.

1870
Fifteenth Amendment to the Constitution ratified, granting African Americans the right to vote

1873
Joseph Glidden invents barbed wire

June 25, 1876
Battle of the Little Bighorn

Aug. 1876
Colorado enters the Union

Nov. 1876
Presidential election undecided

May 21, 1881
Clara Barton founds the American Red Cross

July 2, 1881
Garfield shot by assassin, dies 11 weeks later

Sept. 20, 1881
Chester A. Arthur inaugurated as president

Oct. 1881
Shoot-out at the O.K. Corral

1869 **1870** **1871** **1872** **1873** **1874** **1875** **1876** **1877** **1878** **1879** **1880** **1881**

May 10, 1869
Union Pacific and Central Pacific railroads meet at Promontory Point, Utah

Nov. 1872
Grant reelected president

Mar. 1877
Rutherford B. Hayes declared winner of presidential election

June–Oct. 1877
Flight of Chief Joseph and the Nez Percé

1879
Ponca tribe sues for the return of their land

1880
George Pullman founds Pullman, Illinois

Nov. 1880
James Garfield elected president

SETTLING THE WEST

1869–1900

Americans have always been a frontier people, living on the edge of the unknown. In the late 19th century, the frontier was the area that had been bypassed in the rush to the Pacific earlier in the century. Ranchers and cowboys moved north into the frontier from Texas to be closer to the railheads that shipped cattle east; homesteaders and sheep ranchers settled these lands, too, using new farming technology to overcome difficult conditions; and miners ventured into the Rocky Mountains in search of gold and silver.

This expansion threatened American Indians, especially the Plains tribes who lived by hunting the roaming buffalo herds. Some tribes fought to save their land, but by the late 1870s, all the tribes had been forced onto reservations. In 1890, the U.S. Census reported that the frontier was closed to settlement.

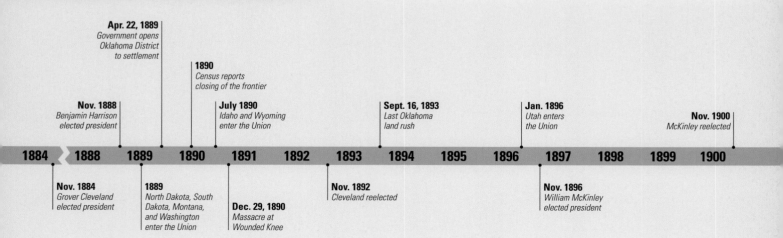

Apr. 22, 1889
Government opens Oklahoma District to settlement

1890
Census reports closing of the frontier

Nov. 1888
Benjamin Harrison elected president

July 1890
Idaho and Wyoming enter the Union

Sept. 16, 1893
Last Oklahoma land rush

Jan. 1896
Utah enters the Union

Nov. 1900
McKinley reelected

1884 1888 1889 1890 1891 1892 1893 1894 1895 1896 1897 1898 1899 1900

Nov. 1884
Grover Cleveland elected president

1889
North Dakota, South Dakota, Montana, and Washington enter the Union

Dec. 29, 1890
Massacre at Wounded Knee

Nov. 1892
Cleveland reelected

Nov. 1896
William McKinley elected president

Railroads

Westward expansion happened slowly before the transcontinental railroad was established. It had long been a goal of politicians, businessmen, and many ordinary Americans to have a network of railroads that would link the coasts of the United States. Once that system was in place, ranchers could ship herds of cattle north and east for big profits; manufactured goods could easily be sent to new towns in the West; and all could travel around the country at a fraction of the time and money it had once cost.

THE PONY EXPRESS

From 1860 to 1862, the Pony Express operated as a mail service between San Francisco, California, and St. Joseph, Missouri, with the U.S. Postal Service carrying the mail east from there. People were captivated by the image of brave riders speeding alone across the landscape, leaping onto fresh horses at every 10-mile station until they had completed their 200 miles. The Pony Express was fast—it took only eight days to get a letter to San Francisco— but it was stopped when the first transcontinental telegraph line was completed in 1862.

A PONY EXPRESS RIDER greets men setting up telegraph poles.

Building the Railroads

On May 10, 1869, in Promontory, Utah, a golden railroad spike was hammered into place, joining the Central Pacific and Union Pacific Railroads and completing a continuous track across the country. The transcontinental railroad followed the natural path of waterways, but it required laborers to level the terrain and blast passages through mountains.

Four more transcontinental railroads and dozens of "feeder" lines followed rapidly. The government gave the railroad companies large tracts of land on either side of their lines for sale to settlers or land companies, promoting the quick development of the West (see p. 100).

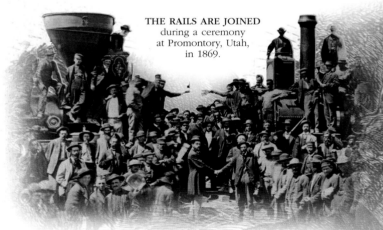

THE RAILS ARE JOINED during a ceremony at Promontory, Utah, in 1869.

Working on the Railroad

The 20,000 workers who labored on the transcontinental railroad included European and Chinese immigrants as well as Civil War veterans. The Chinese—who had immigrated across the Pacific to California—made up about half the work force (see p. 113). They were made to do the most dangerous work and were paid less than other workers. In general, the work was hard, 12-hour work days were common, and Indian attacks were a danger since buffalo-hunting grounds were being ruined by the growing network of tracks. Railroad owners were powerful men who could ignore workers' demands for more pay and better conditions.

A UNION PACIFIC POSTER advertises rail travel to the West in comfort and style, in Pullman Palace Sleeping Cars.

SHOOTING BUFFALO FROM TRAINS became a cruel sport after the railroad system was established. The great herds were seen as hindrances to the settling of western lands. Then, in 1871, a process was developed for tanning buffalo hides. Tanning companies sent teams of hunters to kill the animals for the hides, leaving the meat to rot and threatening the survival of the Plains Indians, who relied on the herds for their livelihood.

Train Travel

Before the expansion of the railroads, trips between the coasts were made by stagecoach, around South America by ship, or across the Isthmus of Panama. These expensive routes took weeks. By train, the trip could be made in five days for a cost of only $150.

Early train travel was uncomfortable and slowed by frequent transfers and stops at meal stations. As railroads grew and train design improved, passengers did not have to switch trains so often, and food was served onboard. The connections between cars were enclosed so that passengers could move through the train. This also improved ventilation, so windows could be shut and passengers—many of whom were traveling to visit family—no longer arrived covered in dirt. Although cheap accommodations did exist, almost all traveled first-class. A first-class trip from New York to Chicago—912 miles—cost $5.

PULLMAN SLEEPING CARS had seats and curtained sleeping compartments.

Pullman Innovations

George Pullman saw a need for more comfortable train cars with both day and night accommodation. The best Pullman cars had electric lights, steam heat, and leather seats.

In 1880, Pullman founded one of the first company towns, Pullman, Illinois, where he owned the houses, shops, and even the church. In 1894, the workers, angry that they were in debt to Pullman's stores and working for low wages, went on strike; though unsuccessful, the effort was supported by railroad workers across the United States (see p. 115).

Wild West: Fact and Legend

For those who were born after the frontiers of the United States had been explored and settled, or never went west of the Mississippi River, the American West was a wild, untamed, and sometimes dangerous place where people lived according to their own rules in a true pioneer spirit. This romantic vision of cowboys and Indians, sheriffs and outlaws, was created in large part by the writers and storytellers of the day, who wanted to satisfy Americans' appetite for adventure.

Cowboys and Cattle Drives

Before the railroads, there was no profitable way to get several million longhorn steers from the grasslands of Texas and northern Mexico to large northeastern cities. Once the system of railroads was established, the cattle drives followed trails north from Texas to railroad towns such as Abilene, Dodge City, and Cheyenne. Cattle were then shipped by train in "stock cars" to the Chicago stockyards, where a steer bought in Texas for $3 sold for $40. Ten million steers were moved on the overland trails in the 20 years of the great cattle drives.

The streets of cattle towns were lined with saloons, hotels, and dance halls eager to help cowboys spend their pay. After two months of battling stampedes, storms, and bands of Indians, cowboys usually needed to blow off some steam. Their rowdiness was spun by writers into exciting stories about the Wild West. Newspapers, magazines, dime novels, and theatrical productions created a West that was more fiction than fact.

NAT LOVE, also known as Deadwood Dick, was a former slave from Tennessee who became a rodeo star. Black cowboys were common in the Old West. In fact, about one in seven cowboys was African American; many of them were former slaves.

> **DEFINITION**
>
> During a **cattle drive**, cowboys on horseback led a herd of cattle across grasslands toward a rail depot.

COWBOY GEAR

Americans learned about handling cattle on the open range from *vaqueros*—Mexican cattle drivers. This is some of the equipment and clothing cowboys used.

ITEM	USE
Bandanna	washcloth, tourniquet, protects eyes and nose from dust
Broad-brimmed hat	provides shade, a pillow, or a bucket for water
Chaps	protect the legs from cactus and sagebrush
High-heeled boots	hold the feet firmly in the stirrups
Lariat, or lasso	long rope used to grab a calf or colt
Pommel (on a saddle)	a knob that the lariat can be wrapped around while riding

Wild West Celebrities

The stars of Wild West legend were the lawmen and outlaws whose exploits—real and imagined—thrilled and enthralled. Wild Bill Hickok was one of the few lawmen who was a great shot. It was said he rarely had to draw his gun because of his reputation. He was killed in Deadwood, Dakota Territory—shot in the back while playing poker. Calamity Jane was buried next to him years later. A crack shot herself, she encouraged the myth that she and Hickok were secretly married. Annie Oakley was another famous sharpshooter. Before she was 15 years old she paid off the mortgage on her mother's farm with the money she made hunting and selling game. She later performed in Buffalo Bill Cody's "Wild West Show."

Wyatt Earp was the most famous lawman of the Old West. His reputation was made by popular fiction and later by television, but the only gunfight he was ever involved in was the notorious "Gunfight at the O.K. Corral" in Arizona.

Wild Bill Hickok

Solid silver badge (c. 1880)

1869–1900

Outlaws

Outlaws were not the romantic heroes portrayed in the dime novels, and later in movies and television. Most were mean-spirited thugs who often shot their foes in the back or when they were unarmed. Billy the Kid was notorious for doing this.

The stories about Jesse James, his brother Frank, and their gang were true in that they robbed railroads and banks, but they were not Western Robin Hoods helping the poor, as they were depicted in legend.

The Wild Bunch was a gang known for robbing trains and banks from Wyoming to New Mexico. Their ringleaders were Robert L. Parker, known as Butch Cassidy, and Harry Longbaugh, the Sundance Kid.

IN SALOONS, settlers, cowboys, and miners met to drink, play card games, and forget the hardships of frontier life.

Jesse James

THE WILD BUNCH had the longest string of successful train and bank robberies in the West.

Robert L. Parker, known as Butch Cassidy

Harry Longbaugh— the Sundance Kid

The Indian Wars

After 1850, the native tribes of the West lost more and more of their lands to frontier settlements. The U.S. government failed to come up with a workable Indian policy, and some tribes turned to warfare. The army slowly forced all the tribes onto reservations, and resistance was ended by 1890.

> **DEFINITION**
>
> A **reservation** is an area of public land set aside for use by a certain group, such as an American Indian tribe.

CHIEF JOSEPH, 1840–1904

One of the most dramatic episodes of the Indian Wars took place in 1877, when the army tried to round up the Nez Percé tribe led by Chief Joseph. Hoping to reach safety in Canada, Chief Joseph took his people on an incredible 1,700-mile march, managing to elude the army for more than three months. The tribe won the sympathy of many Americans. The half-starved families were caught and forced to surrender only 30 miles from the border.

Threatening a Way of Life

Roughly 250,000 American Indians, belonging to many different tribes, lived in the West, with the Plains tribes (see p. 16) being the most numerous. Most of these groups, such as the Sioux, Arapaho, and Cheyenne, lived by following the huge migrating herds of buffalo. Much of the buffalo meat was preserved by smoking or drying; the hides were made into tepees, clothing, and moccasins; and bones and sinews were used for tools, weapons, and decorative items, such as jewelry.

Beginning with the wagon trains and army forts, each wave of westward expansion threatened this way of life. The railroads caused the greatest disruption because they crossed the buffalo migration routes.

Fighting for American Indian Rights

In 1879, a Nebraska journalist named Thomas Tibbles and Susette La Flesche, the daughter of an Omaha chief, sued in court to have reservation land returned to the Ponca tribe. The Ponca won the case, and the court ruled that "an Indian is a person within the laws of the United States."

Tibbles and La Flesche continued to speak out for Indian rights. They inspired a white writer named Helen Hunt Jackson, who devoted her life to working for Indian rights. In *A Century of Dishonor*, she wrote about the Indian treaties the U.S. government had broken. Her novel *Ramona* was about the California Mission Indians.

Conflict Erupts into War

The treaty system, in which the U.S. government designated certain lands as "reserved" for American Indians, was unfair and did not work, especially since the government often did not honor the agreements. As a result, some tribes turned to warfare. From the 1850s through the 1870s, terrible battles between Indian warriors and the U.S. Cavalry broke out on the Great Plains. In 1862, Chief Little Crow led a Sioux band through Minnesota, killing scores of pioneer families. Two years later, Colorado militiamen killed several hundred Cheyenne and Arapaho in the "Sand Creek Massacre."

CHIEF RED HORSE'S PAINTING of Custer's Last Stand at Little Bighorn

GENERAL GEORGE A. CUSTER was widely criticized for taking so few men against the Sioux at the Battle of the Little Bighorn.

PLAINS INDIANS HUNT BUFFALO—bison—on horseback in this period painting. The bison, once numbering at least 50 million, were nearly extinct by 1875.

The Battle of the Little Bighorn

In 1874, the discovery of gold in the Black Hills of Dakota sent thousands of gold seekers through sacred Sioux lands. War parties responded by raiding white settlements. After two years of warfare, a group of Sioux and Cheyenne warriors confronted a U.S. Cavalry column at the Little Bighorn River in Montana territory. Instead of waiting for reinforcements, General George A. Custer led his 264 troopers into battle. They were surrounded, and every last man, including Custer, was killed.

The Battle of the Little Bighorn was the Indians' greatest victory, but it was also their last. By 1881, all the Plains tribes had been forced to move to reservations.

Wounded Knee

In 1889, some Plains Indians turned to a prophetic religious movement based on the "Ghost Dance," a group ritual that was supposed to give followers a vision of the world in 1891, when the whites would disappear and buffalo herds would return.

The movement spread, and army officials feared a Sioux uprising, so they rounded up suspected leaders. Late in 1890, soldiers were holding 350 Sioux at Wounded Knee Creek in South Dakota. Gunfire was heard, and the soldiers opened fire on the Sioux. Nearly 200 men, women, and children were killed or wounded. Organized Indian resistance was at an end.

THE FROZEN BODY of Sioux chief Big Foot at Wounded Knee

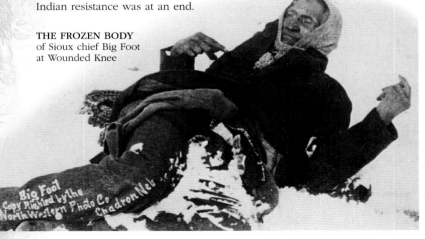

Homesteading

Cheap land and new technology drew growing numbers of homesteaders to the Great Plains. As farmers and sheep ranchers fenced in the land, they ended the open range of the cattle drives, forcing the cattle owners onto settled ranches. By 1890, the Plains region was highly populated and organized into states and territories.

1869–1900

The Homesteaders' Frontier

The explorers' maps of the West labeled the Great Plains as the "Great American Desert." Guidebooks for wagon trains warned of long stretches with no water and no trees, even for firewood.

Still, cheap acreage encouraged farm families to try to make a living from the prairie lands. The Homestead Act of 1862 allowed anyone—even new immigrants—to claim a tract of 160 acres, provided they built a house and lived on the land for five years. In less than 30 years, 80 million acres were claimed. Most of that land was bought by speculators who resold it later for much more than they paid originally.

Railroad companies also charged little for the lands granted to them by the government, because they wanted farms and towns to grow nearby that would provide regular paying customers for the railroad (see p. 94).

In 1890, just a few months after Montana and the Dakotas became states, the U.S. Census reported that there was no more open land that could be called "frontier."

SOD HOUSES were made of the thick prairie sod, which had formed over many years as the grass decomposed. Homesteaders learned to cut the sod into blocks for building their houses, stores, and even churches. The prairie farmers were called "sod busters."

Homesteading Life

Pioneers faced extraordinary hardships in their lives on the Plains. The landscape—flat and treeless—could be overwhelming. Droughts, floods, broiling summer heat, bitterly cold winters, and the loneliness of being miles from a neighbor were just some of the difficulties to be faced. Sometimes, 1884 being the worst case, clouds of grasshoppers descended like a Biblical plague and consumed every blade of grass.

The small size of the land parcels—160 acres—made it necessary for farm families to buy more land or cooperate with others to be able to afford the machinery needed for the large-scale growing of wheat, corn, or oats. Somehow, several million people worked through the hardship and transformed the prairie into one of the world's greatest "breadbaskets."

> ### DEFINITION
>
> A **breadbasket** is an area known for its grain crop—not just wheat, but also corn, oats, rye, and barley.

MILLIONS OF ACRES

PRODUCTS WILL PAY FOR LAND AND IMPROVEMENTS!

View on the Big Blue, between Camden and Crete, representing Valley and Rolling Prairie Land in Nebraska.

IOWA AND NEBRASKA LANDS

FOR SALE ON **10** YEARS CREDIT
BY THE
Burlington & Missouri River R.R. Co.

AT 6 PER CT. INTEREST AND LOW PRICES.
Only One-Seventh of Principal Due Annually, beginning Four Years after purchase.
20 PER CENT. DEDUCTED FROM 10 YEARS PRICE, FOR CASH.

LAND EXPLORING TICKETS SOLD
and Cost allowed in First Interest paid, on Land bought in 30 days from date of ticket.

Address GEO. S. HARRIS, LAND COMMISSIONER,
or T. H. LEAVITT, Ass't Land Comm'r, Burlington, Iowa.
Or apply to

FREE ROOMS for buyers to board themselves are provided at Burlington and Lincoln

"BOOMER" ADVERTISING and literature invited land-hungry farm families to come to "America's New Garden of Eden." State and territorial governments encouraged farmers by offering low-interest loans and even free tools. In the 1870s and 1880s, railroads joined the land boom by advertising in newspapers in the Scandinavian countries, Germany, Holland, and England.

The End of the Open Range

In 1874, an Illinois farmer named Joseph Glidden patented barbed wire. Homesteaders used it to fence in their lands, which made sheep ranching profitable by protecting the sheep from predators and keeping them from getting away. The fencing in of the prairie infuriated cattle owners, and led to occasional gun battles.

The final blow to the open range was the blizzard of 1886–1887, the worst on record. Huge drifts of snow destroyed herds of range cattle, killing an estimated 90 percent. The days of the long cattle drives were over. Cattle owners bought land, fencing it in, and the cowboys became ranch hands.

WHITE SETTLERS RACED TO STAKE CLAIMS during the final Oklahoma land rush, seen in this photo from September 16, 1893.

The Last Land Rush

In 1889, the government responded to public pressure and opened an area called the Oklahoma District, unoccupied land surrounded by the Indian Territory. On April 22, 1889, exactly at noon, a signal was fired and thousands of people rushed to stake claims. By the end of the day, 50,000 people had claimed roughly two million acres. In 1893, the final land rush took place when the government purchased a strip of Oklahoma Territory called the Cherokee Outlet. More than 100,000 people—some even pedaling bicycles—took part in the rush.

Closing the Frontier

So many Americans had moved out West that the 1890 U.S. Census reported that the frontier—the line between settled and unsettled areas—was closed. Frederick Jackson Turner, a historian, saw it as the end of an important era in American history. He argued that the frontier had made settlers independent and self-reliant, and that these traits had promoted a healthy democracy. Turner's writing focused on the frontier's effect on white Americans, but the changing frontier and the movement of settlers into the West had also greatly changed American Indians' way of life (see p. 98).

ADVANCES IN FARMING

Advances in technology were critical for farming prairie grasslands. John Deere's "chilled steel" plow, invented in 1837, could slice through the thick sod. Better windmills could draw water from aquifers 300 feet below the earth's surface. And a new strain of wheat from Turkey could withstand the bitterly cold winters. In addition, a technique called "dry farming"—plowing deep to reach moist soil—made it possible to plant huge fields of wheat. And machines like Cyrus McCormick's reaper could harvest that wheat—doing the work of five or six men.

THE McCORMICK REAPER, seen here in an early version, made harvesting a large wheat crop easier.

SEED CATALOGS enabled farmers to buy by mail.

MULBERRY STREET, a main thoroughfare at the center of the Italian immigrant community in New York City, is filled with vendors' fruit and vegetable stands and people of all ages. Immigrant groups tended to cluster together for support once they arrived in the United States. America's cities grew rapidly because of the influx of immigrants, who provided cheap labor for the industrial age.

Mar. 1867
Nebraska enters the Union

Nov. 1876
Presidential election undecided

Mar. 1877
Rutherford B. Hayes declared winner of presidential election

Dec. 4, 1867
Kelley forms Patrons of Husbandry

1869
Knights of Labor organized

1873
Andrew Carnegie builds Homestead Steel Works

Feb. 22, 1879
First Woolworth five-and-dime opens

July 2, 1881
Garfield shot by assassin, dies 11 weeks later

1865
Thirteenth Amendment to the Constitution ratified, abolishing slavery

Nov. 1868
Ulysses S. Grant elected president

1872
Ward starts mail-order business

Aug. 1876
Colorado enters the Union

July–Aug. 1877
B&O Railroad strike

Sept. 20, 1881
Chester A. Arthur inaugurated as President

1865   **1870**   **1875**   **1880**

1868
Fourteenth Amendment to the Constitution ratified, guaranteeing citizenship to African Americans

1870
Fifteenth Amendment to the Constitution ratified, granting African Americans the right to vote

June 1870
John D. Rockefeller forms Standard Oil of Ohio

Nov. 1872
Grant reelected

1876
John Wanamaker opens the country's first department store

Oct. 21, 1879
Edison makes electric light bulb

1882
Rockefeller forms Standard Oil Trust

Mar. 1876
Alexander Graham Bell invents the telephone

Nov. 1880
James Garfield elected president

May 6, 1882
Chinese Exclusion Act

AMERICA'S INDUSTRIAL AGE

1865–1900

After the Civil War, the American landscape, once dominated by farms and villages, became increasingly industrialized. Factories and mills churned out products on a huge scale.

New inventions created new businesses and helped improve everyday life. Many business leaders drove out competitors, forming monopolies and amassing great fortunes.

Between 1870 and 1900, the nation's population doubled from fewer than 40 million to 76 million, largely because of immigration. But while the growing middle class enjoyed more leisure time, many workers and farmers struggled to make ends meet. They formed unions and other organizations to bring equity and comfort to their lives.

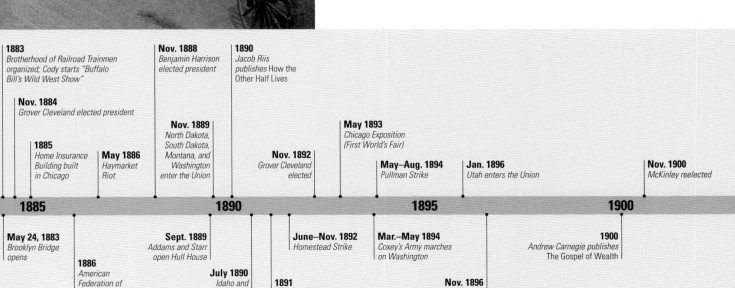

1883
Brotherhood of Railroad Trainmen organized; Cody starts "Buffalo Bill's Wild West Show"

Nov. 1888
Benjamin Harrison elected president

1890
Jacob Riis publishes How the Other Half Lives

Nov. 1884
Grover Cleveland elected president

Nov. 1889
North Dakota, South Dakota, Montana, and Washington enter the Union

May 1893
Chicago Exposition (First World's Fair)

1885
Home Insurance Building built in Chicago

May 1886
Haymarket Riot

Nov. 1892
Grover Cleveland elected

May–Aug. 1894
Pullman Strike

Jan. 1896
Utah enters the Union

Nov. 1900
McKinley reelected

1885　　　　**1890**　　　　**1895**　　　　**1900**

May 24, 1883
Brooklyn Bridge opens

1886
American Federation of Labor (AF of L) organized

Sept. 1889
Addams and Starr open Hull House

July 1890
Idaho and Wyoming enter the Union

1891
Farmers' Alliances form People's Party of the U.S.A.

June–Nov. 1892
Homestead Strike

Mar.–May 1894
Coxey's Army marches on Washington

Nov. 1896
William McKinley elected president

1900
Andrew Carnegie publishes The Gospel of Wealth

An Age of Industry

After the Civil War, America's abundant natural resources, nationwide transportation system, and innovative technology combined to provide for mass production on an enormous scale. The United States of America had entered a period of rapid industrialization.

Companies then developed new methods of selling a wide variety of products to consumers across the country.

1865–1900

A BESSEMER CONVERTER uses incredibly high heat to melt iron ore for steelmaking.

HOW STEEL IS MADE

In 1855, Sir Henry Bessemer developed the Bessemer process for converting iron into steel. A coal fire in a blast furnace heats iron ore to a white-hot temperature; a blast of hot air is then forced through the molten iron, removing impurities and leaving molten steel, which is poured into molds.

Turning Iron into Steel

Steel is much stronger and more durable than iron, so it is a better material to use for building large buildings and bridges, train tracks, and small items such as tools and cooking utensils. In the past, making steel had been slow and expensive and was only used for special items, such as precision instruments and swords. Once an easy method of turning iron into steel was developed with the Bessemer process, steel became fast and cheap to produce. In fact, steel that used to take ten hours to make could now be turned out in 15 minutes.

By 1870, iron ore from deposits near Lake Superior was being transported by lake freighters and railroads to mills in Chicago or Pittsburgh. Then coal from the world's largest coal reserves in Pennsylvania and West Virginia was taken by rail to the mills, to fuel the furnaces. Soon, steelmaking was the nation's largest industry.

COAL MINERS TAKE A BREAK from working to provide the steel mills with the fuel needed to heat iron ore into steel.

THE CEREAL WARS

In the 1880s, Dr. John Kellogg, operator of a sanatorium in Battle Creek, Michigan, developed a ready-to-eat cereal he named Corn Flakes. The nation's first "instant breakfast," packaged by his brother W. K. Kellogg, was an instant success. The Kelloggs soon had competition from Charles W. Post, a former patient at the sanatorium, who began to market a very similar product under the name Post Toasties. The conflict became known as the "Cereal Wars." Both the Post and Kellogg companies survived to become major corporations that still make cereal today.

A CEREAL AD promises convenience and good taste.

SINGER SEWING MACHINES were responsible for one of the largest mass-production businesses—ready-made clothes. Singer also produced a smaller sewing machine that was popular for home use. The Singer Company was among the first to open sales offices in other countries, and it advertised as a worldwide corporation.

Mass Production

When Samuel Colt, inventor of the famous Colt .45 revolver, received a large order from the Texas Rangers (the Texas state police), he turned for help to the company Eli Whitney had started early in the 1800s. He used Whitney's idea of interchangeable parts and added the concept of division of labor—each worker in the assembly line performed just one or two tasks, then the revolver moved on to the next worker. Colt's assembly-line system was the final step needed for the mass production of goods.

Assembly Lines Are Used in Multiple Industries

By the 1870s, assembly lines were used in meatpacking, food processing, clothing manufacture, and many other industries. Singer sewing machines, themselves mass-produced, were used to make clothes in assembly-line processes. And in New England's shoe factories, instead of a shoemaker crafting an entire shoe, he might make one part, such as the heel or sole, while the parts were pieced together on another assembly line. Mass production increased the volume of goods that could be produced and lowered their price.

By 1890, the value of the manufactured goods produced in the United States had for the first time exceeded the value of its agricultural products.

1865–1900

New Ways to Distribute

Once more goods were being produced for sale, business owners devised systems for selling them to a broader market. Department stores and chain stores were two approaches. F. W. Woolworth and J. C. Penney pioneered the chain-store system, each opening stores in dozens of cities in the 1880s and 1890s.

One advantage chain stores held over smaller, local businesses was that they could buy goods in large quantities, which lowered both the cost of buying the item from the manufacturer and the retail price consumers were charged.

Catalogs and Department Stores Arrive

In 1872, Aaron Montgomery Ward began a mail-order business, making it possible for rural Americans who didn't live near chain stores to purchase factory-made goods. He quickly met with competition from Sears, Roebuck & Co (see p. 157). Then, in 1876, John Wanamaker opened Wanamaker Grand Depot—the nation's first department store—in a huge railroad freight station in Philadelphia. In 1886, the store installed electric lights in place of the old gas lamps. Electric lighting was so new and mysterious that some people were afraid the lights might explode.

THE FIRST WOOLWORTH FIVE-AND-DIME store opened in Lancaster, Pennsylvania, on June 21, 1879. By 1911, the chain would have more than 1,000 stores.

Big Business and Great Fortunes

Rapid industrialization offered a unique opportunity for a certain kind of capitalist—such as Cornelius Vanderbilt in railroads, John D. Rockefeller in the oil industry, and Andrew Carnegie in steel. All followed the same pattern: they used tough methods to force competitors out of business, streamlined business operations, accumulated huge fortunes, and lived lives of luxury.

DEFINITION

Capitalism is a system of economic production in which the means of making and distributing goods are privately owned and operated to make profits. A *capitalist* is someone who owns a business or invests money in one in the hope of earning profits.

1865–1900

Vanderbilt and Railroads

In 1865, at the age of 71, Cornelius Vanderbilt entered the railroad business. To do so, he used the $10 million fortune he had made with a fleet of steamships to buy up several railroads, creating a 14,000-mile combination of railroad lines called the New York Central.

When Vanderbilt died 12 years later, he had increased his fortune to $100 million by using ruthless methods. One of them was to drop prices lower than a competitor could afford to drop his; then, when all his business had been taken away, the competitor would be forced to declare bankruptcy or sell out. This led many people to label Vanderbilt a robber baron. Others hailed him as a "captain of industry" because he made railroads more efficient. Before Vanderbilt, travelers and freight had to transfer 17 times between New York and Chicago to complete their journey. After Vanderbilt, one train made the trip—in half the time and at a lower cost.

THE BREAKERS, IN NEWPORT, RHODE ISLAND, was completed in 1895 by Cornelius Vanderbilt's grandson, William. Many wealthy families competed in building second homes called cottages in resort areas such as Newport and Narragansett, Rhode Island. The 70-room Breakers, which cost $11 million, was one of the showiest of these cottages.

THE AMERICUS CLUB BALL shown in this painting was held at the Connecticut Academy of Music, Greenwich, in 1871. For privileged Americans, balls and dinner parties like this were popular entertainment in the late 1800s. The country's wealthiest families took the opportunity to show off their fortunes in events that were much like movie premieres today. Hundreds of people lined the streets to watch the wealthy arrive at a mansion in elegant carriages, while inside, the guests might find favors, such as cigars wrapped in $100 bills, or oysters containing black pearls.

OIL—"BLACK GOLD"

Oil was common on the farms of western Pennsylvania, where it was considered a nuisance because it seeped to the surface of farm fields and pastures, damaging soil with its black ooze. Then, in 1855, a way to refine oil into petroleum that could be used for lamps and heaters was developed. Suddenly, oil had great commercial value. Four years later, "Colonel" E. L. Drake dug the first successful oil well near Titusville, Pennsylvania. Soon, "wildcatters" were drilling all over the state. By 1865, they were producing 40 million barrels a year.

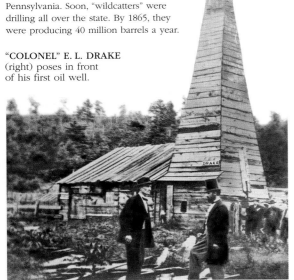

"COLONEL" E. L. DRAKE (right) poses in front of his first oil well.

Rockefeller and Oil

When John D. Rockefeller formed Standard Oil of Ohio in 1870, the oil industry was in chaos, with dozens of companies involved in drilling, refining, selling, and distributing oil. He persuaded the railroads to give rebates—partial refunds—to his company with the promise that they would have all his business when he had consolidated the industry. Cheaper shipping costs let him sell his oil for less, forcing competitors out of business.

Within two years, he controlled one quarter of the nation's oil refining. He then bought steamships, railroads, docks, even barrel companies, to supply his company with everything it needed to distribute oil. He retired at the age of 72, the richest man in America, and began giving away his $530 million to worthy causes.

Trusts and Monopolies

Rockefeller also invented a business arrangement called the trust, in which one board of directors controlled several companies. By 1879, Standard Oil controlled 90 percent of the industry—a monopoly—and Rockefeller said, "The oil industry belongs to us." Under the giant trust he created, no single company in his oil empire could be accused of being a monopoly. People thought trusts were unfair because they enabled companies to charge whatever they pleased for their product. The U.S. government took action against the trusts in the early 1900s.

> **DEFINITION**
>
> A **monopoly** is exclusive control over an industry or economic market by one company or individual.

Carnegie and Steel

Andrew Carnegie, a Scottish immigrant, grew up penniless. He worked his way up fast and became the owner of several ironworks. He was quick to see the value of steel and built the nation's largest Bessemer-process steel plant (see p. 104) in 1873—the Homestead Steel Works—near Pittsburgh, Pennsylvania. Using railroad rebates and bribes, he drove out the competition and expanded into related areas—mining coal and iron ore, and building steamships.

In 1901, with control of 25 percent of the steel industry, Carnegie sold it all for $492 million to a bank headed by financial wizard J. Pierpont Morgan. Morgan combined Homestead with other companies to form United States Steel, then the world's largest corporation.

Carnegie's Philosophy

In his book *The Gospel of Wealth*, Carnegie said he believed rich men deserved their wealth. But he also believed that a person should give away his money to worthy causes, and said, "The man who dies rich, dies thus disgraced." Carnegie donated nearly all of his fortune, using it to build libraries, concert halls, and hospitals.

Still, people who called Carnegie a robber baron pointed out that the wealth he enjoyed was actually created by the workers—men, women, and some children who toiled long hours for low wages—and that Carnegie ignored the welfare of those workers.

CARNEGIE'S FIRST STEEL MILL opened on August 22, 1875, along the Monongahela River in Braddock, Pennsylvania. The railroad tracks ran up to the mill for quick and efficient delivery of iron ore and collection of the finished steel.

Cities and Inventions

Between 1865 and 1900, American cities flourished as industry, business, and populations boomed. Cities grew upward into the first skyscrapers and out into the first suburbs. The invention of electric lighting and telephone communication added to the wonder and excitement of city life.

Skyscrapers

Office buildings began to replace churches in the late 1800s as the cities' tallest buildings. These buildings were said to be so tall they "scraped the sky."

Unlike the highly decorated early Victorian buildings, architects now designed large public structures out of steel and glass, such as Grand Central Station and the Flatiron Building in New York. Chicago architect Louis Sullivan said that the form of a building should follow its function, or use. His assistant, Frank Lloyd Wright, applied that idea to houses, building them to fit into their natural environment.

Constructing buildings taller than four or five stories high required new building materials and a practical way for people to get to the higher floors. Steel, which was lighter and stronger than iron, allowed builders to create taller structures safely.

Otis's Elevators

The first elevators were used only for freight because they crashed often and people were afraid to ride them.

In the mid-1850s, Elisha Otis developed a "safety hoist," which prevented a crash even if the cable broke. This encouraged people to ride Otis elevators. In 1885, the Home Insurance Building in Chicago, with a steel frame and steam-powered Otis elevators, rose to ten stories to become the first skyscraper.

THE 20-STORY FLATIRON BUILDING, one of New York City's first skyscrapers, was outfitted with Otis elevators in 1902.

Trolleys and Suburbs

Frank J. Sprague had worked for Thomas Edison before starting his own company making electric motors. In 1887, he installed trolley cars in Richmond, Virginia, using tracks built for horse-drawn railways. Power for the electric motors was delivered by an overhead wire.

Sprague's quiet, smooth-riding trolleys were an instant success. Within three years, 51 cities had installed his system. Trolleys also provided fast, cheap transportation beyond the city limits, connecting outlying towns to the bigger cities. Urban areas grew even more, since people could now work in the city while living in the suburbs.

Bridges

Steel was made into beams, but it could also be twisted into strong cables for bridge building. The most outstanding work in design and engineering was the Brooklyn Bridge. Started by John Roebling in 1869, it was completed by his son, Washington Roebling, in 1883. The world's longest suspension bridge, it led to combining the separate cities of Manhattan and Brooklyn into one massive metropolis.

IN 1893, HORSE-DRAWN TROLLEYS provided public transportation in Cincinnati, Ohio. Later, overhead wire networks were built to power electric motors, which replaced the horses.

THOMAS EDISON, 1847–1931

Thomas Edison with an early model of his phonograph

Thomas Edison was the most famous inventor during the great age of invention. In his lifetime, he was granted 1,093 patents. His inventions included a telegraph that would send and receive messages simultaneously over the same line; a transmitter for Bell's telephone; the phonograph; the incandescent light bulb; the mimeograph machine; waxed paper; and the basic system for making motion pictures.

Working at his laboratory in Menlo Park, New Jersey, Edison worked long hours, slept little, talked to himself, and became lost in his work. In fact, on his wedding night, he forgot about his bride and went back to his lab to work out a problem.

1865–1900

Electric Lighting and Power

In 1879, Thomas Edison developed the first incandescent light bulb, which was much like the bulb in use today. His genius emerged next when he and his workers created everything needed for a complete lighting system—sockets, fuses, meters, insulated wire, underground cable, and a generator to produce the electricity.

In 1882, after years of trial and error, Edison's team installed the first central power station in New York City. By the early 1900s, electric lighting and power stations were installed in every city.

THIS EARLY EDISON BULB consists of a carbonized bamboo filament inside an airtight globe of blown glass.

BELL'S TELEPHONE

Bell telephones, c. 1876

When Alexander Graham Bell introduced his "speaking telegraph" in 1876, people treated it as a curiosity. For example, when he offered it to the Western Union Telegraph Company, the president was not interested, saying they had no use for an "electrical toy."

Over the next few years, Americans gradually saw the value of the "tele-phone" for personal and business communication. By 1880, there were 50,000 telephones in use; over the next 20 years, the number soared past one million.

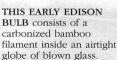

Westinghouse v. Edison

Alternating current, known as AC, was developed by Nikola Tesla in 1888. George Westinghouse, inventor of the airbrake, owned the rights and campaigned to make AC the country's most widely used power system. Edison preferred the direct current system, but AC proved safer, more efficient, and better for sending electricity over long distances. Edison believed he was right, but Westinghouse won out, and most of the U.S. began to use AC.

1870–1901 Victorian America

American society and culture changed significantly during the period of time named for Great Britain's Queen Victoria. Convenient, more comfortable living, new entertainment, literature, art, and diversions—all reflected the tastes of an industrialized and urbanized age.

New Comforts

Visitors to America's large cities were amazed by changes in the way people lived. Streets, shops, and department stores were well lit, and electric trolley cars moved people quietly with ease.

Changes in people's homes were even more astounding. An urban middle-class family usually had servants, such as a maid and nanny, and might also have had indoor plumbing, a telephone, and the first electrical appliances—vacuum cleaners and electric irons.

THE SPACIOUS PARLOR of a Washington, D.C., home, circa 1885, contains elegant furniture and decorations.

MARK TWAIN, 1835–1910

Mark Twain was the pen name of Samuel Clemens, a writer and humorist whose works helped create an American literary style. His novels, short stories, and memoirs dealt with politics, racism, and national identity. Twain was raised in Hannibal, Missouri, and used the Mississippi River of his youth as a setting in his two most famous novels, *The Adventures of Tom Sawyer* and *The Adventures of Huckleberry Finn*.

Art and Literature

John Singer Sargent and James Whistler, who lived in England during their careers, painted evocative portraits and scenes of society life. Winslow Homer retreated to the Maine coast to create seascapes; and Thomas Eakins was known for his photographic realism.

In American literature, regional writing was popular, such as Bret Harte's stories of the gold-mining camps and Mark Twain's Mississippi River tales. Edith Wharton wrote about the tensions between America's established families and the newly rich who had amassed fortunes in industry. Henry James created remarkable studies of Americans living in Europe.

WHISTLER'S MOTHER, by James Whistler, was striking in its stark colors and arrangement. His work displayed a formal style, which was less emotional than was common at the time.

Popular Culture

New forms of entertainment appealed to a wide variety of people. Circuses reached small towns as well as cities, and in 1883, William F. Cody began to dazzle audiences with "Buffalo Bill's Wild West Show."

The latest rage in music was Scott Joplin, known as the "King of Ragtime." His "Maple Leaf Rag" started a new trend in music that would set the stage for jazz, blues, and other uniquely American sounds. Band music was also popular, especially the marches of John Philip Sousa.

Newspapers and magazines began reaching mass audiences during this time, in part by emphasizing sensational stories and introducing comic strips.

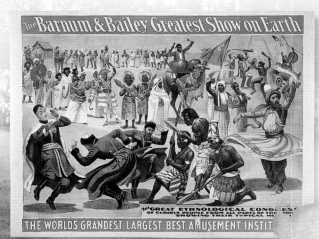

THE RINGLING BROS. AND BARNUM & BAILEY CIRCUS had three rings in which different acts performed simultaneously.

THE CHICAGO EXPOSITION

In 1893, Chicago opened a huge exposition—the World's Columbian Exposition. Twenty-seven million visitors marveled at the bright electric lights and the transportation provided by miles of canals with gondolas from Venice and Thomas Edison's electric trains. Besides exhibits of technical achievements, the exposition included a midway with carnival rides and such oddities as a Venus de Milo sculpture made of 1,500 pounds of chocolate.

THE "FERRIS WHEEL" awed visitors. G. W. Ferris's invention towered 250 feet above the exhibits, and each of its glass cabs held 60 passengers.

Recreation

Bicycle riding, which began as an eccentric fad, became the most popular pastime of the 1890s.

Other outdoor sports became popular, too: badminton, croquet, ice skating, sailing, and recent imports such as tennis from England and golf from Scotland.

A CURRIER & IVES LITHOGRAPH shows a baseball game in progress at the Elysian Fields in Hoboken, New Jersey (background image).

Spectator Sports

Baseball led the way as the most popular spectator sport. By 1900, both the National and American Leagues had been established, and large crowds packed stadiums. College football, along with rowing races, track and field events, and horse racing, was also of growing interest. The first Kentucky Derby took place in 1875. Basketball was invented in 1892, but would not catch on for some time.

Coming to America

One reason cities grew so rapidly in the late 1800s was that immigrants came to the United States in record numbers. Cities could not absorb so many people so fast, and the poor suffered from a lack of basic services. Government was slow to respond, so private groups provided badly needed help.

Waves of Immigrants

Many poor people in southern and eastern Europe envisioned America as a land where the streets were paved with gold. Desperate to escape the poverty of their homelands, they made their way to America—9 million immigrants between 1880 and 1900, and 14.5 million more from 1900 to 1920. In the past, most immigrants had come from western European countries such as Great Britain and Germany, but this new wave was different: They came from eastern European countries such as Poland and Russia, and from southern Europe, especially Italy. Italians made up the largest immigrant group; Jews, many fleeing religious persecution, the next largest.

Immigration to Cities

The influx of newcomers changed the makeup of cities. They helped boost the population of New York City to 3 million by 1900. More than one-third of that number— 1.26 million—had been born outside the United States. The nation's largest cities absorbed the most immigrants, so that in 1900, one out of every 12 Americans lived in New York, Philadelphia, or Chicago.

MULBERRY STREET
was the center of
Italian immigrant life
in New York City.

JACOB RIIS, 1849–1914

Many middle- and upper-class families knew little about immigrants' problems. Jacob Riis, a Danish immigrant—and a photographer and journalist—exposed the suffering experienced by many immigrants. Riis's work, *How the Other Half Lives*, published in 1890, helped people realize that government action was necessary to improve conditions in city slums.

A DIRTY, CROWDED TENEMENT
as photographed by Riis

Coping with Poverty

Most of the immigrants arrived with little or no money, hoping to find work—even though they had few skills outside of farming, and usually spoke no English. The majority were forced to live in slum conditions, often in hastily constructed "tenements"—tall, narrow wooden buildings, poorly lighted and ventilated, with maybe a water faucet in the yard. In New York City in the late 1800s, a mere 4,000 tenements housed more than one million people.

Public Services for the Poor

Most cities had public water systems by 1890. Running water helped to eliminate epidemics of cholera and yellow fever, but large numbers of people living in unclean, cramped conditions turned tuberculosis into a major slum disease. City governments simply could not keep up with the great numbers of people, and never before had they been called upon to deal with such huge amounts of garbage and sewage.

The Demand for Change

People began to demand government action, but the response was slow. Individuals and private organizations found ways to make a difference. In 1889, Jane Addams opened Hull House in Chicago, based on the English idea of "settlement houses" where the poor could find help. Settlement workers showed women how to care for the sick and how to shop for American food; workers gave classes in English, sewing, and dozens of other subjects. Churches and synagogues also became involved and set up welfare agencies; the Salvation Army provided meals, lodging, and prayer.

Although conditions seemed overwhelming for some, most immigrants remained optimistic. City schools offered classes day and night, providing training in English, citizenship, nutrition, and job skills. Newcomers continued to believe in the dream of a better life, if not for themselves, for their children.

A GARMENT WORKER on New York's East Side carries her work home with her. Many women earned meager livings as seamstresses.

1865–1900

CHINESE WORKERS lay track for the new railroad.

Immigrants from China

Beginning with the California Gold Rush in 1849, thousands of Chinese immigrants came to California. About 10,000 Chinese worked on the construction of the transcontinental railroad (see p. 94). By the 1870s, many white workers resented the Chinese, especially since they were often willing to work for lower wages than whites. Anti-Chinese feelings led to riots by mobs. Congress responded to the demands of politicians in California by passing the Chinese Exclusion Act of 1882, which ended Chinese immigration until the act was repealed in 1943.

The Struggles of Labor

With large-scale industrial production, work grew impersonal. Workers hoped to counter management's power by banding together and forming unions—even going on strike if their demands were not met. But the owners had far more power and often used the police or military to break strikes and weaken unions.

1865–1900

The Changing Nature of Work

In the past, workers and owners had labored together in small shops. Now, in the late 1800s, employees toiled in huge factories, taking orders from managers. Jobs were tedious—workers performed the same operation over and over, 10 or 12 hours a day, without the satisfaction of having completed something.

Owners of factories and mines paid little attention to employees' health or safety. Not only adults, but children, too, stood for hours operating dangerous machines or breathing dust or foul air. Laborers who were injured or became too ill to work were fired, and permanently disabled workers received no medical help or wages.

A POSTER for the Brotherhood of Railroad Trainmen, a union organized in 1883

Sweatshops

In slum tenements, people labored in what were called sweatshops. They were paid for each completed item—"piecework"—rather than by the hour. Sometimes entire families worked 12-hour days, sewing garments or making paper flowers for little money; because the pay per item was low, people had to work long hours to make enough money.

Labor Unions and Strikes

Workers tried to form unions and to gain power with collective bargaining—talking to owners as a group about their needs. The owners found ways to get back, such as the blacklist—sharing names of union organizers with other owners—and the lockout—firing workers on strike.

In 1877, the Baltimore and Ohio Railroad and three other railroad companies announced a ten-percent pay cut, and 100,000 workers across the country walked off their jobs. The striking workers became violent, and destroyed millions of dollars worth of property, derailed trains, and burned rail yards. The owners asked the government for help, and police, state militia, and federal troops helped to end the strike. Americans were horrified by the disturbance that the workers caused, and public opinion largely supported the owners.

114

The Homestead Strike, 1892

In 1886, 300,000 members from various trade unions joined together to form the American Federation of Labor, or "AF of L." When the union representing steel workers went on strike against Carnegie Steel's Homestead plant (see p. 107), the owners' agent, Henry Frick, locked out the workers and hired 300 men from the Pinkerton detective agency to enforce the lockout and protect nonunion replacements, or "scabs." A bitter fight resulted; seven guards and nine strikers were killed. After nearly six months, the lockout ended, thousands lost their jobs, and the steel workers' union was destroyed.

HOMESTEAD STRIKERS fight Pinkerton guard, shown in a newspaper illustration from 1892.

The Pullman Strike, 1894

The Pullman Company in Illinois, manufacturer of luxury railroad cars, operated a company town, meaning that it required its workers to live in Pullman housing and buy food and necessities at the Pullman store (see p. 95). In 1893, Pullman cut wages by 25 to 40 percent, but did not lower its rents or store prices. In May 1894, the American Railway Union went on strike. Strikebreakers were brought in, followed by the militia. In the summer of 1894, President Grover Cleveland ordered army troops in, and the strike was finally crushed. The loss in this strike convinced many workers that unions could not help them.

1865–1900

THE HAYMARKET RIOT OF 1886 began when police were called to break up a strike at the McCormick Harvesting Machine Company in Chicago. One worker was killed and several others wounded. The next day, people gathered to protest the police's violence. When the police arrived to break up the meeting, someone threw a bomb, which killed seven police officers and wounded many more. The police opened fire, injuring dozens. Although the Knights of Labor, then one of the largest unions, was blamed for the riot, their involvement has never been proven.

LABOR ORGANIZERS

SAMUEL GOMPERS, 1850–1924

Samuel Gompers rose from work in tenement sweatshops to become the most influential leader of the labor movement. As a young immigrant, he had enjoyed his factory experience as a cigar maker. Gompers and his fellow workers took turns, having one person read aloud while the others rolled cigars, sharing their finished output with the reader.

In his 30s, Gompers helped form the American Federation of Labor. The union grew, and Gompers remained the head of it for 40 years. Although unions were weak at the turn of the century, their membership increased greatly in the 1930s and 1940s. By 1945, the AFL had more than nine million members; the Congress of Industrial Organizations (CIO) had five million. They combined in 1955 to form the AFL-CIO.

MOTHER JONES, 1830–1930

Mary Harris "Mother" Jones was an Irish immigrant who worked for more than 50 years as a labor organizer, mostly for the United Mine Workers. She was so successful that mine owners called her "the most dangerous woman in America."

In 1867, Mother Jones lost her husband and four children in a yellow-fever epidemic. She moved to Chicago and worked as a seamstress but lost all her belongings in the great Chicago fire of 1871. She became a labor organizer in the 1870s and spent much of her time on the road until she retired at 95, living quietly until her death at the age of 100.

Farmers in Trouble

With new machines and other innovations, American farms produced such an abundance of crops that prices plummeted to disastrous levels as supply exceeded demand. Farmers searched for ways to organize to improve their conditions, including taking political action.

1865–1900

The Problems of Overproduction

In the late 1800s, new farm machines, better seeds, and improved methods led to huge increases in output. The production of wheat, for example, soared from 173 million bushels to 635 million bushels in 50 years. Other harvests—corn, cotton, and sugar—grew at similar rates.

The trouble was that, even with the explosive growth of cities, there was more produce than could be used, and the prices plummeted. Prices for some crops fell so low that farmers plowed the harvest back into the ground, since it was worth more as fertilizer than it was at market.

As farm income declined, families fell into debt. They had borrowed money to buy land or machinery that they now could not pay back. Some families sold out. Others had their farms foreclosed by banks. Between 1889 and 1894, banks took over 11,000 farms in Kansas alone.

THE COMBINE

The combine was one of the most amazing inventions of the agricultural revolution. Pulled by a team of 40 horses or mules, it performed every step of the wheat harvest—cutting, gathering, threshing, and bagging the grain, which previously required dozens of men and days of work.

DEFINITION

Supply and *demand* are economic terms that can explain why prices go up or down. If a lot of people want an item, then demand is high; and if there isn't a lot of it, then supply is low. The price will then go up because people will pay more rather than go without.

APPLE HARVESTERS pick the crop in Virginia's Shenandoah Valley.

The Farmers Revolt

In 1867, a postal worker named Oliver Kelley formed the Patrons of Husbandry, better known as the Grange. Kelley's idea was to organize farmers so they could open stores called cooperatives—enterprises owned and operated by the people using them—to buy supplies and machinery at low cost.

By the 1890s, farmers resented the power of banks and the high rates charged by railroads to ship crops. As a result, they began to form regional Farmers' Alliances. In 1889, they had gained control of eight state legislatures and elected three governors and 44 congressmen. Midwestern farmers decided the next step was to form a new political party.

Coxey's Army

In 1894, Jacob Coxey led a group of unemployed workers to Washington to demand government help for the unemployed. This was one of the first mass protests against indifference to the plight of workers and farmers. It wasn't successful, but it brought attention to a previously silent cause.

COXEY'S ARMY approaches Washington on April 30, 1894.

The Populist Party

In 1891, leaders of several Granges and Farmers' Alliances formed the People's Party of the U.S.A., which became known as the Populist Party. The Populists adopted a platform including proposals such as government ownership of railroads, banks, telephones, and telegraphs. They also wanted the coinage of silver to increase the supply of money, making it easier to pay debts. They chose James B. Weaver of Iowa, a former Grange leader, as their presidential candidate for 1892. Although Grover Cleveland easily beat him, the Populists made a strong showing. Weaver received more than one million votes; a dozen Populists were elected to Congress, and three as governors.

A STAMP commemorates the 100th Anniversary of the National Grange.

The Election of 1896

The new Populist Party had high hopes for winning the presidential election of 1896. Then the Populists were dealt a blow when the Democratic Party convention called for the "free and unlimited coinage of silver," which had been a major part of the Populist platform. The Democrats' dynamic new leader, William Jennings Bryan, gave his electrifying "Cross of Gold" speech on the silver issue, and it was clear that the Democrats had taken over a major part of the Populist program. In order not to lose to the Republicans, the Populists endorsed Bryan. Bryan lost the election to the Republican candidate, William McKinley, and the Populist Party was finished.

WILLIAM JENNINGS BRYAN, 1860–1925

Bryan was only 36 when he turned the 1896 presidential campaign into a great crusade of the working people against the rich. In the space of 14 weeks, he traveled 18,000 miles, went to 27 states, and delivered 600 speeches. It is estimated that he spoke to five million people.

He spoke with a simple, folksy eloquence, which had great appeal for rural Americans. Bryan ran against McKinley again in 1900, and lost. In 1912, he became Secretary of State under President Woodrow Wilson.

In 1925, Bryan helped the prosecution in the Scopes Monkey Trial in Tennessee, against teaching Charles Darwin's theory of evolution (see p. 149). Bryan's literal interpretation of the Bible was ridiculed by the famous defense attorney Clarence Darrow. Bryan died five days after the famous trial ended.

BRYAN never won a presidential election, even though he was a popular public speaker.

THE WRIGHT BROTHERS' FIRST FLIGHT, in Kitty Hawk, North Carolina, made the dream of air travel a reality. New inventions such as the airplane and the automobile changed peoples' lives in the early 1900s, as did new ideas. An age of progress in many areas of American life, the Progressive Era saw individuals and government organizations launch programs of social and political reform to the benefit of many.

1900
Galveston, Texas, adopts commission government; Robert M. La Follette elected governor of Wisconsin

Nov. 1900
William McKinley reelected

Sept. 6, 1901
McKinley shot by assassin, dies one week later

Sept. 14, 1901
Theodore Roosevelt inaugurated as president

July 1903
Mother Jones leads a march against child labor

Dec. 17, 1903
Wright brothers make first successful flight at Kitty Hawk, NC

1906
Upton Sinclair publishes The Jungle

July 29, 1906
Hepburn Act passed

July 30, 1906
Meat Inspection Act passed; Pure Food and Drug Act passed

Nov. 1908
William Howard Taft elected president

1900 **1901** **1902** **1903** **1904** **1905** **1906** **1907** **1908** **1909** **1910**

1901
Socialist Party organized

June 17, 1902
Newlands Reclamation Act

Oct. 1902
Roosevelt mediates coal miners' strike

Nov. 1904
Roosevelt elected for a full term

July 1905
W. E. B. DuBois forms Niagara Movement

Nov. 1907
Oklahoma enters the Union

Feb. 12, 1909
NAACP formed

THE PROGRESSIVE ERA

1900–1920

The freewheeling pace of industrial and urban growth after 1865 created huge economic imbalances. One percent of the population controlled 70 percent of the nation's wealth. Americans learned about widespread poverty in magazine articles by journalists called muckrakers, and this information prompted many people to take action. Reform efforts included labor movements, which represented workers against corporations; suffragists, who fought for women's right to vote; and political reformers, who fought for more responsible government services. The combined efforts of reformers for political and social issues was known as the Progressive Movement.

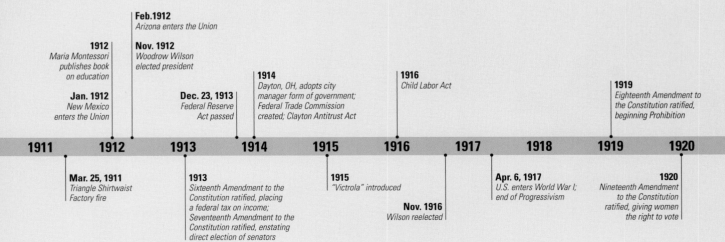

Feb.1912
Arizona enters the Union

1912
Maria Montessori publishes book on education

Nov. 1912
Woodrow Wilson elected president

1914
Dayton, OH, adopts city manager form of government; Federal Trade Commission created; Clayton Antitrust Act

1916
Child Labor Act

1919
Eighteenth Amendment to the Constitution ratified, beginning Prohibition

Jan. 1912
New Mexico enters the Union

Dec. 23, 1913
Federal Reserve Act passed

| 1911 | 1912 | 1913 | 1914 | 1915 | 1916 | 1917 | 1918 | 1919 | 1920 |

Mar. 25, 1911
Triangle Shirtwaist Factory fire

1913
Sixteenth Amendment to the Constitution ratified, placing a federal tax on income; Seventeenth Amendment to the Constitution ratified, enstating direct election of senators

1915
"Victrola" introduced

Nov. 1916
Wilson reelected

Apr. 6, 1917
U.S. enters World War I; end of Progressivism

1920
Nineteenth Amendment to the Constitution ratified, giving women the right to vote

The Spirit of Reform

An antisuffragette button

Beginning about 1900, a desire to change for the better, or reform, American society swept the country. Reformers had high hopes for the century that was just starting. They wanted to improve the relationships between citizens and government and citizens and industry, and also to encourage better behavior in individuals. This period was called the Progressive Era, because those who worked for change hoped society would progress, or move forward, to a higher level of civilization.

1900–1920

Women's Suffrage

Since the Fifteenth Amendment had passed in 1870 (see p. 89), African American men could vote; but at the turn of the century, women of all races were still denied that right. Many thought women were not equipped to handle the responsibility of full citizenship. The drive for women's voting rights, or women's suffrage, gained momentum in the early 1900s. Carrie Chapman Catt provided energetic leadership for the suffragette movement. She urged groups to organize protests and parades, and demanded action by Congress.

SUFFRAGETTE PARADES were heckled by spectators at first, but the women gradually won support. Each year the parades were larger and better organized. By 1913, 12 states had granted voting rights to women, but Congress still held back from passing an amendment to the Constitution. It wasn't until the Nineteenth Amendment was ratified in 1920 that women could vote in all elections at the local, state, and national levels of government.

Women and Prohibition

Many women also felt strongly about prohibiting the sale and consumption of alcoholic drinks, which was known as Prohibition. Groups such as the Women's Christian Temperance Union, or WCTU, and the Anti-Saloon League gained support among middle-class women and many men for banning the drinking of alcohol. By 1916, 23 states had "gone dry," but supporters felt only a national ban would stop alcohol's negative influence on society. Prohibitionists felt alcohol encouraged laziness, irreponsibility, and violent behavior. In 1919, the Eighteenth Amendment was ratified; it prohibited the manufacture and sale of alcoholic beverages.

CARRY NATION, a WCTU leader, used her Bible and her axe (for smashing liquor bottles) to reform drinkers.

Progress for African Americans

W. E. B. DuBois

W. E. B. DuBois emerged as an African American leader for a new generation when he formed the Niagara Movement in 1905. DuBois disagreed with Booker T. Washington, who, in 1895, had urged blacks to seek dignity as farmers. DuBois argued that African Americans deserved more choices. The Niagara Movement fought the job discrimination that prevented them from seeking other work.

Then, in 1908, after a mob terrorized blacks with lynchings in Springfield, Illinois—the home of Abraham Lincoln—several leading progressives, including Jane Addams (see p. 113) and John Dewey, offered to help. They met with DuBois and other black leaders in 1909. The group created the National Association for the Advancement of Colored People, or NAACP, to work for racial equality through the courts. It was a leading civil-rights group throughout the 20th century, and still is today.

DEFINITION

*A **lynching** is a killing by a mob, usually by hanging, and often because of racial hatred or prejudice.*

IDA B. WELLS-BARNETT, 1862–1931

Journalist Ida B. Wells-Barnett launched a campaign against lynching after a white mob lynched three African Americans in 1892 in Memphis. She paid a price for her vocal opposition. The newspaper offices where she worked were wrecked and her life was threatened by racists. She moved to New York and then Chicago, and continued writing and lecturing about lynching until her death in 1931. With the help of the NAACP, the demand for antilynching laws became part of the Progressive agenda. Although more than 3,000 lynchings had been recorded by the 1920s, Southern opposition blocked every anti-lynching bill in Congress.

1900–1920

Crusades for Children

By the 1890s, nearly two million children under age 16 were employed in mines, mills, and factories. Many worked in dangerous conditions, laboring long hours for very low pay. To dramatize their plight, labor organizer "Mother" Jones (see p. 115) led children on a march from Pennsylvania to President Theodore Roosevelt's home in New York in 1903. The "March of the Mill Children" persuaded New York and New Jersey to pass laws limiting child labor. By 1910, 23 states had such laws, but the use of child labor remained a serious problem.

School Reforms

Children's education was another area where reform was needed. Between 1895 and 1910, most states passed laws requiring at least six years of schooling. In Chicago, John Dewey was developing the concept of "progressive education," emphasizing learning by doing, not just by memorizing, and allowing each child to develop at his or her own pace. Another influence on educators began in 1912. Italian teacher Maria Montessori published a book that advocated using toys to make learning fun.

"NEWSIES" were young boys who sold newspapers to earn money—instead of going to school.

MCCLURE'S MUCKRAKERS

In 1902, S. S. McClure put together a staff of outstanding writers for his *McClure's Magazine*. The monthly issues contained some of the most famous articles of the Progressive years. Lincoln Steffens wrote about corruption in St. Louis. The first of Ida M. Tarbell's exposés of the ruthless methods used by John D. Rockefeller was published the next month, along with Ray Stannard Baker's article on abuses in labor unions. And the magazine's assistant editor, Upton Sinclair, was researching his novel *The Jungle*, which would shock Americans by reporting the dangerous and unsanitary conditions in meatpacking plants. Other magazines copied *McClure's Magazine*'s crusading style, but they rarely matched its quality or impact.

President Theodore Roosevelt said McClure reminded him of a character in John Bunyan's 1678 religious allegory, *The Pilgrim's Progress*, who did nothing but rake the mud, or muck. He said this was good for society as long as the "muckrakers" knew when to stop. The writers proudly wore the label.

Government for the People

Progressive reformers wanted to make government more responsive to the needs and desires of the people. Their goals were to limit the power of political bosses, reduce the influence of giant corporations, and give average people a stronger voice in government.

Improving City Life

In most cities at the turn of the century, private companies had exclusive control of, or monopolies on (see p. 107), utilities, including electrical power, water, telephone, and trolley cars. When Samuel Jones was elected mayor of Toledo, Ohio, in 1897, he was determined to put the city in control of the utilities as a first step toward creating honest, efficient government. He succeeded—the city managers put limits on how much the utilities could charge and required that good, reliable service be provided.

Jones wanted to run the city by the Golden Rule, which was printed on a sign in his office: "Do unto others as you would have them do unto you." The city of Toledo also built parks and playgrounds, provided free band concerts, and established a free kindergarten.

Dayton's City Manager System

In 1912, Dayton, Ohio, faced emergency problems because of a flood; the result of fixing the problems was a new form of city government. Instead of having an elected mayor, the city council decided to hire a professional manager. Councilmen elected by the people continued to decide what would happen, but the manager—a person with business experience—was responsible for how the city's various departments were run.

The city manager system was soon adopted throughout the country. Progressives liked hiring outsiders with no connection to political machines or party bosses to run the day-to-day operations of a city or town.

DEFINITION

*A **party machine** is a political party in a city or state tightly controlled by **political bosses**—small groups of men with huge influence who promote policy that benefits them personally.*

SUMMIT STREET, TOLEDO, OHIO, around 1900–1910—including the trolley cars that were brought under city control

State Government Reform

Robert M. La Follette

Robert M. La Follette was the most famous progressive in state government. He fought to overcome the all-powerful political party machines in Wisconsin before being elected governor in 1900. His nickname was "Battling Bob." La Follette's goal was to give the people more control over government. Wisconsin became one of the first states to use a direct primary, where voters rather than political parties choose candidates to run for office. "Battling Bob" also passed a law requiring that civil-service workers take exams to qualify for jobs. That way, party bosses couldn't hire their friends in exchange for political favors.

To reduce the power of utility companies, La Follette established commissions to watch the cost and the quality of service. Professors from the University of Wisconsin served on the commissions, and he worked with the university's president to make sure powerful lumber companies did not overuse the state's forests. La Follette's reforms became known as the Wisconsin Idea.

Other Government Reforms

In Oregon, reformer William S. U'Ren established the referendum, in which the people voted to decide some issues directly.

In New York, Governor Charles Evans Hughes pushed through the first workmen's compensation act, providing benefits for injured workers.

The secret ballot was one of many reforms first proposed by the Populists (see p. 117). In the past, each party had a brightly colored ballot; after marking it, the voter dropped it into a ballot box in full view of everyone in the room. The secret ballots looked the same and were marked in private, so people did not have to reveal how they had voted.

BETTER GOVERNMENT FOR GALVESTON

In September 1900, a deadly hurricane and tidal wave struck Galveston, Texas, killing more than 6,000 people and destroying nearly half the city's buildings. The tragedy itself was terrible, but the widespread looting that followed, including stealing from bodies that washed ashore, made it worse. To speed cleanup and rebuilding, the city hired individual commissioners to direct operations of several departments, including safety, public health, and utilities.

As the city recovered, voters decided to keep the commission form of government. By 1912, more than 200 other communities had adopted the plan. In traditional city governments with elected mayors and councils, it was often hard to tell who was responsible for solving particular problems; the commission system assigned specific jobs to departments, making for a more active and responsive government.

GALVESTON WAS DEVASTATED after a tidal wave struck. This led to a new system of government.

President for Change

Theodore Roosevelt was the first president to use the power of the federal government to work for progressive goals. He attacked giant trusts, helped settle a strike fairly, and improved people's lives with laws demanding safe foods and drugs. Most important, though, his leadership helped reform causes at all levels.

A 1907 POLITICAL CARTOON, "The President's Dream of a Successful Hunt," shows Roosevelt killing off businesses engaged in unfair practices.

THEODORE ROOSEVELT, 1858–1919

Theodore Roosevelt was born to a wealthy New York family that traced its roots back to the Dutch colonial era. Weak and sickly as a boy, he became devoted to physical fitness as a man.

After serving as police commissioner of New York City, assistant secretary of the navy, and hero of the Spanish-American War, he became governor of New York. In 1900, Republican leaders nominated him to run for vice president—usually an unimportant position—with presidential candidate McKinley, to keep him quiet.

Roosevelt was an active and popular president, and at 42, the youngest man to serve in the office. He said the presidency provided a "Bully Pulpit" that allowed him to air his views, using his personality to force the government to take responsibility. Senator La Follette may have summed him up best by saying that "Roosevelt made reform respectable in the United States."

Taking on the Trusts

President William McKinley was assassinated in 1901, and young Vice President Theodore Roosevelt was thrust into the White House. One of his first acts as president was to file a lawsuit against the Northern Securities Company—three railroads that had eliminated competition in a large area of the country. The U.S. government argued that the company violated the Sherman Antitrust Act of 1890. After a two-year legal battle, the Supreme Court ruled that the trust must be dissolved. The Roosevelt government filed 43 more antitrust suits, breaking up monopolies (see p. 107) in beef, oil, tobacco, and other products. Then Roosevelt had Congress create a Department of Commerce and Labor to keep an eye on corporate practices.

The Square Deal

In 1902, a coal miners' strike threatened the nation's supply of heating fuel. Roosevelt invited the mine owners and union officials to the White House, but the owners refused to negotiate. Furious, the president got them to back down, and the strike was settled, with the miners receiving a pay raise and a nine-hour work day, down from 12 hours.

In his bid for reelection in 1904, Roosevelt said that in brokering the settlement he had tried for a "square deal"—a fair result—for both sides. The Square Deal became his motto for the rest of his career. Roosevelt won a landslide election to become president in his own right in 1904.

A PROMOTIONAL POSTER for *The Jungle*

Regulating Foods and Drugs

In 1906, Roosevelt read *The Jungle,* a novel by muckraker Upton Sinclair, which exposed the filth in the nation's meatpacking plants that often ended up in meat products—from floor sweepings to dead rats. The president was skeptical until his investigators confirmed Sinclair's findings; Roosevelt then demanded action. Congress responded with the Meat Inspection Act in June 1906, setting standards for sanitation and federal meat inspection.

The Pure Food and Drug Act was passed in 1906, to force manufacturers to make accurate claims about what was in the food they sold and the benefits their medicines provided.

Conserving Natural Resources

Roosevelt was deeply concerned about how rapidly Americans were using up natural resources. Only 200 million acres of virgin forest remained from the country's original 800 million acres, for example, and three-fourths of the forests were controlled by timber and mining companies. Encouraged by Gifford Pinchot, chief of the Forest Service, the president withdrew from public sale 150 million acres of forest—an area larger than France.

Roosevelt also doubled the number of national parks and pressed Congress to pass the Newlands Reclamation Act, which provided that funds from the sale of public lands would go for irrigation projects to reclaim wasteland in 16 western states.

ORIGIN OF THE TEDDY BEAR

On a hunting trip in 1902, Theodore Roosevelt refused to shoot a bear cub. Reporters made a big story out of it, and an editorial cartoonist drew a picture of the incident. Morris Michton, a store owner in Brooklyn, New York—or his wife—heard about this incident and got the idea of making a cuddly stuffed animal that the Michtons named the "Teddy Bear." The bears were a hit.

A STUFFED TEDDY BEAR, manufactured in 1903 by the Ideal Toy Company

1900–1920

PRESIDENT ROOSEVELT AND JOHN MUIR (right), one of America's greatest naturalists, on a camping trip in Yosemite National Park in 1903. Muir's books and articles in popular magazines helped awaken Americans to the need for conservation, and he urged the president to create more national parks and forests.

More Progress

Other progressive presidents followed Roosevelt. Republican William Howard Taft and Democrat Woodrow Wilson both acted to reduce the power of the trusts, safeguard people's welfare, and conserve natural resources. A series of acts of Congress and amendments to the Constitution made the reforms of the Progressive Era permanent, ensuring they would serve the public far into the future.

William Howard Taft

PROGRESSIVE ERA CONSTITUTIONAL AMENDMENTS

AMENDMENTS	ISSUE	PASSED CONGRESS
Sixteenth	Federal tax on personal income	July 1909 ratified by states 1913
Seventeenth	Direct election of senators	May 1912 ratified by states 1913
Eighteenth	Prohibition—made illegal the sale, manufacture, and transport of alcoholic beverages	December 1917 ratified by states 1919 repealed 1933
Nineteenth	Women's right to vote	June 1919 ratified by states 1920

President Taft's Record of Reform

Roosevelt was the nation's youngest president ever, and William Howard Taft would be the largest at 350 pounds. Roosevelt promised that he would not seek a third term, but he persuaded the Republican Party to nominate Taft, his friend and cabinet member. Taft, an intelligent, easygoing man, breezed to victory over Democrat William Jennings Bryan in 1904 (see p. 117).

Taft continued Roosevelt's progressivism. His attorney general filed 90 antitrust lawsuits against corporations—twice as many as Roosevelt had filed. Taft also initiated reforms in safety standards for railroad workers and miners. In 1909, he proposed a federal income tax to provide a constant stream of revenue for the government. The measure became the 16th Amendment to the Constitution in 1913.

The Election of 1912

Right before the 1912 election, Roosevelt returned home from a trip to Africa and expressed disappointment in decisions Taft had made as president. The rift between the two split the Republican Party, and Roosevelt seemed ready to get back into politics. Meanwhile, the Democrats nominated Woodrow Wilson, a former college president and progressive governor of New Jersey. The Republicans nominated Taft, so Roosevelt's followers formed a new party—the Progressive Party—and nominated Roosevelt. In the election, Roosevelt and Taft split 50.5 percent of the popular vote—which the Republican Party would have normally earned alone. Wilson got only 42 percent of the popular vote, but 82 percent of the electoral vote—and the presidency.

A Bull Moose pull toy

THE BULL MOOSE PARTY—or the Progressive Party—got its nickname when, delighted to be back in politics, Roosevelt declared, "I feel as fit as a bull moose!" Although it didn't last long after its defeat in the 1912 election, the Bull Moose was a rare example of a third party making a good showing in a general election.

1904 SOCIALIST PARTY CAMPAIGN POSTER for Eugene V. Debs and Ben Hanford

The Voice of the Socialist Party

Eugene V. Debs left the labor unions to form the Socialist Party in the early 1900s. The party criticized capitalism for creating social and economic inequalities, and fought for many of the same issues as other progressives: women's suffrage, child labor laws, union rights, and workplace safety. Debs ran for president four times. He never got enough votes to compete against the major parties, but the Socialists' point of view gave working people a voice in the national debate.

Wilson's New Freedom

President Wilson called his kind of reform the New Freedom. He wanted to liberate people from the "tyranny" of big business. He pushed for the 1914 Clayton Antitrust Act, which was more comprehensive than the Sherman Antitrust Act. Then he started the Federal Trade Commission, or FTC, which had the authority to order companies to stop unfair practices.

Wilson also got the Federal Reserve Act passed, which strengthened the nation's banks, and lowered tariffs—the taxes on goods coming into the country. This helped consumers by forcing American companies to lower prices in order to compete with manufacturers in other countries.

THE TRIANGLE SHIRTWAIST COMPANY FIRE in 1911 cost the lives of 146 people, mostly women workers trapped on the upper floors beyond the reach of rescue ladders. Several escape routes failed because of poor planning and disrepair. The fire dramatized the need for government action to ensure workplace safety.

CHILD LABORERS in the Kohinor mine, Shenandoah City, Pennsylvania, 1891

Social Reforms Under Wilson

Although Wilson felt social-welfare programs were the responsibility of the states, progressives urged him to pass national directives. As a result, he signed measures that made it easier for farmers to obtain loans. Next, railroad workers were granted the eight-hour work day, and the Workmen's Compensation Act gave help to injured workers. The Child Labor Law limited the hours children could work. Wilson also formed the National Park Service.

The Progressive Era Ends

Wilson was reelected in 1916, and his second term became increasingly involved with World War I. Many historians mark the Progressive Era's end at 1917—the year America entered the war.

For nearly 20 years, the Progressive Movement had initiated a wide variety of social, economic, and political reforms. Wilson's Child Labor Law was declared unconstitutional, and the direct primary proved to be difficult and costly. But most of the reforms were successful: they required greater honesty from government, reduced the power of big corporations, protected people from unsafe foods and drugs, and took the first steps to protect natural resources. The basic idea—that government could, and should, act to resolve difficult social and economic issues—had been tested and accepted by many Americans.

Lifestyles Change

By 1920, the United States had almost completely changed from a rural, agriculture-based society to the world's leading urban, industrial nation. The country was experiencing unprecedented prosperity, and progressive reforms had helped extend that prosperity to farmers and laborers. In addition, new inventions—and improvements on older ones—were making housework easier and leisure more enjoyable, and were ushering Americans into the modern age.

SINKING OF THE "UNSINKABLE" TITANIC

The RMS *Titanic* began her maiden voyage in Southampton, England, on April 10, 1912. She was headed for New York. The ship hit an iceberg the night of April 14 and sank, along with more than 1,500 passengers and crew. People everywhere were astonished at the destruction of this great example of man's ingenuity.

THE NEW YORK TIMES the day after the disaster

THE WRIGHT BROTHERS' FIRST FLIGHT, in Kitty Hawk, North Carolina

Boom Times for Farmers

Although the number of farms and farmers was beginning to decline, the remaining American farmers were producing far more food than ever before. State agricultural colleges were developing better seeds, scientific methods, and new uses for farm machines. At the same time, the nation's cities were growing, so markets for farm products were expanding. European countries, before and during World War I, needed record amounts of American grain, meat, and other agricultural products.

The value of farmland doubled, then doubled again. This meant farmers could get loans to buy tractors, a new invention. There were about 1,000 farm tractors in use in 1910; by 1920, there were 246,000.

The Automobile

One of the most revolutionary changes in the economy was the arrival of the automobile. At first, cars were expensive toys for the wealthy, but by 1920, they had become affordable enough for average people to own.

One reason for the lower cost of automobiles was the Ford Motor Company's pioneering use of assembly-line production (see pp. 105, 150–151). Assembly lines and specialized machinery reduced the production cost of each car, so that more cars could be made and sold.

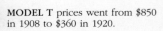

The Multiplier Effect

The manufacture of cars and trucks had an amazing multiplier effect on the economy. Each automobile needed raw materials—steel, glass, rubber, and copper—as well as oil and gasoline. New industries sprang up to produce the parts needed to make cars; pave roads; and supply roadside gas, food, and repairs for America's travelers.

MODEL T prices went from $850 in 1908 to $360 in 1920.

THE TRADEMARK for the Victor Talking Machine Co. shows Nipper the dog listening to a Victrola playing a record. The popular logo was adapted from a painting of a dog hearing his dead master's voice through the Victrola.

A number of labor-saving devices developed in the past were rapidly improved in the early 1900s to make housework less of a burden. However, having washing machines and vacuum cleaners changed Americans' ideas of cleanliness and often created more work for women.

Other inventions allowed people to enjoy their leisure time at little cost. The family car was just coming into vogue, for example, and farm families could drive their Model T's into town on Saturdays.

Thomas Edison's (see p. 109) first motion-picture apparatus, developed in the early 1890s, advanced to silent movies by the early 1900s. Edison's phonograph, invented in 1876, took several years to develop. In 1915, when the Victor Talking Machine Company brought out its first "Victrola," listening to music on records became a favorite pastime. By 1919, Americans were spending more on Victrolas and records than on books and magazines or sporting goods.

An early Edison movie projector

The Dawn of Flight

In October 1903, the head of the U.S. Naval Observatory wrote, "The example of the bird does not prove that man can fly … Aerial flight … is one of that great class of problems with which man can never cope." Two months later, Wilbur and Orville Wright made the first successful flight at Kitty Hawk, North Carolina.

The aircraft industry developed slowly. Tales of air battles between heroic pilots in World War I gave people an idea of what airplanes could do. Then, in 1918, the first experimental air-mail route was opened between New York and Washington, D.C.

Taking Flight

On December 17, 1903, Wilbur and Orville Wright conducted the first flight in an airplane they had built themselves. The brothers had studied engineering and used their experience building bicycles to design and construct an aircraft. Of the four trips they made that day, the longest was 852 feet and lasted 59 seconds. At first, Americans doubted the value of flight. But by 1908, the military realized what airplanes could mean in battle situations and awarded the Wrights a contract.

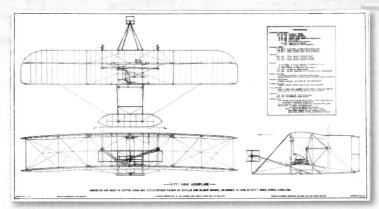

THESE DRAWINGS of the *Wright Flyer* show three views of the airframe.

THE DEATHS OF CIVILIANS aboard the British passenger ship *Lusitania*, sunk by a German submarine, shocked Americans. Although the United States was juggling involvements in many parts of the world, most Americans wanted to stay out of the war in Europe. Two years later, Germany's submarines began to attack America's cargo ships, prompting President Wilson to ask Congress to declare war on Germany.

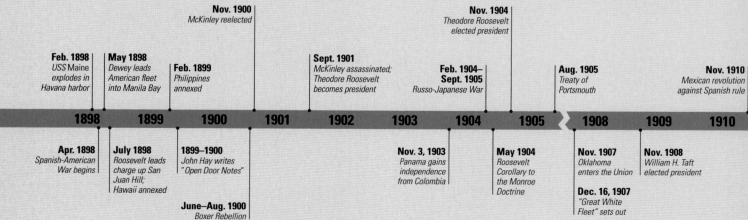

Nov. 1900
McKinley reelected

Nov. 1904
Theodore Roosevelt elected president

Feb. 1898
USS Maine explodes in Havana harbor

May 1898
Dewey leads American fleet into Manila Bay

Feb. 1899
Philippines annexed

Sept. 1901
McKinley assassinated; Theodore Roosevelt becomes president

Feb. 1904–Sept. 1905
Russo-Japanese War

Aug. 1905
Treaty of Portsmouth

Nov. 1910
Mexican revolution against Spanish rule

| 1898 | 1899 | 1900 | 1901 | 1902 | 1903 | 1904 | 1905 | 1908 | 1909 | 1910 |

Apr. 1898
Spanish-American War begins

July 1898
Roosevelt leads charge up San Juan Hill; Hawaii annexed

1899–1900
John Hay writes "Open Door Notes"

Nov. 3, 1903
Panama gains independence from Colombia

May 1904
Roosevelt Corollary to the Monroe Doctrine

Nov. 1907
Oklahoma enters the Union

Dec. 16, 1907
"Great White Fleet" sets out

Nov. 1908
William H. Taft elected president

June–Aug. 1900
Boxer Rebellion

AMERICA BECOMES A WORLD POWER

1898–1920

At the beginning of the 1900s, the nation was focused on foreign affairs. Americans clamored for war to support the Cuban revolt against Spain. From the Spanish-American War, the U.S. acquired a colonial empire that included Puerto Rico, the Philippines, Hawaii, and continued influence over Cuba. Involvement in Pan-American affairs led to foreign ventures, such as the building of the Panama Canal.

As Europe plunged into war in 1914, President Wilson's administration remained neutral until Germany's submarine attacks forced the U.S. to get involved. Though inexperienced, American troops energized the exhausted French and British and played a key role in the final victory.

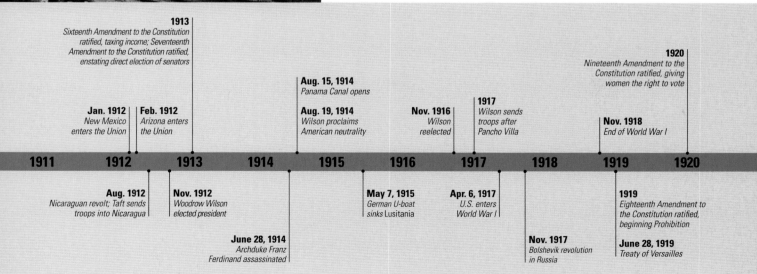

1913
Sixteenth Amendment to the Constitution ratified, taxing income; Seventeenth Amendment to the Constitution ratified, enstating direct election of senators

1920
Nineteenth Amendment to the Constitution ratified, giving women the right to vote

Aug. 15, 1914
Panama Canal opens

Aug. 19, 1914
Wilson proclaims American neutrality

Nov. 1916
Wilson reelected

1917
Wilson sends troops after Pancho Villa

Nov. 1918
End of World War I

Jan. 1912
New Mexico enters the Union

Feb. 1912
Arizona enters the Union

| 1911 | 1912 | 1913 | 1914 | 1915 | 1916 | 1917 | 1918 | 1919 | 1920 |

Aug. 1912
Nicaraguan revolt; Taft sends troops into Nicaragua

Nov. 1912
Woodrow Wilson elected president

May 7, 1915
German U-boat sinks Lusitania

Apr. 6, 1917
U.S. enters World War I

1919
Eighteenth Amendment to the Constitution ratified, beginning Prohibition

June 28, 1914
Archduke Franz Ferdinand assassinated

Nov. 1917
Bolshevik revolution in Russia

June 28, 1919
Treaty of Versailles

The Spanish-American War

Cuba had been a Spanish colony since the 1500s. In 1895, Cubans, wanting their freedom, rebelled against Spanish rule. Three years later, the United States declared war against Spain because American sentiment supported the Cubans. The call for war in America was created in part by the sensationalizing of events by the popular newspapers of the day. American forces easily defeated Spain, and the United States gained an overseas empire.

1898–1920

Building an Empire

In the late 1800s, a small but influential group of Americans led by Massachusetts Senator Henry Cabot Lodge (see p. 145) and newsman William Randolph Hearst were eager for the United States to join the major world powers in colonizing other countries. These expansionists watched as European powers such as England, Germany, and France built huge colonial empires in Africa and other parts of the world.

The Cuban revolt against Spain in 1895 provided an opportunity for the expansionists, since winning a war against Spain might open the door to taking over some of Spain's empire overseas and in the Western Hemisphere.

BUFFALO SOLDIERS

Known for their service on the western frontier, Buffalo Soldiers were segregated regiments of African American soldiers in the U.S. Army. Historians disagree on the origin of their nickname, with some suggesting it was given by Native Americans who compared their hair to that of buffaloes, while others suggest it reflected their fierce fighting skills. Several generations of Buffalo Soldiers fought bravely for the United States across nearly 200 engagements from 1866 to 1951. They were the only African American soldiers to fight in Cuba during the Spanish American War, earning five Medals of Honor among them.

DEFINITION

Expansionists support expanding a nation's territory, national prestige, and economic markets by acquiring colonies and dependencies.

Newspapers Play a Role

Spain put General Valeriano Weyler in charge of crushing the Cuban rebellion. He used ruthless methods to do it, and American newspapers printed graphic stories about "Butcher" Weyler torturing and murdering his victims. At that time, engaged in a fierce competition for readers, newspapers tried to outdo each other with the most dramatic—or sensational—stories. Influenced by the newspaper accounts, Americans demanded a war "to free the Cuban people." Then, on February 15, the U.S. warship *Maine* blew up in Havana harbor, killing 266 Americans. President William McKinley asked Congress for a declaration of war. The war lasted for 10 weeks and ended in the United States' victory. In a startling turn-around, the U.S. then used the same tactics as General Weyler to establish dominance in the Philippines, including the establishment of reconcentration camps.

THE EXPLOSION OF THE *MAINE* in Havana, shown in an 1898 lithograph, remains a mystery. The cause was never determined, but the press blamed the Spanish. "Remember the *Maine*" became a rallying cry for going to war against Spain.

War on Two Sides of the World

The first battle of the Spanish-American War took place on May 1, 1898, six days after Congress declared war. Admiral George Dewey led a fleet into Manila Bay in the Philippines, another Spanish colony. The Americans' new steel ships quickly defeated the older Spanish fleet.

Then, on the island of Cuba, the U.S. army landed near the capital, Santiago, in June 1898. The soldiers faced terrible heat and tropical illnesses, including yellow fever, which proved to be more life-threatening than the enemy.

Then the Americans began their assault against Spanish fortifications in Cuba.

Rough Riders and Victory

Colonel Theodore Roosevelt had resigned from his position as assistant secretary of the navy to create a cavalry regiment of old college friends and athletes. On July 1, Roosevelt led the "Rough Riders" and the African American soldiers of the Ninth and Tenth Cavalry in a charge up San Juan Hill. In taking the hill, 1,572 men were wounded, many fatally, but the army now had a commanding position. Less than a week later, the war was over and Spain was no longer a world power.

The conflict lasted only four months and gave the United States a colonial empire, including the Philippines and the Pacific islands of Guam and Wake Island. Cuba was placed under U.S. occupation, and Puerto Rico became a commonwealth of the U.S. Plus, Congress had voted to annex the Hawaiian Islands, where American sugar planters had established a government five years earlier.

Colonel Theodore "Teddy" Roosevelt

THE ROUGH RIDERS were physically fit and skilled horsemen, most of whom were athletes or old college friends of Roosevelt's.

Victory Over Yellow Fever

In Cuba, 375 Americans were killed in battle, but roughly 5,000 died of disease, primarily yellow fever. Dr. Walter Reed led a team effort to identify the mosquito that carried the deadly disease. Although several volunteers died during the work, the medical team did identify the mosquito and clear the swamps. By 1901, there was not a single case of yellow fever in Cuba.

Aedes aegypi, *the yellow fever mosquito*

THE ASSAULT ON SAN JUAN HILL made Theodore Roosevelt the hero of the Spanish-American War.

A New Role in the World

Americans took pride in their nation's new status as one of the world's great powers, as did President Theodore Roosevelt, who took office after President McKinley was assassinated during the Pan-American Exposition in Buffalo, New York, in 1901. Building the Panama Canal was one show of that power, and of American ingenuity. But power brought responsibility, and safeguarding U.S. interests became a priority.

ROOSEVELT AND THE RUSSO-JAPANESE WAR

In 1904, war broke out between Russia and Japan. Americans were concerned the Japanese might move into American territory in the Philippines to help the anti-American guerilla forces, or even to invade. Those concerns became more real when the Japanese won an impressive naval victory over Russia's fleet in May 1905.

In an effort to keep a balance of power in Asia, President Roosevelt invited leaders of the warring countries to meet with him in Portsmouth, New Hampshire, in August 1905. The result was the Treaty of Portsmouth, which ended the fighting and recognized Japan's territorial gains. The following year, Theodore Roosevelt was awarded the Nobel Peace Prize for his role as mediator.

ROOSEVELT AND ENVOYS from Russia and Japan during peace talks

THE GREAT WHITE FLEET was a group of 16 battleships President Roosevelt sent on a cruise around the world in December 1907 to demonstrate America's military might. Roosevelt was fond of quoting a West African proverb, "Walk softly and carry a big stick." Showing off the Great White Fleet was a way of doing just that.

The Open Door Policy

In the late 1800s, each of the great powers of Europe—Great Britain, Germany, France, and Russia—was eager to increase business opportunities in China, the world's most populous nation and a potentially huge market for trade. In order to avoid conflict, the European leaders agreed to carve the country into "spheres of influence"—specific geographic regions, or spheres, of China in which each nation controlled trade.

Secretary of State John Hay, concerned that U.S. merchants might be shut out, sent a series of "Open Door Notes" to the European powers in 1899 and 1900, asking them to respect China's territory and independence. The leaders agreed to America's Open Door policy to avoid a confrontation. China opposed the policy because the foreign influence was considered excessive. It led to the Boxer Rebellion of 1900, which the U.S. later helped suppress.

The Panama Canal

At the end of the Spanish-American War, the United States had acquired the Philippines and Hawaii. This made the nation a major power in the Pacific. The navy now needed to find a way to move ships from the west coast to the east coast that was more efficient than going around the tip of South America. The solution was to build a canal—a waterway connecting two bodies of water—across Central America to join the Atlantic Ocean and the Pacific Ocean.

In 1903, a revolution in Panama gave the country its independence from Colombia. President Roosevelt now had the opportunity he needed to acquire a route for the canal, since the Isthmus of Panama is the narrowest piece of land in the Americas. The U.S. government instantly recognized the new government of Panama and signed a treaty that gave the United States a ten-mile-wide "Canal Zone" in exchange for a fee of $10 million and an annual payment of $250,000.

Intervening in the Americas

American involvement in Cuba, Puerto Rico, and Panama made the region's stability a national priority. To protect that stability, Roosevelt decided to strengthen the Monroe Doctrine (see p. 62), which had warned European countries not to interfere in North or South America. The Roosevelt Corollary to the Monroe Doctrine became a pillar of American policy. It stated that only the United States could intervene in Latin America.

In the next 30 years, American presidents repeatedly used the corollary to justify intervening in other nations' affairs to protect U.S. interests. The most controversial intervention came in 1917, when President Woodrow Wilson sent troops to hunt down Mexican bandit Pancho Villa.

TEDDY ROOSEVELT OPERATES A STEAM SHOVEL during the digging of the Panama Canal. After the area was cleared of the mosquito that causes yellow fever, American engineers and 40,000 workers began building the 40-mile Panama Canal. Opened in 1914, the canal is still regarded as one of the world's great engineering feats. Military and cargo ships of all nations were able to use it. In 1978, President Jimmy Carter arranged a new treaty with Panama, which ended the U.S. lease in 2000. Panama now runs the canal.

PANCHO VILLA and his gang murdered 16 American engineers in 1917, and then invaded New Mexico, where they burned a town and killed 19 people. Villa, a popular hero in Mexico, was angry that the United States recognized his enemy, Venustiano Carranza, as president of Mexico. In response, President Wilson sent General John J. Pershing and 15,000 troops into Mexico in an effort to hunt down the bandit and his gang. They did not find him, and soon Wilson ordered the troops back to prepare for World War I.

THE CULEBRA CUT of the Panama Canal was nine miles long and crossed through a gap in the Continental Divide—a ridge connecting the highest points of land in North and South America.

The Great War Begins

Tension had been building in Europe when Archduke Franz Ferdinand of Austria-Hungary was assassinated by a Serbian in 1914. A system of alliances existed in Europe at that time, through which the two major empires, Russia and Austria-Hungary, fought for supreme power in the region. Anger over the assassination erupted into war, which, to most Americans, seemed far away from the United States and its interests.

THE NEW YORK TIMES announces the assassination of Archduke Franz Ferdinand.

War in Europe

On Sunday, June 28, 1914, a Serbian nationalist, upset by Austria-Hungary's control of Bosnia-Herzegovina, assassinated Archduke Franz Ferdinand, heir to the Austro-Hungarian throne. Most Americans knew little about the archduke or Serbia, but many were aware that a system of alliances divided Europe. Germany, Austria-Hungary, and Italy had formed the Triple Alliance in 1882; France, Russia, and Great Britain had signed alliances between 1894 and 1907. These agreements guaranteed support if a member was attacked. Following the assassination, nations went to war to support their treaty partners, and, by mid-August, Europe was engulfed in "the Great War."

DEFINITION

A **nationalist** is a person who takes extreme pride in his or her own country, to the exclusion of others.

WHO'S WHO IN WORLD WAR I

The Central Powers and Allied Nations took shape from alliances made years earlier. The Allies also had the support of Portugal, Romania, Serbia, Greece, Montenegro, and Italy (Italy joined the Allies in May 1915). Norway, Sweden, Denmark, Switzerland, Spain, and Albania remained neutral.

CENTRAL POWERS	ALLIED NATIONS
Germany	Great Britain
Austria-Hungary	France
Ottoman Empire	Russia
Bulgaria	United States
	Belgium

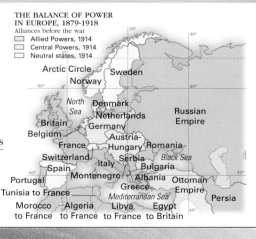

THE BALANCE OF POWER IN EUROPE, 1879-1918
Alliances before the war
- Allied Powers, 1914
- Central Powers, 1914
- Neutral states, 1914

Challenges to American Neutrality

In August 1914, President Woodrow Wilson issued a proclamation of neutrality and asked Americans to remain "impartial in thought as well as in action." The American people, however, were far from neutral in their attitudes. The great majority wanted the Allies to win, in part because of historic ties to both France and Great Britain. Also, the Allies had sold more than $2 billion in bonds to fund their war effort, and they were using it to buy huge amounts of U.S. agricultural and industrial goods.

Strong anti-German sentiment emerged in the United States, at first in reaction to the invasion of Belgium, then to press accounts of atrocities—extremely cruel acts—committed by the German army.

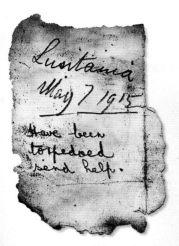

A NOTE IN A BOTTLE written by a passenger says, "Lusitania, May 7, 1915. Have been torpedoed—send help."

THE OCEAN LINER *Lusitania* sinks after being torpedoed by a German submarine. The painting shows lifeboats full of passengers escaping the wreck.

The *Lusitania* and America's Neutrality Are Sunk

In May 1915, a German U-boat, or submarine (see p. 141), torpedoed the British ship *Lusitania*, killing 1,198 civilians, including 128 U.S. citizens. Americans were horrified by Germany's tactics. In past wars, military personnel had avoided harming civilians, but German U-boat commanders fired without warning on ships that carried munitions. The *Lusitania* was registered as an auxiliary cruiser before the war and was known to carry war contraband.

Wilson and other U.S. leaders responded to the *Lusitania* sinking with a series of messages to Germany protesting the action. The United States was in the position of needing to be prepared for war while still advocating a peaceful settlement.

To avoid a rift with the United States, Germany said it would warn merchant ships before attacking, eliminating the U-boats' element of surprise. That agreement led to an easing of tensions that lasted about two years.

ZIMMERMANN TELEGRAM

In January 1917, the German government sent a coded telegram to Mexico's government proposing a military alliance between the two countries. Germany suggested that Mexico should support them if the United States entered World War I. In return, they promised to return Texas, Arizona, and New Mexico to Mexico if Germany won the war. This secret telegram was intercepted by British intelligence, who broke the code, and Americans were enraged by Germany's plans. In March that year, German Foreign Secretary Arthur Zimmermann finally confirmed the telegram was real, which encouraged support in America for entering the war.

America at War

In 1917, Germany sent U-boats after American cargo ships and called on Mexico to invade the United States. Americans were outraged. Congress declared war on Germany in April 1917. America would have to provide men, weapons, and supplies immediately. President Wilson said, "It is not an army that we must shape and train for war, it is a nation."

Mobilizing People

Raising, training, and equipping an army was the first task. The government started by requiring all men to register for military service. Initially only men between the ages of 21 and 31 had to register, but later the law required all men ages 18 to 45—a total of 24 million citizens—to sign up. Then, in the first-ever draft, three million were ordered into the army; roughly two million more volunteered.

> **DEFINITION**
>
> A **draft** is a system of selecting people to **register** (sign up) for required military service. A certain number can then be "drafted," or called to report for duty.

Women and African Americans in the War Effort

With so many white men in the army, huge numbers of jobs became available. Women worked at jobs they had not tried before—delivering mail and driving trolleys and ambulances, for example—and African Americans moved north by the thousands for jobs in factories and shipyards. Blacks still experienced discrimination, but many felt participating in the war effort encouraged others to treat them equally.

President Wilson said women's suffrage was "vital to winning the war." Congress responded by passing the Nineteenth Amendment (see p. 120), giving women voting rights. The amendment would be ratified in 1920.

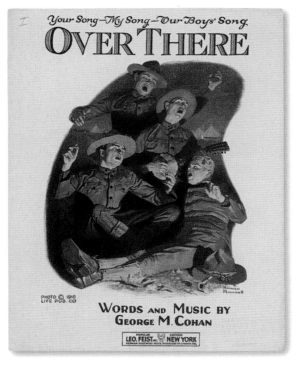

"OVER THERE" by George M. Cohan was the most popular song of its day—with military men and average citizens alike.

"UNCLE SAM" made his most famous appearance on an army recruiting poster by James Montgomery Flagg. He became one of the most recognizable symbols of the U.S. government.

Patriotism

Even without graphic government propaganda, such as "Uncle Sam," the American people exhibited extraordinary patriotism. American soldiers, called doughboys, supposedly in reference to the globular shape of the buttons on their uniforms, were given rousing send-offs with bands playing and crowds cheering and waving American flags.

Songwriter Irving Berlin gave patriotism a musical boost with a play about army life called *Yip-Yip-Yaphank*, which included popular songs such as "Over There," by George M. Cohan, and Berlin's own "God Bless America."

Mobilizing the Economy

The Wilson administration, having been given broad emergency powers by Congress, established special boards, or agencies, to direct the mobilization of all aspects of the economy for the war effort. The War Industries Board increased industrial production and reduced red tape. Director Bernard Baruch established priorities, built new factories, and converted old ones—for example, a piano manufacturer began making parts for airplanes, and a corset maker produced gas masks.

The Food Administration was headed by engineer Herbert Hoover. Aided by a massive advertising campaign, Hoover encouraged Americans to observe meatless Tuesdays, wheatless Mondays and Wednesdays, and porkless Thursdays and Saturdays. Posters with slogans like "Use All Leftovers" and "Be a Member of the Clean-Plate Club" also helped.

Hoover set prices for farm products and determined how much was to be sent to Europe. By "Hooverizing" food supplies, the United States was able to triple its shipments.

A Fuel Administration established daylight savings time, giving workers and farmers an extra hour of daylight at the end of each day in the late spring and summer to cut down on fuel consumption for lighting.

DEFINITION
Red tape *refers to complex paperwork and administrative steps that must be completed before a job can be done.*

OUTLAWING OPPOSITION

With a series of laws that many felt directly opposed the Bill of Rights, particularly the First Amendment, the U.S. government tried to silence anyone who spoke against the war effort. A Sedition Act, for example, made it a crime to use "disloyal … or abusive language" about the government, the Constitution, the flag, and American uniforms. Such laws led to a kind of witch hunt, with people spying on their neighbors. Nearly 6,000 men and women were arrested and 1,500 convicted of acts that may have involved nothing more than making statements against all war. Eugene V. Debs (see p. 126), a founder of the Socialist Party in America, received a prison sentence.

Financing the War Effort

There were many ways in which the U.S. government raised money to pay for the war. One way was selling Liberty bonds. Celebrities appealed to people to buy them; movie star Douglas Fairbanks was a champion salesman. Of the $36 billion needed, roughly half came from Liberty bonds. Children were urged to buy 25-cent Liberty stamps to "help lick the Kaiser"—the German ruler.

THEY KEPT THE SEA LANES OPEN

INVEST IN THE VICTORY LIBERTY LOAN

POSTERS spoke to American military pride to encourage the buying of war bonds.

Propaganda Builds Support

In April 1917, a Committee on Public Information, headed by newsman George Creel, began using a variety of methods to promote patriotism and develop a negative image of the enemy. Creel hired 75,000 "four-minute men" to give patriotic talks in theaters and at public gatherings. Artists, writers, and photographers were employed to create posters, pamphlets, and silent movies with themes supporting the war effort.

Propaganda Creates Hatred

Some of the anti-German propaganda went so far as to promote hatred of Germans and their culture. Two million Americans who were born in Germany and several million of German descent were made to feel ashamed of their heritage. Several states banned teaching the German language, and books by German authors were removed from some libraries. German-born orchestra conductors in Chicago and Boston were replaced.

DEFINITION
Propaganda *is visual or audio material used to spread political ideas, often playing on prejudice toward a particular group.*

Waging Modern War

Since the last major war in Europe—the Napoleonic Wars 100 years earlier—the development of modern industry and science had produced weapons of frightening destructive power, including machine guns, tanks, torpedoes, and mustard gas. Many thought the very existence of such weapons would make their use unthinkable. As late as July 28, 1914, the *New York Times* declared that "war is now so dreadful, it cannot happen." It did, and the new weapons were used to fight it.

SIMULATED GAS ATTACKS were used in basic training of recruits.

A GUN CREW from Regimental Headquarters Company, 23rd Infantry, fires a 37-millimeter gun against German soldiers in 1918.

Invade and Entrench

By the summer of 1914, the leaders of Germany became convinced that they were about to be attacked and decided to strike first. The Germans hoped that they could make a fast approach through neutral Belgium, invade France, and conquer Paris before the Allies could respond. But the French and British stopped the invasion at the Marne River on September 5, and both sides were forced to "dig in," creating an elaborate system of trenches that eventually stretched 450 miles from the North Sea to the Swiss border. Neither side gained much ground, and a stalemate on the western front continued for three years.

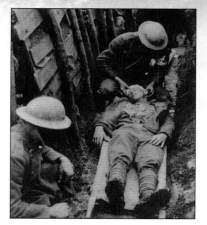

TRENCHES sometimes became hospitals.

The Nightmare of Trench Warfare

Until the final offensives in mid-1918, troops on the western front lived in narrow trenches; rain created standing water that gave soldiers "trench foot," and rats ran rampant. An attack by either side resulted in hours, sometimes days, of artillery fire that wore soldiers' nerves to the breaking point. Then, the attacking army would go "over the top"—climb out of the trenches and run across a barren no-man's-land toward the barbed wire and machine guns that guarded the enemy trenches. If an attack was successful, a few hundred yards might be gained.

The War in the Air

When the war began, the United States had 55 fragile airplanes and 130 pilots. By the time the country joined the war in 1917, the fleet had expanded, and rapid advancements had been made in technology and pilots' skill. In 1914, Allied pilots began shooting pistols at each other in flight. In less than two years, planes were carrying bombs—some of which pilots simply dropped over the side of the aircraft—and mounted machine guns. Occasionally, French, British, or German planes were used to drop mustard gas, which choked or blinded anyone not wearing a gas mask.

A GERMAN BIPLANE—the "Fokker D.VII"

CAPTAIN EDDIE RICKENBACKER, 1890–1973

Eddie Rickenbacker was a businessman and race car driver before he joined the American Expeditionary Force (AEF) (see p. 142) to fly combat planes in France. He was America's top "ace" in the AEF because of his 26 "scores"—enemy planes he shot down. Rickenbacker received both the French Croix de Guerre award and the Congressional Medal of Honor.

Capt. Rickenbacker with his plane

SUBMARINES PLAY A ROLE IN THE WAR

During World War I, Germany used U-boats, or submarines, to attack merchant ships, hoping to prevent shipments of supplies and troops from reaching Great Britain. Unannounced attacks on American merchant ships shocked Americans and forced the United States into the war (see p. 137). U-boats traveled above or below the water's surface, and they were mounted with deck cannons for destroying enemy ships. German U-boats sank more than 5,000 merchant ships and many warships. But the Allies fought back, tracking U-boats by aircraft and bombing or capturing many of those in Germany's fleet.

CAPTURED GERMAN SUBMARINES idly docked in a Brooklyn, New York, harbor

America in Battle

American troops did not reach Europe in large numbers until late 1917, and most needed more training. Since American, British, and French leaders knew that the Germans hoped to end the war with one massive offensive in spring 1918, before the Americans could arrive in force, the United States rushed to get as many soldiers to France as possible.

GENERAL JOHN J. PERSHING, 1860–1948

General John "Black Jack" Pershing, commander of the U.S. forces, was one of a few American officers with combat experience. He had served in the Spanish-American War and led the U.S. force against Pancho Villa (see p. 135). While he was in Mexico, his wife and three children died in a fire, and he became a silent, taciturn man. But Pershing was a strong leader with great organizational skills, and he turned his raw recruits into an effective fighting force.

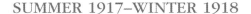

SUMMER 1917–WINTER 1918

The "Yanks" Arrive

American soldiers began arriving in France in the summer of 1917. Their commander, General John J. Pershing, wanted the American Expeditionary Force (AEF) to fight as a separate formation, but the Allied commanders were desperate for help, so Pershing allowed U.S. troops to be mixed into British and French formations. The Americans' freshness and fighting spirit provided a morale boost to the war-weary Allies.

Soon, two events tipped the scales in Germany's favor. First, the Austro-Hungarian army broke through Italy's defensive line on the eastern front, forcing the British and French to move troops from battle lines in the west to the Italian border. Then, early in 1918, the Russian Revolution—which had started in 1917—ended with the Bolshevik wing of the Communist Party seizing control of the government. The Bolsheviks signed a treaty with Germany, and 500,000 German soldiers who had been fighting in Russia began to move to the western front.

ALVIN YORK, 1887–1964

Alvin York was one of the most famous American war heroes of World War I. Born in 1887 in Tennessee, he was drafted into the army in 1918. He soon proved himself noteworthy among the 17 soldiers sent to infiltrate German lines and capture a machine gun position. After many on his team died in the confrontation, he singlehandedly captured the gun, killing several German soldiers. The German officer in charge of the gun surrendered, and York marched more than 130 German soldiers back to his camp as prisoners of war. He was lauded as a national hero and earned the Medal of Honor. After the war, some businessmen purchased a farm for York and his family in Tennessee, where he lived until his death in 1964. His story was made into a film *Sergeant York* in 1941.

MAY–NOVEMBER 1918

The Allied Counteroffensive

The Germans had reinforcements arriving by railroad from the Russian front by the spring of 1918, so they tried to end the three-year stalemate on the western front. German lines advanced to within 50 miles of Paris and expected the Allies to surrender at any moment. But the Allies, strengthened by the arrival of 100,000 American troops, were ready to fight. They won an impressive battle at the town of Chateau-Thierry; then U.S. Marines drove back the experienced German troops.

In mid-July, the Germans made a final assault and again were pushed back in fierce fighting. In September, with the Americans fighting as their own unit for the first time, the Allies began a huge counteroffensive. They captured the vital railroad junction of St. Mihiel. Then, in the Argonne Forest, more than a million U.S. soldiers inched their way through rain, fog, mud, and German machine guns. Nearly 120,000 Americans were killed, wounded, or went missing in the Meuse-Argonne Offensive, but they won the battle and cut the Germans' main supply line on November 7, 1918. Four days later, German commanders signed the armistice that ended the war.

1898–1920

U.S. MARINES CAPTURE BELLEAU WOOD, Chateau-Thierry, France, preventing Germany's advance toward Paris, 30 miles away.

THE NAVY'S "BRIDGE OF SHIPS"

The U.S. Navy was ready for action as soon as war was declared, and played a major role in reducing the submarine menace. American and British fleets laid some 70,000 mines in the North Sea, which made it difficult for U-boats to get to the Atlantic Ocean from Germany.

The Americans also persuaded the British to use a convoy system in which many ships traveled in a pack and were protected by destroyers equipped with antisubmarine weapons. The convoy system was so effective that during a seven-month period from late 1917 through spring 1918, the navy's "bridge of ships" carried two million soldiers and four million tons of supplies across the Atlantic without losing a single ship.

The Search for a Lasting Peace

In January 1918, President Wilson presented his plan for creating a lasting peace after the war. He called it the Fourteen Points. People around the world liked the plan, but for the French and British, who had suffered so much during the war, its terms were too lenient toward the Germans. At home, Republicans also thought the Fourteen Points were too easy on the Germans; and they opposed Wilson's idea for the League of Nations.

Wilson's Fourteen Points

Wilson presented his Fourteen Points to Congress in January 1918. He believed this plan was part of America's special mission to "aid in the

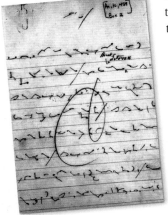

establishment of a just democracy throughout the world." Pamphlets about it were circulated throughout Europe and dropped behind Central Power lines from aircraft.

Wilson insisted that only elected governments could negotiate and sign peace treaties. German socialists, encouraged by the lenient terms in Wilson's plan, established the Weimar Republic; the Kaiser stepped down, and the new government signed an armistice based on the Fourteen Points on November 11, 1918.

The treaty included the right of "self-determination"—that people of the same national background should be allowed to establish their own nation—and the creation of a world organization, the League of Nations, to provide a peaceful forum for international relations.

WILSON'S SHORTHAND NOTES
on the Fourteen Points

EDITH WILSON, 1872–1961

While on the road gathering support for his peace plan, President Wilson fell ill and suffered a stroke. First Lady Edith Wilson took control of his affairs at the beginning of the illness. She decided who could visit him and for how long. Many people felt her involvement was inappropriate, and some thought it was unconstitutional since she had not been elected to office. But it set a precedent for other first ladies to take an active role in their husbands' administrations.

Woodrow and Edith Wilson

A NEW EUROPE IS CREATED

After World War I, Europe looked very different. Four huge empires—German, Austro-Hungarian, Russian, and Ottoman—had been dissolved. Nations with individual cultural identities were reborn as independent states.

Nations formed from the collapse of the **Russian Empire:** Finland, Latvia, Poland (formerly divided between Russia and Germany), Estonia, Lithuania

Nations formed from the breakup of the **Austro-Hungarian Empire:** Czechoslovakia, Hungary, Austria, Yugoslavia

—— German borders 1914
—— Russian borders 1914
—— Austro-Hungarian borders 1914
—— Borders 1923   ▢ New states

EUROPE AFTER WORLD WAR I

Norway
Sweden
Finland
North Sea
Northern Ireland
Irish Free State
Britain
Estonia
Latvia
Lithuania
Baltic Sea
Netherlands
Belgium
Germany
East Prussia
Poland
USSR
Atlantic Ocean
Luxembourg
Ruhr
Saar
Czechoslovakia
Alsace-Lorraine
Switzerland
Austria
Hungary
France
Romania
Portugal
Spain
Italy
Yugoslavia
Bulgaria
Black Sea
Albania
Mediterranean Sea
Greece
Turkey

Negotiating the Treaty of Versailles

The peace talks were held in the Palace of Versailles, outside Paris. As each new point in Wilson's plan was discussed, his idealism collided with the realism of the British and French, and the American president was forced to compromise. He was confident, however, that the League of Nations would correct injustices. There were some important victories for the Fourteen Points. The concept of self-determination led to the formation of a number of new nations. And the Allies approved the formation of a League of Nations, which was the 14th point.

But Wilson's hopes for lenient treatment of Germany were shattered. The defeated nation was stripped of one-eighth of its territory and all its colonies, which would be ruled by Great Britain, France, and Japan. Germany was disarmed and would be occupied by Allied troops. Also, Germany was ordered to pay for the damage caused during the war, including making payments for Allied soldiers killed or wounded, and had to accept full responsibility for starting the war.

The Effect of the War

The United States emerged from World War I as the world's leading industrial and military power. But it did not enter the League of Nations, which limited American influence in world events at a crucial time. In addition, the wartime emphasis on conformity and suppressing dissent led many to feel that criticism of the government was dangerous or un-American—a viewpoint that persisted for years.

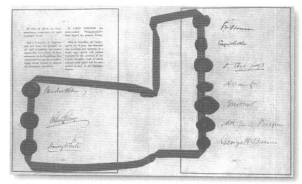

The Treaty of Versailles

The Treaty Is Defeated at Home

President Wilson didn't anticipate how the treaty would be received in the United States. Many Americans, led by Senator Henry Cabot Lodge of Massachusetts (see p. 132) and other Senate Republicans, did not like the way the League of Nations would operate, especially the part of the league's charter that provided for the use of force against aggressive nations. Lodge feared America could be led into another European war. And since the league was part of the treaty, they opposed the treaty in general.

President Wilson took the issue straight to the American people, starting a nationwide speaking tour to 29 cities in 22 days. At every stop, an opposition speaker countered Wilson's arguments. In Colorado, the exhausted president collapsed. He was rushed back to Washington, where he suffered a stroke that left him partially paralyzed.

The Senate voted twice, but, even after a number of amendments were added, the treaty and the league were defeated. The League of Nations went into operation without the participation of the United States.

1898–1920

PEACE TALKS at the Palace of Versailles, as depicted in a 1919 painting by J. C. Johnson

A PROHIBITION ENFORCER pours out confiscated kegs of beer. Following World War I, Americans faced an uncertain future. The economy was unstable, and social changes made many people restless. Supporters of Prohibition felt that banning alcohol would bring a return to traditional values.

Nov. 1920
Warren G. Harding elected president

May 1921
Sacco-Vanzetti trial

Feb. 1924
Teapot Dome scandal breaks

1920

1921

1923

1924

1920
Great Red Scare; Nineteenth Amendment to the Constitution ratified, beginning Prohibition

Aug. 2, 1923
Harding dies; Calvin Coolidge becomes president

AMERICA'S GOLDEN DECADE

1920–1929

Most Americans prospered in the decade after World War I. It seemed anyone could get rich quickly on the stock market or in real estate. Prohibition was in effect, but people ignored the law and drank at illegal clubs, called speakeasies. Young people danced the Charleston all night, listening to the new sounds of jazz.

The fun didn't last, though. Some Americans longed for a return to small-town living among friendly neighbors and were increasingly wary of outsiders. Much of the new wealth was temporary, created by risky loans on stock and worthless real estate deals. Farm families struggled as prices dropped and debts rose. When the stock market crashed in 1929, the nation headed into the Great Depression.

Nov. 1924
Calvin Coolidge elected president

Aug. 6, 1926
Gertrude Ederle swims the English Channel in 14½ hours

May 20–21, 1927
Charles Lindbergh makes first solo nonstop flight across Atlantic

Sept. 22, 1927
Gene Tunney wins rematch against Dempsey

1925   **1926**   **1927**   **1928**   **1929**

July 1925
Scopes trial on teaching evolution in Tennessee schools

Sept. 23, 1926
Gene Tunney wins boxing title from Jack Dempsey

Aug. 1927
First "talkie," The Jazz Singer, released

Aug. 23, 1927
Sacco and Vanzetti executed

Sept. 30, 1927
Babe Ruth hits his 60th home run in one season

Nov. 1928
Herbert Hoover elected president

Fear and Unrest

With the end of World War I in 1918, there was a downturn in the economy, and then a sudden surge upward. Workers were suspicious that the recovery would not last. Labor unions launched a series of strikes to win higher wages for their workers. Many Americans were frightened by the widespread labor unrest. They blamed foreigners for the trouble and demanded that the government stop the flood of immigrants that had been pouring into the country since the 1880s (see pp. 112–13).

Strikes and the Great Red Scare

When a series of labor strikes swept the country in 1919, many people felt that America was in serious trouble. They were afraid the strikes might be the start of a Communist revolution, in part because the recent revolution in Russia had started with strikes.

During the months of unrest, package bombs were mailed to prominent Americans, including J. P. Morgan and John D. Rockefeller (see p. 107). Nearly all of the bombs were detected by postal workers and no one was killed, but the incidents fed the hysteria.

Attorney General A. Mitchell Palmer decided to go after the "immigrant trouble-makers" many blamed. On January 2, 1920, he set in motion police raids in 33 cities and arrested 4,000 suspected "Reds," as Communists were called. Some of the suspects were deported and many were jailed for weeks without being charged, then released. Most Americans were outraged by this violation of constitutional rights.

Palmer then said there would be an attempt to overthrow the government on May 1, 1920. Nothing happened. By late 1920, what people called the Great Red Scare had faded away.

The Sacco-Vanzetti Trial

In May 1920, two Italian immigrants were arrested and charged with murdering two clerks during a payroll robbery in Massachusetts. The accused—Nicola Sacco and Bartolomeo Vanzetti—were anarchists, who believed in getting rid of all government, and had been involved in several strikes. Because of the mood of the times, the two men were convicted and sentenced to death, although the evidence against them was not conclusive. Many people protested that Sacco and Vanzetti had been convicted because of their beliefs, rather than any crime they committed. Years of court appeals failed, and the two men were executed in 1927.

PROHIBITION AND AMERICAN VALUES

Early in 1919, the states ratified the Eighteenth Amendment to the U.S. Constitution, outlawing the manufacture, transport, or sale of alcoholic drinks. For supporters of temperance, banning alcohol was a way to strengthen values, such as hard work and thrift. But by 1920, Americans treated Prohibition as a joke or a nuisance. In December 1933, the states ratified the Twenty-first Amendment to the Constitution, which repealed—or revoked—the Eighteenth.

A PROHIBITION ENFORCER empties beer kegs into the street.

SACCO AND VANZETTI leave jail in Dedham, Massachusetts, on their way to the courthouse in 1927. The pair often were surrounded by policemen, journalists, and protesters.

Rebirth of the Ku Klux Klan

The KKK, which had terrorized Southern blacks after the Civil War, was reestablished in Georgia in 1915. The new Klan claimed it was protecting America's "pioneer heritage" from not only blacks but also radicals, foreigners, Jews, and Catholics. Membership soared following a series of antiblack riots in 1919, when white mobs rampaged through black neighborhoods in Chicago and Washington, D.C., killing at least 100 African Americans.

Money poured into the Ku Klux Klan treasury, and its membership swelled to more than four million. For a few years the Klan was a political force in small towns in the South, Midwest, and Southwest, helping elect senators and governors in several states. By 1925, economic prosperity and full employment reduced fear of radicals, and the popularity of the Klan went into a steep decline. By 1930, membership had dropped below 10,000.

Restricting Immigration

Many Americans wanted to limit the number of foreigners let into the country. This led Congress to pass a series of immigration laws in the 1920s. Unlimited numbers of immigrants could still come from Canada and Latin America, but only 150,000 per year were allowed from the rest of the world, excluding Asia. Each country had a quota—a share of the 150,000—roughly related to the number of American people who traced their ancestry to that country.

KLANSMEN BURNED CROSSES on their victims' land to terrify them.

THE SCOPES TRIAL

In 1925, a Tennessee teacher named John T. Scopes was arrested for teaching Charles Darwin's theory of evolution, which said that "higher" forms of life, such as humans, evolved from "lower" life forms, such as apes. Many rural Americans felt this theory was at odds with the creationism they believed in and their traditional Christian values.

William Jennings Bryan, the great Populist hero (see p. 117), spoke for the prosecution. Scopes was defended by famous defense attorney Clarence Darrow. In his questioning, Darrow made Bryan seem foolish and ignorant. The trial settled nothing, though. Scopes was fined $100, and the ruling was later reversed on a technicality.

DEFINITION

Creationism is the belief that the world was created by God out of nothing, as described in the Bible.

DARROW AND BRYAN during the trial. The strain of the trial was too much for Bryan (right), who died soon after.

The Economy Booms

During the 1920s, the nation enjoyed the greatest burst of prosperity in its history, promising the fulfillment of the American dream. Three consecutive Republican presidents took the credit. Warren G. Harding started the probusiness Republican dynasty in 1920—which was also the first presidential election in which women could vote. Harding was followed by Calvin Coolidge and Herbert Hoover. Most people enjoyed the good times and ignored the weaknesses in the economic system that began to emerge late in the decade.

New Economics

World War I was followed by a brief recession as industries adjusted to the end of profitable government contracts struck a few years earlier to produce goods for the war. These agreements paid companies—and, in turn, their workers—well. The economy recovered quickly with the support of the Republican government.

America was now operating under a different economic policy. While the Progressives (see pp. 120–127) attempted to regulate business to protect workers and consumers, Republicans felt that government agencies should help business when they could and stay out of its way when they couldn't.

Paradise for Consumers

Americans had never had so much money or so many things to spend it on. Wages rose steadily in the 1920s, and the cost of living decreased as goods became cheaper due to technology and more efficient production methods. In fact, a dollar in 1927 could buy one-third more than it could in 1914, making it possible for working-class families to buy household goods, such as electrical appliances, that they could not have afforded a few years earlier.

In addition to the assembly line (see p. 105), innovative car manufacturer Henry Ford (see p. 128) introduced the idea of buying on credit. A family could make an initial down payment on a car, then pay the rest in weekly or monthly installments. Buying on credit was soon accepted practice for the purchase of appliances, furniture, and homes, as well.

WOMEN IN THE WORK FORCE

Women had joined the work force in big numbers during the war, but many lost their jobs when men returned home from fighting. The number of women in the work force continued to grow in the 1920s, but they worked in less-skilled, lower paid jobs. By the late 1920s, women made up more than 25 percent of the work force, but most women earned less than half the average weekly wage.

A FEMALE HIGH SCHOOL STUDENT works on an automobile engine. It was uncommon that women worked in such technical jobs.

The Florida Land Boom

In the early 1920s, people with extra money began investing it in Florida real estate—not to build vacation houses, but to make money by selling the land later. The "Dixie Highway" running down the East Coast became crowded as people rushed to get in on the boom. Those who invested and sold quickly made small fortunes, but many others lost money to swindlers who sold swamp land that was sometimes infested with alligators. Sales slumped in 1926, and a devastating hurricane in September ended the boom. Many Florida banks failed, and thousands of investors were left with worthless land.

Uneven Prosperity

The great affluence of the decade did not reach everyone. The nation's farm families, for example, had enjoyed two decades of prosperity, but, by 1920, they faced the problem of overproduction and falling crop prices. More than three million people left farms for cities or towns, and roughly 13 million acres of farmland were abandoned. Of those who remained in agriculture, about half became tenant farmers and worked land belonging to others.

The times were also difficult for many African Americans. An estimated one million left the South for the North and West, where they continued to encounter discrimination. Many found a haven in Harlem, a neighborhood in New York, where their freedom and creativity flourished. In addition, throughout the country, more than 70,000 businesses were started by African Americans.

During the 1920s, about 500,000 Mexicans crossed the border into the American Southwest. Lacking skills, many became migrant farmworkers and lived in camps with squalid conditions—poor sanitation and a lack of fresh water.

> **DEFINITION**
>
> **Migrant farmworkers** move with the seasons to different regions—wherever they are needed—to harvest fruits, vegetables, and other crops.

HENRY FORD'S FIRST ASSEMBLY LINE for the Model T Ford in 1913. By 1929, 26 million motor vehicles were registered, about half of them Fords.

HARDING ADMINISTRATION SCANDALS

A CAMPAIGN CARD for the 1924 Democratic presidential ticket reminds voters of the scandal.

Warren G. Harding was an honest politician who was insecure with his abilities. He relied heavily on friends from home but didn't realize that members of this "Ohio gang" were dishonest. His administration suffered a series of scandals. The worst one, called the Teapot Dome Scandal, involved Secretary of the Interior Albert Fall, who was convicted of granting rights to the Teapot Dome, Wyoming, oil reserves in exchange for contributions to the Republican presidential campaign.

The public and press paid little attention to the scandals, but Harding was devastated. To restore his spirits, he went on a speaking tour in the West. On August 2, 1923, he died in San Francisco.

The Jazz Age

The majority of Americans in the 1920s were hardworking, family-oriented, churchgoing, and law-abiding. Many others, especially the younger generation, were bent on having fun, defying traditions, and living what were considered "fast" lives. For them, this decade was the Roaring Twenties or the Jazz Age. More conservative people found much to enjoy, too, including movies, radio, and spectator sports. The 1920s seemed to offer something for everyone.

1920–1929

ALVIN "SHIPWRECK" KELLY atop a flagpole in 1929. Kelly continued to seek fame by performing stunts throughout his life.

Jazz-Age Lifestyles

Edna St. Vincent Millay began her most famous poem with the line, "My candle burns at both ends." She was speaking for a generation of young people who wanted to live exciting, fast-paced lives and seek pleasure wherever they could find it.

Young women called flappers typically cut their hair short and wore short skirts with stockings rolled below their knees. They also defied convention—and their parents—by smoking cigarettes, often from long holders.

Wealthier young people with money to spend enjoyed country-club lives. They liked fast, open cars—called roadsters—and dancing the latest dances, like the lindy and the Charleston, at all-night parties.

FLAPPERS were known for wearing cloche hats and short skirts and for leading wild lives. The origin of the term "flapper" is uncertain.

Fads and Crazes

With more free time and a growing fondness for entertainment, Americans enjoyed a colorful variety of fads, such as beauty contests—including the first Miss America pageant—dance marathons, contract bridge, and crossword puzzles.

There were also some strange crazes. For example, an ex-boxer named Alvin "Shipwreck" Kelly started the practice of flagpole-sitting, staying on a narrow perch for days at a time. As the *New Republic* reported, "almost any form of imbecility becomes important in these States."

Jazz-Age Literature

The 1920s was a time of great literary energy. Ernest Hemingway, for example, had experienced World War I firsthand, and his novels shattered romantic images held by many at home. Gertrude Stein, an American poet who lived in Paris, called writers such as Hemingway and F. Scott Fitzgerald part of a "lost generation."

Zora Neale Hurston and Langston Hughes wrote about the struggles of blacks in America; William Faulkner examined race and family roots in the Deep South. Sinclair Lewis ridiculed middle-class values, and a group of writers in New York known for their meeting place, the Algonquin Round Table—including playwright George S. Kaufman (see p. 168), poet Dorothy Parker, and novelist Edna Ferber—inspired interest with riveting writing and cliquish ways.

(see p. 168)

RUDOLPH VALENTINO appears on a 1925 poster for the film *The Black Eagle*.

ARTISTS OF THE HARLEM RENAISSANCE

A number of African American writers used poetry, novels, short stories, and essays to examine the gap between American ideals and the realities of blacks' lives. The works of Langston Hughes, Claude McKay, and Zora Neale Hurston were part of a burst of creative energy in New York City that became known as the Harlem Renaissance. This cultural movement included composers, playwrights, actors, dancers, and musicians.

ZORA NEALE HURSTON, 1891–1960

LANGSTON HUGHES, 1902–1967

KING OLIVER'S DIXIE SYNCOPATORS, one of the first highly popular jazz bands, and other musicians created the music that defined this age and gave it its name: jazz. New Orleans is considered the birthplace of jazz; it emerged from different strands of African American music, including traditional African rhythms, folk songs, gospel music, the blues, and ragtime. King Oliver's Dixieland Band was one of its earliest innovators. Jazz quickly traveled all over the country, and Chicago; Kansas City, Missouri; and New York, among other towns, became famous for their own brands of the uniquely American jazz sound.

Movies and Radio

As motion-picture technology improved in the years after the war, production companies moved to Hollywood and created "silent" films with elaborate sets and costumes. Even without sound, stars emerged and drew huge audiences. In 1927, *The Jazz Singer* was the first "talkie." Films were shown in opulent movie palaces, some seating more than 4,000. An estimated 20 million people enjoyed this splendor every week.

Radio played an important part in people's lives. Two years after the first broadcast, 522 stations were airing news, music, sports, and more. For millions of families, an evening now involved clustering around the radio. Radio and movies were ending rural Americans' isolation. People around the country listened to the same radio shows and saw the same movies, which helped create a more uniform American culture.

1920s Boom-Time Heroes

Americans were eager to enjoy themselves in the years after the war. The economy was booming and there was extra money to spend on entertainment. A new, popular culture emerged, and with it a new brand of hero-entertainers who thrilled the nation with their talent—rather than the war heroes of the past. The new mass media told stories of the exploits of movie, music, and sports stars, describing them in larger-than-life language.

Louis "Satchmo" Armstrong

Jazz Heroes

Many of the best musicians and singers of the 1920s would be headliners for several decades. Trumpeter and band leader Louis Armstrong was still playing in the 1960s and had extended his career to movies and TV.

BESSIE SMITH sheet music

More Jazz Greats

Bessie Smith was known for her slow, soulful renditions of early jazz hits. Duke Ellington and George Gershwin gave jazz a loftier status by including it in classical compositions performed by symphony orchestras.

Mary Pickford

Movie Stars

In this era, Hollywood became the glittering motion-picture capital of the world. By the 1920s, the stars loomed larger than life with the help of their press agents and the media. Two of the biggest stars were Mary Pickford, "America's Sweetheart," and her real-life husband Douglas Fairbanks, a handsome action hero. A third outstanding performer was Charlie Chaplin. In a costume of baggy pants, frock coat, derby hat, cane, and mustache, Chaplin created his signature role, the "Little Tramp." He, Pickford, and Fairbanks joined forces to form United Artists, a successful production company.

Charlie Chaplin

The Legends of Sports

Spectator sports, which first emerged around the turn of the century, became remarkably popular in the 1920s. Huge crowds gathered to watch outstanding athletes in every sport set performance standards for future generations to try to surpass.

JACK DEMPSEY AND GENE TUNNEY (standing) fought twice in the 1920s for the heavyweight boxing championship. Tunney used "scientific" boxing to take the title from Dempsey, a rough-and-tumble fighter.

GERTRUDE EDERLE created a sensation in 1926 when, at age 19, she became the first woman to swim the English Channel—in 14½ hours, nearly two hours faster than the men's record.

GEORGE HERMAN "BABE" RUTH was the 1920s sports figure who loomed above all others. Originally one of the best left-handed pitchers, Ruth was even more impressive at bat. In 1927, he set a home-run record of 60 in a season, which wouldn't be broken until 1961. His reputation for fast living added to his legend.

FLYING SOLO ACROSS THE ATLANTIC

On May 20–21, 1927, aviator Charles A. Lindbergh flew a single-engine plane nonstop from New York to Paris—the first solo flight across the Atlantic. It took him 33½ hours at a top speed of only 100 miles per hour. Exactly five years later, Amelia Earhart became the first female pilot to fly solo across the Atlantic, flying from Newfoundland to Ireland in just 14 hours, 56 minutes.

Amelia Earhart

Charles A. Lindbergh

"Let the Good Times Roll"

As the 1920s drew to a close, most Americans were confident that the good times would go on and on. Factories churned out mountains of new products, and consumers bought houses, automobiles, and appliances at a record pace. There were signs that the economy might be headed for trouble—such as the failure of thousands of family-owned farms—but practically no one paid attention.

A CAMPAIGN BUTTON from 1932 reminds voters of Hoover's public service.

Confidence in the American Dream

In 1928, when President Calvin Coolidge decided not to seek reelection, the Republicans nominated Herbert Hoover, who had served in a variety of government posts since World War I. Voters elected Hoover in a landslide victory over New York's governor, Democrat Al Smith.

Even before his election, Hoover had expressed confidence that the prosperity would never end. "We in America today," he stated, "are nearer to the final triumph over poverty than ever before in the history of any land." American consumers seemed to share this faith. New business developments—brand names, advertising, and buying on credit—urged them to enjoy life more by buying more.

AN ADVERTISEMENT for the Lincoln Sedan shows a wealthy lifestyle to attract buyers.

The Power of Advertising

A new kind of advertising and a new generation of salespeople emerged during the decade, presenting Americans with "the hard sell." Radio advertisements bombarded listeners with catchy jingles and endless messages to "buy your share of the American Dream." Billboards lined the nation's highways and neon lights blared advertising in every city and town. The message to buy was everywhere.

In addition, salespeople in showrooms for cars, furniture, and appliances were trained in the hard sell. As one manual advised, "Look the customer straight in the eye. Don't give him the time to reflect or the chance to say no."

CORNER DRUGSTORES, like this one in New York City's Pennsylvania Station, gave way to big chain stores as the economy grew.

Chain Stores and Brand Names

The steady consolidation of the economy under control by a few large corporations had an influence on consumers' spending habits. Hundreds of small retail outlets were replaced or dominated by chain stores—Rexall Drugstores; A&P Grocery Stores; and Sears, Roebuck & Company, for example. By buying in massive quantities, the chain stores were able to offer lower prices. Also, the large corporations that manufactured consumer products now offered "brand names"—a well-known name being a guarantee of quality. The combination of chain stores and brand names gave people confidence in their purchases, especially for more costly products like furniture and appliances.

Chain stores also facilitated buying on credit, which grew rapidly during the 1920s. Instead of saving to buy a refrigerator or a new car, consumers could buy things that they could not afford right away—paying a small amount up front and owing the rest in installments.

Playing the Stock Market

The value of shares in the stock market climbed steadily upward, and this encouraged some investors to take the risk of buying "on margin"—much like buying on credit. Instead of paying cash for stocks, the investor paid part of the price, called the margin, and borrowed the rest from the stockbroker. The broker, in turn, borrowed from banks. The investor hoped to pay off the balance by selling the stock at a profit in a few months or years when the price rose. This seemed a sure bet, as long as the stock market went up in value.

Countless stories circulated about average people who made $10,000, $20,000, or $30,000 in only a few months. Thousands joined in "playing" the stock market, but, even at its peak, only about one of every 20 Americans owned stock. The loans seemed safe to the banks, and investors were confident that the stock market would keep on rising.

A 1920S STOCK CERTIFICATE represented the wealth that many Americans hoped to have.

1920–1929

Warning Signs

Most Americans felt the economic outlook was perfect, but several areas carried potential for trouble.

Farm overproduction and the loss of European markets for crops brought prices down.

Germany was having trouble paying the huge war debt it owed the Allies. And the Allies—Great Britain and France—were borrowing from American investors to pay the debts they owed the U.S. government.

Lastly, surpluses were beginning to pile up. Customers had bought all the products they wanted, but factories were still making more.

FARMS like this one in Germantown, Pennsylvania, saw the boom times of World War I disappear by the end of the 1920s.

DEFINITION

*A **surplus** is the amount of an item left over after the need for that item has been satisfied.*

THE WORKS PROGRESS ADMINISTRATION
employed artists on community projects such as public
murals. The WPA was formed as part of President
Roosevelt's Second New Deal, which included additional
programs to provide employment and assistance in
response to the Great Depression. Roosevelt's creative
relief and reform efforts got Americans back on their
feet and back to work.

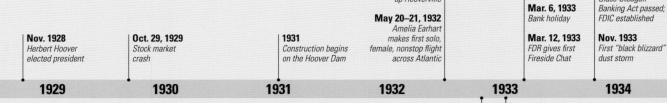

May 1932
*Bonus Army marches
on Washington, sets
up Hooverville*

Mar. 1933
*Hundred Days
legislation begins*

June 16, 1933
*Glass-Steagall
Banking Act passed;
FDIC established*

May 20–21, 1932
*Amelia Earhart
makes first solo,
female, nonstop flight
across Atlantic*

Mar. 6, 1933
Bank holiday

Nov. 1928
*Herbert Hoover
elected president*

Oct. 29, 1929
*Stock market
crash*

1931
*Construction begins
on the Hoover Dam*

Mar. 12, 1933
*FDR gives first
Fireside Chat*

Nov. 1933
*First "black blizzard"
dust storm*

1929	1930	1931	1932	1933	1934

Nov. 1932
*Franklin D. Roosevelt
elected president*

1933
*Twenty-first Amendment to the
Constitution ratified, ending Prohibition*

Feb. 15, 1933
Assassination attempt on FDR

THE GREAT DEPRESSION

1929–1939

As the nation slid rapidly into the Great Depression, Americans lost their money and their jobs, as well as their hope and confidence. Banks failed, factories cut wages, and unemployment soared. President Hoover's calls for voluntary measures to provide jobs had little effect.

In the 1932 presidential election, voters were attracted to Democrat Franklin D. Roosevelt's promise of a New Deal. In his first months in office, Roosevelt pushed emergency measures through Congress that eased suffering and put thousands to work.

The depression persisted despite Roosevelt's efforts until 1939, when the nation neared full employment. As World War II engulfed Europe, U.S. defense plants and shipyards operated 24 hours a day to rebuild the military, ensuring economic recovery.

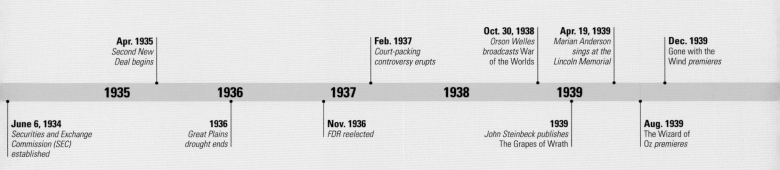

Apr. 1935
Second New Deal begins

Feb. 1937
Court-packing controversy erupts

Oct. 30, 1938
Orson Welles broadcasts War of the Worlds

Apr. 19, 1939
Marian Anderson sings at the Lincoln Memorial

Dec. 1939
Gone with the Wind premieres

1935   **1936**   **1937**   **1938**   **1939**

June 6, 1934
Securities and Exchange Commission (SEC) established

1936
Great Plains drought ends

Nov. 1936
FDR reelected

1939
John Steinbeck publishes The Grapes of Wrath

Aug. 1939
The Wizard of Oz premieres

Boom to Bust

In October 1929, when stock prices suddenly collapsed with little warning, the nation was plunged into the Great Depression. President Hoover's response failed to stop the downward spiral, and the depression got steadily worse. In reaction, worried Americans elected Democrat Franklin D. Roosevelt to the presidency, hoping he could make a difference.

The Stock Market Crash

During the summer of 1929, the stock market reached record highs. There were hints of problems ahead, but few people paid attention. For one thing, too many people's wealth depended on buying stocks on margin (see p. 157), creating a debt that would be hard to repay if stock prices fell. Another hint was the slowdown in buying—most families had already bought a car, furniture, and an array of household appliances, and did not need any more. But factories continued to produce goods at record rates, creating huge inventories of unsold products that just sat in warehouses and on store shelves. Also, farms continued to fail at an alarming rate as prices dropped and money stopped coming in.

In the fall of 1929, the prices of stocks dropped sharply, then recovered—until October 29, 1929, when they collapsed. Stocks that had sold for $90 a share or more were suddenly almost worthless. Investors lost nearly $8 billion on that one day.

Panic

Once people lost confidence in the stock market, it touched off a chain reaction. Brokers demanded that investors pay their margin loans, and banks asked for the money they had loaned the brokers. Millions of people withdrew their money from banks. This "run" on the banks caused hundreds of banks to run out of cash and forced them to close temporarily. In the aftermath of the stock market crash, there were stories about people who jumped out of windows and killed themselves—which did happen, although the stories often exaggerated the numbers of victims.

OUT OF WORK DURING THE DEPRESSION

Unemployment—the calculation of how many people, or what percentage of people, are out of work—is an important factor in determining if an economy is healthy. During the depression, unemployment was at record high levels. In 1932, almost one-quarter of American workers did not have a job, and since the United States did not have unemployment insurance at that time, most of those people did not have a way to support themselves or their families.

Unemployment, 1920–1932, as a percentage of the work force

1920 1921 1922 1923 1924 1925 1926 1927 1928 1929 1930 1931 1932

A CROWD GATHERS ON WALL STREET in downtown New York City on October 29, 1929, after the stock market crash.

A DESPERATE CAR OWNER tries to raise money. Situations such as this were common after the crash.

$100. WILL BUY THIS CAR MUST HAVE CASH LOST ALL ON THE STOCK MARKET

From Crash to Depression

The stock market crash did not actually cause the Great Depression, but it did expose serious weaknesses in the economy. Even without the crash, there would have been layoffs and factory closings to reduce the effects of overproduction. Also, too many farm families, migrant workers, and African Americans had been left out of the prosperity of the 1920s.

The stock market crash sped up the process, though, and unemployment soared. Local governments and charities did what they could to help people, but they soon ran out of funds. By then, 86,000 businesses had failed, including many banks. People with accounts in those banks lost their life savings. And wages for people still employed had been cut by 60 percent.

THE BONUS ARMY

In the spring of 1932, thousands of World War I veterans marched on the nation's capital to demand payment of bonuses that had been approved by Congress in 1924, but which the government didn't plan to pay until 1945.

When Congress refused to act, some of the veterans set up a camp of cardboard and tin shacks near the capitol. They called it Hooverville. In response, Hoover called in the army. Though no shots were fired, troops leveled the camp on the orders of Army Chief of Staff General Douglas MacArthur, shocking Americans and leading many to consider Hoover a heartless man who ignored the problems of average people.

CAMPED OUTSIDE THE CAPITOL in Washington, D.C., the Bonus Army demanded attention.

Hoover's Voluntary Programs

President Hoover was concerned that using social programs to pull the country out of the depression would make people permanently dependent on the government. Instead, he asked state governors to fund construction projects such as building highways and bridges to create jobs. In addition, in 1930, Congress voted to provide money for the construction of harbors, public buildings, and the huge Boulder Dam on the Colorado River—later renamed the Hoover Dam. Hoover's loans-for-farmers program failed, as did his appeals to business owners to avoid layoffs or factory closings. These efforts weren't enough to push the economy toward recovery.

Herbert Hoover

The Presidential Election of 1932

Hoover's reputation could not have been in worse shape going into the election of 1932. Homeless people built Hoovervilles in city parks. They called the newspapers they used to cover themselves Hoover blankets. And people were angry at Hoover for using troops against the war veterans of the Bonus Army.

Democratic nominee Franklin D. Roosevelt campaigned vigorously, promising a "New Deal for the American people." He won a landslide victory, carrying all but six states, winning the electoral vote 472 to 59, and ending 12 years of Republican presidents.

DEFINITION

*A **landslide** occurs when an election is won by a huge margin.*

FDR Comes to Power

From Franklin D. Roosevelt's election in November 1932 until his inauguration the following March, the American people anxiously wondered what kind of president he would be. Most journalists did not expect much. One famous writer, H. L. Mencken, wrote, "He is far too feeble and wishy-washy ... to make a really effective fight." Soon after Roosevelt took office, however, opinions changed dramatically. One of his harshest critics, journalist Walter Lippmann, declared, "In one week the nation, which had lost confidence in everything and everybody, has regained confidence in the government and in itself."

People changed their minds about FDR—as Roosevelt was popularly called—because he brought energy, compassion, and new ideas to the challenging job of leading the nation during the Great Depression.

Privilege and Politics

Franklin Delano Roosevelt was born in 1882 into one of New York State's old land-owning families. When he married Eleanor Roosevelt, a distant cousin, in 1905, her uncle, President Theodore Roosevelt, gave the bride away.

The young FDR was rich, good-looking, well connected, and ambitious— useful qualities for a political career, which he began soon after he graduated from Columbia Law School. After serving in the New York State Senate, he was appointed assistant secretary of the navy under President Woodrow Wilson. In 1920, he was the Democratic nominee for vice president on the losing ticket with James M. Cox. In these early years, there were few signs of Roosevelt's future importance. While he had personal charm, many people found him to be arrogant.

ROOSEVELT'S OFFICIAL PORTRAIT, painted by Douglas Granville Chandor in 1945

The Polio Crisis

In 1921, at the age of 39, FDR was stricken with poliomyelitis. The energetic, vigorous father of five became paralyzed from the waist down. Months of agonizing physical pain and uncertainty about his political future followed. Eleanor Roosevelt, a shy woman, turned out to be a tower of strength, helping him fight the effects of polio and restore his political career.

Roosevelt recuperated at a spa in Georgia, where he fought to build up his strength. He managed to disguise his disability, and newspaper editors were careful not to print pictures showing his heavy steel braces or, later, his wheelchair.

At the Democratic National Convention in 1928, Roosevelt was cheered as a returning hero. There, he agreed to run for governor of New York—and he won. During his term as governor, it was clear that FDR had changed. His arrogance gone, he showed genuine concern for the suffering of others.

ELEANOR ROOSEVELT (right) visiting coal miners in Appalachia. Mrs. Roosevelt often acted as FDR's "legs," traveling around the country to places he couldn't.

RIDING THE RAILS became a way of life for many jobless people during the depression. They traveled in boxcars and stopped at town after town looking for work and food.

FOR THE DEMOCRATIC NATIONAL CONVENTION in 1932, Roosevelt chartered a plane to fly him from Albany to Chicago in order to accept the nomination in person. In the past, nominees had waited at home until a delegation from the convention arrived to give them the official word. Since Roosevelt, candidates have accepted the nomination at the convention.

"Lame-Duck" Months

In the four months between Roosevelt's election to the presidency and his inauguration—Hoover's "lame-duck" months—FDR surrounded himself with experts in economics, agriculture, and law. These men became known as the "brain trust," and many stayed on to help FDR draft legislation to send to Congress. Roosevelt also formed his cabinet during this time, which included Frances Perkins as secretary of labor—the first woman to hold a cabinet post.

The depression deepened during these four months, and 13 million people were unemployed. A "Vagabond Army," which included about 200,000 homeless teenagers, roamed the country. The Southern Pacific Railroad reported that it had ejected 683,000 trespassers in 1932—men, women, and young people riding empty boxcars from city to city. Massive cash withdrawals at banks also increased. By Inauguration Day, 5,000 banks had failed, and most states declared "bank holidays," in which all the state's banks were closed or their hours reduced.

DEFINITION

*During the period between the election and inauguration of a new official, the current office holder becomes known as a **lame duck**. The origin of the expression is unknown.*

163

The Hundred Days

Inauguration Day, March 4, 1933, was rainy and gloomy, matching the mood of the country. The depression had people feeling defeated. Franklin Delano Roosevelt, however, couldn't wait to face the challenge. In his inaugural address, which was broadcast over the radio, FDR declared, "Let me assert my firm belief that the only thing we have to fear is fear itself—nameless, unreasoning, unjustified terror." Those words marked the beginning of a remarkable period in American history. Over the next 100 days, Roosevelt launched his New Deal—a series of legislative proposals that produced dramatic changes across the nation.

1929–1939

Restoring Banks—and Confidence

Roosevelt's immediate goal was to restore confidence as quickly as possible. First, he announced a nationwide bank holiday, closing all banks for four days. This stopped a "run" on the banks, which happens when huge numbers of people rush to withdraw their money for fear of losing it if the banks run out of cash. FDR also called Congress into an emergency session and pushed through the Emergency Banking Relief Act, which stated that banks would reopen when the Treasury Department ruled that they were sound.

Within a week, three quarters of the nation's banks had reopened, money was circulating again, and a wave of confidence swept the country.

FDR'S "FIRESIDE CHATS" were his way of addressing the American people directly. On the first Sunday evening of his presidency, Roosevelt delivered a radio address to the nation. He emphasized that it was not a speech but what he called a fireside chat. These informal talks gave FDR a chance to explain his actions, and they became very popular.

The Three R's of the New Deal

At the heart of the New Deal were programs that fell into one of three categories: relief, recovery, or reform. Relief programs were aimed at reducing suffering; recovery programs were broader efforts to revive business and agriculture; and reform programs instituted new regulations to correct problems that had contributed to the depression.

Relief Programs

The Civilian Conservation Corps (CCC) hired jobless young men and put them to work clearing roads and trails, fighting fires, and building picnic areas. Another relief project started during FDR's first 100 days was the Public Works Administration (PWA), which funded public works such as the construction of schools, city halls, and public gardens.

BOYS ENROLLED IN THE CCC (Civilian Conservation Corps) learn forestry.

Reform Programs

Two early reform programs were designed to make banking and stock-market investing safer and more reliable. In June 1933, the Glass-Steagall Banking Act set up rules to reduce bank failures by preventing risky investments. It also established the Federal Deposit Insurance Corporation (FDIC). This meant that the federal government would insure people's bank deposits against bank failure up to $5,000 per account, so that they would feel confident about keeping their money in the bank.

The Federal Securities Act provided investors with information about newly issued stocks. A year later, the Securities and Exchange Commission (SEC) was set up to discourage speculation, stop secret trades, and issue licenses for each of the nation's stock exchanges.

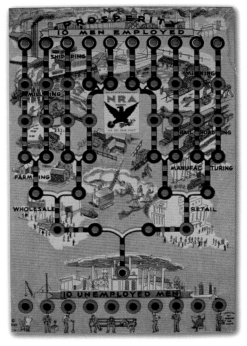

AN NRA BOARD GAME shows how the program puts people to work.

Recovery Programs

Two of the most revolutionary programs were efforts to help agriculture and business. The Agricultural Adjustment Administration (AAA) aimed to boost farm prices by reducing production. Farmers were paid to plant fewer acres and to raise fewer animals. From 1933 to 1934, the prices farmers received for wheat and cotton doubled. Thousands of farm families had money to spend for the first time in years.

The National Recovery Administration (NRA) worked with business owners and labor unions to establish codes of fair hours and wages. Employers who accepted the codes could display an attractive new symbol—the NRA "Blue Eagle"—and its motto, "We do our part." For nearly three years, the NRA was a striking success. The program ended child labor and established the right of unions to bargain collectively.

AN "ALPHABET SOUP" OF LEGISLATION FROM THE HUNDRED DAYS IN 1933

DATE	AGENCY	PROGRAM	PURPOSE	STATUS
March 3	CCC	Civilian Conservation Corps	Provide employment for men aged 18–25	Ended in 1941 Program largely ended in 1936
May 12	AAA	Agricultural Adjustment Administration	Advise and assist farmers	Ended in 1936
May 12	FERA	Federal Emergency Relief Administration	Provide direct relief, such as money or food	Ended in 1936
May 18	TVA	Tennessee Valley Authority	Help develop resources of Tennessee Valley	Still in operation
June 13	HOLC	Home Owners Loan Corporation	Help people refinance mortgages	Ended in 1950
June 13	NRA	National Recovery Administration	Revive American business	Ended in 1935
June 13	PWA	Public Works Administration	Provide employment on public works	Ended in 1937
June 16	FCA	Farm Credit Administration	Set up a credit system for farmers	Became part of the Department of Agriculture in 1939
June 16	FDIC	Federal Deposit Insurance Corporation	Set up a system to guarantee individual bank deposits	Still in operation

Rural Reforms

During the mid-1930s, there were signs that some of Roosevelt's New Deal programs were beginning to ease suffering and to revive both the economy and people's confidence. The Great Depression was far from over, however, especially in rural America, including the part of the Great Plains that became known as the "Dust Bowl." FDR and his advisors continued to devise new programs; two of the most successful— the Tennessee Valley Authority and the Rural Electrification Administration—transformed much of the nation's farmland.

"MIGRANT MOTHER," photo taken in California in 1936

Dorothea Lange was a successful portrait photographer in San Francisco until the sight of jobless people in a bread line drove her to start recording the suffering she saw. She became one of the most famous Depression-era photographers, many of whom contributed to the "historical section" of the Farm Security Administration (FSA). FSA pictures were published in newspapers and magazines, giving Americans a haunting visual record of the Dust Bowl and its aftermath. Lange's best-known photograph—"Migrant Mother"— became an enduring symbol of hard rural life during the Great Depression.

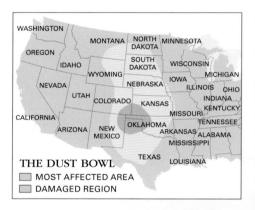

THE DUST BOWL
- MOST AFFECTED AREA
- DAMAGED REGION

The Dust Bowl

Since the prairie sod had first been plowed on the flat and treeless plains in the mid-1800s, overfarming had been a problem. Farmers made no attempt to conserve the topsoil by planting trees or rotating crops to rest the soil. Then in 1933, over a huge area, no rain fell. The drought continued through 1936. The soil turned to dust, and disastrous dust storms became common throughout a 150,000-square-mile area that covered parts of ten states, from the Dakotas south to Texas. The hardest-hit area, which became known as the Dust Bowl, included parts of Kansas, Oklahoma, Texas, New Mexico, and Colorado.

Killing Dust

In November 1933, a massive dust storm called a black blizzard lifted an estimated 300 million tons of topsoil into the air. The dark, swirling cloud turned day to night as it slowly moved east, dropping a layer of gray dust all the way to the Atlantic Ocean. In county after county, farm families had no crops to harvest and no way to make a living. Farms were taken over by banks, which hired big companies to plow up everything, even houses and barns, to try to squeeze another crop or two out of the lifeless land.

A FARMER AND HIS SONS seek shelter from a dust storm. Rural Americans whose land and livelihood were ruined by dust and dry weather had little choice but to move away.

Dust Bowl Migrants

Many farm families piled their belongings on whatever vehicle they owned and headed west to find work. They became known as "Okies," or sometimes "Arkies," although many migrants came from states other than Oklahoma or Arkansas. During the 1930s, more than a million people took to the road. About half went to California, where they hoped to find jobs.

By 1937, the government began providing emergency relief for migrants through a newly created Farm Security Administration (FSA). The FSA helped the migrants establish camps with adequate water and sanitation, which supported more than 30,000 families at a time.

Transforming Rural America

The Tennessee Valley Authority (TVA) was one of the most revolutionary programs of the New Deal. It changed the lives of rural Americans living in poverty-stricken areas throughout Tennessee and in six other states.

The TVA took over the Wilson dam on the Tennessee River, and it built 20 more dams on the Tennessee and its tributaries. The dams provided flood control, created lakes for fishing and recreation, and brought low-cost electricity to a region where only two percent of the farms had previously had electric lights and power. The power plants, in turn, made the valley an appealing location for new industries.

JOHN STEINBECK'S *THE GRAPES OF WRATH*

Many Americans were unaware of the hardship created by the Dust Bowl until John Steinbeck's novel *The Grapes of Wrath* was published in 1939, with a movie following a few months later. The story presented a realistic picture of the suffering and pride of an Okie family from the loss of their farm to their struggles in California.

IN THE FILM VERSION of *The Grapes of Wrath*, Henry Fonda portrayed Tom Joad, a man driven to protest injustices such as poverty and the exploitation of workers.

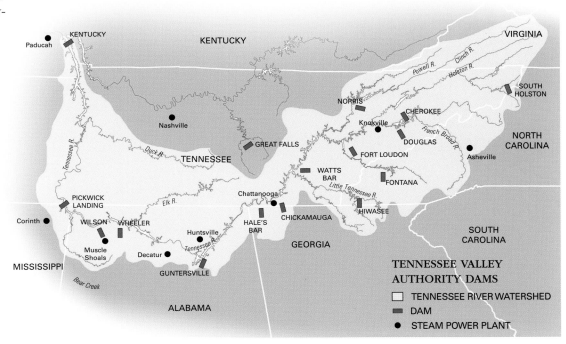

Electrical Power for American Farmland

When Roosevelt took office, only one out of every ten American farms had electricity. The president planned to change that with the Rural Electrification Administration (REA), started in 1935. The REA provided money for local agencies to string wires between farms, which then encouraged the large utility companies to complete the construction of utility poles and relay stations. The federal government also funded new dams and hydroelectric plants in the Northwest and on the Missouri River. Fifteen years later, 90 percent of the nation's farms had electricity.

1930s That's Entertainment

Everyone, whether they weathered the depression well or had a hard time, needed a break from the politics and economics of the 1930s. People found it in the richness and variety of American entertainment. Even though money was tight, Americans managed to see movies and theater, listen to the radio, and dance to the big bands.

Depression-Era Popular Culture

The establishment of the five-day work week, combined with high unemployment, gave Americans more free time than ever before in history. Entertainment offered rich and varied ways to use the leisure hours.

EDGAR BERGEN, the voice of puppet Charlie McCarthy, was a star of stage and radio.

ORSON WELLES performs during a radio broadcast.

The "Monster" Radio

Critics often called radio "the monster." Most families had radios in more than one room of the house, but the big console was usually in the center of the living room. During the day, housewives kept up with soap operas such as *Just Plain Bill* and *Ma Perkins*. In the evening, a family might spend two or three hours listening to variety shows or comedies from favorites such as Jack Benny or Charlie McCarthy.

A CONTEMPORARY ILLUSTRATION for *The War of the Worlds*

THE WAR OF THE WORLDS

In 1938, radio itself made news when a young producer named Orson Welles put on a show about an invasion from Mars that was so realistic that many people panicked and flooded police stations with calls, not realizing it was a dramatization of the novel *The War of the Worlds* by H. G. Wells.

Theater

In the 1930s, popular interest in theater swelled. Visitors flocked to Broadway, the Great White Way, to see spectacular song and dance in musicals such as *Anything Goes*. Playwrights such as George S. Kaufman (see p. 153) presented plays that addressed social issues in witty dialogue; Kaufman won the Pulitzer Prize in 1937 for his play *You Can't Take It with You*. Other plays were more serious in tone, such as Eugene O'Neill's *Mourning Becomes Electra* and Lillian Hellman's *The Children's Hour*.

TIMES SQUARE, the heart of the theater district, in 1938

Movies

The movie industry had more than 15,000 theaters across America. Hollywood produced extravagant full-color films such as *Gone with the Wind* and *The Wizard of Oz*, and Walt Disney used drawings—250,000, in fact—to create the first full-length animated film, *Snow White and the Seven Dwarfs*. Other depression-era film fare included child wonder Shirley Temple, Westerns starring John Wayne, slapstick featuring the Marx Brothers, and musicals with teams such as Fred Astaire and Ginger Rogers.

Movies at most theaters cost a dime, and theater owners offered a range of giveaways to lure customers, such as sets of dishes or bags of groceries.

THE WIZARD OF OZ, 1939, starred Bert Lahr, Jack Haley, Judy Garland, and Ray Bolger.

A MOVIE POSTER from 1939's *Gone With the Wind*

GINGER ROGERS AND FRED ASTAIRE in *Swing Time*

The Big Bands

The music that characterized the 1930s was created by the big bands—big in volume as well as size. These music makers turned the 1930s into the age of swing. Benny Goodman, Tommy Dorsey, Glenn Miller, and many others produced the lively, upbeat songs that led to a wave of new dances known collectively as the jitterbug. In some marathon battles of the bands, as many as 25 or 30 bands might take turns playing for five or six hours.

CONDUCTOR DUKE ELLINGTON AND HIS BAND played gigs in the United States and 65 other countries.

Closing the Deal

One of the most painful lessons of the depression was that the American economy was at the mercy of uncontrollable forces that no one seemed to understand.

In the late 1930s, Americans learned another difficult lesson: although they could now turn to the government for help in hard times, not even the billions of dollars spent on New Deal programs could bring an end to unemployment and poverty. Roosevelt's New Deal had been a remarkable success—but not a complete one.

The Second New Deal

President Roosevelt changed his approach to the country's problems in his 1936 reelection campaign. In 1935, he asked Congress for broad legislation aimed at both work relief and reform. This became known as the Second New Deal and represented some of the most important acts of the New Deal years, including the Social Security Act, the creation of the National Labor Relations Board (NLRB), and the establishment of the Works Progress Administration (WPA).

The Social Security Act

The landmark Social Security Act was a step toward creating a "welfare state," which assured the basic welfare of every man, woman, and child. The act provided monthly retirement pensions for the elderly, unemployment insurance for the jobless, and assistance for the dependent and disabled.

WPA ARTISTS AT WORK in a painting by Raphael Soyer

The Works Progress Administration

The WPA emphasized "work with dignity" through immediate employment on small-scale projects such as building playgrounds, schools, and libraries. It also tried to put people to work in their chosen fields: actors put on community plays, artists created murals for public buildings, and photographers documented their work.

The National Labor Relations Board

The NLRB guaranteed workers the right to form unions and to bargain collectively—as a group, rather than as individuals—to achieve better wages or conditions. The board could take action against companies that fired workers because of their union activities or that refused to bargain with unions. By 1939, several large labor organizations gave workers more power than ever before.

African Americans and the New Deal

New Deal policies toward African Americans provided limited support. The president was cautious because he didn't want to alienate Southern whites. He would not, for example, support antilynching legislation, but his administration was open to black leaders, such as Mary McLeod Bethune.

In general, blacks supported FDR and the New Deal because of its efforts to help the poor and unemployed. Until the 1930s, most blacks had voted Republican in honor of Abraham Lincoln, who played a key role in ending slavery, but the Republican party in the 1930s offered African Americans little to win their votes.

SINGER MARIAN ANDERSON was barred from giving a recital in a private hall in 1939 because she was black. Eleanor Roosevelt helped arrange a concert on the steps of the Lincoln Memorial; 75,000 people attended. Later, in a historic moment in 1955, Anderson was the first African American to perform at the Metropolitan Opera House in New York City.

MARY MCLEOD BETHUNE was director of Negro Affairs for the National Youth Administration (NYA), a consultant to the U.S. secretary of war, and a consultant for the United Nations charter conference. She founded the National Council of Negro Women and served as vice president of the NAACP (see p. 121).

1929–1939

NLRB EMPLOYEES monitor votes in a union election.

The End of the New Deal

Although Roosevelt won reelection by a landslide in 1936, his popularity and authority eroded during his second term, for three main reasons.

First, Roosevelt was criticized for trying to add more justices to the Supreme Court to avoid judicial opinions against New Deal programs. This "court-packing" scheme was unconstitutional.

Second, many Americans had become worried by the expansion of the government's power, especially the president's, and felt that the New Deal should not get any bigger.

Third, the economy weakened even more in 1937 and 1938, and a growing number of voters decided that more New Deal measures wouldn't make a difference. Although the economy started to recover by mid-1938, many Southern Democrats joined with Republicans to form a powerful conservative coalition to block New Deal legislation.

COMPLETING THE NEW DEAL IN 1935

DATE	AGENCY	PROGRAM/PURPOSE	STATUS
April 8	NYA	National Youth Administration Provide jobs and training for Americans 16–25 years of age	Ended in 1942
April 8	WPA	Works Progress Administration Provide employment on public works projects	Ended in 1942
May 11	REA	Rural Electrification Administration Help farmers to electrify homes	Became part of the Department of Agriculture in 1939
July 5	NLRB	National Labor Relations Board Guarantee rights of workers	Still in operation
August 14	SSB	Social Security Board Provide a social security system	Still in operation

OMAHA BEACH in Normandy was the setting for Operation Overlord, the Allies' ambitious plan for invading Nazi-occupied France. On D-Day, American soldiers waded toward shore from ships and troop-carriers to launch a surprise attack. Europe had been at war for five years, but the Allies had been unable to contain Hitler's forces. Once the Allied forces set up a position in France, they advanced quickly and soon reached Germany.

Aug. 14, 1941
Roosevelt and Churchill write Atlantic Charter

Sept. 1, 1939
Germany invades Poland

Oct. 1941
FDR allows Navy to shoot enemy ships on sight

Dec. 7, 1941
Japanese attack Pearl Harbor; U.S. enters war

Sept. 3, 1939
Great Britain and France declare war on Germany

Nov. 1940
Roosevelt reelected

June 22, 1941
Germany invades Soviet Union

Mar. 1939
Germany takes over Czechoslovakia

Mar. 1942
Relocation of Japanese-Americans begins

1939   **1940**   **1941**   **1942**

Nov. 4, 1939
Congress passes Neutrality Act

Spring–Summer 1940
German troops conquer Denmark, Norway, the Netherlands, Belgium, Luxembourg, and France; The Battle of Britain

Mar. 11, 1941
Lend-Lease Act is passed

1942
Allies begin to bomb German cities

Jan. 1, 1942
Declaration of the United Nations

WORLD WAR II
1939–1945

Ⅰn the 1930s, powerful dictatorships came to power in Germany, Italy, and Japan, and the political and military ambitions of these leaders erupted in World War II. The U.S. abruptly abandoned its policy of avoiding all foreign wars when, on December 7, 1941, Japanese warplanes launched a surprise attack on the U.S. naval base at Pearl Harbor, Hawaii.

The American-led alliance of Britain, Russia, and the United States slowly pushed back Axis forces in Europe and the Pacific. In May 1945, Germany surrendered and the world discovered the full horror of Hitler's effort to eliminate Europe's Jews.

The United States dropped two atomic bombs on the Japanese cities of Hiroshima and Nagasaki, forcing Japan to surrender in September 1945 and ending the war.

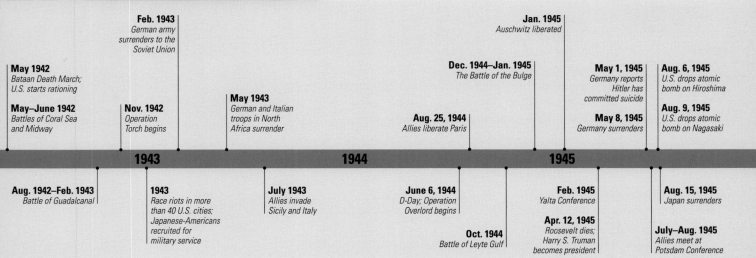

Feb. 1943
German army surrenders to the Soviet Union

Jan. 1945
Auschwitz liberated

May 1942
Bataan Death March; U.S. starts rationing

May–June 1942
Battles of Coral Sea and Midway

Nov. 1942
Operation Torch begins

May 1943
German and Italian troops in North Africa surrender

Dec. 1944–Jan. 1945
The Battle of the Bulge

Aug. 25, 1944
Allies liberate Paris

May 1, 1945
Germany reports Hitler has committed suicide

May 8, 1945
Germany surrenders

Aug. 6, 1945
U.S. drops atomic bomb on Hiroshima

Aug. 9, 1945
U.S. drops atomic bomb on Nagasaki

1943   **1944**   **1945**

Aug. 1942–Feb. 1943
Battle of Guadalcanal

1943
Race riots in more than 40 U.S. cities; Japanese-Americans recruited for military service

July 1943
Allies invade Sicily and Italy

June 6, 1944
D-Day; Operation Overlord begins

Oct. 1944
Battle of Leyte Gulf

Feb. 1945
Yalta Conference

Apr. 12, 1945
Roosevelt dies; Harry S. Truman becomes president

Aug. 15, 1945
Japan surrenders

July–Aug. 1945
Allies meet at Potsdam Conference

The Rise of Dictators

The League of Nations, formed after World War I to promote peaceful international problem-solving, was a weak organization—in part because the U.S. did not join (see p. 145). When military dictators rose to power in Italy, Germany, and Japan, neither the U.S. government nor the American people protested. By the mid-1930s, those three nations were ready to start campaigns of conquest, and no country seemed to have the will to stop them.

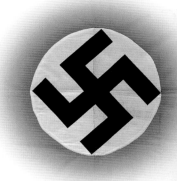

THE SWASTIKA was the main symbol of Hitler's Nazi Party.

America's Peace Proposals

The U.S. did try to promote peace in other ways. In 1921, at the Washington Naval Conference, the U.S. proposed treaties that would decrease the number of warships owned by the world's navies. Then in 1928, Secretary of State Frank B. Kellogg, in partnership with France, agreed to outlaw war through the Kellogg-Briand Pact. The problem was, there was no way to enforce treaties and pacts such as these, so they were ultimately unsuccessful.

ADOLF HITLER used intimidation and violence in Germany to make his National Socialist, or Nazi, Party the largest in Germany.

Good Neighbors in the Western Hemisphere

Since 1898, the U.S. had been sending troops into Latin American countries to protect American interests. In the early 1930s, President Roosevelt began the "Good Neighbor" policy, in which the U.S. withdrew troops from Latin America and established new treaties. When the U.S. became engaged in World War II, most of America's good neighbors in Latin America joined the alliance against the dictators.

A New Kind of Dictator

BENITO MUSSOLINI restored order in Italy using violence and his private army.

When World War I ended in 1918, much of Europe was in crisis. Economic chaos, widespread unemployment, and fear of revolution made many people willing to follow a strong leader. In Italy, fascist dictator Benito Mussolini marched on Rome in 1924 and took over the government. Adolf Hitler in Germany was elected chancellor in 1933, but soon wielded dictatorial power over his countrymen. In Japan during the 1930s, military leaders tightened their grip on power following the assassinations of politicians and government officials. Each of the three dictatorships developed into a totalitarian state, in which a single party controls the government, the economy, and the means of shaping opinion—radio, newspapers, and schools.

DEFINITION

Fascist and *communist* states both involve total control of a nation by a single political party; both are examples of *totalitarian* states.

GENERAL HIDEKI TOJO was the most important military leader in Japan after 1931 and led Japan during World War II.

German Anti-Semitism

The brutality of Nazi Germany's dictatorship was made clear by its vicious discrimination and persecution of Jews. Hitler believed in the racial superiority of Aryan, or purebred, Germans. Scapegoating the successful Jewish population for Germany's economic problems, Hitler rallied support for eliminating the country's "impure" races to restore national supremacy. In 1935, Hitler made anti-Semitism (discrimination against Jews and Arabs) official policy with the Nuremberg Laws, which stripped German Jews of their citizenship. In 1938, the government organized a nationwide night of violence called Kristallnacht, or the "night of broken glass." Mobs roamed the streets, smashing windows in Jewish houses and businesses, setting synagogues on fire, and beating Jews; hundreds were killed and some 20,000 were sent to concentration camps on that night.

America is Silent

The American government did little to help Jews who wanted to escape from Germany. Several thousand families managed to send their children out of Germany—about 10,000 went to Great Britain—but only a few hundred made it to America. The U.S. Congress refused to change its immigration laws to allow more Jews to come. Many in Congress were anxious to avoid conflict with Germany; some shared the anti-Semitism of the German government. In 1938, Germany closed its borders, forbidding Jews to leave.

GERMANY'S NUREMBERG LAWS forced Jews over age six to wear yellow stars on their clothes. Jude is the German word for "Jew."

NAZIS INTERROGATE JEWS IN THE WARSAW GHETTO in 1942. During the war, the anti-Semitic policies established with the Nuremberg Laws extended to Jews living in Nazi-occupied countries, such as Poland. The Warsaw Ghetto was an overcrowded, sealed-off corner of the city, created by the government to separate Jews from the general population and restrict their movements.

America Stands Aside

Throughout the 1930s, America and the League of Nations were reluctant to oppose the dictators threatening world peace. Japan conquered the Chinese province of Manchuria in 1931; Italy invaded Ethiopia in 1935; and the U.S. and the League responded only with written protests. The U.S. stood by as Hitler ignored the Treaty of Versailles (see p. 145), began a huge military buildup, and formed an alliance with Mussolini called the Rome-Berlin Axis (Tokyo was added later). America, France, and Great Britain upheld policies of nonintervention as fascists won the Spanish Civil War. Up to this point, firm action by the Allies might have stopped the dictators, but after 1936, they ran out of chances to prevent war.

JESSE OWENS, 1913–1980

In 1936, the Olympic Summer Games were held in Germany, and Hitler wanted it to be a great showcase of German—or Aryan—racial superiority. But Jesse Owens, an African American track and field star, stole the show, setting records and winning four gold medals.

JESSE OWENS at the starting line

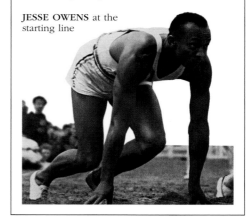

The Outbreak of War

Throughout the 1930s, Congress and the American people were determined not to get involved in the problems in Europe. They ignored President Roosevelt's warnings that the U.S. could not remain isolated. In Europe, Britain and France tried to avoid war by giving in to Hitler's demands. But when he broke his promises by invading Poland in September 1939, they finally declared war.

American Neutrality

The aggressive actions of Italy, Germany, and Japan led Congress to search for ways to guarantee America's neutrality. The Neutrality Act of 1935 banned selling weapons to warring nations. A second Neutrality Act in 1936 prevented American companies from making loans to any nation at war.

Roosevelt's Warnings

In what became known as his Quarantine Speech, FDR said that fascist aggression was like an epidemic of a disease and quarantine was needed to keep it from spreading. Isolationists were upset by the speech, especially when the President said, "Let no one imagine that America will escape."

MARCH 1938–MARCH 1939

Appeasing Fascist Aggression

In March 1938, Hitler sent troops into Austria and annexed, or took over, that German-speaking nation. France and Great Britain protested, but took no action.

Hitler next demanded the Sudeten region of Czechoslovakia, claiming that the three million Germans living there wanted to be part of Germany. In September 1938, at a meeting with British and French leaders in Munich, Hitler promised that this was "the last territorial claim I have to make in Europe." After persuading the Czech government to give up the land, the British prime minister claimed that he had brought "peace in our time." Six months later, in March 1939, Hitler's troops took over the rest of Czechoslovakia.

BRITISH PRIME MINISTER Neville Chamberlain was welcomed to Munich in 1938.

DEFINITIONS

Giving in to a hostile nation in return for peace is called **appeasement**. **Isolationism** *is a deliberate policy of staying out of international affairs.*

THE BOMBING OF SHANGHAI

Japan's war of conquest in China seemed more remote to Americans than the aggression in Europe. However, when the Japanese bombed the city of Shanghai in 1937, Americans were shocked by the newsreels and news photos showing the first full-scale air attacks on a populated city.

THIS PHOTO was taken moments after Shanghai South railway station was bombed, killing 1,800 people.

1939–1945

SEPTEMBER 1939

Blitzkrieg!

At 4:45 am on September 1, 1939, Germany attacked Poland. Germany's Blitzkrieg—or "lightning-war"—assault of fast-moving tanks supported by fighter planes and 1.8 million troops took Poland by surprise. Two days later, Britain and France declared war on Germany, marking the official beginning of World War II.

President Roosevelt called Congress into a special session as soon as the war became official. He asked for emergency changes to the Neutrality Act so that Britain and France could receive weapons and ammunition from the U.S. Congress passed a new Neutrality Act allowing nations at war to buy military supplies, but only on a "cash-and-carry" basis—that is, paying for the supplies, rather than using a loan, and taking them away in non-American ships.

HITLER REVIEWS a long column of German soldiers marching into Poland in the early hours of the invasion on September 1, 1939.

A GERMAN SOLDIER lobs a grenade on the front lines. Germany's blitzkrieg tactics depended on fast-moving tanks and mobilized troops to punch holes through the enemy's lines and avoid the stalemate of World War I's trench warfare.

The End of Isolation

As the German blitzkrieg swept across northern Europe in 1940, the war suddenly seemed very close and menacing to the American people. By summer, only Great Britain stood between Hitler and his total control of the continent. Some isolationists continued to insist on neutrality, but most members of Congress were finally ready to build up the nation's defenses.

1939–1945

SPRING 1940

German Conquests

In April 1940, Hitler's troops conquered Denmark, Norway, the Netherlands, Belgium, and Luxembourg. The Nazis invaded France in May, and pinned down the retreating British and French armies at the French port of Dunkirk. The new prime minister, Winston Churchill, urged the British people to help rescue the trapped men. Hundreds responded; they crossed the English Channel in fishing boats, tugboats, and yachts, and helped pluck 340,000 troops off the beaches. France surrendered to the Germans on June 22, 1940.

THE 1940 ELECTION

In the midst of Roosevelt's campaign to help the British, he faced the presidential election of 1940 against Republican Wendell Willkie. This was the first time anyone had run for a third term. Some people voted against Roosevelt for this reason, and the popular vote was fairly close. But the president won a decisive victory with an electoral vote of 449 to 82. He considered this to be a mandate for his policies toward Great Britain.

President Franklin Delano Roosevelt

JULY 1940–OCTOBER 1940

The Battle of Britain

Great Britain stood alone against the military might of Nazi Germany. Hitler boasted that his troops would be in London in three months. However, before the Germans could invade, they first had to defeat the British Royal Air Force (RAF). The bombing of British airfields began in July 1940. In October, after four months of battling the RAF in the skies over Britain, the Germans abandoned their invasion plans.

THE UNDERGROUND SHELTERED more than 170,000 Londoners during air raids. Some disused underground "tube" or subway stations were specially reopened to act as shelters; concrete floors were laid over the tracks and cots installed.

MAY 1940–MARCH 1941

American Actions

In May 1940, Congress finally voted to provide funds to build up America's military forces, and, in September, approved the nation's first peacetime draft. The same month, to help the British combat Nazi submarines, the United States traded 50 old destroyers for British naval bases in the Caribbean and Newfoundland.

President Roosevelt wanted to help the British on a more regular basis. In March 1941, Congress passed his "Lend Lease" program, in which the United States would lend weapons and supplies to the British, who would replace them after the war, since they had no ready cash to pay for them. Grateful Britons displayed American flags as a token of thanks.

Roosevelt and Churchill: The Atlantic Charter

In August 1941, Roosevelt and Churchill met on a warship off the coast of Newfoundland for talks. They agreed on the Atlantic Charter, a statement saying that the Allied nations were not interested in taking any territory, but rather in restoring peace. The Atlantic Charter included FDR's idea of the "Four Freedoms": The Allies were fighting for freedom of speech and religion, and freedom from fear and want. The Atlantic Charter, and especially the Four Freedoms, gave Americans a sense of being part of the European war.

Winston Churchill

1939-1945

WHO'S WHO IN WWII

Other nations joined one side or the other during the war, but these were the main participants. Some countries, such as Switzerland and Sweden, remained neutral throughout the war.

AXIS POWERS	ALLIED POWERS
Germany	Great Britain
Italy	France
Japan	Soviet Union
	Unites States

FIRES RAGE IN LONDON after the first mass German air raid on the city on September 7, 1940. In what became known as the blitz, Germany hoped to force a surrender by bombing major British cities. Between September 1940 and May 1941, the Germans launched 127 large-scale night raids against London and other British cities, killing 60,000 civilians.

A DEPTH CHARGE is fired from an American naval vessel patrolling the North Atlantic for German submarines.

SPRING 1941–FALL 1941

War in the North Atlantic

Hitler believed that Germany needed new land to grow and expand economically. It was one of Hitler's war goals to take this land—which the Nazis called *Lebensraum*, or "room to live"—from neighboring countries, especially the Soviet Union. So, in the spring of 1941, Hitler suddenly turned on his former treaty partner, sending troops deep into Soviet territory. The bombing raids against Great Britain stopped, but the Germans intensified their submarine attacks in the Atlantic. By the autumn of 1941, FDR issued "shoot-on-sight" orders to the U.S. Navy, freeing it to fire on German naval vessels. There was no declaration of war, but America was now fully involved in the Battle of the North Atlantic.

Pearl Harbor: War!

The Roosevelt administration was worried about the Japanese. Japan had joined the Axis powers, Germany and Italy, in September 1940; all three Axis powers had agreed to declare war on America if it went to war with any of them. Fears about an invasion on the West Coast were realized in part when the Japanese attacked Pearl Harbor. As America geared up for war, fear also led the U.S. government to forcibly move thousands of Japanese-Americans into internment camps.

1939–1945

DECEMBER 7, 1941

A Unified and Determined Nation

Early on Sunday, December 7, 1941, Americans were stunned by a radio bulletin from Hawaii: At 7:55 am, Hawaii time, nearly 400 Japanese planes bombed the U.S. naval base at Pearl Harbor, near Honolulu. The surprise attack destroyed most of the nation's Pacific fleet and killed more than 2,000 people. Only the aircraft carriers, at sea for maneuvers, were spared.

The next day, President Roosevelt asked Congress for a declaration of war, calling December 7 "a date which will live in infamy."

War Jitters

American anger about the attack was mixed with anxiety. The attack raised the fear that the U.S. mainland was no longer protected by the oceans. German submarines were operating close to the Atlantic coast. U-boats sank more than 100 Allied cargo ships every month in early 1942, often within sight of American coastal communities. The greatest danger of air attack was thought to be on the West Coast. Daily air-raid drills and nighttime blackouts quickly became routine across the country.

AIR RAID PRECAUTIONS
KEEP COOL
DON'T SCREAM
DON'T RUN
PREVENT DISORDER
OBEY ALL INSTRUCTIONS

A POSTER tells citizens what to do in the event of an air raid on the United States.

HOW MUCH DID THE U.S. GOVERNMENT KNOW?

Some critics argued that President Roosevelt knew of the coming attack on Pearl Harbor but allowed it to happen because it would force America into the war. However, nearly all historians reject this theory. U.S. code experts had broken Japan's secret code and had read several messages about a planned attack on the United States, but Pearl Harbor did not seem to be a likely target. It is also clear, however, that American officers at all the Pacific bases, including Pearl Harbor, missed numerous warning signals.

THE JAPANESE ATTACK on Pearl Harbor devastated the U.S. naval base located there. Ten days after the attack, the flames still burned at the naval air station, which lost 177 planes. Nineteen ships were destroyed, and 2,403 sailors were killed.

THESE JAPANESE-AMERICANS were brought to the Santa Anita racetrack in California, where they lived before being moved inland to relocation camps.

Mobilizing for War

In the first few months after Pearl Harbor, FDR's goals were straightforward but enormous in scale: develop with America's new allies a military strategy to defeat the Axis powers, and focus U.S. industrial might on producing the goods needed to wage war. This war would be fought not only on the battlefields of Europe but also on factory floors throughout the nation.

The Long Road Ahead

Two weeks after Pearl Harbor, British prime minister Winston Churchill arrived in Washington for planning sessions with FDR—a partnership that continued until Roosevelt's death in April 1945. They produced the Declaration of the United Nations, signed on January 1, 1942, to present a united front against the Axis powers. More than 40 nations signed the declaration—the basis for the United Nations Organization formed at the end of the war.

Striking Back

FDR and Churchill also decided on military priorities. The two leaders agreed to keep Japan at bay while concentrating on defeating Hitler. They knew that eventually they would land an invasion force in Europe. This would relieve pressure on the Soviet Union, but more importantly it would force the Nazis to fight on two fronts—against the Russians in the east and against the Americans and British in the west.

WOMEN IN THE MILITARY

About 300,000 women served in the military during World War II. There were many organizations in which women could work such noncombat jobs as radio operators, clerks, and truck drivers. For instance, the WAFS flew new aircraft from factories to bases and towed targets for gunnery practice.

Nancy Harkness Love, founder of the WAFS

Army: WAAC (Women's Auxiliary Army Corps)
Navy: WAVES (Women Appointed for Voluntary Emergency Service)
Air Corps: WAFS (Women's Auxiliary Ferrying Squadron)
Coast Guard: Women's Reserves
Marine Corps: Women Marines

WOMEN, SUCH AS THESE MACHINISTS, entered the work force in great numbers to replace the 16 million men who joined the armed services. Women worked in factories making bombs, airplanes, ships, and tanks—playing a crucial role in the war effort.

THE MIRACLE OF PRODUCTION

The enormous output of American industries between 1941 and 1945 became known as a "miracle of production." The military equipment produced included:

87,620 warships
102,351 tanks and self-propelled guns
296,429 airplanes
372,431 artillery pieces
2.4 million military trucks
44 billion rounds of small-arms ammunition

Making the Tools for War

The U.S. government moved with amazing speed to convert industries to war production. Automobile companies turned to making tanks, landing craft, and airplanes. A manufacturer of model trains produced bomb fuses; a merry-go-round company made revolving gun mounts; and, somehow, the leading manufacturer of facial tissues retooled to make .50-caliber machine guns.

Within two years of the Pearl Harbor attack, American industries were outproducing Germany, Japan, and Italy combined. U.S. aircraft companies, for example, had produced 6,000 planes in 1939. By 1944, they were turning out 8,000 planes every month. The extraordinary commitment of American industry to the war effort was a sign of the nation's resolve. American troops would confront the Axis powers overseas; at home, American workers would produce the goods needed to win the war.

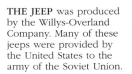

THE JEEP was produced by the Willys-Overland Company. Many of these jeeps were provided by the United States to the army of the Soviet Union.

Worldwide War

At the beginning of 1942, the war news seemed to get worse each day, with the Axis powers threatening the Allies all over the world. The Germans had plunged deep into the Soviet Union and now threatened Moscow; in North Africa, German and Italian tank divisions pushed the British back toward Egypt; and in Asia and the Pacific, the Japanese were overpowering Allied defenses. This widening global war would eventually involve nearly 70 nations in total.

1939–1945

EUROPEAN RESISTANCE

In every European nation conquered by Hitler's armies, small groups worked in secret to resist the Nazi occupation. These resistance fighters engaged in sabotage, such as ambushing truck convoys and blowing up bridges. Nazi reprisals were vicious; civilians were often killed for hiding resistance fighters. Each occupied country also had small military forces, such as the Free French and Free Dutch, made up of people who had escaped the occupation to fight with the Allies.

Free French resistance armband

WINTER 1942–SUMMER 1943

Turning the Tide in Europe

In February 1942, while the Russians were fighting desperately to avoid conquest by the Germans, the Allies began bombing raids over German industrial centers and cities. They also landed troops on the Italian island of Sicily in July 1943 to try and establish a second front in Europe. In the fall, the Allies invaded mainland Italy. When Mussolini's own government overthrew him and asked for peace, Hitler's forces took over the defense of Italy and slowed the advance of the Allies.

AN AMERICAN SOLDIER STANDS GUARD over Nazi soldiers captured in Germany.

Field Marshal Erwin Rommel

FALL 1942–SPRING 1943

The Battle for North Africa

A new kind of warfare involving hundreds of tanks was waged in North Africa. The German Africa Corps, led by Field Marshal Erwin Rommel—called the Desert Fox—nearly conquered all of North Africa. On November 8, 1942, British Field Marshal Bernard Montgomery launched Operation Torch, aided by 500 American tanks. A large invasion force, led by American General Dwight D. Eisenhower, landed in Algeria. In May 1943, the Axis forces in North Africa surrendered. The Allied victory was a devastating loss for Hitler and gave the Allies a place to prepare to invade Italy. At that point, the Nazis would be fighting Allied forces on two fronts—in Russia to the east and Italy to the west.

SUMMER 1942–SPRING 1943

The Heroic Russians

In the summer of 1942, a year after invading the Soviet Union, Germany launched a dramatic offensive and nearly took over the city of Stalingrad. But the Russian forces dug in, and their defense of Stalingrad became a symbol of their determination and strength. In the winter of 1942–1943, the Russians launched a massive counterattack, forcing an entire German army to surrender in February. For the next two years, the Russians drove relentlessly to the west, slowly regaining lands from German occupation.

THE ORDER OF THE RED STAR was awarded to Soviet soldiers and sailors for outstanding service in defense of the Soviet Union.

ASIA

• Stalingrad

JAPAN

Midway Island

PACIFIC OCEAN

Wake Island

Hawaii

Bataan Peninsula

Corregidor Island

PHILIPPINES

Guam

INDIAN OCEAN

MAY 4–7, JUNE 6, 1942

Coral Sea and Midway

Over May 4–7, 1942, American warplanes launched from carriers in the Coral Sea devastated a Japanese invasion fleet headed toward New Guinea, forcing Japan to cancel the invasion. A month later, American planes met a larger Japanese fleet at Midway Island and destroyed four of Japan's five aircraft carriers. The battles of Coral Sea and Midway changed the Pacific War—the Japanese were now on the defensive. And the American people finally had something to cheer about.

NEW GUINEA

WINTER–SPRING 1943

The Pacific War

Days after the Pearl Harbor attack, Japanese forces overran the American bases on Wake Island and Guam, and then invaded the Philippines. The American troops, commanded by General Douglas MacArthur, were forced to retreat with their Filipino allies to the Bataan Peninsula, where they held out for three months. When the island of Corregidor fell in May 1942, the survivors were sent on what became known as the Bataan Death March. Hundreds of Americans died on the 70-mile march to Japanese prison camps.

CORAL SEA

AUSTRALIA

A PLANE TAKES OFF from an aircraft-carrier flight deck in the Pacific Ocean.

Victory at Home

The American people responded to the war with a strong sense of unity and purpose. They knew that their cause was just—helping liberate people from the iron rule of totalitarian dictatorship. Despite some shameful incidents of racial prejudice, America's war effort was an extraordinary achievement.

A Total Commitment

In his speech declaring war, President Roosevelt said, "Every man, woman, and child is a partner." Americans rapidly learned how much sacrifice and effort was required. A total of 15 million men and women—more than one out of every ten Americans—served in the military. Most other sacrifices were primarily material. People learned to do without major items such as new cars and refrigerators, plus dozens of little everyday items, such as toothpaste tubes, dish soap, safety pins, and coat hangers.

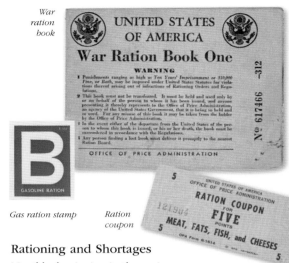

War ration book

UNITED STATES OF AMERICA
War Ration Book One
WARNING

N° 617466 -312

OFFICE OF PRICE ADMINISTRATION

B GASOLINE RATION

Gas ration stamp

UNITED STATES OF AMERICA
OFFICE OF PRICE ADMINISTRATION
RATION COUPON FOR
FIVE POINTS
5 MEAT, FATS, FISH, and CHEESES 5
121904
OPA Form R-1614

Ration coupon

Rationing and Shortages

Monthly, beginning in the spring of 1942, Americans received books of ration stamps for such items as meat, coffee, and gasoline. The rationing system helped keep prices from soaring and also achieved a fair distribution of scarce items. Even with rationing, shortages still occurred.

FACTORY WORKERS finish the transparent noses of A-20 attack bombers at a California aircraft plant.

"JUNK WILL WIN THE WAR"

Bing Crosby's song, "Junk Will Win the War," was an exaggeration of the fact that scrap materials were vital to the war effort. In June 1942, after Japan had cut off 90 percent of America's rubber supply, President Roosevelt made an emergency plea for scrap rubber. In just four weeks, Americans responded by collecting 450,000 tons of rubber to help fill the gap until synthetic rubber could be developed.

Scrap collection became a regular part of every family's routine. People flattened tin cans, bundled newspapers, and collected kitchen oils, which were used to make explosives.

New Roles for Women

In the first six months after Pearl Harbor, 750,000 women applied for jobs in defense plants, but only 80,000 were hired. Factory managers said that women couldn't operate machines, but the shortage of male workers forced them to rethink their views. Over the next two years, six million women were added to the work force.

Women also volunteered in large numbers for the Office of Civilian Defense (OCD), which provided air-raid wardens and ambulance drivers as well as many other services. Others joined the Red Cross and more than one million volunteered at United Service Organizations (USO) canteens, where servicemen came for entertainment and company.

ROSIE THE RIVETER, from a painting by Norman Rockwell, became a favorite wartime symbol of women ably taking over men's jobs.

1939–1945

The Struggle Against Prejudice

African Americans, many of whom moved north during the war years to work in factories, made greater progress toward equality during this period than at any time since post–Civil War Reconstruction (see pp. 88–89). African American employment in government increased from 40,000 to 300,000, and in industry from 500,000 to more than 1.2 million. While nearly 500,000 African Americans joined the armed services, their service was restricted, and facilities remained segregated until 1944.

Fair Employment for African Americans

In 1941, FDR issued Executive Order 8802 forbidding racial discrimination in defense hiring, and established the Fair Employment Practices Commission (FEPC). The FEPC represented the first time the government had actively promoted racial equality in more than 75 years.

SEGREGATED DRINKING FOUNTAINS (see p. 212) were just one of the countless ways that African Americans were affected by discrimination in everyday life. Racial equality was still a long way off.

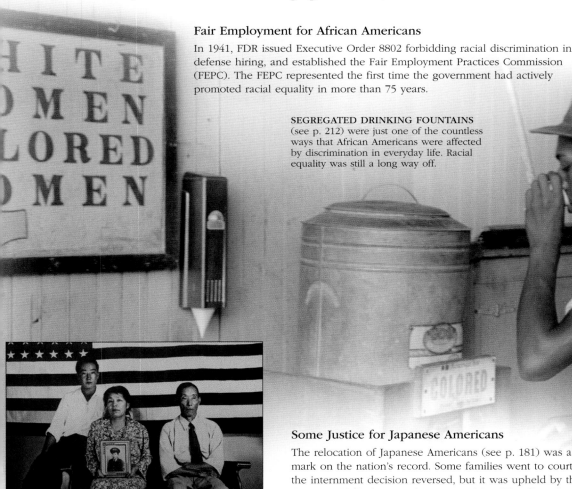

THE FAMILY OF A *NISEI* SOLDIER sits out the war at a relocation camp. About 25,000 Japanese Americans entered the army, most serving in segregated units.

Some Justice for Japanese Americans

The relocation of Japanese Americans (see p. 181) was a black mark on the nation's record. Some families went to court to have the internment decision reversed, but it was upheld by the Supreme Court. In 1943, the army began recruiting *Nisei* (American-born Japanese Americans) to serve in segregated military units. The *Nisei* 442nd Regimental Combat Team, fighting in Italy, earned more military decorations than any unit in America's history.

187

D-Day

By the spring of 1944, the countryside of Great Britain had been transformed into a gigantic armed camp and supply depot. The Allies were now prepared for Operation Overlord. Allied troops would cross the English Channel and invade occupied France. This would force Hitler to fight a two-front war, since the Russian Allied force was keeping most of the German army busy in eastern Europe. Over the previous year, the Americans and British had gained the upper hand over German U-boats in the Atlantic, and their planes had destroyed much of Hitler's air force. Now the Allies faced their greatest challenge—cracking Hitler's land defenses in Europe.

GENERAL DWIGHT D. EISENHOWER, Supreme Commander of the Allied forces in Europe, talks to a few of the three million men under his command, just before D-day.

SPRING 1944

Operation Overlord

Operation Overlord required incredibly detailed planning, as well as perfect coordination and timing. The final decisions were made by American general Dwight D. Eisenhower, nicknamed "Ike." He was the Supreme Commander of the Allied Expeditionary Force (AEF). Weather was Ike's biggest headache. There were only a few days each month when the tides were right for the invasion, and, as June approached, storms howled out of the North Sea and into the English Channel.

Secrecy was also vital. Hitler's forces had built a wall of concrete bunkers and gun emplacements along the French coast, and had lain tank traps, mines, and miles of barbed wire. Through a variety of deceptions, the Allies convinced Hitler that the landing target was not Normandy, but farther north where the Channel narrowed.

JUNE 6, 1944

"The Longest Day"

The invasion began just after midnight, June 6, when weather forecasters told Eisenhower there would be a break in the storms. First, paratroopers and glider troops landed in the dark behind enemy lines to disrupt communications. Next, bombers and warships pounded the coastline with explosives. As dawn broke, the English Channel filled with ships and landing craft. Overhead, American and British planes outnumbered the Germans 30 to 1 and provided covering fire.

Even so, the 176,000 troops who hit the beaches of Normandy met ferocious resistance and suffered tremendous losses. Finally, they established a beachhead, a secure area on the coast that would allow the Allies to safely bring in more troops and supplies. The soldiers called it "the longest day."

THIS IS A PATCH of the United States Strategic Air Forces in Europe (USSTAF). The USSTAF fought the Luftwaffe (the German air force) during Operation Overlord.

AMERICAN TROOPS wade ashore from the Coast Guard landing station on D-day. 2,500 American, British, and Canadian troops were killed during the invasion of Omaha Beach in Normandy.

1939–1945

Victory in Europe

Once the Allies landed in France, they moved swiftly to liberate western Europe from Nazi rule. At the same time, Soviet troops were racing westward, forcing their way into Poland and the countries of eastern Europe. In April of 1945, the Russians entered Berlin and Germany surrendered soon after, bringing an Allied victory in Europe.

1939–1945

JUNE 1944–MAY 1945

The Destruction of Nazi Germany

In the weeks following D-day, soldiers, supplies, and equipment were brought ashore. The Allies liberated Paris on August 25, then Brussels, Antwerp, and Luxembourg. The Nazis were on the run, and with Russian troops pushing from the east, it seemed only a matter of time before Allied troops were inside Germany. However, in December 1944, a powerful Nazi counterattack in the Ardennes, a forest region in Belgium, punched a bulge 50 miles deep into the Allied line, trapping the 101st Airborne Division, among many others. Reinforcements arrived in time to free the half-frozen, half-starved men, but the Battle of the Bulge was costly, claiming about 77,000 Allied casualties.

MAY 8, 1945

German Surrender and V-E Day

Russian troops entered Berlin on April 23, 1945. On May 1, the German government reported that Hitler had committed suicide. German troops in Italy, the Netherlands, Denmark, and Austria laid down their arms. On May 8, 1945—Victory in Europe Day— Eisenhower accepted Germany's unconditional surrender, marking the end of the war in Europe.

THE SECOND LONDON "BLITZ"

War-weary London was stunned in the summer of 1944 by a new round of air raids. First, in June, the city was hit by small, unmanned aircraft, called V-1s, which flew noisily overhead until the motor suddenly stopped and the craft plummeted to earth as a bomb. Even more dangerous was the V-2, a rocket that soared across the English Channel at 3,600 miles per hour, making interception impossible. Many Germans thought the V-2, first launched in September 1944, was the secret weapon Hitler was said to be holding in reserve. The Allies soon captured the launch sites and the danger was over.

The V-2 rocket

V-E DAY was celebrated in New York City with ticker-tape streamers on Wall Street. The day after Germany surrendered, people poured into the streets and celebrated across America and in liberated European cities. But with Japan still fighting, the war was not yet over.

LIBERATING HITLER'S DEATH CAMPS

In early 1945, as the Allied troops drove the German army out of occupied Europe, they came across what they thought were labor camps. But inside the camp gates they found emaciated bodies stacked in great piles, rows of ovens stuffed with bodies, and a few gaunt survivors. Allied troops had discovered nearly 20 German death camps, including Auschwitz in Poland, and Dachau and Buchenwald in Germany. The world would finally see the evidence of Hitler's scheme to exterminate six million Jews, plus five million other "undesirables"—including Gypsies, Catholics, Lutherans, Slavs, gays and lesbians, and the handicapped.

Oven at Buchenwald *Holocaust survivors*

The Yalta Conference

In February 1945, the "Big Three" Allied leaders—Roosevelt, Churchill, and Stalin—met at Yalta on the Black Sea. There they agreed that, when the war in Europe was over, Germany would be divided into four occupation zones, to be controlled by American, British, French, and Soviet forces. They also made plans for a United Nations organization, as a successor to the failed League of Nations, this time with the United States as a founding member. Stalin was promised pieces of Japan's empire in exchange for Soviet help against Japan after Germany's surrender.

Unlike the Treaty of Versailles (see p. 145), which punished Germany harshly after World War I, this agreement emphasized rebuilding postwar Europe.

Churchill   *Roosevelt*   *Stalin*

Closing in on Japan

From late 1942 to early 1945, U.S. troops had moved through the Central Pacific, destroying Japan's military strongholds. Roosevelt's death in April 1945 left his successor, Harry S. Truman, with a difficult decision: invade Japan, or use a top-secret new weapon of devastating power—the atomic bomb. The "A-bomb" destruction of Hiroshima and Nagasaki forced Japan to surrender and brought an end to World War II.

1939–1945

FALL 1942–SPRING 1945

Sweeping Through the Pacific

Throughout 1943 and 1944, the Allies advanced from island to island. By the summer of 1945, U.S. forces had captured three important Japanese island bases—Guadalcanal, Iwo Jima, and Okinawa—at great cost to both sides. In October 1944, the MacArthur and Nimitz forces landed in the Philippines. At the Battle of Leyte Gulf—the largest naval battle in history—the Japanese lost most of their remaining ships. Five months later on March 7, the Allies liberated Manila, the capital of the Philippines, from the Japanese. The casualties suffered by both sides in the Pacific campaign were enormous.

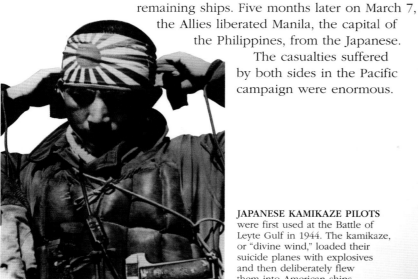

JAPANESE KAMIKAZE PILOTS were first used at the Battle of Leyte Gulf in 1944. The kamikaze, or "divine wind," loaded their suicide planes with explosives and then deliberately flew them into American ships.

AUGUST 1942–FEBRUARY 1943

The Lesson of Guadalcanal

In August 1942, U.S. Marines landed on the island of Guadalcanal and were introduced to a new kind of warfare—steamy jungle, malarial swamps with poisonous snakes, and an enemy that refused to surrender. The battle dragged on for seven months before the Japanese finally evacuated in February 1943. This long struggle over one island led American commanders to an important decision. Instead of invading every island, they adopted a strategy they called "island-hopping" or "leapfrogging." They would invade certain key outposts but bypass others, which American warplanes would then isolate from the Japanese and prevent from being resupplied or evacuated.

THE MUSHROOM CLOUD created by the atomic-bomb blast at Hiroshima

The Atomic Bomb

In July 1945, at a meeting of the Allied leaders in Potsdam, Germany, President Truman received word that the world's first atomic bomb had been tested in the New Mexico desert. The bomb was the result of the top-secret Manhattan Project, started by Roosevelt in 1942 after learning that German scientists were working on such a bomb.

Truman faced one of history's most difficult decisions: to invade Japan, the Allies would need Soviet help, but Truman did not trust the Soviet Union. Additionally, America's victories in the Pacific had involved so many casualties that U.S. military leaders were concerned about the loss of life that would come with a full-scale invasion. If America used this terrifying new weapon, it might force Japan to surrender without an invasion. However, it would mean a tremendous loss of life and property for the Japanese. With Great Britain's support, Truman decided to use the bomb.

AUGUST–SEPTEMBER 1945

The Japanese Surrender

On August 6, 1945, the first atomic bomb was dropped on the Japanese city of Hiroshima by the *Enola Gay*, a B-29 bomber. A four-square-mile area of the city was destroyed, killing 80,000 people. The Japanese military leaders refused to surrender. On August 8, the Soviet Union declared war on Japan. On August 9, the United States dropped a second bomb on Nagasaki, killing 35,000. The Japanese finally surrendered. August 15 was V-J day—Victory over Japan— and World War II was over.

SEPTEMBER 1945

"The Guns Are Silent"

With those words, General MacArthur announced the Japanese signing of the surrender on the deck of the battleship USS *Missouri*. MacArthur added, "A great tragedy has ended." America had almost 400,000 war dead. Across the world, 55 million people had been killed, including civilian casualties. Millions were left homeless, some in relief camps, others wandering aimlessly through the bombed-out ruins of cities. Rebuilding in Europe and Japan would take years.

GENERAL MACARTHUR signs the instrument of Japanese surrender aboard the USS *Missouri*.

IMPRISONED ALLIED TROOPS celebrate liberation from a Japanese prison camp.

IN THE 1950S, MANY AMERICAN FAMILIES worked toward a middle-class dream of a house in the suburbs and their own car. World War II had just ended, but the United States was again involved in international conflicts—in Russia, Korea, Vietnam, and at home, in a campaign to rid the world of Communism.

Nov. 1948
Harry S. Truman elected president

Apr. 25, 1945
United Nations Organization established

May 14, 1948
Israel created

Apr. 4, 1949
NATO formed

Feb. 1950
McCarthy hearings begin

Oct. 1951
I Love Lucy premieres

1945	1946	1947	1948	1949	1950	1951	1952

Mar. 1945
Vietnam claims independence from France

1948
First Arab-Israeli War; Marshall Plan begins

June 1948
Berlin Airlift begins

Oct. 1949
People's Republic of China established

June 1950
North Korea invades South Korea, sparking the Korean War

Apr. 11, 1951
General Douglas MacArthur dismissed from duty by President Truman

COLD WAR ANXIETY

1945–1960

As World War II ended, Americans were happy to return to peacetime routines. Most people thrived in the postwar economy of the world's wealthiest nation. This time, America did not turn its back on the world as it had done in the 1920s. The U.S. provided massive relief to war-ravaged countries and helped create the United Nations.

However, by the late 1950s, the Cold War pitted the Communist bloc countries against the "Free World"— America and its allies. This Cold War was an ideological conflict, not a traditional military fight, although Americans and others lived with the constant threat of military action or nuclear war, and fear caused some people to search for scapegoats. However, the gnawing anxiety of the Cold War did not prevent Americans from enjoying the greatest period of prosperity in their history.

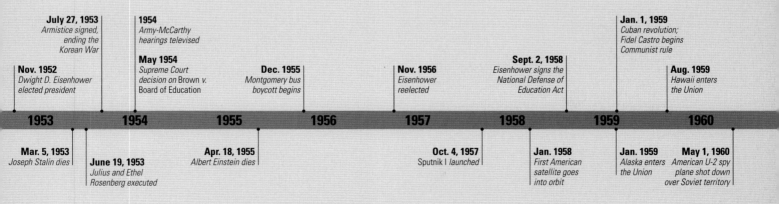

July 27, 1953
Armistice signed, ending the Korean War

1954
Army-McCarthy hearings televised

Jan. 1, 1959
Cuban revolution; Fidel Castro begins Communist rule

Nov. 1952
Dwight D. Eisenhower elected president

May 1954
Supreme Court decision on Brown v. Board of Education

Dec. 1955
Montgomery bus boycott begins

Nov. 1956
Eisenhower reelected

Sept. 2, 1958
Eisenhower signs the National Defense of Education Act

Aug. 1959
Hawaii enters the Union

1953	1954	1955	1956	1957	1958	1959	1960

Mar. 5, 1953
Joseph Stalin dies

June 19, 1953
Julius and Ethel Rosenberg executed

Apr. 18, 1955
Albert Einstein dies

Oct. 4, 1957
Sputnik I launched

Jan. 1958
First American satellite goes into orbit

Jan. 1959
Alaska enters the Union

May 1, 1960
American U-2 spy plane shot down over Soviet territory

Aftermath of the War

In 1945, Americans were keen to put World War II behind them and get on with their lives. The United States helped to rebuild war-torn Europe and Asia, actively participated in the founding of the United Nations, and played a leading role in bringing fugitive Nazi leaders to justice. The devastation of the Holocaust and sympathy for Jewish refugees from Hitler's murderous regime deeply influenced the shape of the postwar world, leading in 1948 to the creation of a homeland for the Jews—the state of Israel.

ELEANOR ROOSEVELT, 1884–1962

Eleanor Roosevelt, in addition to being FDR's eyes and ears, also worked for equal rights for African Americans and other minorities. After President Roosevelt's death in 1945, she spent many years working as a member of the U.S. delegation to the United Nations. As chairman of its Human Rights Commission, she spent months debating the Russian delegation over the wording of a UN Declaration of Human Rights. She is credited with producing a document that both Americans and Russians would accept.

Building Peace

To help the devastated areas of Europe and Asia, America became the major supporter of the United Nations Relief and Rehabilitation Administration (UNRRA), established in 1943, before the United Nations itself. The UNRRA provided shelter for millions of people displaced by the war, and delivered 22 million tons of supplies and tools to rebuild farms, villages, and cities.

REFLECTING THE SPIRIT OF THE TIMES, this painting commemorating the founding of the United Nations is titled "U.N.O.—The Hope of the World."

The United Nations

President Roosevelt believed that once the Axis powers were defeated, world peace could only be guaranteed if the Allies created a new international organization to replace the League of Nations. A joint statement issued by the United States and the Allies on November 1, 1943, recognized the "necessity of establishing … a general international organization" dedicated to "international peace and security." Two weeks after FDR's death in April 1945, the United Nations Organization was founded. A conference of 800 delegates from 50 nations met in San Francisco and produced the Charter of the United Nations, which was approved by the U.S. Senate 89 to 2.

Jewish Refugees and American Attitudes

As World War II ended, Americans showed little interest in opening the nation's doors to Holocaust survivors. This attitude changed as people learned more about death-camp atrocities. The testimony of survivors at the Nuremberg Trials contributed to a wave of sympathy for Europe's Jews. In addition, newsreels showed courageous bands of Jews overcoming all obstacles to make their way to Palestine, a state on the eastern shore of the Mediterranean Sea that is the site of the Biblical Jewish homeland (including areas sacred to Christians and Muslims as well). The determination of Jews in Palestine to build an independent nation struck a responsive chord in Americans. By 1947, when the United Nations proposed dividing Palestine into separate Jewish and Arab states, many Americans were eager for the United States to champion the new state of Israel.

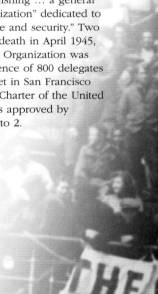

JEWISH REFUGEES arrive in Palestine on the cargo ship *Theodor Herzl* in April 1947. The banner running alongside the ship's railing says, "The Germans destroyed our families and homes—don't you destroy our hopes."

ISRAEL'S FIRST LEADERS, David Ben-Gurion (left) and Chaim Weizmann (right), review Israeli army units during a parade in July 1949.

The State of Israel

During World War I, Great Britain took control of Palestine from Turkey, which was fighting with Germany against the British. At the end of the war, the League of Nations assigned the governing of Palestine to Great Britain, but also entrusted to the British the establishment within Palestine of "a national home for the Jewish people." Both Arabs and Jews lived in this largely desert land, and neither group was willing to form a government with the other.

During Hitler's dictatorship, thousands of European Jews fled to Palestine. In 1947, the UN proposed that separate Arab and Jewish states be created out of Palestine. The Jews living in Palestine immediately accepted and announced the formation of the state of Israel on May 14, 1948.

The First Arab-Israeli War

Palestinian Arabs rejected the UN decision and declared war on Israel. Several Arab nations sent troops to destroy Israel, but the Israelis held their own. During the conflict, more than 500,000 Palestinian Arabs fled to neighboring Arab countries. The UN negotiated a truce in July 1949, but the Arab countries still refused to recognize Israel.

THE ARAB ARMIES of Egypt, Syria, Transjordan, Lebanon, and Iraq invaded the new state of Israel shortly after it announced its formation. Here, Arab soldiers shell Jewish positions in June 1948.

THE WAR CRIMES TRIALS

In 1945 and 1946, 22 top Nazi leaders were tried by an international court in Nuremberg, Germany. They were charged with "crimes against humanity" committed during the Holocaust. The testimony of concentration-camp survivors left the world with unforgettable images of Nazi brutality. The trials ended in 19 convictions, including 12 death sentences.

HERMANN GOERING, Hitler's right-hand man, stands on trial at Nuremberg. Goering was convicted and sentenced to death, but he committed suicide on the night before his execution by swallowing a capsule of cyanide, a powerful poison.

The Cold War Heats Up

During World War II, most Americans thought of the Soviet Union as a close ally. Few people worried about Communism, which had not been seen as a threat in this country since the "Red scare" of 1920 (see p. 148). Wartime political cartoons depicted Joseph Stalin, the Soviet dictator, as a jovial Russian bear, or as kindly "Uncle Joe." Beginning in 1946, Americans experienced a series of shocks as the Russians sought to exert control over nations in Europe and Asia. The United States was now involved in a strange new conflict called the Cold War.

The Soviet "Iron Curtain"

In 1945, Soviet troops remained in the nations they had liberated from the Germans. Stalin ignored American demands for free elections in those countries and, by 1948, Communist governments were established throughout Eastern Europe—in Poland, Czechoslovakia, Hungary, Romania, and Bulgaria.

In 1946, British prime minister Winston Churchill helped awaken many Americans to the danger posed by the Soviet Union. Churchill warned that an "Iron Curtain" had descended across Europe; behind that curtain, basic freedoms and free elections had disappeared, and all opposition to Communist rule was being crushed.

JOSEPH STALIN ruled as dictator of the Soviet Union from 1924 until his death in 1953. He maintained his grip on power by murdering his political opponents and repressing any segments of the population that he considered disloyal.

NATO

On April 4, 1949, the United States joined 11 other nations—primarily western European nations such as Great Britain and France, plus Canada—to form the North Atlantic Treaty Organization (NATO). The NATO members agreed that an attack on one would be considered an attack against all. They also agreed to form a military force, with headquarters in Paris and General Dwight Eisenhower as Supreme Commander.

A POSTAGE STAMP commemorating the establishment of NATO shows North America and Europe united.

The Truman Doctrine

Late in 1946, the Soviet Union began demanding land from Turkey, and also encouraged Greece's Communist neighbors—Albania, Bulgaria, and Yugoslavia—to overthrow the Greek monarchy. President Truman responded with a policy of containment—that is, containing Communism where it already existed, so it would not spread further. The president said, "I believe it must be the policy of the United States to support free peoples who are resisting attempted subjugation by armed minorities or by outside pressures." This policy would be the basis for the United States getting involved later in Korea and in Vietnam (see pp. 200–201, 226–229).

The Marshall Plan

In June 1947, General George C. Marshall, Truman's secretary of state, proposed a huge war-recovery program of money, food, clothing, and machinery to help Europe overcome "hunger, poverty, desperation, and chaos." Marshall invited all of Europe to participate, but the Soviet-bloc countries refused, calling it an American scheme to take over Europe.

With 16 nations participating, the Marshall Plan was a great success. Between 1948 and 1952, U.S. aid amounting to $13 billion helped to rebuild cities, factories, roads, and railroads throughout Europe.

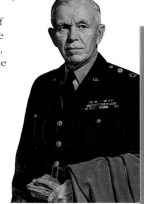

General George C. Marshall

SOME NEWSPAPERS were so sure that Dewey would win the election that they printed the next day's papers before the final election results were in.

The 1948 Election

By the time the Democratic and Republican Conventions nominated their presidential candidates, the news media and the polls were sure that Republican Governor Thomas E. Dewey of New York would win a landslide victory over President Truman. Truman responded by campaigning hard, traveling 22,000 miles by train, and delivering up to ten speeches a day. In one of the most surprising elections in history, Truman won a solid victory, with 303 electoral votes to Dewey's 189.

The Berlin Airlift

Soviet dictator Stalin was infuriated when the United States, Britain, and France announced plans to unify their postwar occupation zones in Germany and establish a democratic government for West Germany. In June 1948, the Russians closed all roads, railroads, and canals into West Berlin, which was 110 miles inside Soviet-controlled East Germany.

The Americans and British responded with the Berlin airlift. For more than a year, planes flew in every three minutes, bringing food, medicine, clothing, and heating fuel to the 2.5 million people trapped in the western sectors of Berlin. In May 1949, the Soviets gave up and lifted the blockade. A year later, the West German Federal Republic was formed. In turn, the Soviets created the East German Democratic Republic, with East Berlin as the capital. This division of Germany would last more than 40 years (see p. 246). In 1961, the East German government built the Berlin Wall as a physical barrier between East and West Berlin, to stop citizens from fleeing to West Berlin.

THE BERLIN AIRLIFT delivered more than two million tons of goods to West Berliners in about 275,000 emergency flights.

The Korean War

From the late 1940s through the 1950s, new Cold War trouble spots were often in places Americans didn't know much about. A civil war in China led to a Communist takeover of that country—the most populous in the world. Communist North Korea invaded South Korea. Many of the U.S. soldiers who shipped out to help defend South Korea did not know where it was. They would fight for almost three years to preserve South Korea's independence and stop Communist expansion.

MAO ZEDONG, leader of China's Communists, addresses followers in 1944. Mao led the Chinese Communist Party from 1935 until his death in 1976.

Communist Victory in China

China's Nationalist government, led by Chiang Kai-shek, had been fighting a Communist force led by Mao Zedong since the late 1920s. The Communists and Nationalists formed an uneasy truce to fight the Japanese in World War II, but by 1945 the truce had failed and the United States was spending huge sums to help Chiang's government—a government thought by the Chinese people themselves to be corrupt. In 1949, the Communists won control of China and forced the Nationalists to flee to the island of Formosa, which was renamed Taiwan.

THE DIVISION OF KOREA

During World War II, Japan controlled Korea. At the end of the war, the Russians accepted Japan's surrender in Korea north of the 38th parallel, and the Americans accepted it south of that line. This agreement avoided a conflict over which superpower would control the country. Then, the Soviet Union would not allow a national election, so Korea became divided into two countries—the Communist Democratic Republic of Korea, or North Korea; and the Republic of Korea, or South Korea, which was supported by the U.S. and United Nations forces.

KOREA IN 1950

- NORTH KOREA
- SOUTH KOREA
- CHINA
- JAPAN
- USSR

A No-War in Korea

On June 25, 1950, Communist North Korean troops stormed over the 38th-parallel border into South Korea. The South Korean troops fled south, and President Truman ordered General Douglas MacArthur to support South Korea with U.S. forces (see p. 199). By August, General MacArthur's troops—a UN force of 16 nations, but primarily Americans and Koreans—pushed the North Koreans above the 38th parallel. By November, they controlled most of North Korea and were close to the Yalu River on the Chinese border.

Then, on November 26, 1950, thousands of Chinese Communist troops swarmed across the Yalu, forcing the UN troops to retreat. President Truman realized that the war would have to be fought against China—and that the Soviets might intervene to help China. Because of this, the American and UN goal became not victory, but stalemate—and a lasting truce.

Truman and MacArthur Disagree on Strategy

By early 1951, the UN troops had regained ground and were again close to the 38th parallel. Truman decided the time had come to try for a cease-fire. General MacArthur refused to cooperate. He believed the United States should use atomic bombs on China, and then have Chiang Kai-shek's Nationalists invade the Chinese mainland—or, at the least, the U.S. forces should bomb Chinese troops north of the Yalu. Truman thought these ideas were too radical, and as commander-in-chief, he did not want MacArthur to stay in charge. On April 11, 1951, Truman dismissed MacArthur.

An Election and a Truce

Truman chose not to run for reelection. The Republican candidate for president in 1952, Dwight Eisenhower, promised to go to Korea if elected, and seek peace. "Ike," as Eisenhower was called, was a popular war hero, and he easily defeated Democrat Adlai Stevenson, governor of Illinois. After months of negotiation, an armistice was finally signed on July 27, 1953. This ended the war in Korea.

The Korean peninsula was again divided, with the 38th parallel as the border. Fifty-four thousand Americans had been killed and 100,000 wounded. The Cold War goal had been achieved, however—preventing Communist expansion while avoiding World War III.

PRESIDENT TRUMAN AND GENERAL MACARTHUR talk on Wake Island in the Pacific. On October 13, 1950, Truman flew 7,500 miles to Wake Island to meet with MacArthur and award him the Distinguished Service Medal. Truman praised MacArthur's "vision, judgment, indomitable will, gallantry, and tenacity." Six months later, Truman fired MacArthur.

THE KOREAN WAR MEMORIAL in Washington, D.C., was completed in 1995. The 19 soldiers, representing a unit on patrol, head uphill toward the Pool of Remembrance, where an inscription reads: "Our nation honors her sons and daughters who answered the call to defend a country they never knew and a people they never met."

New Cold War Anxieties

More and more countries around the world were being led by Communist governments during the 1950s, and this made Americans anxious. The Communist system was seen as the opposite of the American political system and most Americans' values concerning freedom and liberty. All over the globe the United States appeared to be in increasing conflict with the Soviet Union and China.

Vietnam

At the end of World War II, much of Vietnam was still the French colony it had been since 1867. But in 1945, the Viet Minh, a Vietnamese nationalist coalition, declared Vietnam to be an independent nation, free of French control. After a decade of warfare, the Viet Minh, led by the Communist Ho Chi Minh (and supported by China), defeated the French—with America paying 80 percent of France's expenses. In July 1954, an international conference divided the country into North and South Vietnam, with the boundary at the 17th parallel. Hoping to prevent the Communist North from taking the entire country, the United States began sending financial aid to South Vietnam, and, later, military personnel to train its armed forces.

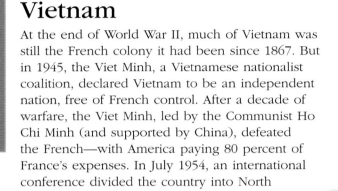

MAO ZEDONG AND NIKITA KHRUSHCHEV, the leaders of China and the Soviet Union, meet in Beijing in 1958. The two Communist countries worked closely together. That year, Soviet nuclear experts were sent to China to show Chinese scientists how to make nuclear weapons.

SPUTNIK I (a replica is shown here) beat America into space by almost four months. The first American satellite—*Explorer I*—wasn't launched until January 31, 1958.

Sputnik I

In October 1957, Americans learned that the Soviet Union had launched *Sputnik I*, the world's first earth-orbiting, man-made satellite. This Russian success convinced many Americans that the Soviet Union was winning the Cold War with more advanced scientific knowledge. One reaction was the National Defense Education Act, passed in 1958, which gave $280 million to the states for loans to college students.

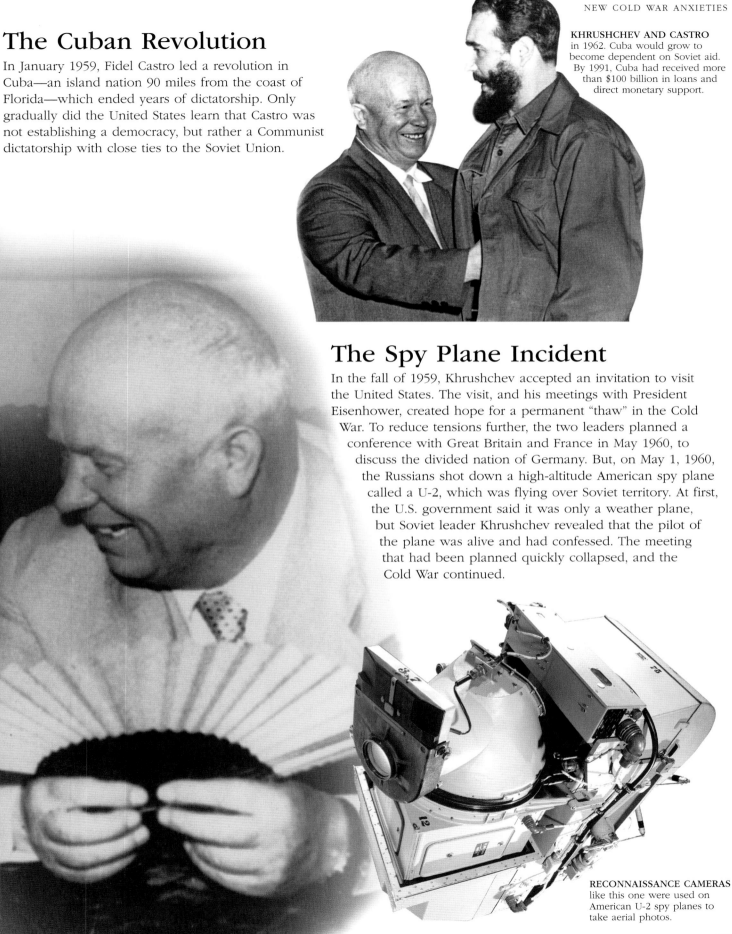

The Cuban Revolution

In January 1959, Fidel Castro led a revolution in Cuba—an island nation 90 miles from the coast of Florida—which ended years of dictatorship. Only gradually did the United States learn that Castro was not establishing a democracy, but rather a Communist dictatorship with close ties to the Soviet Union.

KHRUSHCHEV AND CASTRO in 1962. Cuba would grow to become dependent on Soviet aid. By 1991, Cuba had received more than $100 billion in loans and direct monetary support.

1945–1960

The Spy Plane Incident

In the fall of 1959, Khrushchev accepted an invitation to visit the United States. The visit, and his meetings with President Eisenhower, created hope for a permanent "thaw" in the Cold War. To reduce tensions further, the two leaders planned a conference with Great Britain and France in May 1960, to discuss the divided nation of Germany. But, on May 1, 1960, the Russians shot down a high-altitude American spy plane called a U-2, which was flying over Soviet territory. At first, the U.S. government said it was only a weather plane, but Soviet leader Khrushchev revealed that the pilot of the plane was alive and had confessed. The meeting that had been planned quickly collapsed, and the Cold War continued.

RECONNAISSANCE CAMERAS like this one were used on American U-2 spy planes to take aerial photos.

The Cold War at Home

The rapid expansion of Communism in Europe and Asia in the late 1940s led to the fear that Communist agents had infiltrated the United States. People worried that Communists were organizing labor movements to disrupt American industry, leaking vital secrets back to the Soviets, and planning to overthrow the government. Hysteria nearly took hold as government officials tried to weed the Communists out of the country before they put an end to the American way of life.

IN 1954, SENATOR RALPH E. FLANDERS (shown standing) compared fellow senator Joseph McCarthy (seated at far right next to attorney Roy Cohn) to cartoon character Dennis the Menace, describing both as "children who blunder into the most appalling situations as they ramble through the world of adults." In response, McCarthy threatened to call Flanders before his Senate committee investigating Communism to determine what he knew about "the [Red] Menace."

FBI DIRECTOR J. Edgar Hoover warned in 1950 that there were Communists "gnawing away like termites at the very foundations of American society."

DEFINITION

Subversion is the attempt to overthrow a government by undermining it from within.

The Search for Internal Enemies

Fear of Communist subversion led President Truman to create, in March 1947, the Loyalty Review Board, which investigated three million government employees from 1947 to 1951. No spies were found, but 212 employees were fired for being "security risks." The House Un-American Activities Committee, a congressional investigation team, also held hearings in the search for spies.

In 1948, Alger Hiss, a senior State Department employee, was accused of being a Communist agent. A confessed former spy named Whittaker Chambers provided evidence that helped convict Hiss of perjury—lying to the jury—but not spying. News reports of the trial convinced many that there really was a danger of Communist subversion.

ETHEL AND JULIUS ROSENBERG were convicted of espionage in April 1951. Here they sit in a police van shortly after learning of their conviction.

HUAC and the Power of Blacklisting

In 1947, the House Un-American Activities Committee (HUAC) opened a series of hearings in Hollywood, California. The committee tried to embarrass the Truman administration by demonstrating its ability to "expose and ferret out Communists." The movie industry provided headline-grabbing publicity when a group called the "Hollywood Ten" loudly denounced the committee, saying that it had no right to question them. The writers, producers, and directors of the Hollywood Ten were fined and jailed for contempt of Congress because they wouldn't answer questions asked them under oath. They were also "blacklisted"—that is, the movie studios refused to hire them. The ban lasted more than ten years. After that, blacklisting proved to be an effective means of punishing those who refused to testify.

Atomic Secret

In Great Britain, a physicist named Klaus Fuchs was convicted in 1950 of giving atomic-bomb secrets to the Russians during World War II. His conviction led to the arrest in New York of Julius and Ethel Rosenberg on the same charge. They were convicted and, in 1953, executed. Historians still debate whether the Rosenbergs were guilty or innocent.

The McCarthy Era

Early in 1950, Wisconsin senator Joseph R. McCarthy claimed to know the names of 205 Communists working for the government in the State Department. His accusations led to a series of Senate committee hearings that launched a reign of fear known as "McCarthyism."

In public speeches, McCarthy recklessly lashed out at individuals, including the secretary of state and President Truman. In committee hearings, he verbally attacked witnesses and tried to show guilt by association. As each accusation was disproved, he came up with new ones. Despite his aggressive tactics, he never succeeded in exposing a single Communist agent working in the U.S. government.

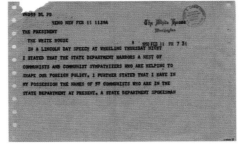

THIS TELEGRAM sent by McCarthy to Truman alleges Communist infiltration in the government.

MARGARET CHASE SMITH, 1897–1995

Senator Margaret Chase Smith, a Republican who represented Maine in the U.S. Senate from 1949 to 1973, was one of the first to speak out against Senator McCarthy. In June 1950, she said, "The American people are sick and tired of being afraid to speak their minds." She and six other Republican senators signed a "Declaration of Conscience" against McCarthy's irresponsible attacks. He was already so feared, however, that the opposition of his colleagues did not slow him down.

The Spell Is Broken

Senator McCarthy finally went too far in December 1953, when his charges included high-ranking army officers. Public hearings were broadcast on television in the spring of 1954. They lasted for 35 days and revealed McCarthy to be a rude, insulting bully. In a dramatic moment, the army's attorney, mild-mannered Joseph Welch, became angry and demanded, "Have you no sense of decency, sir? At long last, have you left no sense of decency?" A long silence followed, and then everyone in the room broke into wild applause. Somehow, that broke the McCarthy spell. The hysteria died down and, with it, the senator's reputation. In December 1954, the Senate voted to "condemn" his behavior for bringing "dishonor and disrepute" to the Senate.

1945–1960

1950s Dreams of Affluence

After suffering the hardships of the Great Depression and the sacrifices of the war years, Americans welcomed the chance to work at good jobs for better wages and find new ways to have fun. For many, the chance to live the 1950s "American Dream" meant owning a home in the suburbs with kids playing in the yard and a shiny new car in the garage. Part of this new lifestyle was enjoying entertainment on television, at the movies, and on the radio, which created a new, easy-to-absorb popular culture for the middle class.

The Arrival of Television

During the 1950s, television became a dominant force in American culture and entertainment. Almost every suburban house and city apartment sprouted a TV antenna. Between 1950 and 1955, the number of TV sets increased by nearly 30 million.

Fads and Fashions

Television helped fads develop and spread nationwide with great speed. For example, *Davy Crockett*, a popular TV show about the famous frontiersman, started a craze that had boys and girls all over the country wearing coonskin caps. A tent manufacturer with 20,000 unsold tents stenciled a Crockett cap on the side of the tents and sold them all within a few days. Some fads, such as hula hoops and Barbie dolls, became enduring classics.

Television's Golden Age

The 1950s were a golden age for television. Favorite TV shows included Westerns like *Gunsmoke*, comedies like *I Love Lucy*, and family series like *Leave It to Beaver*. Although critics called television "chewing gum for the mind," the studios also produced outstanding documentary programs, and more live drama in a year than Broadway. In 1952, the networks broadcast the Republican and Democratic national conventions for the first time, which involved average voters in the election process more than ever before.

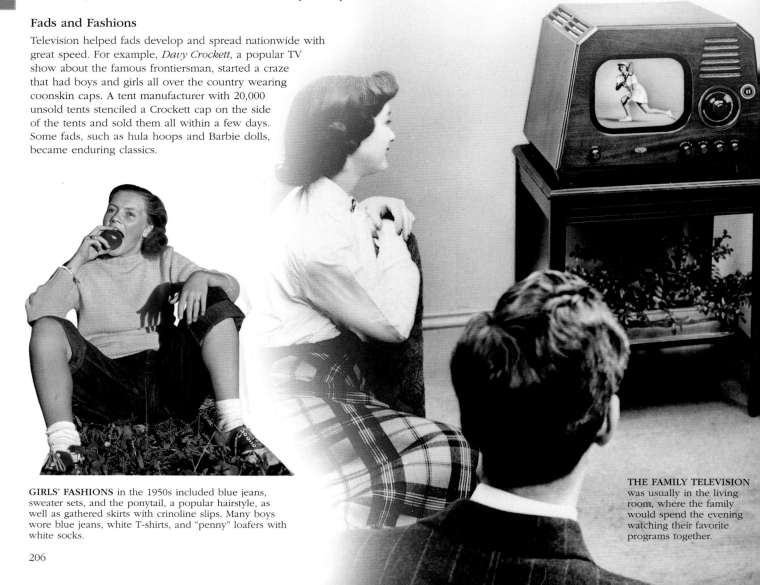

GIRLS' FASHIONS in the 1950s included blue jeans, sweater sets, and the ponytail, a popular hairstyle, as well as gathered skirts with crinoline slips. Many boys wore blue jeans, white T-shirts, and "penny" loafers with white socks.

THE FAMILY TELEVISION was usually in the living room, where the family would spend the evening watching their favorite programs together.

Getting and Spending

A number of factors led Americans to make these years a great age for spending. During the war, Americans received high wages, but there were few things to buy, so people saved their money. After the war, Americans were eager to spend, and they did so as fast as companies could make new products. Advertisers helped convince people that it was now all right to spend money to satisfy personal whims. Congress aided prosperity by passing the Servicemen's Readjustment Act, known as the GI Bill of Rights. This gave veterans low-interest loans for buying a house or farm, starting a business, or paying for college.

Suburbs and Automobiles

A housing shortage beginning in 1945—caused in part by servicemen returning from war and starting families—led to the building of suburban developments such as Levittown, Long Island. By the late 1950s, more than one third of Americans lived in the suburbs. And while the population grew by 36 percent between 1940 and 1960, home ownership grew much faster—by 92 percent.

THE AUTOMOBILE was the main way to get around in the suburbs. Cars led to drive-in movies, fast-food restaurants, and shopping malls—places you needed to have a car to go to.

ELVIS PRESLEY, shown here on a 1956 album cover, became a teen idol with hits such as "Don't Be Cruel" and "All Shook Up." Parents regarded Elvis Presley as a symbol of rebellious youth.

1950s Music

During the 1950s, a generation of clean-cut, all-American pop singers emerged, including Pat Boone and Debbie Reynolds. But in 1955, a popular music revolution started when Bill Haley recorded "Rock Around the Clock"—a mixture of African American sounds and country music. A year later, a young truck driver named Elvis Presley began belting out "rock and roll" hits, changing music forever. "Doo-wop," with its intricate harmonies, also thrilled young people.

1950s Movies

The film industry found creative ways to lure people away from their TVs. Huge, outdoor drive-in theaters, with space for up to 2,000 cars, featured family picnic areas and playgrounds in addition to movies. Indoor theaters were redesigned with extra-large screens to show spectacular epics, such as *Ben-Hur,* and wide-screen musicals, such as *The Sound of Music*, which set attendance records everywhere. Moviegoers also liked seeing their favorite stars, such as Marilyn Monroe and James Dean, on the "big screen," an experience that couldn't be duplicated on small TV screens.

MARILYN MONROE became a movie star in the 1950s in such films as *The Seven-Year Itch* (1955) and *Some Like It Hot* (1959). Here she entertains American soldiers in 1954.

THE 1963 BIRMINGHAM DEMONSTRATIONS against segregation involved thousands of people. The activists of the civil rights movement of the 1960s marched, sat, rode, and spoke in favor of equal rights for African Americans. Their efforts brought about the 1964 Civil Rights Act and Economic Opportunity Act as well as many other governmental attempts to secure equality for all Americans.

Aug. 1961
Construction of Berlin Wall begins

Oct. 1962
Cuban Missile Crisis

1963
The Feminist Mystique, by Betty Friedan, published

July 2, 1964
President Johnson signs the Civil Rights Act

Feb. 1, 1960
Lunch counter sit-ins begin in Greensboro, NC

Apr. 17–19, 1961
The invasion of the Bay of Pigs by American-trained Cubans fails to overthrow Fidel Castro's government

1962
Silent Spring, by Rachel Carson, published

Apr. 1963
Birmingham demonstrations against segregation

Aug. 7, 1964
Gulf of Tonkin Resolution

1960 **1961** **1962** **1963** **1964**

Nov. 1960
John F. Kennedy elected president

Mar. 1, 1961
Peace Corps created

May 1961
Freedom Riders ride from Washington, D.C., to New Orleans

June 1962
Supreme Court outlaws prayer in public schools

Aug. 28, 1963
March on Washington

Nov. 22, 1963
President Kennedy assassinated; Johnson sworn in as president

1964
Economic Opportunity Act creates Head Start, VISTA, EEOC, OEO

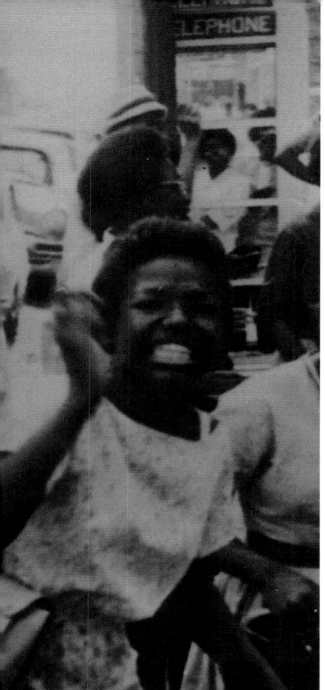

TURBULENT TIMES

1960–1969

The 1960 election of President John F. Kennedy inspired many Americans to hope for progress and security at home and around the world. Americans were devastated by the assassination of the young president, but the change and upheaval of the 1960s required their attention. Inspiring leaders such as Martin Luther King, Jr. fought prejudice with non-violent demonstrations and legislative change, while other activists turned to violence.

President Lyndon Johnson tried to focus on the war on poverty and ambitious civil rights legislation, but his presidency was overwhelmed by the demands of waging an unpopular war in Vietnam. Protests against the war influenced the arts, politics, and daily life of the late 1960s.

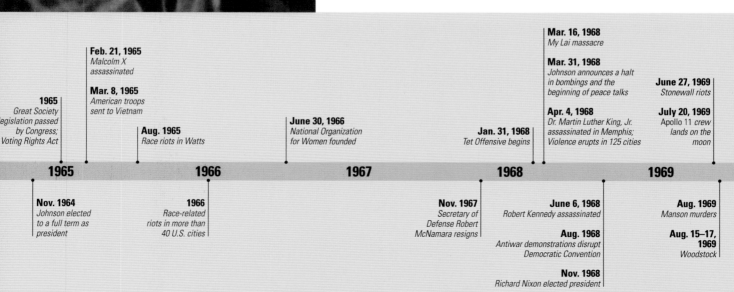

1965
Great Society legislation passed by Congress; Voting Rights Act

Feb. 21, 1965
Malcolm X assassinated

Mar. 8, 1965
American troops sent to Vietnam

Aug. 1965
Race riots in Watts

June 30, 1966
National Organization for Women founded

Jan. 31, 1968
Tet Offensive begins

Mar. 16, 1968
My Lai massacre

Mar. 31, 1968
Johnson announces a halt in bombings and the beginning of peace talks

Apr. 4, 1968
Dr. Martin Luther King, Jr. assassinated in Memphis; Violence erupts in 125 cities

June 27, 1969
Stonewall riots

July 20, 1969
Apollo 11 crew lands on the moon

1965 1966 1967 1968 1969

Nov. 1964
Johnson elected to a full term as president

1966
Race-related riots in more than 40 U.S. cities

Nov. 1967
Secretary of Defense Robert McNamara resigns

June 6, 1968
Robert Kennedy assassinated

Aug. 1968
Antiwar demonstrations disrupt Democratic Convention

Nov. 1968
Richard Nixon elected president

Aug. 1969
Manson murders

Aug. 15–17, 1969
Woodstock

The New Frontier

The election of John F. Kennedy, who was known as "JFK," brought a refreshing youthfulness to the White House. JFK said the 1960s were a New Frontier, and he challenged Americans to be pioneers, giving many a renewed sense of purpose and inspiring people to contribute to society.

In November 1963, the new mood was shattered when the young president was shot and killed as his motorcade toured the streets of Dallas, Texas. Few events in the nation's history have given Americans a deeper or more painful feeling of loss.

THE 1960 PRESIDENTIAL ELECTION

The 1960 presidential election was one of the closest in history. Republican Richard M. Nixon seemed to have an edge with eight years' experience as Eisenhower's vice president, while Democrat John F. Kennedy, a Roman Catholic, struggled against anti-Catholic prejudice.

Kennedy, however, attracted voters with his sense of mission. He also gained votes in the first-ever TV debates by appearing fresh and energetic, while Nixon looked pale, unshaven, and tired.

Kennedy's words on January 20, 1961—Inauguration Day, the formal celebration marking the first day of a presidency—set the tone for his administration: "Now the trumpet summons us again … against the common enemies of man—tyranny, poverty, disease, and war itself."

A SOUVENIR BUTTON with ribbon from Kennedy's inauguration

Kennedy's New Frontier

Kennedy wanted to use his presidency to create a new energy and spirit of possibility in the American people. Two new programs were typical of his New Frontier.

The Peace Corps was established on March 1, 1961. More than 18,000 Americans volunteered to go abroad for two years to contribute their skills and energy to helping others.

The Alliance for Progress, first proposed on March 13, 1961, was a ten-year program in which the United States worked with 19 Latin American countries to improve regional economic and social conditions. The alliance fostered a new spirit of cooperation, though not all programs were successful.

The Bay of Pigs Fiasco

In world affairs, Kennedy got off to a rocky start. In April 1961, the Central Intelligence Agency (CIA) arranged for 1,500 anticommunist Cuban refugees to invade Cuba in an effort to overthrow the government of Fidel Castro. The invasion force landed at a place called the Bay of Pigs and was quickly overwhelmed by Castro's troops. World opinion criticized the United States for its role in what became known as the "Bay of Pigs fiasco." Kennedy tried to repair some of the damage to his administration by publicly accepting full responsibility for the disaster.

PRESIDENT KENNEDY greets Peace Corps volunteers on the White House lawn.

Dealing with Cold War Tensions

In the summer of 1961, the Soviet Union began building a physical barrier between East and West Berlin to stop refugees from fleeing the East German Communist dictatorship. The Berlin Wall remained a source of Cold War hostility for nearly 30 years. In 1963, Kennedy visited West Berlin and renewed America's commitment to keep the city free. Standing at the wall, the president told a cheering crowd, *"Ich bin ein Berliner"*—"I am a Berliner."

The Cuban Missile Crisis

In October 1962, another crisis brought America—and the world—to the brink of nuclear war. The crisis began when the United States learned that the Soviets were installing nuclear missiles in Cuba, just 90 miles from the American coast.

Kennedy immediately put U.S. armed forces on alert. Several of his military advisers suggested an air strike to knock out the missiles, followed by an invasion with ground troops. Kennedy rejected that, fearing it would trigger World War III. Instead, he demanded removal of all missiles and told Khrushchev, the Soviet leader, that any Soviet ships carrying military supplies to Cuba would be stopped by a U.S. naval blockade.

An American fleet of 19 warships had formed a line in the Atlantic 500 miles from Cuba, and a Soviet fleet was steaming toward that barricade. For the next few days, the world teetered on the edge of a nuclear conflict. Then the Soviet ships stopped and turned around. On October 28, Khrushchev agreed to remove the missiles; in return, Kennedy said U.S. forces would not invade Cuba.

JACQUELINE KENNEDY, 1929–1994

Jackie—as the first lady was popularly known—remodeled the White House during her husband's presidency, exploring the attics and scouring the country for furnishings that had once belonged there. She made the Executive Mansion more inviting while recalling its illustrious past. She then led a television tour of the restored building, captivating millions of viewers. Her beauty, style, and intelligence also made her an excellent goodwill ambassador to other countries.

The Assassination

By 1963, President Kennedy seemed more popular than ever. The nation was prosperous, and Americans generally supported his handling of the Cold War crises and his strong backing of the civil-rights movement. In November, he and Mrs. Kennedy flew to Dallas, hoping to meet with Texas Democrats who opposed his stand on civil rights.

On Friday, November 22, 1963, shots were fired on the president's motorcade as it passed near the Texas State School Book Depository, striking him in the head. Kennedy was pronounced dead within the hour. Lee Harvey Oswald, an employee at the book depository, had fled the scene. He was arrested for the crime a few hours later.

KENNEDY'S ASSASSINATION dominated newspaper headlines for weeks while the American people wrestled with shock and grief from the event.

THE AFTERMATH OF THE ASSASSINATION

Two days after Kennedy was shot, in a scene captured on live television, the police were leading Oswald out of a Dallas jail when nightclub owner Jack Ruby stepped out of a crowd of journalists and photographers, drew a gun, and shot and killed Oswald. For many years afterward, official and amateur investigators explored various conspiracy theories about how and why the president was killed, but no solid evidence was ever found.

JACK RUBY SHOOTS Lee Harvey Oswald in front of stunned onlookers.

Marching for Civil Rights

When John F. Kennedy took office in 1961, exactly 100 years had passed since the start of the Civil War. That war had abolished slavery, but it had not ended prejudice and discrimination. In the 20th century there had been some progress, such as the desegregation of the armed forces begun by President Truman in 1948. But throughout the South, all public facilities, from drinking fountains to schools, remained strictly segregated—and blacks and whites did not have equal rights and opportunities in any area of the country. Beginning in the mid-1950s, black Americans began a peaceful and determined march for civil rights.

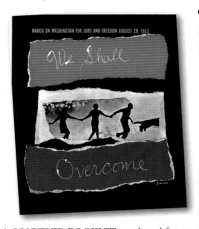

A SOUVENIR BOOKLET produced for participants in the March on Washington for Jobs and Freedom, August 28, 1963, during which Dr. King delivered his historic "I Have a Dream" speech.

PASSIVE RESISTANCE

MOHANDAS K. GANDHI'S nonviolent protest tactics helped win India's independence from Great Britain in 1947.

In a Montgomery, Alabama, church in 1955, a 26-year-old minister named Dr. Martin Luther King, Jr. electrified an audience of blacks who were trying to organize a boycott of the city's buses. People were impressed by the power of his spoken words and by his emphasis on nonviolent protest and passive resistance, concepts King had learned from studying the life of Mohandas K. Gandhi, the leader of India's independence movement.

DEFINITION

*The policy of separating people by race in schools, housing, industry, and public facilities is called **segregation**.*

Peaceful Action, Violent Reaction

The NAACP (National Association for the Advancement of Colored People) scored a victory in 1954 when the Supreme Court ruled in *Brown v. the Board of Education of Topeka, Kansas,* that separate schools for blacks were unconstitutional because "racially segregated schools are inherently unequal." This ruling brought down the 60-year-old "separate but equal" doctrine, which held that segregation was not unequal treatment. Some states took steps to integrate their schools, but there was resistance in much of the Deep South. In 1957, President Eisenhower sent troops to Arkansas to enforce the integration of Little Rock High School.

The Montgomery Bus Boycott

The march for social justice began in earnest in 1955. African Americans in Montgomery, Alabama, stopped riding city buses after Rosa Parks was arrested for not giving up her seat to a white passenger. The boycott, led by Dr. King, lasted a year. The boycotters responded to repeated harassment with nonviolent resistance. In 1956, the Supreme Court ruled that segregated buses were unconstitutional.

ROSA PARKS became a heroine in the struggle for racial equality.

The Continuing Fight

In February 1960, four black college students sat down at a whites-only lunch counter in Greensboro, North Carolina, to protest segregation. They did not leave, even though they were repeatedly refused service because of their race. "Sit-ins" spread throughout the South. Within a month, more than 1,000 protesters were arrested. As a result, many chain stores integrated their lunch counters.

In the spring of 1960, black college students, many of them veterans of the sit-ins, formed the Student Nonviolent Coordinating Committee (SNCC—pronounced "snick"). They helped Southern blacks form self-help organizations and register to vote.

In May 1961, a group of students set out to test the Supreme Court's segregation rulings by making an interstate bus trip from Washington, D.C., to New Orleans. The "Freedom Riders" journey was successful, despite riders being beaten, and one bus they rode being burned. By fall, many bus companies and railroads had begun to integrate their facilities.

EXTRA **REGISTER** EXTR

FOR SERVICE

Students Stag Sitdown Deman

THE GREENSBORO SIT-IN of 1960 inspired similar protests throughout the South.

Crisis at Birmingham

In April 1963, Dr. King went to Birmingham, Alabama, to lead protests in what he called "probably the most thoroughly segregated city in the U.S." As the demonstrators marched peacefully through the streets, the police attacked them with dogs and fire hoses. Dozens were jailed, including King.

While King's Southern Christian Leadership Conference (SCLC) and city leaders were negotiating, King's hotel and his brother's house were bombed. President Kennedy moved troops close to the city. Peace was established, and the city government agreed to partial desegregation. The courage displayed by King and the demonstrators inspired other nonviolent protests throughout the South.

CIVIL RIGHTS CASUALTY COUNT

In 1963, white racists planted 35 bombs that killed 10 people, including four young black girls in a Birmingham church. Nonetheless, civil rights protestors persevered with nonviolent demonstrations. By the fall of 1963, about 14,000 demonstrators had been arrested in 75 cities in the South.

MORE THAN 3,300 AFRICAN AMERICAN protesters were arrested during demonstrations in Birmingham in the spring of 1963.

MARTIN LUTHER KING, JR. addresses supporters in Selma, Alabama, in March 1963, at the start of a march to Montgomery.

The Civil Rights Act of 1964

The segregationists' resistance to change and their continued use of violence led President Kennedy to announce on June 11, 1963, that he was sending a bill to Congress that would make discrimination on the basis of race illegal. On August 28, 1963, the "March on Washington for Jobs and Freedom" drew more than 200,000 people to the nation's capital in support of the bill. There, Dr. King delivered his famous speech: I Have A Dream.

Still, many Americans continued to reject integration. Fewer than three weeks after the march, a bomb shattered a Birmingham church, killing four young black girls and injuring 20 others.

President Johnson pushed the Civil Rights Act of 1964 through Congress. It outlawed discrimination in all public places, established an Equal Employment Opportunity Commission (EEOC), and authorized the attorney general to prosecute schools that failed to integrate. Many called the act the "second Emancipation Proclamation."

Johnson's Great Society

As the nation reeled in shock from President Kennedy's assassination, Lyndon Johnson boarded the plane that would take him and the president's body to Washington, D.C. His voice trembling, Johnson took the oath of office with Mrs. Kennedy standing next to him, still wearing her blood-stained suit. Then, the oath completed, his voice became firm: "Let's get this ____ thing airborne." The former senator from Texas knew it was time to take the lead. And for the next four years he piloted the nation toward his vision of the "Great Society."

1960–1969

The War on Poverty

In 1962, a book called *The Other America* by Michael Harrington described the nation's poor as being trapped in a cycle of poverty, and reported that nearly 20 percent of the population lived below the government-established poverty line. The book inspired President Kennedy and led him to call for a "war on poverty."

President Johnson waged the War on Poverty with the Economic Opportunity Act of 1964. This bill created a Job Corps, which provided job training for unemployed young people; a program called VISTA, for Volunteers in Service to America, a domestic Peace Corps; and the Office of Economic Opportunity (OEO), with a $1 billion budget to wipe out poverty. Another ambitious program called Head Start established preschools to help children from poor families prepare for kindergarten.

LYNDON BAINES JOHNSON takes the oath of office aboard Air Force One just hours after Kennedy was shot in Dallas. His wife and new first lady, Lady Bird Johnson, stands to his right; Mrs. Kennedy stands to his left.

FIRST LADY "LADY BIRD" JOHNSON became the honorary chairman of Head Start after passage of the Economic Opportunity Act in 1964. Here she meets children involved in the program.

LYNDON BAINES JOHNSON, 1908–1973

Lyndon Johnson had known hard times growing up in a depressed rural area of Texas. After a short spell as a schoolteacher, he became a congressman. In his 25 years as a representative in the House and a senator, he developed such remarkable skill in nudging a measure through Congress that he became known as the Great Persuader.

Tall, rugged, and full of energy, Johnson gave 22 speeches in one day during the 1964 campaign. He liked people to know that he was in charge. For example, when a young corporal guiding him past rows of helicopters said, "This one's yours, Mr. President," Johnson smiled and replied, "Son, they're all mine."

Election for the Great Society

During the 1964 election campaign, Johnson proposed a huge reform agenda. He predicted that his program would bring "an end to poverty and racial injustice" and would create a "Great Society" based on "abundance and liberty for all."

The Republican Party, long opposed to big government spending programs, named Arizona senator Barry Goldwater to run against Johnson. Democrats attacked Goldwater's conservative voting record, including his opposition to civil-rights legislation, and warned that he would escalate the war in Vietnam. Johnson breezed to victory with 61 percent of the popular vote and an electoral margin of 486 to 52.

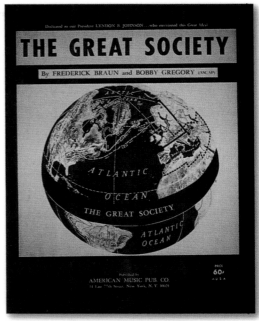

JOHNSON'S AMBITIOUS REFORM AGENDA inspired at least one musical composition, a march called "The Great Society." The dedication at the top of this sheet music cover reads: "Dedicated to our President LYNDON B. JOHNSON ... who envisioned the Great Ideal."

The Warren Court

The 1960s Supreme Court reflected the nation's desire for social change. Under the leadership of Chief Justice Earl Warren, the court passed a number of landmark rulings.

One such case in 1962 outlawed prayer in public schools, calling for the separation of church and state. The court also ruled to redraw districts for electing members of Congress, in order to take into account the growth of the nation's cities. Many decisions created controversy. When the court ruled to protect the rights of individuals accused of a crime, conservatives argued that this interfered with the work of the police. They said the court was making law instead of interpreting it.

CHIEF JUSTICE EARL WARREN led the Supreme Court (shown here in 1955) from 1953 to 1969.

Justice Sherman Minton

Justice Harold H. Burton

Justice Thomas C. Clark

Justice John Marshall Harlan

Justice Hugo L. Black

Chief Justice Earl Warren

Justice Stanley F. Reid

Justice William O. Douglas

Justice Felix Frankfurter

1960s The Counter-Culture

By the 1960s, America's economy was booming. Many middle-class Americans had high-paying jobs and could afford to own a house in the suburbs. Some of the children of this affluent white middle class rejected what their parents had built. Instead, they went in search of alternative lifestyles, creating what became known as the counter-culture.

POET ALLEN GINSBERG was at the 1968 Democratic Convention in Chicago, where anti–Vietnam War protesters clashed with police. According to *Time* magazine, Ginsberg "went about dispensing his Buddhist oms through the tear gas."

The Generation Gap

The number of young people between the ages of 14 and 24 grew from 27 million in 1960 to 40 million by the end of the decade. Many in this new generation saw their own lifestyle as selfish and unfair when other Americans experienced poverty and racism. Parents were bewildered by their children's rejection of the life they worked hard to provide for their families. The breakdown in communication that resulted became known as the generation gap.

Counter-Culture Lifestyles

Many young people rebelled against figures of authority—called the Establishment—who they held responsible for social injustice and the war in Vietnam. Young protesters joined civil rights marches and antiwar demonstrations. They also dropped out of school and moved to counter-culture meccas like New York's Greenwich Village or Berkeley, California.

DR. TIMOTHY LEARY, the one-time Harvard professor who coined the phrase "turn on, tune in, drop out," advocated the use of powerful hallucinogenic drugs such as LSD (lysergic acid diethylamide).

Living on the Fringe

To express their freedom, many rebellious young people created new lifestyles. Groups of young people sometimes rented an apartment or house and shared almost everything, even income. Some people engaged in "free love," which involved switching sexual partners frequently. However, this practice spread diseases. Pursuing a spiritually based lifestyle was a goal for some. They joined religious groups based on a range of major religions, including Christianity and Buddhism.

YOUNG AMERICANS dance at an outdoor festival in Los Angeles, California, in 1967.

Art, Music, and Literature

The artists, writers, and song composers of the Sixties expressed the views of the counter-culture. Some attacked middle-class values and the war in Vietnam. Others searched for new values based on peace and love.

Art

Andy Warhol led a new artistic trend called "Pop Art." He painted everyday—or popular—subjects such as soup cans and celebrities. Another New York artist, Roy Lichtenstein, became popular for painting large images that called to mind comic strips.

PETER MAX, a young commercial artist, produced posters that were explosions of color. Much of the "hippie art" of the decade involved variations on the Max approach to the peace symbol seen here.

WOODSTOCK

In mid-August 1969, a half-million young people traveled to a 600-acre farm in Bethel, New York, for an event called the Woodstock Music and Art Fair.

For three days punctuated by rainstorms that turned the fields into mud pools, the hippies listened to one famous singer or group after another. Communes set up free kitchens and free clinics. It became a great be-in, love-in, and sleep-in with no fights and no arrests.

COLORFUL POSTERS promised Woodstock ticketholders "an Aquarian Exposition" featuring "3 Days of Peace & Music."

1960-1969

ANDY WARHOL, shown here with friends at a museum exhibition opening, became an international art icon in the 1960s for his pop art depicting consumer goods, such as his paintings "Five Coke Bottles" (1962) and "Can of Campbell's Soup" (1964).

Literature

One of the favorite novels of the counter-culture was Herman Hesse's *Steppenwolf*, which drew on Asian religions in the search for inner peace. Other writers, such as Joseph Heller (*Catch-22*) and Ken Kesey (*One Flew Over the Cuckoo's Nest*), used biting humor to poke fun at the Establishment. In poetry, Allen Ginsberg became a hero for his outrageous language in poems like "Howl."

BOB DYLAN AND JOAN BAEZ in London in 1965

Music

Folk singers expressed the generation's anti-materialist and antiwar sentiments in music. The folk songs of Bob Dylan led the way, followed by Joan Baez; Arlo Guthrie; and the trio of Peter, Paul, and Mary. Some preferred the harder-driving rock of Jimi Hendrix and Janis Joplin, while almost everyone loved the Beatles—an English import.

A Movement Divided

In 1964 and 1965, the civil-rights movement began changing in dramatic ways. In the South, civil-rights workers encountered renewed opposition and violence. African Americans in the North, frustrated that marches, demonstrations, and acts of Congress had not changed life in the urban ghettos, erupted in violence. New leaders emerged. Some spoke of armed rebellion, but most advocated what they called "black power" and the creation of a separate black society.

DEFINITION

*A **ghetto** is a section of a city occupied by a minority group. Ghettos are often formed because of social, economic, or legal pressure. The first ghetto was founded in Venice, Italy, in 1516 to forcibly restrict the movement of Jews.*

The Black Vote

By 1960, only one-quarter of eligible African Americans in the South were actually registered to vote. In 1964, civil-rights organizations participated in a voter registration drive in Mississippi called Freedom Summer. In June, three young white volunteers were kidnapped and murdered by a Ku Klux Klan gang. Martin Luther King and the Southern

Christian Leadership Conference (SCLC) joined the drive in 1965 with a march on Montgomery, Alabama. At the start of their march, just outside Selma, state police attacked the 600 marchers. TV pictures of white brutality generated support for the cause. Two weeks later, 25,000 people marched to Montgomery, protected by the National Guard.

The Voting Rights Act of 1965 was subsequently passed, guaranteeing African Americans the right to vote. By 1967, 430,000 new voters were registered.

MARTIN LUTHER KING, JR., the leading spokesman for nonviolent protest, would become a victim of violence. He was gunned down by an assassin on April 4, 1968.

KU KLUX KLAN members march in Atlanta, Georgia, in 1964. In the 1920s, the Klan had 5 million members; by the 1960s, fewer than 45,000 were still active.

URBAN RIOTS

Less than a week after the 1965 Voting Rights Act went into effect, an African American neighborhood in Los Angeles called Watts erupted in rioting and flames. Watts, like many urban African American enclaves, had been shaped by virtual segregation, since people would not rent or sell property to African American families in white neighborhoods. The rioting started over rumors of police brutality in arresting a black truck driver. The burning and looting continued for six days.

Over the next two years, African American neighborhoods in city after city erupted in violence, with the worst rioting in Chicago and Cleveland. In 1967, more than 80 people were killed by gunfire during riots. Rioting mobs attacked and looted white-owned businesses, started fires, and battled the police and National Guard.

THE WATTS RIOTS resulted in 34 deaths, several hundred injuries, and millions of dollars in property damage.

Black Nationalism

In the mid-1960s, many African Americans began to advocate complete separation of the races rather than integration. This idea had roots in Marcus Garvey's "Back to Africa" movement of the early 1900s. Garvey encouraged pride in African heritage and introduced the slogan, "Black is beautiful." Black Muslims formed the largest separatist movement. Many African Americans took Muslim names to replace their "slave names." They denounced Christianity, opposed violence, and followed a strict code of conduct (no alcohol, smoking, or gambling). By 1967, there were an estimated 400,000 in the movement.

The Movement Splinters

Malcolm X, a powerful speaker in the Nation of Islam, a black Muslim group, broke with the separatists in 1964 and formed the Organization of Afro-American Unity. He began cooperating with radical groups of all races, but his promising start was cut short when he was assassinated in February 1965.

Some African Americans started questioning the government's desire to enforce the civil-rights laws. To them, the nonviolent approach was not creating any real change. Stokely Carmichael challenged King's leadership in the South. His phrase "black power" expressed African Americans' hopes for control over their own communities. By the end of the decade, the Black Power movement had helped elect 1,500 blacks to political office.

STOKELY CARMICHAEL, standing at the podium, addresses a Black Power rally at the University of California at Berkeley in 1966.

The Assassination of King

Martin Luther King, Jr. supported the development of black pride and increased political involvement, but he continued to oppose separatism. In 1967, he began to fight poverty as well as racism.

On April 4, 1968, King was assassinated in Memphis, Tennessee. While the nation mourned its loss, black neighborhoods in 125 cities broke out in violence. Police, the National Guard, and federal troops eventually ended the riots, but only after 46 deaths and more than 20,000 arrests.

The new black nationalism and Black Power movements turned their energies to rebuilding communities damaged by the riots.

MALCOLM X, shown here on the streets of New York in 1963, strove to educate the public about injustices done to blacks.

1960–1969

Science Leaps Forward

President Kennedy had predicted that the 1960s would be a "frontier of unknown opportunities and perils—a frontier of unfulfilled hopes and threats." Wartime developments had required rapid advances in science and technology, which led to many of these hopes and opportunities, as well as the perils and threats. Nuclear power, for example, offered the hope of readily available, cheap energy, but it also raised the threat of a nuclear war that could destroy much of the world.

Technology Changes the Economy

During the 1960s, advances in technology were rapidly transforming the workplace. In factories, the first computers ran new machines that performed most of the assembly-line tasks needed to produce steel, automobiles, airplanes, and dozens of other products.

While automation made the production of goods faster and cheaper, it also made the skills of thousands of industrial workers unnecessary. To find work, they had to be retrained or move into lower-paying jobs in service industries, such as fast-food restaurant chains.

PEACEFUL USES OF NUCLEAR ENERGY

The United States played a major role in developing peaceful uses for nuclear energy. In 1957, the first nuclear submarine, USS *Nautilus*, was launched, and the first nuclear plant for generating electricity went into operation at Shippenport, Pennsylvania. By 1970, more plants had been built and accounted for about 10 percent of the country's electricity, despite the fears of many people that they were not safe from accidental meltdowns of their radioactive materials (see p. 234).

USS *NAUTILUS* on its initial sea trials in 1955

TV DINNERS were invented in 1954. By the end of the 1960s, sales had soared and continued to grow, making them a staple in many American homes.

Ready-to-Serve Foods

The food-processing industry was transformed by automation and other technological changes that allowed manufacturers to create a great variety of elaborately packaged foods requiring little time or labor to serve. Americans rapidly became fond of these ready-to-serve foods. In 1955, the manufacturing of processed foods—mostly frozen vegetables and fruit juices—was a $2 billion-a-year industry; by 1967, it had become a $53 billion industrial giant. And Americans' craving for new, hassle-free food would continue to grow. More than half the foods available in the supermarkets of 1970 did not exist in 1950.

Scientific Farming

Agriculture was also revolutionized in the years between 1950 and 1970. The number of farms decreased, but the average acreage of remaining farms increased enormously. Many family-owned farms were replaced by agricultural corporations. By 1970, 10 percent of the nation's farms produced roughly 60 percent of the nation's foods and farm products.

Farms now needed more specialized equipment—combines, mechanized pickers for cotton and corn, milking machines—along with hybrid seeds, feeds with special hormones, chemical fertilizers, and insecticides. Many small farms survived by turning to organic, or chemical-free, farming.

APOLLO 16 lifts off from its launch pad at Kennedy Space Center in Florida on April 16, 1972. It was the fifth mission to land men on the Moon and bring them safely back to Earth.

The Space Race

In 1961, President Kennedy said Americans would succeed in "landing a man on the Moon and returning him safely to Earth" by the end of the decade. It sounded like science fiction, but the American people's spirits received a great boost from Kennedy's idea. Over the previous four years, they had watched the Soviet Union take the lead in the race to conquer space.

In April 1961, a Russian cosmonaut was sent into orbit around the Earth; America didn't catch up until 1962, when John Glenn became the first American in space. Glenn's earth orbit was part of the Mercury Program at NASA (National Aeronautics and Space Administration).

The program's dramatic climax came on July 20, 1969, when Apollo astronauts Neil Armstrong and Edwin "Buzz" Aldrin left their lunar module *Eagle* and became the first humans to stand on the Moon.

1960–1969

BUZZ ALDRIN on the surface of the Moon, July 21, 1969. The televised Moon landing was watched by more than 600 million people around the world.

1970
Environmental Protection Agency (EPA) established; César Chávez wins negotiation rights for United Farm Workers

Feb. 1972
Nixon visits People's Republic of China

Mar. 1972
The Godfather premieres

Nov. 1972
Nixon reelected; American Indian Movement (AIM) occupies Bureau of Indian Affairs

1973
OPEC stops oil shipments to the U.S.

Jan. 17, 1973
Paris Peace Accords signed

Jan. 22, 1973
U.S. Supreme Court decides Roe v. Wade

Oct. 10, 1973
Vice President Spiro Agnew resigns

Oct. 20, 1973
Nixon's Saturday Night Massacre firings

1970   1971   1972   1973   1974

Apr. 22, 1970
First Earth Day celebrated

May 4, 1970
Four student protesters killed by National Guardsmen at Kent State University

Mar. 22, 1972
Equal Rights Amendment (ERA) passed by Congress

June 17, 1972
Watergate break-in

Feb. 1973
Operation Homecoming begins

Mar. 1973
Last U.S. combat troops withdrawn from Vietnam

Sept. 20, 1973
Battle of the Sexes tennis match

July 1974
House Judiciary Committee adopts articles of impeachment against Nixon

WAR AND PROTEST

1970–1979

In the 1970s, the nation wavered between the belief that Americans could solve global problems and the sense that events had spun out of control. Groups fought for greater equality and better environmental protections, but the war in Vietnam sapped the country's energy and spirit. The antiwar movement involved all segments of society.

President Richard M. Nixon, elected in 1968, thought he could stabilize the military situation; instead, he broadened the war and extended America's involvement. Americans were further disillusioned by the Watergate scandal and Nixon's resignation in 1974.

New crises continued to emerge throughout the decade; Presidents Gerald Ford and Jimmy Carter struggled with an energy shortage and international tension over issues such as the continuing Cold War and the seizure of American hostages in Iran.

VIETNAMESE REFUGEES flee Saigon after the fall of South Vietnam. As the war ended and America's forces were pulled out of Vietnam, many North Vietnamese tried to escape to safety. Americans at home were affected by the war, too. Protestors clashed with the war's supporters, and the soldiers who returned often had a hard time finding their way in a changed America.

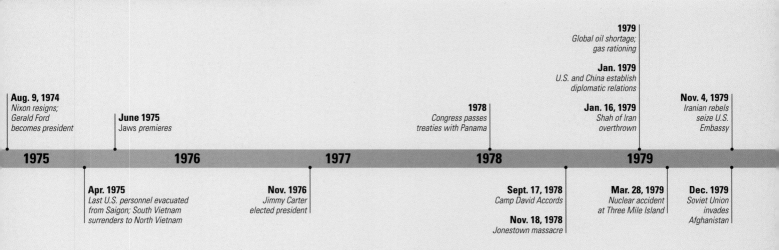

Aug. 9, 1974
Nixon resigns;
Gerald Ford
becomes president

June 1975
Jaws premieres

1978
Congress passes
treaties with Panama

1979
Global oil shortage;
gas rationing

Jan. 1979
U.S. and China establish
diplomatic relations

Jan. 16, 1979
Shah of Iran
overthrown

Nov. 4, 1979
Iranian rebels
seize U.S.
Embassy

1975   **1976**   **1977**   **1978**   **1979**

Apr. 1975
Last U.S. personnel evacuated
from Saigon; South Vietnam
surrenders to North Vietnam

Nov. 1976
Jimmy Carter
elected president

Sept. 17, 1978
Camp David Accords

Nov. 18, 1978
Jonestown massacre

Mar. 28, 1979
Nuclear accident
at Three Mile Island

Dec. 1979
Soviet Union
invades
Afghanistan

Movements for Change

The civil rights movement inspired other groups to launch movements for greater equality. Women, Hispanics, American Indians, and others made use of protest marches, court cases, and sit-ins to advance their causes. Many people also came together over issues such as environmental pollution and the safety of consumer products. All of these groups, in various ways, contributed to the colorful, sometimes angry turmoil of the 1970s.

1970–1979

BETTY FRIEDAN, 1921–2006

In 1963, Betty Friedan's book *The Feminine Mystique* marked the beginning of the modern movement for women's rights, or feminism. In its pages she attacked the idea that women could only find fulfillment in the home as housewives and mothers. In 1966, Friedan helped found the National Organization for Women (NOW)—the largest women's rights organization— which, among other goals, pursued equality for women in the workplace and championed the Equal Rights Amendment.

The Modern Women's Movement

The summer of 1970 marked the 50th anniversary of the Nineteenth Amendment, which had given women the right to vote. Across the country, the occasion was marked with protest marches, whose banners and signs demanded greater job opportunities, protested the sexist nature of advertising, and called for an end to all-male organizations (see p. 230).

By 1970, roughly half the nation's women worked outside the home, but their income was only about 60 percent of what men earned in similar jobs. "Equal pay for equal work" was one of their most vocal demands.

The Equal Rights Amendment (ERA)

One of the major items on the agenda of the women's movement was an Equal Rights Amendment, or ERA. Congress passed it as a simple 24-word addition to the Constitution: "Equality of rights under the law shall not be denied or abridged by the United States or any state on account of sex." Out of the required 38 states needed, only 35 ratified it; the amendment did not pass.

NOW MEMBERS PICKET the White House in May 1969. NOW vigorously campaigned for the pro-choice cause, which supported a woman's legal right to terminate a dangerous or unwanted pregnancy, on the grounds that approximately 10,000 women died every year from illegal abortions. Pro-life activists opposed legal abortions and believed that life begins at conception, making abortion a form of murder. In the 1973 case *Roe v. Wade*, the Supreme Court ruled that abortions were constitutional and guaranteed legal abortions.

STONEWALL STARTS GAY RIGHTS

The movement for gay rights was triggered by the Stonewall riot on June 27, 1969. Throughout the 1960s, police routinely raided gay bars and arrested the patrons. But on that night in June, a group of patrons of the Stonewall Inn, a bar in New York's Greenwich Village, had had enough. When the police came to harass them, they took to the streets, trapping the police in the bar. By the end of the night, the riot had grown to more than 2,000 people. The news that gays and lesbians had fought back led to organized protests for gay rights in cities around the world.

THIS POSTER from 1971 protests society's open hostility toward gays.

Hispanic Movements

Mexican-Americans are the largest Hispanic group in the U.S. Some of their organizations, such as *La Raza Unida,* became active in politics in the 1970s, especially in the Southwest, registering "Chicanos" to vote and run for local office. They also convinced several states to offer bilingual education in schools, so students could learn in both English and Spanish.

One of the most successful movements was led by César Chávez, who worked to unionize California's migrant farm-workers. In 1970, after many protests and boycotts, Chávez's United Farm Workers won the right to represent the workers in contract negotiations with the state's grape growers.

A UNITED FARM WORKERS POSTER encourages migrant workers to demand better conditions.

American Indian Movements

In the early 1970s, half of America's one million American Indians lived on reservations (see p. 98), where living conditions were as bad as in the worst urban slums. In 1972, leaders of the American Indian Movement (AIM) attracted national attention when they took over the offices of the Bureau of Indian Affairs in Washington, D.C.

Other tribes and political groups turned to legal action, suing for their rights under treaties signed in the 1800s. The South Dakota Sioux were awarded $100 million for land they lost in dishonorable dealings. Other tribes were able to enlarge their reservations. In the West, several tribes stopped companies from strip-mining coal and also gained ownership of minerals located beneath their lands.

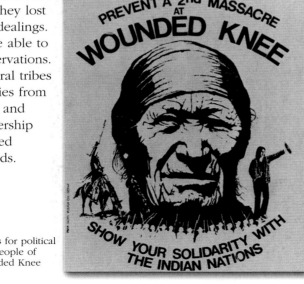

AN AIM POSTER calls for political action by reminding people of the massacre at Wounded Knee Creek in 1890.

Consumers and Environmentalists

In the late 1960s and early 1970s, activists pushed the government into taking action on both consumer-product safety and industrial pollution of the environment. Ralph Nader, a lawyer, pioneered product safety by publicizing automakers' lack of concern about the safety of their automobiles.

In 1962, marine biologist Rachel Carson published a book called *Silent Spring*, in which she warned of the harm caused to the environment by lethal poisons like pesticides. The work of activists such as Carson led to the establishment in 1970 of the Environmental Protection Agency (EPA) to monitor environmental conditions and enforce legal standards. After decades of industrial pollution, public demand finally led Congress to pass the first laws setting standards for clean air and water.

America in Vietnam

America's involvement in Vietnam grew out of the containment policy—a deep commitment to stopping the spread of Communism. Despite escalations of the war in Vietnam—sending more troops and increasing bombings—victory was elusive. Opposition to the war grew steadily. When the Communists launched a massive and successful offensive in January 1968, many Americans began to feel that the war could not be won.

Escalating America's Role

U.S. involvement in Vietnam began in the 1950s when President Eisenhower sent military advisors to South Vietnam (see p. 202). Presidents Kennedy and Johnson had increased troop strength in Vietnam, but little changed until mid-1964.

In August 1964, President Johnson asked Congress for a resolution that would permit him to "take all necessary measures to repel attacks" against U.S. forces and to "prevent further aggression." The president's request was based on reports that North Vietnamese gunboats had fired on two U.S. destroyers in the Gulf of Tonkin.

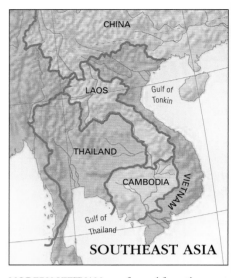

MODERN VIETNAM was formed from the area colonized by France in the late 19th century, which was called French Indochina.

The Gulf of Tonkin Resolution

Congress passed the Gulf of Tonkin Resolution by a huge majority, giving Johnson the ability to pursue large-scale military action in Vietnam. Only Oregon's Wayne Morse warned that they were giving Johnson the power to wage war without a declaration of war by Congress. Johnson could now escalate the war whenever he wished. By late 1965, there were 180,000 American soldiers in Vietnam; by 1968 the number was more than 500,000.

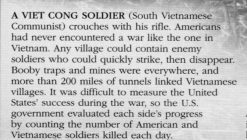

A VIET CONG SOLDIER (South Vietnamese Communist) crouches with his rifle. Americans had never encountered a war like the one in Vietnam. Any village could contain enemy soldiers who could quickly strike, then disappear. Booby traps and mines were everywhere, and more than 200 miles of tunnels linked Vietnamese villages. It was difficult to measure the United States' success during the war, so the U.S. government evaluated each side's progress by counting the number of American and Vietnamese soldiers killed each day.

AN AMERICAN SOLDIER in the field runs to board a helicopter in November 1968.

The Antiwar Movement

Following a series of bombing raids in Vietnam by U.S. troops in 1965, 30,000 people attended an October peace march in Washington. They showed that opposition to the war was not limited to "radicals" on college campuses.

But more than half the country continued to support the war. Many agreed with the "domino theory"—if South Vietnam fell to Communism, then Laos, Cambodia, and other countries would fall, too, like a row of dominoes. In October, former vice president Richard Nixon warned in a letter to the *New York Times* that a Viet Cong victory would mean the "destruction of freedom of speech for all men for all time."

However, public opinion changed over the next two years, as Americans saw innocent civilians killed by American bombs on the evening news night after night. In November 1967, Secretary of Defense Robert McNamara resigned, saying that continuing the war was a grave mistake.

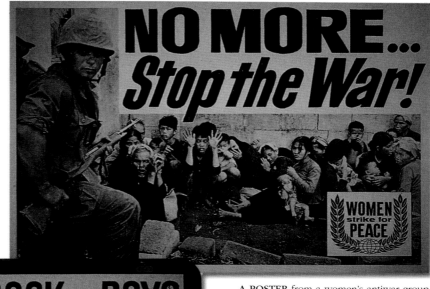

A POSTER from a women's antiwar group.

A CUSTOM LICENSE PLATE shows support for U.S. troops.

A Divided Nation

The war drove deep divisions in American society. Some young men publicly burned their draft cards—or the American flag. Others fled to Canada or Sweden rather than serve. Marchers chanted, "Hey, hey, LBJ: How many kids did you kill today?"

In cities and towns across the nation many Americans marched in support of the war effort. Construction workers—"hard hats"—sometimes clashed with antiwar demonstrators.

The Tet Offensive

On January 31, 1968, the Viet Cong shocked American and South Vietnamese forces by attacking 36 major cities and towns in Vietnam, as well as American bases and the U.S. Embassy in Saigon. Although U.S. and South Vietnamese troops restored order, the Tet Offensive—named because it was launched on the first day of the Vietnamese New Year, or Tet—was a turning point in the war. On March 31, Johnson announced a halt in the bombing and the start of peace talks to be held in Paris. He then said he would not run for reelection in November. The war, however, was not over; it would continue for five more painful years.

CHOLON, a Saigon suburb, lies in ruin after the Tet Offensive in January, 1968.

MUHAMMAD ALI, 1942–2016

Muhammad Ali, the heavyweight boxing champion, was stripped of his title and jailed for draft evasion for refusing to serve in the U.S. military. Ali would not back down and became a hero of the antiwar movement.

ALI IS ESCORTED OUT of the Armed Forces Examining and Entrance Station in Houston, Texas, in 1967.

Ending Vietnam

In 1968, the discord created over the Vietnam War led to political chaos and violence. Robert Kennedy was assassinated in June. During the Democratic Convention in Chicago, protesters taunted National Guardsmen and police wielding nightsticks. TV viewers were horrified by the scenes of hurt and bloodied young people trying to get away from policemen they called "the pigs."

Richard M. Nixon emerged from the chaos as president. His efforts to end the conflict in Vietnam actually broadened it. Finally, in 1973, America pulled out of Vietnam, ending a painful and costly lesson in the limits of military and political power.

THE 1968 PRESIDENTIAL ELECTION

In March 1968, President Johnson said he would not seek reelection. Robert Kennedy was the likely candidate for the Democratic nomination, but, shortly after winning the California primary, he was shot and killed by an assassin.

Vice President Hubert Humphrey won the Democratic nomination, but then lost the election to Republican Richard Nixon.

Robert Kennedy

Edward Kennedy

John Kennedy

ROBERT "BOBBY" KENNEDY, pictured with his brothers in 1962, was heir to the Kennedy political dynasty.

PRESIDENT NIXON explains his Vietnam plan to the press.

Nixon's Vietnam Policy

President Nixon said his goal in Vietnam was "peace with honor." In June 1969, he ordered the withdrawal of 25,000 American soldiers, while continuing the Paris peace talks started by Johnson. But at the same time, Nixon carried on a secret bombing campaign in neighboring Cambodia to stop the North Vietnamese from transporting men and supplies through Cambodia into South Vietnam. Early in 1970, when Cambodia, too, was threatened by a Communist take-over, the president ordered American troops to invade.

The invasion and secret bombing sparked a new wave of antiwar protests. On May 4, 1970, Ohio National Guard troops at Kent State University fired at student protesters, killing four (see p. 231). Two more students were killed in protests at Jackson State in Mississippi. To many Americans, the deaths suggested the government was waging war against its own people.

BUTTONS from the March on Washington, April 24, 1971

Signs of Despair

The antiwar movement continued into 1971. In Washington, D.C., more than 200,000 marchers, including 4,000 veterans, demanded an end to U.S. involvement. In Vietnam, the morale of American troops broke down because of the problems at home and the unclear military goals. Some antiwar protesters alleged that white racism led to higher casualty rates for African Americans, arguing that, while African Americans made up only 11 percent of the population, black soldiers accounted for 23 percent of the casualties.

ANTIWAR PROTESTERS march in front of the White House in 1965.

The Fall of South Vietnam

By 1972, Nixon had reduced American troop strength by half. The bombing raids continued in North Vietnam, Laos, and Cambodia, but they may, in fact, have advanced the peace talks. In January 1973, the two sides signed the Paris Peace Accords, entitled an "Agreement on Ending the War and Restoring Peace in Vietnam." All U.S. forces were withdrawn, and more than 500 American prisoners of war (POWs) were returned.

The end was sudden. A few thousand American civilians remained in Vietnam, along with a small military staff at the embassy in Saigon. In March 1975, the Communists broke the truce and made their final assault on city after city throughout South Vietnam, as millions of refugees fled to Saigon or the coast.

On April 29, 1975, Saigon's American radio station played "White Christmas"—a signal to evacuate. As helicopters lifted the last Americans off the roof of the embassy, the government of South Vietnam surrendered. The long war for Vietnam was over, and the Communists, who had begun their war of liberation against the Japanese in the 1940s, finally controlled a unified country.

THE MY LAI MASSACRE

Late in 1969, Americans learned that, a year earlier, an American lieutenant and his unit had opened fire on a Vietnamese village they thought was held by Communists. They killed an estimated 400 innocent villagers, mostly women and children. Descriptions of the My Lai massacre were so shocking that in a poll taken in one U.S. city, only 12 percent of the people believed it was true.

BURNING VILLAGES, set on fire by American soldiers, were frequently in the news but did not prepare the public for the My Lai massacre.

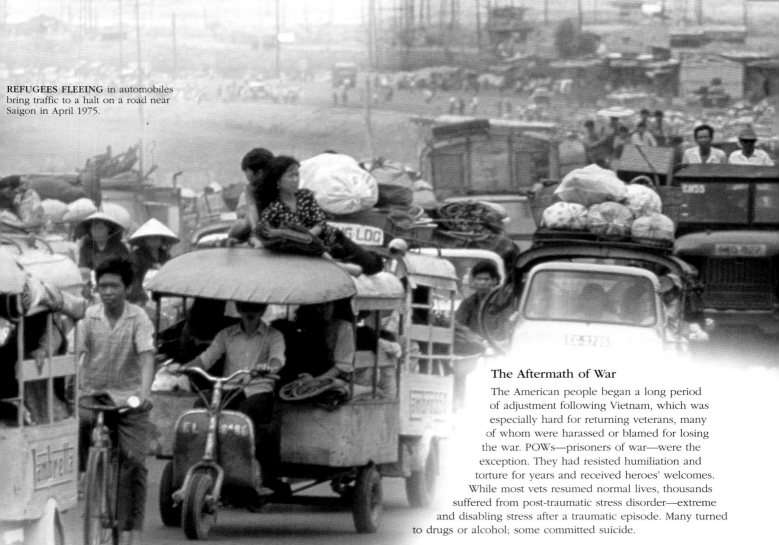

REFUGEES FLEEING in automobiles bring traffic to a halt on a road near Saigon in April 1975.

The Aftermath of War

The American people began a long period of adjustment following Vietnam, which was especially hard for returning veterans, many of whom were harassed or blamed for losing the war. POWs—prisoners of war—were the exception. They had resisted humiliation and torture for years and received heroes' welcomes. While most vets resumed normal lives, thousands suffered from post-traumatic stress disorder—extreme and disabling stress after a traumatic episode. Many turned to drugs or alcohol; some committed suicide.

1970s Politics Gets Personal

Political unrest in the 1970s caused current events and pop culture to blend together, and popular entertainment both reflected and helped define the decade's social changes. Young people responded to cultural influences by seeking new communities and opportunities.

Cults

During the 1970s, some Americans joined cults, close-knit groups, often based in religion, that required extreme devotion, discipline, and isolation from family and friends. In 1974, publishing heiress Patty Hearst was kidnapped and brainwashed by the Symbionese Liberation Army. Distraught parents who feared that their children were being similarly pressured formed anticult movements, hiring "deprogrammers" to bring their children back into the mainstream. Several gruesome incidents illustrated the power of cults. In 1978, more than 900 followers of Jim Jones, founder of the People's Temple, committed suicide at the group's commune in Jonestown, Guyana. The 1969 murder of actress Sharon Tate and others by the followers of cult leader Charles Manson received extensive media coverage in the 1970s during the circuslike trials.

PATTY HEARST was kidnapped by the Symbionese Liberation Army in 1974. She was kept in a closet for two months, then forced to help rob a bank. During the ensuing robbery trials, her defense lawyer used psychiatric testimony to prove that she had been brainwashed.

Showing Equality

Across the country, women proved they could compete with men in the classroom and the boardroom. Women's enrollment in higher education was catching up to men's, and a number of women with business degrees began to join men at the top levels of big corporations. Billie Jean King's victory over fellow tennis champ Bobby Riggs in the Battle of the Sexes exhibition match proved that women could perform as well as men in many areas. Many women fought hard for the Equal Rights Amendment (see p. 224), which would have guaranteed equality of the sexes. Although Congress passed the bill with President Nixon's support, the ERA was defeated because not enough states ratified it.

BILLIE JEAN KING, left, and Bobby Riggs after King's victory in the Battle of the Sexes on September 20, 1973.

Entertainment

The 1970s were a time of great creativity in the entertainment business. Young directors and musicians produced new and innovative works that appealed to the American public. On television, politics was serious comedy; on the radio, punk music vented anger at the mainstream.

THE EAGLES, one of the biggest bands of the 1970s, sold millions of albums with hit songs like "Hotel California" and "Take It Easy."

Television and Film

The best television shows of the 1970s were the sitcoms, or situation comedies. Unlike earlier shows, half-hour comedies such as *All in the Family* and *Maude* had realistic characters who discussed current social and political issues. Women, especially, had better roles: Mary Richards, as depicted on *The Mary Tyler Moore Show*, was an independent career woman.

THE CAST of *All in the Family*

In the 1970s, a talented group of film directors became famous by creating blockbuster movies that were and still are critical hits. This golden age of film produced classics like Martin Scorsese's *Taxi Driver*, Francis Ford Coppola's *The Godfather*, Woody Allen's *Annie Hall*, Robert Altman's *Nashville*, and Steven Spielberg's *Jaws*.

Music

Rock and roll was still big in the 1970s, but so were other kinds of rock and pop music. Music became a whole lifestyle—identity, politics, and clothing were all connected to certain types of music. People danced all night to disco music in clubs like Studio 54. The Ramones popularized punk rock's fast, angry chords in America, as the Sex Pistols had done in England.

ROLLER DISCO FANS roller-skated at clubs and discos in towns across the United States. Young people who listened to this kind of dance music created clothing and dance styles to go with it.

KENT STATE STUDENTS protesting Nixon's invasion of Cambodia are met with tear gas on May 4, 1970. The National Guard was called in to confront the peaceful protest, and four students were shot dead. The baby-boom generation had swelled college campuses, and students and their parents were horrified by this tragedy (see p. 228).

231

Triumph and Tragedy

President Richard Nixon made history by opening relations with China and improving relations with the Soviet Union. He easily won reelection in 1972. Then the Watergate scandal broke and everything seemed to go wrong. Nixon's attempts to cover up the wrongdoing only made things worse. Gradually, facts emerged about dozens of crimes committed by the White House staff to make sure no one threatened their power. Facing impeachment, Nixon chose to resign.

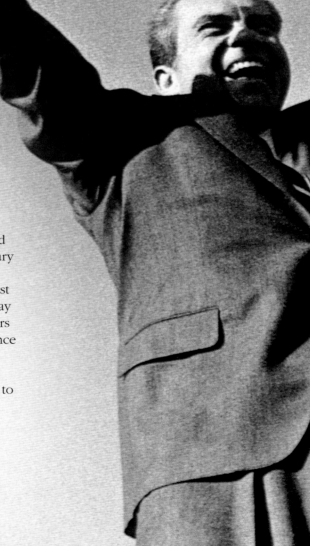

DURING HIS CAMPAIGN for reelection, Nixon greets supporters with his famous "V for victory" gesture.

1970–1979

WATERGATE

During the 1972 election campaign, five men were arrested trying to break into Democratic Party headquarters in the Watergate complex in Washington, D.C. The electronic eavesdropping equipment they carried suggested that they were not ordinary burglars. President Nixon assured the nation that his administration was not involved, and the event was dismissed as a "third-rate burglary attempt" by the White House press secretary.

The matter was quickly forgotten by the public, and Nixon went on to win reelection over the Democrats' candidate, George McGovern.

EAVESDROPPING equipment used at Watergate

Peace with Communists

In 1971, President Nixon startled the nation by announcing his plan to visit China. Since the Communist take-over in 1948 (see p. 200), the U.S. had refused to recognize the People's Republic of China. Now Nixon, the staunch anticommunist, intended to reopen relations. His visit to China in 1972 was a success, and the two countries agreed to economic and diplomatic exchanges.

The historic trip was part of a new foreign policy called *détente*—increasing contact to create a better understanding between two countries—devised by the president and his secretary of state, Henry Kissinger. In the next step, Nixon became the first president to visit Moscow, in May 1972, when the two superpowers agreed to joint ventures in science and space exploration. Easing tensions with the Communist world was personally satisfying to the president, who hoped to go down in history as a great peacemaker.

PRESIDENT NIXON (center left) and First Lady Pat Nixon (center right) at the Great Wall of China in 1972

Unraveling Watergate

The White House cover-up began to unravel in 1973, as Nixon began his second term. One of the convicted burglars wrote to the trial judge, John J. Sirica, claiming that high administration officials were behind the break-in.

Nixon tried to calm suspicions by appointing a special prosecutor, Archibald Cox, to conduct an investigation. Unsatisfied, the Senate in May 1973 formed its own Select Committee on Presidential Campaign Activities.

In the televised Senate hearings, a complicated story emerged of illegal wiretaps, political spying, and a paranoid White House desperate to cover up the Watergate burglary. The one detail that could not be pried out of any witness was how deeply the president was involved.

SPIRO AGNEW, 1918–1996

In the fall of 1973, federal investigators charged that Vice President Agnew had accepted bribes while he was governor of Maryland. He resigned on October 10, 1973, pleaded "no contest" to income-tax evasion, and was ordered to pay a $10,000 fine.

The Twenty-Fifth Amendment, ratified in 1967, set up procedures for choosing a new president or vice president if one resigned. Accordingly, Nixon named Michigan Congressman Gerald R. Ford to replace Agnew, with the approval of Congress.

SPIRO AGNEW leaves a funeral the day after his resignation in October 1973.

The Battle for the Tapes

When it became known that President Nixon secretly taped all of his Oval Office conversations, both the Senate committee and Special Prosecutor Cox demanded to hear the tapes. Nixon refused and ordered his attorney general to fire Cox. When the attorney general refused, Nixon fired him and two other members of the Justice Department. The firings, called the Saturday Night Massacre, raised a storm of protest, prompting Nixon to insist on national television, "I am not a crook!"

The president finally hired a new special prosecutor, Leon Jaworski, but when Jaworski also demanded the tapes in April 1974, Nixon still refused to hand them over. In July, the Supreme Court ruled unanimously that the president must surrender the tapes.

The Final Act

In July 1974, the House of Representatives Judiciary Committee adopted three articles of impeachment against Nixon. He finally released the tapes, which connected him to the break-in and revealed that he had lied to the public about his administration's involvement, blocked an FBI investigation, and started the cover-up.

Nixon seemed certain to be impeached by the House and convicted by the Senate. To avoid this, on August 8, 1974, Nixon became the first American president to resign. Vice President Gerald Ford became the new president.

GERALD FORD takes the oath of office in the White House on August 9, 1974.

Coping with New Realities

After Vietnam and the Watergate scandal in the 1970s, Americans felt a lack of national confidence they had not experienced since the dark days of the Great Depression.

The limits of U.S. power, which Vietnam had demonstrated, were reinforced when the United States could not stop oil-producing countries from raising oil prices to shockingly high levels, causing severe energy crises. Similarly, Presidents Ford and Carter discovered that they could do little to revive a sluggish economy. The 1970s became a time of adjusting to new realities and limitations.

THREE MILE ISLAND

By the 1970s, 12 percent of the nation's electricity was produced by 72 nuclear plants, and more plants were under construction (see p. 220). But, in the midst of the 1979 energy crisis, an accident at the Three Mile Island plant in Pennsylvania created doubts about the promise of nuclear energy. A combination of mechanical failure and human error raised the alarm of a "meltdown." Although the situation was quickly corrected, the accident strengthened the arguments of the antinuclear movement.

THREE MILE ISLAND nuclear power plant on the Susquehanna River

OPEC Strikes Back

The enormous demands of the American economy led the nation to start importing oil around 1960. By the 1970s, nearly 40 percent of the oil used was imported, much of it from countries that were members of OPEC—the Organization of Petroleum Exporting Countries.

Actions by OPEC caused the nation's two worst energy crises. First, in 1973, the price of oil skyrocketed when OPEC members stopped shipments to the United States for a few months, in retaliation for American support of Israel in that country's war against Syria and Egypt. Then, in 1979, a global oil shortage led OPEC to raise prices a staggering 60 percent.

Learning to Conserve Energy

The oil shortages and high prices of the energy crises affected Americans' living standards. Motorists suddenly found themselves sitting in long lines to buy gasoline. Homeowners were paying twice as much for home heating oil.

In response, people turned down thermostats, carpooled, and bought smaller, fuel-efficient cars. Congress passed legislation lowering the highway speed limit and offering tax cuts for the purchase of appliances that used less energy. By 1984, Americans were using less oil than in 1974. But some energy needs were unavoidable, and people still had to accept higher prices.

MOTORISTS LINE UP to fill their tanks on the first day of gas rationing in Los Angeles on May 9, 1979. No tank was filled unless it was more than half empty. This crisis was a direct result of the revolution in Iran, which caused a shortage of crude oil.

TO CONSERVE ENERGY, people resorted to old-fashioned means, such as using kerosene lamps instead of light bulbs for interior lighting.

Foreign Policy and Human Rights

When former Georgia governor Jimmy Carter was elected president over Gerald Ford in 1976, he planned to use U.S. foreign policy to promote respect for human rights in all dealings with other countries.

Carter's first move was to sign new treaties with Panama, ending America's "perpetual" control of the Panama Canal and giving ownership to Panama in the year 2000. Although many Americans felt it was foolish to give up control of the vital waterway, the treaties squeaked through the Senate in 1978.

That same year, Carter announced that, on January 1, 1979, the U.S. would establish full diplomatic relations with Communist China and cut formal ties with Taiwan, raising a storm of protest. Many people felt Carter was betraying the Nationalist Chinese government in Taiwan; others believed that this was the best way to maintain peace in Asia.

Hoping to strengthen the spirit of *détente*—the new policy of relaxing tense relations through diplomatic communication—Carter negotiated an arms-limitation treaty with the Soviet Union. Before the Senate could act, however, Russian troops invaded Afghanistan to aid a pro-Soviet government. Carter denounced the invasion and placed an embargo on all shipments of grain and technology to the Soviet Union.

The Iran Hostage Crisis

The 1970s ended on a somber note. The Shah of Iran, an American ally, was overthrown in a bloody revolt early in 1979. Muslim religious fundamentalists took power, declaring a government based on the rules of Islam.

In 1979, the dying Shah came to the United States for medical treatment. To force his return, Iranian revolutionaries stormed the U.S. embassy in Iran in November 1979 and took 52 Americans hostage. Despite the Shah's death from illness, the hostages were held until Carter arranged for the return of Iranian assets frozen by the United States after the Shah's fall. The hostages returned home after 444 days in captivity, on January 31, 1981, the day Republican Ronald Reagan was sworn in as president.

BOYCOTTING THE OLYMPICS

President Carter announced that the United States would not take part in the 1980 Summer Olympics in Moscow unless Soviet troops withdrew from Afghanistan. The Soviet government ignored the warning. Sixty-five nations joined America in boycotting the games. Athletes and fans were devastated by the boycott, but most Americans felt Carter had made a responsible decision.

The Camp David Accords

The greatest success of Carter's foreign policy came late in 1978, when he helped hammer out an agreement between Egyptian president Anwar el-Sadat and Israeli prime minister Menachem Begin. Meeting at the presidential retreat, Camp David, in Maryland, the three men emerged with

a treaty ending the state of war that had existed between Egypt and Israel for 30 years. Israel also agreed to return to Egypt the Sinai Peninsula, which Israel had occupied since the Six Days War in 1967.

PRESIDENT CARTER looks on as Begin (right) and Sadat (left) shake hands at the White House on March 26, 1979.

1970–1979

SUPPORTERS OF THE AYATOLLAH KHOMEINI, an Islamic fundamentalist leader, celebrate in Iran after the fall of the Shah in a bloody revolt in January 1979.

THE NAMES PROJECT created an enormous quilt whose panels remembered and honored the victims of AIDS. Many Americans came to see the AIDS memorial quilt when it went on display on the National Mall in Washington, D.C. The 1980s were an aggressive era, in which Americans energetically pursued economic success at home and defeating Communism abroad. Projects such as the AIDS quilt reminded the country of the social issues still affecting America.

July 13, 1985
Live Aid concert for famine relief

1980
U.S. boycotts Moscow Olympic Summer Games

1981
Scientists identify Acquired Immune Deficiency Syndrome (AIDS)

Mar. 30, 1981
John Hinckley, Jr. attempts to assassinate President Reagan

Mar. 23, 1982
Reagan proposes Strategic Defense Initiative (SDI), a.k.a. "Star Wars"

Apr. 18, 1983
U.S. embassy bombing in Beirut, Lebanon

Mar. 11, 1985
Mikhail Gorbachev becomes president of the Soviet Union

1980 **1981** **1982** **1983** **1984** **1985**

Nov. 1980
Ronald Reagan elected president

Aug. 1, 1981
MTV premieres

1982
Oil prices and interest rates drop; Economy begins to rebound

Oct. 23, 1983
Truck bomb kills 241 members of the U.S. peacekeeping force in Beirut

Nov. 1984
Reagan reelected

June 14, 1985
Terrorists hijack TWA flight 847 from Athens to Rome

Jan. 20, 1981
Reagan's first inauguration; Iran releases American hostages

Oct. 25, 1983
U.S. troops invade Grenada

THE GLOBAL AGE

1980–1991

As the 1980s began, Americans felt stressed. The economy was sluggish and people lived with the threat of nuclear war. The ongoing Iran hostage crisis added to a feeling of declining national power. But when the economy revived in the mid-1980s, some Americans amassed great wealth. Not since the 1920s had so many millionaires been created so fast.

Americans watched as the power of the Soviet Union and its Communist-bloc allies crumbled rapidly. After 30 years, the Cold War came to a sudden end. Many Americans credited President Reagan, the most popular president since FDR, with these changes.

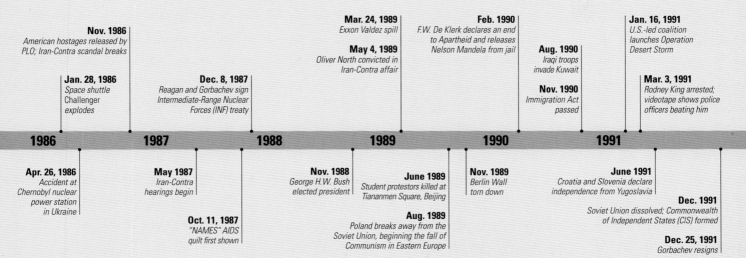

Nov. 1986
American hostages released by PLO; Iran-Contra scandal breaks

Mar. 24, 1989
Exxon Valdez spill

May 4, 1989
Oliver North convicted in Iran-Contra affair

Feb. 1990
F.W. De Klerk declares an end to Apartheid and releases Nelson Mandela from jail

Jan. 16, 1991
U.S.-led coalition launches Operation Desert Storm

Jan. 28, 1986
Space shuttle Challenger explodes

Dec. 8, 1987
Reagan and Gorbachev sign Intermediate-Range Nuclear Forces (INF) treaty

Aug. 1990
Iraqi troops invade Kuwait

Nov. 1990
Immigration Act passed

Mar. 3, 1991
Rodney King arrested; videotape shows police officers beating him

1986 **1987** **1988** **1989** **1990** **1991**

Apr. 26, 1986
Accident at Chernobyl nuclear power station in Ukraine

May 1987
Iran-Contra hearings begin

Nov. 1988
George H.W. Bush elected president

June 1989
Student protestors killed at Tiananmen Square, Beijing

Nov. 1989
Berlin Wall torn down

June 1991
Croatia and Slovenia declare independence from Yugoslavia

Oct. 11, 1987
"NAMES" AIDS quilt first shown

Aug. 1989
Poland breaks away from the Soviet Union, beginning the fall of Communism in Eastern Europe

Dec. 1991
Soviet Union dissolved; Commonwealth of Independent States (CIS) formed

Dec. 25, 1991
Gorbachev resigns

The Reagan Revolution

By 1980, many Americans felt that the federal government was too large and taxes were too high. Republicans, especially, thought that too much of their income tax was spent on costly social programs designed to help the unemployed and the poor. When Republican Ronald Reagan promised in the 1980 presidential election to reduce government size and spending, he beat Democrat Jimmy Carter by the huge electoral vote margin of 489 to 49. On the day of his inauguration, Iran released 52 American hostages who had been held captive for 444 days.

"Reaganomics"

Reagan wanted to shrink government's role in American life by cutting taxes, relaxing regulations on business, and reducing the amount of money spent on social programs. He began his first term by pushing through Congress a $280 billion tax cut—the largest in history. A tax cut decreases the amount of money that the government takes from every worker's paycheck. Reagan hoped these policies, dubbed "Reaganomics," would help the economy grow, because people would have more money to spend on goods and services.

OUR NATIONAL DEBT:
$5,257,470,112,2#8.
YOUR *Family share* $58,112.
THE NATIONAL DEBT CLOCK
NATIONAL DEBT INCREASE PER SECOND $ 10,000
1992 INTEREST COST – $292 BILLION

THIS NATIONAL DEBT "CLOCK" was an electronic billboard that stood in New York City's Times Square from 1989 to 2000. It kept a running count of the size of the national debt—the money borrowed from banks by the government—which exploded under Reagan, despite his program to shrink government.

Economic Recovery

In 1980, the economy was still suffering from the sharp rise in oil prices in 1979 (see p. 234). Then, late in 1982, oil prices and interest rates dropped, starting an economic recovery. By 1984, companies were hiring new workers and people were spending money again. It was the start of a long period of economic prosperity.

Shrinking Government

In order to "get government off the backs of the people," and businesses, Reagan reduced the regulatory power of government agencies such as the Securities and Exchange Commission (SEC) (see p. 165) and the Environmental Protection Agency (EPA) (see p. 225).

Reagan also tried to limit the size of the federal government. Responsibility for managing and funding government programs— such as low-income housing and mass-transit systems—was transferred from Washington to the states. Federal spending decreased, but states were forced to come up with new funding or reduce—or eliminate—programs.

RONALD REAGAN, 1911–2004

When Ronald Reagan was sworn in as president on January 20, 1981, he was 69 years old—the oldest president in America's history. Reagan's age did not seem to matter; to the American people he appeared to be bursting with energy. A former movie actor, he had a persuasive speaking style that led people to call him the Great Communicator.

Reagan was also called the Teflon president because criticism never seemed to stick to him. When Reagan left office in 1989, he was one of the most popular presidents in history.

DURING THE ASSASSINATION ATTEMPT on Ronald Reagan, the president was shot in the chest, but his wounds were not serious. Three others were badly hurt, including Press Secretary James Brady, when John W. Hinckley, Jr. opened fire outside the Washington Hilton on March 30, 1981.

PRESIDENT RONALD REAGAN gives a speech at a rally for Senator David Durenburger in Minneapolis, Minnesota, on February 2, 1982. Reagan was popular with most Americans, including many registered Democrats who voted for him even though he was a Republican. They became known as "Reagan Democrats."

The Lopsided Prosperity

Despite the economic success experienced by many Americans in the 1980s, prosperity was not felt by all. Relaxed government regulations led to widespread speculation on the stock market and in real estate development, and some people made big fortunes in a short time. But a congressional study late in the decade showed a widening gap between the incomes of rich and poor Americans.

Another sign of an economy out of balance was the incredible growth of the national debt, which had soared to above $3 trillion. This meant that more of the tax dollars collected by the government would be needed to pay interest on the debt instead of funding government services. To many middle-class and wealthy Americans, however, these were the best of times.

THE NUMBER OF HOMELESS PEOPLE grew at an alarming rate in the 1980s, according to a congressional study. Here, with the White House in the background, homeless people in Washington, D.C.'s Lafayette Park eat a free Thanksgiving meal provided by a local community group.

1980–1991

THE 1984 PRESIDENTIAL ELECTION

Ronald Reagan ran for reelection in 1984, claiming credit for the nation's return to prosperity. His opponent, Minnesota Democrat Walter Mondale, who had been Carter's vice president, argued that Reagan was creating the largest national debt in history. No one paid much attention, and the Democrats could not cut into Reagan's remarkable popularity. Reagan won every state's votes except Minnesota—Mondale's home state—and Washington, D.C.

GERALDINE FERRARO, Mondale's running mate, was the first woman to be nominated to high office by a major party.

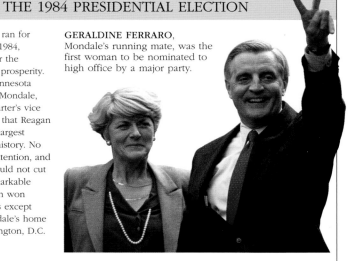

Changing Times

The pace of life seemed to speed up in the 1980s. Innovations like personal computers, fax machines, and overnight delivery services allowed people to conduct business much more swiftly. Reducing government regulations also smoothed business transactions and investing. Many "baby boomers"—people born during the population explosion after World War II—enjoyed urban life and the chance to make money quickly.

Life in the fast lane had its problems, though. Drug use reached epidemic proportions, as did cases of a new disease called AIDS, which was identified in 1981.

The Changing Business World

Thanks to the tech boom of the 1980s, America became even more dominated by cities and suburbs during the decade. Between 1970 and 1990, more than 750,000 farms disappeared. Fewer people lived on farms than at any time since the Civil War.

The business world was changing, too. More than 400,000 businesses went bankrupt in the 1980s—four times as many as in the 1970s. But entrepreneurs also thrived, and nearly 250,000 new businesses started up each year. Business mergers—when one company buys out another—were increasingly common. In 1985, a record 24 mergers occurred, involving more than $1 billion each.

As the business world changed, so did America's view of money. The 1980s was a decade that embraced power, wealth, and status. Many Americans seemed to agree with the line from the popular movie *Wall Street*, "Greed is good!", while others saw it as the embodiment of the worst excesses of the era.

THE WAR ON DRUGS

While drug use had long been associated with urban poverty and the 1960's counter-culture, for several million Americans in the 1980s, cocaine use was part of the lifestyle of yuppies—the slang term for young urban professionals (see p. 242). Drug traffickers like Pablo Escobar took advantage of the new market for cocaine in the U.S. and became billionaires off the trade.

President Reagan and, later, President George H. W. Bush declared a war on drugs; Bush sent military aid to drug-producing Latin American countries to stop the flow of drugs at its source. These efforts, however, made little impact. In 1988, 55 percent of high school seniors admitted to using drugs in the previous 30 days. And by 1990, Americans were spending an estimated $100 billion a year on illegal drugs.

FIRST LADY NANCY REAGAN'S "Just Say No" campaign, designed to keep kids off drugs, was unsuccessful.

The Savings and Loan Crisis

The problem of greed was not limited to Wall Street. In the late 1980s, many of the nation's savings and loan banks—called "S&Ls"—failed. After the recession in the late 1970s, Reagan's administration had eased regulations on businesses in order to help them recover, which also helped the tech boom. But the managers of many S&Ls took advantage of these relaxed regulations to make loans that were either too risky or dishonest, or both. An added problem was that the government guaranteed people's bank deposits, so the nation's taxpayers ended up paying for what was later called a "savings and loan debacle." By 1992, the bill was as high as $500 billion.

THE *CHALLENGER* DISASTER

Innovations in space travel led to 133 successful flights of reusable spacecraft—better known as the Space Shuttle—between 1977 and 2011. However, the technology was not always perfect. On January 28, 1986, the space shuttle *Challenger* took off from Cape Canaveral, Florida, with a crew of seven, including Christa McAuliffe, a schoolteacher from New Hampshire. Seventy-four seconds after lift-off, millions watched as the shuttle burst into flames and exploded, killing everyone on board. The disaster was blamed on a faulty O-ring seal, so NASA canceled all scheduled launches while the space program was reviewed for better shuttle construction and safety control plans.

A NEW ELECTRONIC AGE

Innovations in technology in the 1980s influenced almost every American family's way of life. Personal computers, developed in the 1970s, had limited sales until a college dropout named Bill Gates developed a "graphical user interface" that simplified computer use. By the late 1980s, one out of every five families owned a PC, and Gates had earned his first billion dollars.

Other innovations became successful even faster. The first cellular phones for automobiles appeared and could soon be found in 1.5 million cars. Other new arrivals included ATMs, VCRs, microwave ovens, Sony Walkmans, camcorders, overnight package delivery, fax machines, and toll-free 800 numbers.

THE FIRST CELL PHONES weighed as much as two pounds.

THE WALKMAN was introduced by Sony in 1979 and sold for $200.

COMPACT DISCS (CDS) were introduced in 1983; by 1988, more than 150 million had been sold.

The AIDS Epidemic

In 1981, 269 Americans died of a condition with strange new symptoms that became known as AIDS (Acquired Immune Deficiency Syndrome). By 1990, AIDS, caused by HIV, the human immunodeficiency virus, had claimed more than 100,000 lives in the United States. By 2000, the death toll reached nearly 450,000 Americans. At first, people associated HIV and AIDS with gay men because the first cases were identified in the homosexual male community. Gradually, it became clear that the virus was also transmitted by blood transfusions, shared drug needles, and heterosexual sex. As Americans learned more about the disease and ways to decrease the risk of contracting it, fear began to subside. People joined in raising money for research into cures and a possible vaccine (see p. 243).

THE NAMES PROJECT FOUNDATION AIDS MEMORIAL QUILT was shown for the first time over the weekend of October 11, 1987, on the National Mall in Washington, D.C. More than 500,000 people visited the quilt that weekend to view the 1,920 panels commemorating the lives of individuals who had died of AIDS.

1980s Go-Go Years

Americans prospered in the heady economy of the "go-go '80s," but many people became aware of the misfortune suffered by others at home and abroad. Famine relief and antiapartheid campaigns received wide support—and produced results. At the same time, Americans discovered new trends, such as the fitness craze and rap music, that would have a lasting influence on American culture.

The Fitness Craze

The 1980s fitness fad that swept the country led Americans to take up jogging or bicycling, or to try aerobics, a dance-based exercise. The trend was fueled by medical reports on the benefits of exercise and advertising campaigns promoting sneakers and sports drinks. Although many quickly abandoned the sports they had taken up, more Americans became aware of the need for physical fitness. Today, many people participate in sports and activities first popularized in the 1980s.

YUPPIE LIFESTYLES

The baby boomers—born after 1945, when the postwar population soared—reached their thirties and forties in the 1980s. Many were at the top in their professions and making a lot of money. Their fast-paced, upscale ways of living led to the name yuppies—young urban professionals.

Yuppies enjoyed spending their money. They bought second homes, expensive cars, luxury foods, and designer clothes. Those who moved to the suburbs to raise their children took their lavish lifestyles with them. For example, the landscape and gardening industry grew 47 percent between 1982 and 1985.

THE DELOREAN, a very expensive sports car manufactured only in 1981 and 1982, became a symbol of new wealth in the 1980s.

LOW-IMPACT AEROBICS improves general fitness without harming joints such as knees and ankles.

The Real Estate Boom

As the stock market prospered, banks and investors were eager to put their money into real estate. New buildings and developments began to crop up everywhere, and many people, such as Donald Trump, made their fortunes. However, too much construction led to unoccupied buildings. In late 1987, the real estate market crashed as the U.S. economy moved into a recession.

Rap Music

Rap music began in New York City in 1970 as a combination of spoken rhymes and recorded music. It was part of an urban African American culture that included break dancing and graffiti art. Early songs, like the Sugar Hill Gang's "Rapper's Delight," reached a mostly black audience. MTV, which began to broadcast music videos in 1981, was initially notorious for not showing black performers. Eventually this changed, and a wide audience could watch music videos by rap acts such as Run-DMC. By the late 1980s, rap was popular with listeners of all races.

RUN-DMC AND THE BEASTIE BOYS were two of the first rap acts to become popular with both black and white audiences

Celebrities Get Involved

Suffering around the world alarmed many Americans, and celebrities helped out by organizing and joining campaigns for change. Their high profiles made more people pay attention. The AIDS awareness movement, for example, began at the grassroots level, but soon actors and musicians such as Michael Jackson were lending support.

TENNIS GREAT ARTHUR ASHE (left) and musician Harry Belafonte (right) march against apartheid.

Ending Apartheid

Since 1948, apartheid, or separateness, had been the official policy in South Africa. Under this system of segregation, an all-white government led the black majority. Laws restricted blacks' access to housing, jobs, and education, and denied them political representation. Most Americans were horrified by this system, and many famous people joined the campaign against apartheid. The United States and other countries imposed economic sanctions on South Africa, hoping to pressure the government by limiting trade. In 1990, with public opinion clearly against his government, South African president F. W. DeKlerk declared an end to apartheid and released Nelson Mandela, a black activist imprisoned since 1964 for protesting government policy. In 1994, Mandela became the country's first black leader.

Live Aid

In 1984, Irish musician Bob Geldof was shocked by reports of the brutal famine in Ethiopia. To raise money to help the victims, Geldof organized the Live Aid concert on July 13, 1985. More than 40 bands and musicians, including Sting, Elton John, Paul McCartney, the Pretenders, U2, Madonna, and Eric Clapton, participated in the biggest rock concert up to that time. Live Aid took place simultaneously in Philadelphia, Pennsylvania, and London, England. Television footage was broadcast live between the two stadiums and around the world via satellite. $70 million was raised from the sale of tickets and souvenirs and the telethon held throughout the broadcast.

THE STAGE AT LIVE AID, Philadelphia, Pennsylvania

AIDS Awareness

During the 1980s, as AIDS and HIV infection reached epidemic proportions, many people did not know the facts about transmission and treatment (see p. 241). The AIDS Coalition to Unleash Power (ACT UP), founded in 1986, created public spectacles to encourage government support for AIDS research. Ryan White, an Indiana teenager who contracted the HIV virus from a blood transfusion, became the new face of AIDS when he was blocked from attending public school. In 1990, the government passed the Ryan White Comprehensive AIDS Resources Emergency (CARE) Act to fund AIDS treatment for Americans without health insurance.

RYAN WHITE on his first day back at school. When his school's administrators found out Ryan had AIDS, he was barred from attending classes. The case received widespread attention, and eventually he was allowed to return to school.

America Abroad

The 1980s were a difficult time in world affairs, as the United States developed diplomatic and military programs to combat new problems. In the Middle East, Americans were targeted by terrorists opposed to U.S. support of Israel. The arms race between the two superpowers—the United States and the Soviet Union—threatened the whole world with nuclear war, and the Iran-Contra affair scandalized President Reagan's administration.

The "Evil Empire"

The Soviet Union's invasion of Afghanistan in 1979 led many Americans to think that the eased relations of the late 1970s had been ineffective. When President Reagan entered office in January 1981, he took a hard line against the Soviet Union, which he called an "evil empire" because of its opposition to individual freedom, religion, and democracy. Reagan pressed Congress to increase America's arsenal of nuclear missiles and to develop new weapons, like the B-1 bomber. He also proposed a futuristic defense system called the Strategic Defense Initiative (SDI), nicknamed "Star Wars." SDI, which planned to use lasers to destroy incoming missiles, would be a multibillion-dollar experiment.

THE U.S. EMBASSY IN BEIRUT, LEBANON, was bombed on April 18, 1983, killing more than 40 people. Six months later, on October 23, 1983, 241 Americans were killed when a suicide squad drove a bomb-laden truck into U.S. Marines headquarters in Beirut. During the 1980s, Arab terrorists who opposed U.S. intervention on behalf of Israel in Arab-Israeli conflicts targeted Americans living in the Middle East.

President Reagan was criticized for keeping the marines in Lebanon without a clear mission. The difficulty of responding to renegade terrorists would plague Americans through the end of the 1990s and into the new millennium.

THE GRENADA INVASION

Two days after the Beirut truck bomb in October 1983, marines invaded the Caribbean island of Grenada, where a communist government was being formed with the help of Cuba. Although some Americans—and Latin Americans—criticized the U.S. intervention, the marines ousted the Cubans and stayed long enough to ensure the creation of an anticommunist government.

U.S. SOLDIERS APPREHEND a man on Grenada in 1983.

AN MX "PEACEKEEPER" INTERCONTINENTAL BALLISTIC MISSILE is launched from its silo during a test in March 1986. The "Peacekeeper" was developed as part of Reagan's modernization of America's nuclear-missile arsenal.

The Iran-Contra Scandal

The Iran-Contra affair began early in Reagan's presidency and grew out of his desire to help anti-communist guerrillas—called the Contras—in Nicaragua. When Congress ordered a stop to all funding for the Contras, a special group of Reagan's advisers, called the Enterprise, devised a scheme to keep the money flowing. Weapons were illegally sold to Iran in exchange for money and the release of hostages. The money was then used to fund the Contras. Once this scheme was exposed, the extent of the president's involvement remained unclear.

The Middle East Connection

In November 1986, an American hostage being held in Beirut, Lebanon, by the Palestine Liberation Organization (PLO) was released. On the same day, newspapers reported that the United States had secretly sold millions of dollars worth of weapons to Iran, with whom America had broken off relations in 1980 during the Iranian hostage crisis (see p. 235). President Reagan denied that the American government was trading weapons for hostages. Three weeks later, however, there was a third revelation: Money from the weapons sales had somehow ended up in the hands of the Contras.

The Iran-Contra Hearings

In 1987, a congressional committee held televised hearings to find the truth of what was now called the Iran-Contra scandal. The hearings never clarified the president's role, and he suffered only a temporary decline in popularity. However, six members of the Enterprise were found guilty of minor crimes and fined or placed on probation.

MARINE LIEUTENANT COLONEL OLIVER NORTH, a key figure in the Iran-Contra scandal, claimed he thought the scheme for circumventing the law, and Congress, was simply "a neat idea." On May 4, 1989, North was convicted in federal court of destroying and falsifying documents, taking public funds for personal use, and aiding the obstruction of Congress.

1980–1991

A Thaw in the Cold War

America's relations with the Soviet Union changed entirely in 1985 when a reformer named Mikhail Gorbachev came to power in the USSR. At that time, the Soviet Union was in the midst of a severe financial crisis and could no longer afford the huge defense expenditures required to fight the Cold War. The USSR was also bogged down in an unpopular and costly war in Afghanistan, which some people called Russia's Vietnam.

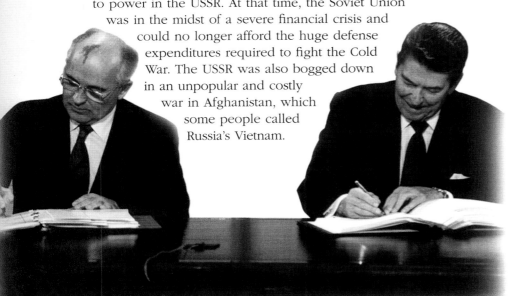

Ronnie and Mikhail

In two highly publicized meetings in 1985 and 1986, President Reagan and Mikhail Gorbachev discussed an end to the nuclear arms race between the USSR and the USA. But by 1987, not much had changed. In June that year, President Reagan gave a speech at the Berlin Wall, which had been built to separate communist East Germany from democratic West Germany, asking Gorbachev to "Tear down this wall!" and again called for an end to the arms race. Gorbachev responded positively and the two increased their efforts to ease Cold War hostilities and to reduce nuclear weapons. Their 1987 agreement became the Intermediate-Range Nuclear Forces (INF) Treaty. It was the first reduction in weapons since the start of the Cold War and suggested a new, optimistic relationship between the once bitter rivals.

THE TWO SUPERPOWER LEADERS sign the INF Treaty in 1987. It eliminated an entire class of nuclear missiles. Americans welcomed the treaty and the improved relations between the two superpowers. But no one realized that this was the beginning of the end of the Cold War.

Iron Curtain Falls

George Herbert Walker Bush took office in January 1989, after serving two terms as Ronald Reagan's vice president. The Cold War standoff, which had shaped U.S. foreign policy for four decades, was cooling down as people's desire for freedom caused turmoil in Communist countries. The eastern European nations broke away from the Soviet Union, and the former superpower divided into 15 separate republics. America faced other challenges as well, including the 1991 Persian Gulf War.

IN BEIJING'S TIANANMEN SQUARE in June 1989, the Communist government crushed a pro-democracy demonstration by storming the square with troops and tanks. Hundreds of demonstrators were killed in the massacre and thousands were arrested.

Americans were horrified by the Chinese government's action. Many wanted the Bush administration to respond with a ban on trade, but the White House insisted that maintaining relations was the best way to influence China's policies.

The End of the Cold War

When Mikhail Gorbachev came to power in 1985, he introduced two reforms in the Soviet Union: *glasnost*, a Russian word for "openness," allowed greater freedom in the media; *perestroika*, or restructuring, allowed limited free enterprise to boost the economy and increase the flow of consumer goods into Russia. Demand for such liberties spread to the nations of eastern Europe, including Czechoslovakia, East Germany, and Romania. Beginning with Poland in August 1989, country after country threw out their communist rulers and formed democratic governments.

In November 1989, Germans tore down the Berlin Wall, which separated democratic West Berlin from Communist East Berlin and the rest of East Germany (see p. 199). Within a year, Germany was reunited under a single democratic government, the Federal Republic of Germany.

THE BERLIN WALL, shown here hours before it was knocked down in November 1989, was a symbol of Communist repression for 28 years.

The Breakup of the Soviet Union

Late in 1991, the Soviet Union itself collapsed. In September, deputies in the Soviet congress voted to dissolve the Union of Soviet Socialist Republics and form 15 independent republics. In the upheaval that followed, Boris Yeltsin, president of the Russian Republic, became the leader of a loose alliance of ten of the republics, which were called the Commonwealth of Independent States (CIS). Many of the new republics, such as Lithuania, had been independent countries before falling under Russian or Soviet rule, and they celebrated their return to self-government. Although the Soviet Union no longer existed, Russia—the largest new republic—retained influence and military power.

Americans cheered the move toward freer societies, but there was concern over what would happen with the huge supply of Soviet nuclear weapons. Yeltsin and President Bush agreed to a treaty in June 1992 to reduce both of their nuclear arsenals by half, but tensions lingered into the 21st century.

The Persian Gulf War

In August 1990, Iraqi dictator Saddam Hussein sent 120,000 troops into neighboring Kuwait, a tiny, oil-rich nation on the Persian Gulf. The Bush administration organized a coalition of 28 nations to block trade with Iraq and protect the region's vital oil supplies. In November, the UN approved the use of force if Iraq did not withdraw its troops by January 15, 1991.

PRESIDENT GEORGE BUSH and First Lady Barbara Bush visit U.S troops during the Gulf War. Bush enjoyed enormous popularity following the war, but his ratings declined steadily in 1992, an election year. Economic concerns and the national debt, which Bush had inherited from Reagan, dominated the election (see p. 238).

Operation Desert Storm

On the morning of January 16, 1991, a U.S.-led coalition launched the first air strikes of Operation Desert Storm. Bombs and guided missiles destroyed military installations throughout Iraq, and most of Hussein's air force was eliminated.

After a month of air war, ground troops were sent into action late in February. Exactly 100 hours later, Iraq surrendered and Kuwait was liberated. For many Americans, the easy victory, with fewer than 600 American casualties, restored confidence in the nation's military might. But many believed the coalition should have kept going until Hussein was driven from power.

HIGH-TECH MILITARY

During the Gulf War, Americans could follow 24-hour cable television coverage of U.S. military action. The press was not allowed near the fighting, so Americans watched the war from a distance. Dramatic video footage of bombs striking their targets showed viewers the sophisticated weaponry being used. New terms were needed to describe the high-tech hardware: smart bombs (which could zero in on a single building from miles away); SAMs (surface-to-air missiles); navy Prowler and air force Raven aircraft (used to confuse enemy radar); Tomahawk cruise missiles; and Patriot anti-missile systems.

PATRIOT MISSILES are stored in transportation containers that also serve as launchers. Each launcher holds four missiles.

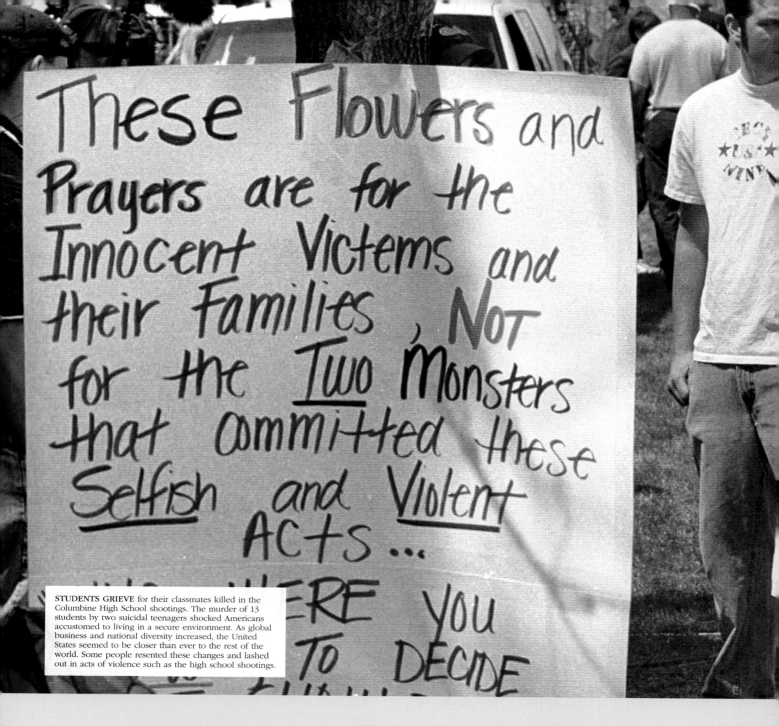

These Flowers and Prayers are for the Innocent Victems and their Families, Not for the Two Monsters that committed these Selfish and Violent Acts... WHERE YOU TO DECIDE

STUDENTS GRIEVE for their classmates killed in the Columbine High School shootings. The murder of 13 students by two suicidal teenagers shocked Americans accustomed to living in a secure environment. As global business and national diversity increased, the United States seemed to be closer than ever to the rest of the world. Some people resented these changes and lashed out in acts of violence such as the high school shootings.

Apr. 6, 1992
Bosnian Serbs lay siege to Sarajevo

Apr. 29, 1992
Police officers acquitted in Rodney King trial, leading to riots in Los Angeles

Dec. 1992
U.S. troops arrive in Somalia to join UN mission

Apr. 19, 1993
Federal authorities storm Branch Davidian compound in Waco, TX

Oct. 3, 1993
Battle of Mogadishu

Mar. 25, 1994
Last U.S. troops leave Somalia

1995
U.S. and NATO conduct airstrikes against Serbia

1992   **1993**   **1994**   **1995**

June 1992
Earth Summit on the Environment held in Rio de Janeiro, Brazil

Nov. 1992
Bill Clinton elected president

Mar. 29, 1993
A car bomb explodes in the World Trade Center garage

Nov. 1993
Congress approves NAFTA

1994
Kenneth Starr appointed to investigate Whitewater

June 18, 1994
O. J. Simpson arrested

Apr. 19, 1995
Oklahoma City bombing

BRIDGES TO THE FUTURE

1992–1999

The economic success and political scandals of the 1990s took most Americans by surprise. Bill Clinton's youthful administration reminded many people of the idealism of the Kennedy years, but his two terms were marked by shocking personal missteps. When Clinton took office in January 1993, the budget deficit seemed a permanent barrier to prosperity. Yet, by the end of the decade, the deficit was gone and the economy seemed stronger than ever. The Internet boom flooded the market with promising new companies, and millions of people were online at home and at work.

As the only superpower, the United States intervened in armed conflicts overseas when its interests were threatened—with mixed results.

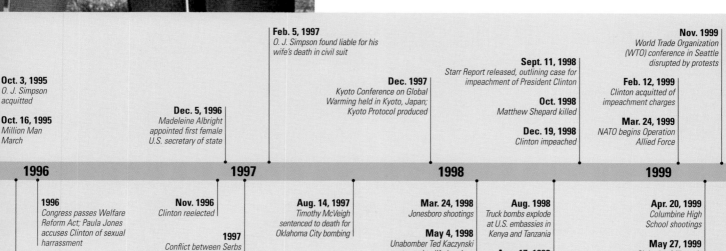

Feb. 5, 1997
O. J. Simpson found liable for his wife's death in civil suit

Nov. 1999
World Trade Organization (WTO) conference in Seattle disrupted by protests

Oct. 3, 1995
O. J. Simpson acquitted

Oct. 16, 1995
Million Man March

Dec. 5, 1996
Madeleine Albright appointed first female U.S. secretary of state

Dec. 1997
Kyoto Conference on Global Warming held in Kyoto, Japan; Kyoto Protocol produced

Sept. 11, 1998
Starr Report released, outlining case for impeachment of President Clinton

Oct. 1998
Matthew Shepard killed

Dec. 19, 1998
Clinton impeached

Feb. 12, 1999
Clinton acquitted of impeachment charges

Mar. 24, 1999
NATO begins Operation Allied Force

1996

1997

1998

1999

1996
Congress passes Welfare Reform Act; Paula Jones accuses Clinton of sexual harrassment

Dec. 14, 1995
Dayton Peace Accord signed

Nov. 1996
Clinton reelected

1997
Conflict between Serbs and Kosovar Albanians

Aug. 14, 1997
Timothy McVeigh sentenced to death for Oklahoma City bombing

Mar. 24, 1998
Jonesboro shootings

May 4, 1998
Unabomber Ted Kaczynski sentenced to life in prison

Aug. 1998
Truck bombs explode at U.S. embassies in Kenya and Tanzania

Aug. 17, 1998
Clinton admits to affair with intern Monica Lewinsky

Apr. 20, 1999
Columbine High School shootings

May 27, 1999
Slobodan Milosevic indicted by the UN

The Clinton Era

After the 1991 Persian Gulf War, President George H. W. Bush enjoyed enormous popularity. As the 1992 election neared, he benefited further from being in office when democracy swept eastern Europe. But American voters were more concerned with an economic recession that had started in 1990. Democratic candidate Bill Clinton and his running mate, Tennessee senator Al Gore, made improving the economy the central goal of their campaign. They became the first "baby boomers" (see p. 240) to reach the White House.

BUSINESSMAN ROSS PEROT ran as an independent candidate in the 1992 presidential election. His focus on the budget deficit attracted 19 percent of the vote—a huge number for a third-party candidate.

The Limits of Presidential Power

President Clinton was confident that his legislative program, including his plan to reform America's health-care system, would be approved by Congress. But his 12 years as governor of Arkansas had not prepared him for working with Washington politicians. Few of Clinton's proposals made their way through the conservative legislature. However, Congress did accept his plan for a controversial North American Free Trade Agreement (NAFTA) with Mexico and Canada that would gradually end all trade restrictions among the three countries.

The Shrinking Deficit

Despite his battles with Congress, Clinton remained popular, in part because he was in office during the U.S. economy's longest period of uninterrupted growth. Congress approved Clinton's plan for reducing the budget deficit, and this allowed him to take some credit for the growth and prosperity. The economic growth, in turn, lowered the deficit because more tax money was flowing into Washington.

Welfare Reform

Clinton felt strongly about another piece of legislation, the Welfare Reform Act, which Congress passed in 1996. Clinton wanted to decrease government spending on unemployed citizens and encourage them to find jobs. The act handed the control of welfare over to individual states; limited the amount of time that people could receive benefits to five years (requiring adults to work after two); and denied assistance to noncitizens. Clinton's more liberal Democratic supporters thought these reforms would punish people for being poor.

BILL CLINTON was the first Democratic president to win reelection since Franklin Roosevelt. Clinton served in the White House from 1992 to 2000.

The Clinton Scandals

Even before election day in 1992, scandal threatened to derail Clinton's campaign. Confronted with evidence, he admitted that he had avoided the draft during the Vietnam War and that he had been unfaithful to his wife. But Clinton persuaded voters that these mistakes were not as important as what he could bring to the presidency.

In another scandal, Clinton and his wife Hillary were accused of unethical activity in a failed Arkansas real estate development called Whitewater. The investigation lasted eight years and concluded in March 2002, having found insufficient evidence for legal charges.

1992–1999

KENNETH STARR, 1946–

Before the post of independent counsel was created in 1978, in response to Nixon's Watergate scandal, the president could fire prosecutors who were investigating him, since they were actually working for him. But the independent counsel is appointed by a three-judge panel selected by the U.S. attorney general, and reports only to the panel.

In 1994, Kenneth Starr was appointed by Janet Reno to investigate the charges related to Whitewater. Starr never managed to make a provable case against the president, but he did obtain convictions of seven other Whitewater defendants.

KENNETH STARR during the Whitewater hearings

Among those found guilty were the Clintons' two business partners and the governor of Arkansas.

MONICA LEWINSKY hugs President Clinton at a press event in 1996. It was a video moment that would be shown again and again in 1998. A Pentagon employee released to the press audio tapes of telephone conversations in which Lewinsky detailed her extended affair with the president, breaking the news to the world.

Riding out the Scandals

During Clinton's 1996 campaign for reelection, Paula Jones, a former Arkansas employee, accused him of sexually harassing her when he was governor. Clinton denied the charges and went on to win the election.

The worst scandal of the Clinton years erupted in 1998 when it was reported that Clinton had had an affair with a young White House intern named Monica Lewinsky. Clinton denied the affair at first, but he eventually admitted to an "inappropriate relationship." Since he had denied the affair with Lewinsky in his sworn statement to the jury in the Jones case, it now appeared that he had committed perjury—or lied in court. For Republicans in the House of Representatives, this represented a serious offense. On December 18, 1998, they voted to impeach the president.

Impeachment

Clinton's impeachment proceedings on perjury charges—with the House prosecuting and the Senate as a jury—were humiliating for the president. Even though the Senate voted to acquit Clinton on February 12, 1999, his conduct led to the suspension of his Arkansas law license. He also resigned from the U.S. Supreme Court bar to avoid being disbarred, or prevented from arguing cases before the Supreme Court.

DEFINITION

To **impeach** a public official is to charge that official with improper conduct in office.

IMPEACHMENT IS BIG NEWS: Bill Clinton was only the second president to be impeached. The first was Andrew Johnson after the Civil War.

A New Economic Age

In his inaugural address on January 20, 1993, Bill Clinton said, "The urgent question of our time is whether we can make change our friend and not our enemy." Most Americans embraced the changes, such as the increased use of computers and the Internet, quickly adapting to business in a worldwide marketplace. The 1990s were a period of remarkable growth and prosperity.

Changing Ways of Working

The kinds of jobs and workplaces that emerged in the 1990s would not have been recognizable to workers earlier in the century. From developing software to designing sites for the World Wide Web, more and more jobs were becoming computer-related. Assembly-line factory jobs were increasingly performed in developing countries, where labor costs were much lower, or workers were replaced by computer-operated robots. Unskilled and semi-skilled jobs continued to be available in service-oriented businesses, such as hotels, fast-food chains, and janitorial services.

The Computer-Internet Revolution

The Internet began in 1969 as a Defense Department experiment to link together four computers. In the 1990s, advances in hardware and software transformed that early trial into the "information superhighway." By 1994, about three million people, mostly in the United States, were making use of the Internet; by the year 2000, more than 300 million people worldwide were connected, and the number was expected to reach one billion by 2005. Americans became enthusiastic Internet users—exchanging e-mail, joining chat rooms, reading the news (the Internet offering 5,000 newspapers and 4,000 magazines to choose from), and even paying bills and banking online.

Challenges to the Internet

Like any new system, the Internet was not perfect. People soon learned that hackers, computer-savvy people capable of breaking into or hacking computer networks, could damage or steal information on their computers. New security systems were developed, but hackers proved remarkably inventive.

Another problem was the difficulty of protecting the rights of authors, composers, and others engaged in creative work. For example, record companies complained that Internet users should not be able to exchange digital music online without paying them a royalty, or fee. Also, since anyone could publish anything on the Internet, there were no standards for quality or accuracy.

THE Y2K SCARE

For decades, computer programmers had written programs using the last two digits of a year to stand in for the full year—for example, "99" instead of "1999." But as the year 2000 approached, many people feared that computers would read the date "00" as "1900" instead of "2000," shutting down computer systems all over the world. In the late 1990s, governments and businesses worldwide spent more than $350 billion on different solutions. In the end, as the clocks ticked past midnight into the year 2000, nothing happened. But the scare did make people aware of how humans had come to depend on computers and the Internet.

The Global Economy

Throughout the 1990s, businesses became increasingly global. Multinational companies, with offices and operations in more than one country, were growing rapidly. Spreading the manufacture of its products over several countries, a corporation would try to conduct business wherever it could be most cheaply done—for example, buying steel in Japan, shipping it to the Philippines to make components, then finishing assembly in Mexico using electronic parts from the United States. A giant multinational corporation, such as ITT or Microsoft, might have stockholders from 20 countries and offices in 80 countries.

1992-1999

AUTO WORKERS assemble a Buick sedan at a General Motors plant in Shanghai, China. Regular production of Buick automobiles in China began in April 1999.

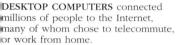

DESKTOP COMPUTERS connected millions of people to the Internet, many of whom chose to telecommute, or work from home.

Resistance to Globalization

Globalization concerned people in many countries. American labor unions opposed having assembly-line work move from the U.S. to Mexico or Southeast Asia. Corporations saved money, but Americans lost jobs. Some people objected when foreign automotive companies set up factories in the U.S., but this hostility diminished when Toyota or Mercedes plants created new American jobs. Other objections focused on environmental and cultural losses due to globalization.

THE DOT-COM REVOLUTION

THIS OPEN LOFT-STYLE OFFICE was typical of 1990s Internet companies.

In the 1990s, the typical office became one of computer work stations, sometimes dozens or hundreds of them in a single warehouselike building. The work people engaged in involved services such as buying and selling everything from toys to real estate; trading stocks, bonds, or other securities; providing banking services; and dispensing information.

Hundreds of new companies emerged that did business solely over the Internet. Many of these "dot coms" were unable to attract customers or keep up with operating costs, and failed within months of starting up.

The New Americans

Amererica's population in the 1990s was more diverse than at any other time in its history. Whites of European background still made up a majority of the population, but minorities—particularly those of Asian and Hispanic descent—were growing fast. The American family was also undergoing profound changes, with increasing numbers of single-parent families and same-sex parents. Despite America's evolving face, old forms of prejudice remained, sometimes triggering new forms of violence.

THE 2010 CENSUS

The Constitution states that every ten years the U.S. government must conduct a census, or population count. A form is sent to every household in the country requesting information about the number, age, sex, and race of the people living there. The 2010 Census estimated America's total population to be 308.7 million.

U.S. POPULATION BY RACE
(in percentages of total population of 308.7 million)

- White: 63.7%
- Hispanic or Latino: 16.3%
- African American: 12.2%
- Asian: 4.8%
- Two or more races: 1.9%
- American Indian and Alaska Native: 0.7%
- Other races: 0.2%
- Native Hawaiian and other Pacific Islanders: 0.2%

The Impact of Immigration

Changes in U.S. immigration law led to changes in the American population. Since 1965, immigration had been limited to 120,000 each year from the Western Hemisphere (North America, Central America, and South America) and 170,000 from the Eastern Hemisphere (Europe, Asia, and Africa). A new law in 1990 more than doubled those limits, greatly increasing the number of immigrants arriving from Asia and Central America. In the last half-century, more than 13 million newcomers arrived from those two regions, compared to fewer than four million from Europe. Hispanic Americans, the fastest growing minority group, now account for 12.5 percent of the population.

THE SWEARING-IN CEREMONY, when immigrants take the oath of allegiance to the United States, is the final step in the citizenship process. Federal legislation prohibiting benefits to illegal aliens spurred many to become U.S. citizens in the 1990s.

The Changing Family

In 1970, more than half of American families followed a "traditional" model – that is made up of husband, wife, and one or more children. By the late 1990s this number had decreased to 35 percent, as other family models became more common. The number of single-parent families, including single fathers raising children, grew during the decade, as did the number of unmarried couples and same-sex couples, some raising children.

Racial Tension Boils Over

Although there were many successes for diversity and acceptance in the 1990s, racial prejudice was still a big concern. In April 1992, a video camera caught Los Angeles police beating a black motorist named Rodney King. King had been pulled over for driving while intoxicated; he resisted arrest and the police responded with excessive force. When a jury found the policemen not guilty of assault, black neighborhoods in Los Angeles erupted in violent riots that resulted in 58 deaths and $1 billion in property damage.

RIOTERS IN LOS ANGELES push over a car after the Rodney King verdict.

Bias Crime

In October 1998, Matthew Shepard, an openly gay student at the University of Wyoming, was strapped to a fence on the outskirts of Laramie and beaten. He was found 18 hours later and rushed to a hospital, but he eventually died. While police claimed that Shepard's death was the result of a robbery attempt gone awry, many people maintained that Shepard was targeted for being homosexual. Arthur Henderson and Aaron McKinney were arrested, found guilty of first-degree murder, and sentenced to life in prison. The event led legislators to take steps toward a more effective Hate Crimes Prevention Act. The act would give authorities more power to prosecute violent crimes motivated by prejudice against race, religion, gender, or sexual orientation.

THE BOY SCOUTS OF AMERICA (BSA), like many American institutions, has tried to adapt to America's changing face by developing programs to meet the needs of boys from a variety of backgrounds, such as young Muslims and boys from urban areas. Gay youths can join the scouts. However, the BSA has attracted public criticism for excluding gay scoutmasters, even though the U.S. Supreme Court upheld its right to do so.

AT THE TRIAL FOR MATTHEW SHEPARD'S KILLERS in October 1999, antigay protesters stood outside the courthouse with signs condemning homosexuals. In response, a number of people dressed up as angels to combat the words of hate with a message of love.

Violence at Home

A s the United States grew more diverse, many people felt threatened by its "melting pot" of races and religions. Some of these people were extremists who claimed they wanted change and tried to achieve it using violence. Americans attacking their own country, which had once been unthinkable, suddenly became a new and overwhelming threat. The availability of weapons dramatically heightened the violent nature of the acts.

Militants

Some extreme right-wing groups created small private armies to "protect" white, Protestant America from blacks, Jews, and foreigners. Such hate groups often saw the government of the United States as the enemy and believed that acts of violence against the government were patriotic acts.

> **DEFINITIONS**
>
> *In politics, **right-wing** groups tend to be conservative and reluctant to change; **left-wing** groups tend to be liberal and want changes made to the established order.*

Standoff with the Branch Davidians

In Waco, Texas, a fringe religious group called the Branch Davidians, led by a charismatic minister named David Koresh, gathered in their compound, a group of fence-enclosed buildings, to prepare for the end of the world. In February 1993, federal agents attempted to raid the compound to search for illegal weapons. A shootout ensued in which four agents were killed. Cult members stood off federal agents, led by the FBI, for 51 days. But on April 19, as the FBI attempted to use tear gas to force an end to the standoff, a fire apparently set by the Davidians destroyed the compound, killing 75 group members.

FIRE ENGULFS THE BRANCH DAVIDIAN COMPOUND near Waco, Texas, in 1993. Twenty-five children died in the blaze. The FBI and Attorney General Janet Reno came under public criticism for allowing the standoff to get out of control.

Oklahoma City Bombing

In April 1995, a 27-year-old Gulf War veteran named Timothy McVeigh detonated a truck full of explosives in front of a federal office building in Oklahoma City, killing 168 people. McVeigh was inspired by the Davidians' militant stand against the federal government. He thought that the government was abusing its power and hoped that this attack would cause others across the country to join his revolt. Nobody did. The crime left people feeling angry and deeply saddened. McVeigh and Terry Nichols, a co-conspirator, were soon caught, tried, and found guilty. Nichols was sentenced to life in prison. McVeigh was sentenced to death and executed in 2001.

THE ALFRED P. MURRAH FEDERAL BUILDING in Oklahoma City, Oklahoma, was almost completely destroyed by the bomb blast. McVeigh later referred to the 19 children killed in the bombing as "collateral damage."

Guns in Schools

By the late 1990s, violent crime in schools was declining. Government statistics show that in 1992 there were 48 reported victims of crime for every 1,000 students. By 1998 that number had dropped to 43. However, a few sensational and tragic events focused national attention on the extreme and violent nature of crimes in schools—particularly crimes involving guns. Many blamed films such as *Natural Born Killers* (1994), which seemed to glamorize violence, while others pointed to the ease with which young people could obtain guns. The events led President Clinton to improve gun safety laws for minors.

AT THE MILLION MOM MARCH in Washington, D.C., on May 14, 2000, hundreds of thousands of protesters demanded that Congress pass common-sense gun control laws. One feature of the march was this memory wall, containing the names of gun-violence victims.

Jonesboro and Columbine

On March 24, 1998, two young boys, aged 11 and 13, opened fire on students after setting off the fire alarm in a Jonesboro, Arkansas, middle school. Andrew Golden and Mitchell Johnson killed four schoolgirls and an English teacher, and injured 12 others.

One year later, on April 20, 1999, Eric Harris, 18, and Dylan Klebold, 17, opened fire on classmates at Columbine High School in Littleton, Colorado. The boys—part of a group called the Trench Coat Mafia—were filled with hate and wanted to strike fear in the hearts of their peers. They planned their attack to occur on Adolf Hitler's birthday. The teenagers killed 13 people and injured 23 others before shooting themselves.

COLUMBINE HIGH SCHOOL students embrace near a memorial for the victims in Littleton, Colorado, on the day after the school shootings.

TED KACZYNSKI, 1942–

Between 1978 and 1995, Ted Kaczynski, also known as the Unabomber, used homemade bombs to attack universities and airlines. He targeted educational and technological institutions because he thought technological advancement would destroy the human race. His bombs killed three people and injured 23 others. The FBI spent more than $50 million trying to capture the 53-year-old Harvard graduate. It was not until his brother contacted authorities that the FBI finally located him in a shack in western Montana. Kaczynski eventually confessed and pleaded guilty to all charges.

UNABOMBER TED KACZYNSKI outside federal court in Helena, Montana, on April 19, 1996

Foreign Affairs

Since the end of World War II, American foreign policy had focused on preventing the expansion of Communism. When the Soviet Union dissolved in 1991, this threat disappeared. The nation's focus shifted to political and humanitarian crises around the world. The United States joined with other nations on missions such as preventing starvation in famine-stricken Somalia. Other crises were closer to home: In the 1990s, for the first time, America faced terrorism on its own soil.

SLOBODAN MILOSEVIC, the first former head of state to be charged with genocide, went on trial in The Hague (Netherlands) in February 2002.

The Breakup of Yugoslavia

In the early 1990s, the former Communist nation of Yugoslavia began to splinter into groups separated by deep animosities. One region, Croatia, declared its independence in 1991, touching off warfare with Serbians ("Serbs") living there.

In 1992, the president of Yugoslavia, Slobodan Milosevic, sent Serb armies into Croatia and Bosnia, which was also trying to break away. Milosevic's troops practiced "ethnic cleansing;" this policy was actually genocide, an attempt to destroy an entire culture, much as Hitler had done with his death camps in World War II.

In 1995, U.S. warplanes led NATO air strikes (see p. 198) against Serbia, forcing Milosevic to the bargaining table. At meetings in Dayton, Ohio, in 1995, President Clinton helped Bosnia and Croatia sign a truce with Serbia. At the same time, a UN court was established in the Netherlands to hear testimony about war crimes, or "crimes against humanity," committed in Bosnia.

Intervention in Kosovo

Trouble erupted in Yugoslavia again in 1997, when the Serbs tried to exercise more control over Kosovo, a province made up largely of Albanian Muslims. The Kosovo Liberation Army launched a fierce counterattack. NATO leaders tried to pressure Milosevic into backing down. When that failed, NATO launched Operation Allied Force on March 24, 1999, bombing Belgrade for 78 days. In June 1999, a 50,000-man peacekeeping force arrived. By September, order was restored and Milosevic was forced out of power.

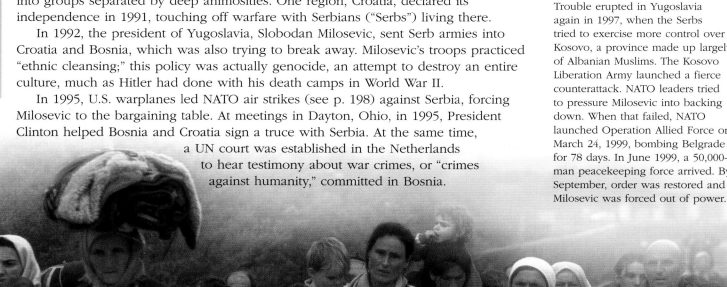

Somalia: Famine and Warlords

In 1992, severe drought and the chaos of civil war led to famine in the African nation of Somalia. More than a third of Somalia's population was at risk of starving to death. In August 1992, President George H. W. Bush, in one of the last foreign policy initiatives of his presidency, announced that U.S. troops would join a UN relief mission to Somalia. When the troops arrived in Mogadishu, the capital of Somalia, in December, their goal was to prevent warring clans from stealing food and relief aid from starving Somalians.

But in time, American and UN troops clashed with the local clans, particularly the Habr Gedir clan and its warlord General Mohamed Farrah Aidid. On October 3, 1993, a raid aimed at arresting some of Aidid's men quickly turned into a full-scale battle (later called the Battle of Mogadishu), in which 18 U.S. soldiers and 1,000 to 2,000 Somalians were killed.

Many Americans were outraged to hear of combat deaths during a humanitarian mission and questioned whether American lives should be risked without clear military objectives. The public outcry led President Clinton to bring the U.S. troops home. On March 25, 1994, the last American troops left Somalia.

A U.S. MARINE stands guard over sacks of food in Mogadishu in December 1992. By the time American troops pulled out in 1994, 40 American soldiers had been killed in battles and skirmishes in Somalia.

Acts of Terror

Islamic fundamentalist groups throughout the Middle East, North Africa, and parts of Asia hated America for its wealth and power as well as its support of Israel, the Jewish homeland (see p. 197).

Fundamentalist Muslims aimed a number of attacks at the United States to show their anger. In January 1993, terrorists exploded a car bomb in the garage of the World Trade Center in New York City, killing six people. In August 1998, truck bombs exploded at U.S. embassies in Kenya and Tanzania, killing 250 people, including 12 Americans, and injuring thousands. Then, in October 2000, a navy ship, the USS *Cole*, was bombed off the coast of Yemen.

American intelligence experts identified and began hunting for the mastermind of the attacks: a millionaire businessman from Saudi Arabia named Osama bin Laden (see p. 265).

ETHNIC ALBANIANS were displaced from their homes by the hundreds of thousands as a result of the war in Yugoslavia. Most of them, like this family, were forced to flee on foot, taking only what they could carry to refugee camps.

THE 1993 ATTACK ON THE WORLD TRADE CENTER left many Americans feeling vulnerable.

THE DESTRUCTION OF THE WORLD TRADE CENTER threw Americans into a state of shock. The events of September 11, 2001, were unexpected and unimaginable. These events consumed American life and shaped much of public and governmental action for the rest of the decade.

Sept. 11, 2001
Two hijacked planes destroy the World Trade Center, another hits the Pentagon, and a fourth crashes in a field

Oct. 2001
USA PATRIOT Act approved

Oct. 7, 2001
U.S. and Britain begin bombing Taliban and Al-Qaeda positions in Afghanistan

Oct. 8, 2001
Office of Homeland Security created

Dec. 12, 2000
Supreme Court halts Florida ballot recount

Dec. 13, 2000
Gore concedes election to Bush

Feb. 1, 2003
Space shuttle Columbia's 28th mission breaks up on reentering the atmosphere

Aug. 2005
More than 1,000 people are killed by Hurricane Katrina

Apr.–May 2006
Millions of immigrants protest against plans to criminalize illegal immigrants

Sept. 2008
Lehman Brothers collapses, causing turmoil in international financial markets—U.S. faces its worst recession since the 1930s

Mar. 2010
Democrats succeed in passing Obamacare bill

2000	2001	2002	2003	2005	2006	2008	2009	2010

May 14, 2000
Million Mom March

Nov. 7, 2000
Presidential election between Al Gore and George W. Bush is undecided

May 24, 2001
Senator James Jeffords leaves the Republican Party to become an Independent

Dec. 9, 2001
Taliban government in Afghanistan collapses

Feb. 2002
Slobodan Milosevic stands trial on genocide charges

2002
Accounting scandals uncovered at several major U.S. companies

Mar. 20, 2003
The Iraq War begins with a U.S. missile attack on Baghdad

Nov. 6, 2006
Saddam Hussein is sentenced to death by hanging after he is found guilty of crimes against humanity

Nov. 4, 2008
Democratic Senator Barack Obama becomes the first African American to win a U.S. presidential election

Jan. 20, 2009
Barack Obama sworn in as president

Apr. 20, 2010
Deepwater Horizon oil disaster begins in the Gulf of Mexico

A NEW MILLENNIUM

2000–2018

New Year's Eve 1999 marked the beginning of a new century and a new millennium. Confident after the Cold War victory a decade earlier, at peace with the world, and with a healthy economy, America was in good shape.

Two years later, terrorists shattered that sense of optimism when they destroyed New York's World Trade Center and damaged the Pentagon, killing thousands. America struck back, forming an international coalition to destroy terrorist networks around the world. But it soon found itself bogged down in two wars, in Afghanistan and Iraq, and its economy suffered in 2008, causing many to wonder what the new century would mean for the United States of America.

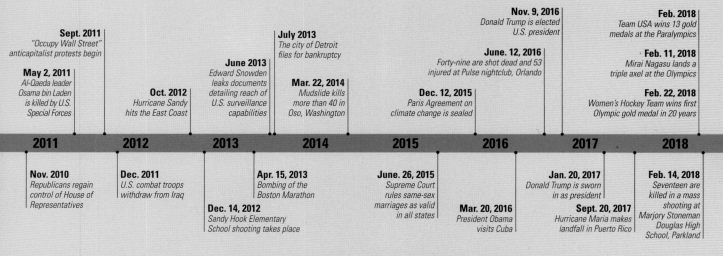

Sept. 2011
"Occupy Wall Street" anticapitalist protests begin

May 2, 2011
Al-Qaeda leader Osama bin Laden is killed by U.S. Special Forces

Oct. 2012
Hurricane Sandy hits the East Coast

July 2013
The city of Detroit files for bankruptcy

June 2013
Edward Snowden leaks documents detailing reach of U.S. surveillance capabilities

Mar. 22, 2014
Mudslide kills more than 40 in Oso, Washington

Dec. 12, 2015
Paris Agreement on climate change is sealed

June. 12, 2016
Forty-nine are shot dead and 53 injured at Pulse nightclub, Orlando

Nov. 9, 2016
Donald Trump is elected U.S. president

Feb. 2018
Team USA wins 13 gold medals at the Paralympics

Feb. 11, 2018
Mirai Nagasu lands a triple axel at the Olympics

Feb. 22, 2018
Women's Hockey Team wins first Olympic gold medal in 20 years

| 2011 | 2012 | 2013 | 2014 | 2015 | 2016 | 2017 | 2018 |

Nov. 2010
Republicans regain control of House of Representatives

Dec. 2011
U.S. combat troops withdraw from Iraq

Apr. 15, 2013
Bombing of the Boston Marathon

Dec. 14, 2012
Sandy Hook Elementary School shooting takes place

June. 26, 2015
Supreme Court rules same-sex marriages as valid in all states

Mar. 20, 2016
President Obama visits Cuba

Jan. 20, 2017
Donald Trump is sworn in as president

Sept. 20, 2017
Hurricane Maria makes landfall in Puerto Rico

Feb. 14, 2018
Seventeen are killed in a mass shooting at Marjory Stoneman Douglas High School, Parkland

Politics Takes a Conservative Turn

I n the 2000 presidential election, Democrat Al Gore stepped out of the shadow of Bill Clinton. He had been Clinton's vice president for eight years. His Republican opponent was George W. Bush, son of former President George H. W. Bush. Neither candidate inspired much voter enthusiasm; barely half the eligible voters went to the polls. On election day, November 7, the vote was so close that no winner was determined until weeks after the polls closed.

MANY VOTERS IN WEST PALM BEACH COUNTY in Florida found this ballot confusing because it was unclear whether the second or third hole from the top should be punched to vote for Gore. Some worried later that they had voted incorrectly.

The Closest Election in History

On election night, Gore had a narrow lead—255 to 246 in the electoral vote, and a slim lead of 200,000 in the popular vote. The outcome of the election would depend on Florida, where the state's 25 electoral votes could make either candidate the next president. Early in the evening, Gore was declared the winner; then that call was withdrawn. Later, Bush was called the winner of Florida; but that, too, was withdrawn.

On the morning of November 8, there was still no new president. The counts were so close between the two candidates that Gore asked the Florida Supreme Court for a recount. The court agreed, and recounting began for the entire state on December 8. Four days later, the U.S. Supreme Court stopped the recount, having decided there wasn't enough time to examine all the ballots equally. The original count would stand, giving Bush Florida's electoral votes. On December 13, 2000, Gore conceded the election and Bush became America's new president.

PRESIDENT-ELECT BUSH and former Vice President Gore meet for the first time after the presidential election of 2000. Even though Gore had led the popular vote—more people across the nation had voted for him—Bush had more electoral votes, and won the election.

JAMES JEFFORDS, 1934–2014

Senator James Jeffords, a Republican from Vermont, shook up the Senate when he announced on May 24, 2001, that he would switch parties. The Senate had been evenly divided—50 Republicans and 50 Democrats. Republicans were the majority party because Vice President Dick Cheney, as the presiding officer of the Senate, would cast the deciding vote in case of a tie. When Jeffords quit the Republican Party to become an independent, he said he would vote with the Democrats on organizational matters—meaning that Democrats now held the majority and controlled most Senate committees.

SENATOR JAMES JEFFORDS announces his decision to leave the Republican Party as Massachusetts Democratic senator Edward Kennedy looks on.

The Return of the Republicans

After eight years of a Democratic administration, the Republicans were eager to leave their mark on the White House. In the closing weeks of his term, Clinton had issued executive orders setting aside thousands of acres of forest land and wilderness to protect them from mining or lumbering. One of President Bush's first actions was to reverse many of those executive orders.

The conservative turn of the Bush presidency was also revealed in the president's choices for his cabinet and other administrative posts. Some of the conservative Republicans he selected had served under his father; in addition, his vice president, Richard B. Cheney, had been in the senior Bush's cabinet.

The Disappearing Surplus

The Clinton administration's budget for 2001 showed a surplus of $184 billion. Bush asked Congress to use that sum for a large tax cut. Congressional Democrats balked at the proposed cut because Bush's plan gave most of the money to the wealthiest Americans.

Then, the surplus itself began to shrink. The economy had turned sluggish and the stock market fell dramatically; this meant that tax revenues did not measure up to the numbers counted on in the annual budget. By the summer of 2001, the surplus had almost completely disappeared and the economy seemed to be heading into a recession.

Economic Growth *v.* the Environment

With the economy tipping toward a recession and an energy crisis in California that suggested a future energy shortage, President Bush withdrew the United States from the Kyoto Protocol. This was the international agreement to reduce atmospheric pollutants (see p. 275), which many Republicans and Democrats felt would hold back the U.S. economy.

Environmentalists were furious. Bush remained firm. "I will not do anything to harm our economy," he declared. He went further and said that to reduce American dependence on foreign oil, he wanted to build 1,900 new power plants to generate electricity, using the nation's abundant supplies of coal as fuel.

In February 2002, President Bush announced his own climate-change plan, which relied on voluntary reductions of pollutants. But many environmentalists argued that voluntary reductions would be unenforceable and ineffective.

PROTESTING THE GLOBAL ECONOMY

In 2000 and 2001, the world's developing countries were becoming desperate over crises such as AIDS and the huge debts they owed developed nations. When the International Monetary Fund and the World Bank held meetings in Washington, D.C., in April 2000, thousands of demonstrators protested that wealthy organizations placed corporate profits above social issues. These protests prompted world leaders to commit more money to combat AIDS. While Europe and Japan also promised to do more to stop global warming, the United States declined to take part.

THOUSANDS OF PROTESTERS gathered in Washington, D.C., to demonstrate at the International Monetary Fund and World Bank meetings. More than 1,100 were arrested.

Terrorism Strikes Home

On the morning of September 11, 2001, Americans were shocked as news of a terrorist attack on the United States unfolded. At 8:46 am, a hijacked airliner crashed into the north tower of the World Trade Center in New York City. Sixteen and a half minutes later, more suicide hijackers steered a second airliner into the south tower. At 9:37 am, in Washington, D.C., a third plane plowed into the Pentagon—the nerve center of the U.S. military—killing 125. A fourth plane, believed to have been heading toward the Capitol building, plunged into a Pennsylvania field after passengers fought back against the hijackers.

"Evil, Despicable Acts of Terror"

The two 110-story towers collapsed within minutes of each other, killing all those still in the buildings, including more than 400 firefighters, police, and city rescue personnel. Miraculously, almost all who were on the floors below the points of impact were evacuated before the towers collapsed.

For his safety, the Secret Service moved the president to a secure location while he stayed in contact with Vice President Cheney and coordinated the nation's response. The attacks, which President Bush called "evil, despicable acts of terror," launched the nation into a new kind of war—against terrorism and those who harbor terrorists.

FIREFIGHTERS SEARCH FOR SURVIVORS in the rubble of the World Trade Center. New York City's firemen and policemen became heroes to many Americans for their brave service during and after the attacks.

The Impact on America

More than three thousand office workers and rescuers lost their lives in the destruction. The heart of New York's financial district was reduced to 16 acres of ash and rubble. With a recession at hand, the stock market—which closed for four days after September 11—experienced the worst week-long drop since the crash of 1929. In the wake of the hijackings, many Americans were reluctant to fly. Each of the major airlines was forced to lay off 10,000 or more employees. The government made a generous loan to the companies to keep them operating. The government also began the complicated process of compensating victims' families.

THE DEATH TOLL

It took authorities weeks to determine how many people had been in the towers at the time of the attack. Although the final count was much less than initially reported, the loss of life is still staggering:

- 2,753 in the towers (including 343 New York City firefighters, 37 Port Authority of New York and New Jersey officers, and 23 New York City police officers)
- 40 in the airline crash in Pennsylvania
- 184 in the Pentagon

Staying Alert

After 9/11, there were more terrorist attempts on flights in the United States. In December 2001, Richard Reid tried to destroy a plane traveling from Paris to Miami by hiding explosives in his shoe. Eight years later, on Christmas Day 2009, Umar Farouk Abdulmutallab attempted to bring down a Northwest Airlines flight as it landed in Detroit, using explosives hidden in his underpants. Both these men were subdued by air crew and passengers before they were able to detonate the bombs successfully.

OSAMA BIN LADEN delivers a videotaped message that was broadcast shortly after the September 11 attacks.

Striking Back

Intelligence sources quickly determined that the man behind the attacks was Osama bin Laden—the Saudi multimillionaire who led an international organization called Al Qaeda—meaning "the Base"—that had launched other attacks on American targets (see p. 259). He was living in Afghanistan, protected by an extremist Muslim group—the Taliban—which had ruled that country for five years. Bin Laden hated American lifestyles and politics, particularly its support of Israel, and had declared a *jihad*, or holy war, against the United States "to kill Americans and plunder their money."

2000–2018

BALLS OF FLAMES shoot out from the south tower (right) moments after being struck by the second airliner; the north tower, struck earlier, billows smoke. By 10:30 am, both buildings, which had each stood 110 stories high, lay in ruins.

The Boston Bombing

The Boston Marathon takes place on Patriot's Day each year, with more than 30,000 competitors and thousands of spectators lining the streets. It shocked the world when this peaceful race ended in tragedy on April 15, 2013. Two Chechen brothers, Dzhokhar and Tamerlan Tsarnaev, aged 19 and 26, exploded two pressure cooker bombs near the finish line, killing three people and injuring 264. Tamerlan was killed evading arrest. When Dzhokhar was caught, he claimed the attack was motivated by Islamic beliefs and revenge on the U.S. for the Afghanistan and Iraq wars.

A BOMB EXPLODES during the Boston Marathon in 2013, as runners approach the finish line—usually a scene of celebration.

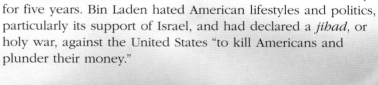

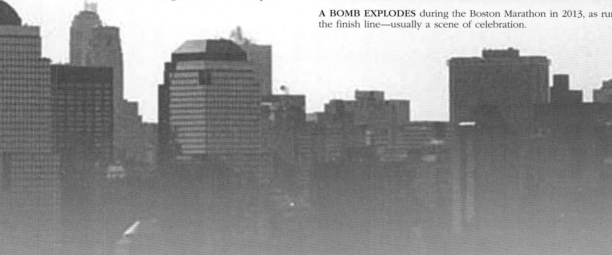

War on Terror

After the 9/11 attacks, the Bush administration decided to take the fight to the enemy, arguing that the best form of defense was offense. As a result, the U.S. would become involved in two wars—one in Afghanistan and a more controversial war in Iraq—along with a broader "war on terror." The costs would prove enormous, with more than 6,000 American troops killed, and the combined expenditures of the war in Afghanistan and Iraq put at between $4 and $6 trillion.

SECRETARY OF STATE COLIN POWELL meets Morocco's King Mohammed VI in April 2002 on a mission to build support for America's war on terrorism.

Protecting Americans

The USA PATRIOT Act was passed in 2001 to help detect and deter terrorist acts. Although it could claim some successes, it was criticized for allowing intelligence services too many opportunities to invade the privacy of individuals, something that was exposed by Edward Snowden, who controversially leaked details of America's surveillance operations to the press.

   The Act was just one of a number of actions designed to improve the safety of Americans. Airport security was tightened, and included the use of full-body scanners in some airports.

Full body scanner

The Bush Doctrine

President Bush pursued a policy to tackle terrorism and so-called rogue states that were a threat to the U.S. It included the right to strike an enemy before the U.S. was attacked first (known as preemption); a belief in regime change (removing leaders from power in countries that the U.S. regarded as a threat); the promotion of democracy overseas; a more unilateralist foreign policy (which meant America was willing to go it alone rather than relying on other countries); and a massive increase in the defense budget.

GUANTÁNAMO BAY

One of the most controversial elements of the war on terror was Guantánamo Bay, a U.S. military prison in Cuba, where suspected terrorists and Al-Qaeda sympathizers were detained. As "unlawful enemy combatants," the suspects were not given the rights of ordinary prisoners of war because they were considered a great threat. There were also accusations made that U.S. security forces engaged in torture to gain information about possible terrorist attacks. The international community widely criticized imprisoning people at Guantánamo, but the Bush administration argued that it was necessary to protect Americans.

IN THIS HOLDING AREA IN GUANTÁNAMO, orange-suited detainees await a medical checkup to assess their health upon entering the prison.

Next stop, Iraq

In March 2003, the U.S. invaded Iraq, accusing its leader, Saddam Hussein, of developing weapons of mass destruction (WMDs) and sponsoring terrorism. Iraqi forces were defeated quickly, and Saddam was tried and executed by his own people. After his removal, the country descended into civil war as different groups competed for power. There were questions as to why U.S. troops remained, because no WMDs were ever found. By the time they left in 2011, more than 4,000 Americans had been killed and 30,000 injured.

A STATUE OF SADDAM HUSSEIN is brought down by U.S. troops in Baghdad on April 9, 2003.

The death of Bin Laden

After years of painstaking work by the U.S. intelligence agencies, Osama bin Laden was tracked to a small compound in Abbottabad, Pakistan. In May 2011, he was killed as he attempted to escape capture by U.S. Special Forces. After his death was confirmed, his body was buried at sea. For many Americans, it felt like the end of a very long journey that had begun on 9/11, but, even after bin Laden's death, Al-Qaeda continued to be a threat.

Afghanistan

The first application of the Bush Doctrine was the invasion of Afghanistan in 2001. Called "Operation Enduring Freedom," the United States led an international coalition to remove the Taliban government that was harboring bin Laden and his Al-Qaeda network. Although the Taliban was quickly defeated, bin Laden escaped, and America found itself bogged down in an increasingly unpopular war that would last for more than a decade. Despite democracy being brought to Afghanistan, terrorist attacks remained commonplace, and more than 2,100 American troops were killed.

A BATTALION OF U.S. TROOPS is transported back to base after fighting the Taliban in the eastern Kumar Province of Afghanistan.

PRESIDENT OBAMA and members of the national security team, including Vice President Joe Biden (left) and Secretary of State Hillary Clinton (second from right), receive an update on the bin Laden mission on May 2, 2011.

2000s A Global Society

Since the year 2000, technology has become a major part of American life. People are more connected to one another and the world than ever before. The rise of the Internet created a global means for people to share ideas, goods, and services, and the development of sites such as Wikipedia opened up opportunities to share knowledge. Digital technology affected all aspects of culture, from photography, music, and politics, to computer games, television, and movies.

Small and Portable

The development of wireless technology allowed people to access the Internet on the go. This pushed hardware, such as cell phones, laptops, e-readers, and tablets, to become smaller, thinner, and lighter. The use of texts, e-mails, and social networks expanded rapidly. Facebook dominated the new social media, growing from a small network of college students at Harvard University in 2004 to more than a billion users worldwide within ten years.

At Your Service

People began to want products at the click of a button. On-demand services allowed live television to be paused, recorded, or downloaded for watching later. Music sales from traditional stores declined as listeners streamed music or bought from a growing number of web retailers, the most successful of which was Amazon, which started in a garage and grew into a multimillion dollar global business with next-day delivery.

Smart Moves and Googling

In 2007, Apple launched its iPhone, a cell phone with a built-in computer and a touch screen. The highly successful iPad followed in 2010. Soon, a third of all Americans would own a smartphone—an iPhone or a phone with similar technology. Through Google's Android and Apple's iOS platforms, apps could be downloaded for social networking, games, news, maps, and much more. Google even gave its name to a search on the Internet—Americans would now "Google it."

APPLE PRODUCTS with their iconic design and simple user interface remained in great demand. Whenever a new Apple product was released, people in the U.S. and many parts of the world lined up overnight to buy the first products off the shelves.

NETFLIX began as a video rental service by mail in 1997. A decade later, it began streaming videos online. Netflix now creates its own Web television series, such as *House of Cards*, and has more than 55 million subscribed viewers in the U.S.

WATSON ON *JEOPARDY*

In 2007, a research project by IBM sought to build a supercomputer that could understand questions accurately and quickly, with data fed into it from books and the Internet. In 2011, the result of this project, Watson, defeated the two biggest winners on *Jeopardy*, a TV game show in which the host provides the answers and the contestants provide the questions. Watson won a $1 million prize, which IBM gave to charity.

Fun for the Whole Family

Where once computer games had been relegated to playrooms and bedrooms, they became an activity for the whole family. Games moved from static computers to cell phones, and they could be played on televisions via linked-in games consoles, such as Playstation, Xbox, and the Nintendo Wii. The Wii, in particular, with its interactive technology, from tennis to Super Mario, encouraged wider gameplay from young children to grandparents.

MINECRAFT, a game about breaking and placing blocks, captured millions of imaginations. People played the game together online across the world. Minecraft was the top game download for both Android and iOS at the start of 2014.

Reality and 3-D

Television viewers watched reality-based programs, such as *American Idol* and *America's Got Talent*, in the millions. On the big screen, advances in movie technology reinvigorated the moviegoing experience and saw box office records broken. In 2009, James Cameron's *Avatar*, which featured characters created by computer-generated imagery, plus 3-D technology, became the biggest-grossing movie of all time.

DANIEL RADCLIFFE, the star of *Harry Potter*, at the movie premiere of *Harry Potter and the Deathly Hallows: Part 1*. J.K. Rowling's *Harry Potter* series of eight movies from seven novels turned into one of the highest-grossing movie franchises. The *Hunger Games* trilogy, a popular young adult series, also became a multimillion dollar global franchise.

Sports

Enthusiasm for sports remained strong, and although baseball and football still led the way, more extreme sports were embraced and new audiences were sought around the world. U.S. football teams played league games in London, England, while new sports, such as snowboarding, attracted younger fans.

Going for Gold

U.S. swimmer Michael Phelps became the most decorated Olympian of all time in 2012 by winning 22 medals, including 18 golds, beating a record that had stood for 48 years. His winning streak continued at the Rio de Janeiro Olympics in 2016. Phelps won his medals in individual and team swimming, including the butterfly, the individual medley, and the freestyle relay over 100, 200, and 400 meters.

Salt Lake City, 2002

The Winter Olympics came to Salt Lake City in February of 2002. Watched by a global audience of two billion people, the U.S. set a record for the most gold medals won in a home Olympics. America found two new heroes in Jim O'Shea Jr., who won the skeleton, and Sarah Hughes who, at only 16 years of age, made a dramatic comeback to win the gold medal for figure skating.

DURING A MOVING OPENING CEREMONY, athletes carried a flag rescued from the September 11 attacks. The games were a healing moment for America.

PHELPS won eight medals in 2004 (Athens), eight again in 2008 (Beijing), six in 2012 (London), and six in 2016 (Rio), taking his total medal tally at the Olympics to 28.

Sportswomen

High-school athletics saw 3.4 million girls taking part in sports in 2017–2018. Soccer soared in popularity, with the U.S. women's team winning their fourth Olympic gold in 2012. The women's hockey team won gold in the 2018 Winter Olympics. Mirai Nagasu created history in ice skating. In 2018, she became the first American woman to land a triple axel at the Olympics. In tennis, Serena Williams earned the most Grand Slam titles.

THE U.S. WOMEN'S NATIONAL SOCCER TEAM led the world with Olympic gold wins in 1996, 2004, 2008, and 2012 (above).

PARALYMPICS

The Paralympic Games, which celebrate the accomplishments of athletes with disabilities, have grown in popularity since their American debut in 2002 at Salt Lake City, Utah. At the 2018 games in PyeongChang, 569 athletes representing 49 countries participated in 80 medal events in total, including snowboarding, skiing, and ice hockey. The United States topped the medal table with 36 medals—13 of them gold. More than 2 billion people watched part of the television broadcast of the Games.

AT THE SLEDGE HOCKEY FINAL IN 2002, America beat Norway 4–3 to take Olympic gold in front of 8,315 excited fans.

The Rise of X Men and X Women

An exciting development was the growing popularity of extreme sports, which led to the introduction of the X Games. Founded in 1995, and first televised in 2002, the X Games brought global attention to sports such as BMX (biking), snowboarding, skateboarding, rally racing, motocross, and snowmobiling. Snowboarding became an Olympic event in 1998. At the 2018 PyeongChang games, Shaun White—winner of 13 X Game winter titles—won his third Olympic gold in snowboarding.

CHLOE KIM—a four-time X Game gold medalist—is the youngest woman to win an Olympic gold for snowboarding and the first woman to win two medals at the Winter Youth Olympics for snowboarding.

Baseball Strikes Out

One of the worrying trends uncovered was the growing use of banned substances by sportsmen. Baseball was rocked in December 2007 by the Mitchell Report, which linked 89 Major League Baseball players to the use of illegal, performance-enhancing drugs. Mitchell condemned what he called "baseball's steroids era" and called for unannounced year-round testing by an independent body to help clean up the game. The players angrily denied his accusations.

LANCE ARMSTRONG was stripped of his titles and banned for life from any future cycling competitions.

ROGER CLEMENS of the New York Yankees, one of the game's greatest pitchers, was the most prominent player accused of illegal drug taking.

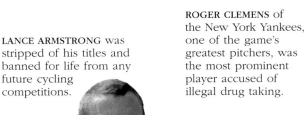

Cycling Shame

The most dramatic fall from grace for any sportsman in the modern era was probably that of cyclist Lance Armstrong, who won a record seven titles in the Tour de France—all after he had successfully battled cancer. Armstrong earned millions from sponsorship and was admired by many for his athleticism and sheer determination. However, this came crashing down when, after denying it for many years, he admitted he was involved in a doping scandal.

Natural Disasters

America has many different geographical features and diverse weather patterns, from hot deserts to cold mountains and vast, blue-sky prairies to raging waters in deep canyons. The beauty of the country is immense. But the country has also experienced catastrophic natural disasters that caused heartache and devastation, and continued to remind Americans of the power of Mother Nature.

2000–2018

HURRICANE KATRINA'S STORM SURGE overwhelmed the flood defenses of New Orleans—80 percent of the city was under water. Thousands of people were displaced, and many were still unable to return a year later.

Hurricane Katrina

On August 29, 2005, Hurricane Katrina hit the Gulf Coast, causing damage from central Florida to Texas. It affected more than 90,000 square miles, with water surging 12 miles inland. Worst hit was New Orleans, where, despite a mandatory evacuation, many thousands were trapped—1,833 people died from the storm and flooding that followed. The Federal Emergency Management Agency (FEMA) was criticized for failing to prepare for the aftermath, as was President Bush for not realizing how bad the situation was. In 2017, President Trump was also blamed for failing to provide adequate care for the people of Puerto Rico after another hurricane, Maria, devastated the island.

Hurricane Sandy

If Hurricane Katrina was not enough, America found itself battered again seven years later by Hurricane Sandy, which caused extensive damage across several northeastern states, killing 159 people. New Jersey and New York were hit the hardest on October 29, 2012. In New York City, record storm surges flooded streets, tunnels, and subway lines. The New York Stock Exchange closed for two days, the first time since 1888, and the presidential election campaign was suspended.

MORE THAN EIGHT MILLION PEOPLE lost power and 650,000 homes were damaged or destroyed. The hurricane was so powerful it was nicknamed "Frankenstorm" and "Superstorm Sandy."

A GLOBAL COMMUNITY

When disaster strikes at home, communities pull together. During Hurricane Katrina, people offered their homes to evacuees, while those with boats rescued thousands trapped in the floodwaters. Americans have also helped those less fortunate overseas. After the tsunamis in Indonesia in 2004 and 2018, and Japan in 2011, the U.S. offered logistical support and expertise to help clear up the devastation. USAID continues to support projects around the world to tackle disease and famine, and provide education and medical supplies.

U.S. FAIRFAX COUNTY SEARCH AND RESCUE search rubble in Kamaishi, Japan, in the aftermath of the tsunami of 2011.

Mudslides

On March 22, 2014, a huge mudslide in the state of Washington killed 42 people. Caused by heavy rains, it engulfed more than 30 houses in a rural community near the town of Oso, 55 miles north of Seattle. Another mudflow, with 15-ft tall walls of debris, swept through the town of Montecito, in Santa Barbara County, California, on January 9, 2018. The mudslide killed at least 21 people and destroyed more than 100 homes.

THE OSO MUDSLIDE ripped through a small community of 180 people, destroying buildings, blocking roads, and damming a local river. Little sign of the community remained afterward.

Tornadoes

Tornadoes are a regular feature in the U.S., but 2011 was an unusually active and deadly year, with 1,691 touching down. April set a new record of 758 tornadoes, with April 25–28 being particularly destructive, when 312 touched down in a single 24-hour period. Four of the tornadoes were strong enough to be given the highest rating of category EF5, with winds in excess of 200 miles an hour. The tornadoes killed at least 350 people, flattening farm buildings and downing power lines, causing $11 billion of damage.

A TORNADO HEADS NORTH across Nebraska on June 20, 2011. The most destructive tornado in 2011 was much larger than this at 1.5 miles wide, with a track 80 miles long. It hit Tuscaloosa, killing 65 people, making it the deadliest tornado since 1955.

Environment

The 21st century has brought greater awareness of the environmental concerns facing both the United States and the rest of the world. Climate change continues to affect the environment across the U.S., particularly in contributing to droughts, wildfires, and hurricanes, all of which have increasingly plagued the country. New initiatives, such as investment in renewable energy, have been launched to better protect the planet and its resources.

2000–2018

A HELICOPTER DROPS FLAME RETARDANT to try and put out raging California fires in 2007. A combination of a drought, hot weather, and the strong Santa Ana winds were most likely to blame for the fires—conditions that were expected to be repeated in the future.

Climate Change

In the 1980s, scientists started to speak of global warming, caused mainly by the "greenhouse effect"—the trapping of heat by a layer of carbon dioxide and other gases in the atmosphere. The steadily rising temperatures across the planet have, in turn, led to changes in the climate. As a result, the U.S. has seen an increase in extreme weather patterns, such as more intense hurricanes and droughts. Recognizing the seriousness of the situation, Barack Obama became the first president to introduce environmental laws to regulate carbon pollution from power plants and provided investments for renewable, or green, energy.

Wildfires

Always a problem in western U.S., wildfires have worsened in the 21st century due to climate change. States like California have had highly destructive fire seasons. More than 30 wildfires occurred there in 2007, spreading across 970,000 acres of land. In October 2018, the state had the deadliest wildfire to date when Camp Fire—named after Camp Creek Road where it originated—destroyed around 17,000 habitable structures, including homes and schools, and killed more than 85 people.

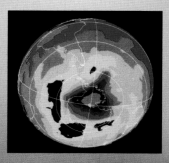

THE HOLE IN THE OZONE LAYER is shown over Antarctica in this computer-enhanced satellite photo. Ozone helps protect Earth from the sun's radiation. After bans on the manufactured chemicals that caused the hole, it has begun to recover.

Biodiversity Loss

Coined in 1985, the term "biodiversity loss" refers to the extinction of plant and animal species, as well as their reduction in certain areas. The rate of global biodiversity loss is estimated to be at least 100 times higher at present than it naturally should be. Climate change, pollution, and a decline in habitats are a few of the key factors that have endangered wildlife and flora. In America, the population of common birds has declined over the years, and freshwater fish, bumblebees, butterflies, and even polar bears are some of the animals whose existence is threatened. Scientists estimate that one-third of all U.S. species are at risk of extinction.

ENDANGERED SPECIES, such as the polar bears found in parts of Alaska, are declining at an increasingly rapid rate.

Deepwater Horizon

On April 20, 2010, the Deepwater Horizon drilling rig exploded in the Gulf of Mexico, killing 11 workers. After burning for 36 hours, the rig sank, causing an oil spill that would become the worst environmental disaster in American history, surpassing even the 1989 Exxon Valdez oil spill. It took three months to plug the leak, during which 4.9 million barrels of oil escaped, threatening marine life and hundreds of miles of coastline.

THE DEEPWATER HORIZON oil spill harmed seabirds, such as this pelican. Scientists warned the environmental impact of the disaster would not be fully known for years.

2000–2018

RISING TEMPERATURES IN THE U.S.

Temperatures have been rising in the U.S., reflecting the general global pattern. On average, current temperatures in America have been 1.5°F warmer than in past centuries. The year 2017 was the third-warmest year on record after 2016 and 2015, indicating an increasing trend. The rise in temperatures contributes not just to hotter, longer summers, but also to longer allergy seasons, more intensive droughts (which, in turn, feed wildfires), a decline in livestock, and the easier spread of tropical diseases.

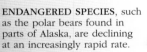

U.S. AVERAGE

(graph: Temperature Change (°F) on y-axis from -2 to 2; x-axis years 1900 to 2020)

THIS GRAPH shows the average temperature difference during 1900–2017, taking 52°F as the average temperature. There is a large rise toward the start of the new century.

Green Initiatives

Efforts are being made in the United States to reduce carbons—which contribute to climate change—emitted by human activities. The U.S. signed the Kyoto Protocol in 1998, which was an international treaty pledging to reduce the emission of heat-trapping greenhouse gases, but Congress did not approve the treaty. Later, in 2015, the U.S. joined many countries in agreeing to combat climate change and bring about a low-carbon future by signing the United Nations' Paris Agreement. Green energy, rather than fossil fuels, and biofuels made from sustainable sources such as animal or food waste were given an investment boost. Americans began to think of conserving energy in their daily lives to save the environment, such as by recycling. However, President Trump announced in 2017 that the U.S. would withdraw from the Paris Agreement. In response, many American governors and mayors redoubled their support of green initiatives; 84 cities or counties have pledged to use 100% renewable energy in the near future.

ELECTRIC CARS powered by large, rechargeable batteries and hybrid cars, which combine a small gasoline engine with an electric motor and batteries, are steadily rising in number on America's roads.

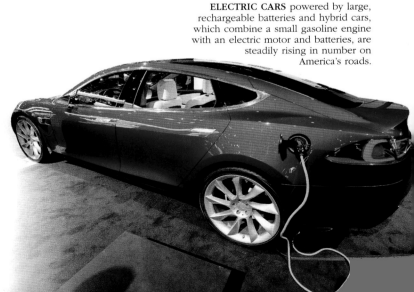

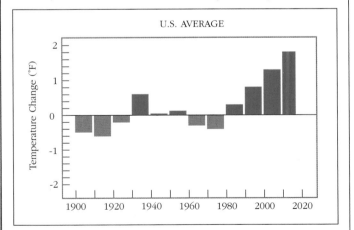

Obama Wins the Election

In 2009, Barack Obama became the first African American president of the United States. Initially, he inspired confidence with the campaign messages "Change we can believe in" and "Yes we can," winning 53 percent of the vote and big majorities in both houses of Congress. But he would soon find it difficult to govern a country that was increasingly polarized. Within two years, the Democrats would lose control of the House.

MORE THAN ONE MILLION PEOPLE came to Washington, D.C., to see Barack Obama take the oath of office. He became the 44th President of the United States of America, with his wife, Michelle, by his side.

Economic Collapse

In 2007, economists began to worry about the increasing number of Americans who were struggling with their mortgage payments. The banks responded by limiting the amount of money that could be borrowed, creating a "credit crunch." This began an economic slowdown, which would see one of America's most powerful banks, Lehman Brothers, collapse in September 2008, followed by a large fall in the U.S. stock market. The economy went into the worst recession since the Great Depression.

DURING THE RECESSION, many people lost their homes, unemployment reached ten percent, and food banks became commonplace. Obama launched a stimulus package, opposed by many Republicans, to kick-start the economy.

The End of the American Dream?

Though the U.S. economy remained the largest in the world, the recession saw Americans begin to worry about whether their children would be worse off than themselves. Middle class and blue collar incomes flatlined, or fell. The divide between the richest and poorest in America was at its widest since 1927. Many feared the increasing challenge posed by the rise of the BRIC countries (Brazil, Russia, India, and China). Of these, China seemed to be the strongest competitor to America.

DESPITE THE RECESSION, the world's largest companies, many leading universities, and the world's strongest military were in America.

2000–2018

GAY RIGHTS BILL

In 2004, Massachusetts became the first state to legalize same-sex marriages. A number of other states would follow, reflecting growing public support. In 2010, the military's "Don't Ask, Don't Tell" policy was repealed. In 2012, Tammy Baldwin from Wisconsin became the first openly gay politician elected to the Senate. Many religious groups opposed these changes, taking their battle to state legislatures and to the courts. Though well organized, they increasingly found themselves in the minority.

A COUPLE CELEBRATES the U.S. Supreme Court ruling in favor of gay marriage.

The Tea Party Movement

In 2010, the traditional two-party system was shaken up by the election successes of the "Tea Party." Taking its name from the Boston Tea Party of 1773, it was a populist, anti-Washington movement that believed the federal government had become too powerful. Its supporters tended to oppose high taxes, and often had evangelical religious values. Although many believed Barack Obama was not fully committed to the U.S., they also attacked well-established Republicans who they felt needed to do a better job.

Cuban Thaw

In December 2014, President Barack Obama and the Cuban President Raúl Castro announced that Cuba and America would begin to normalize relations, ending 54 years of hostility. Obama became the first American president to visit Cuba since 1928, traveling with his family and a group of Cuban-American leaders for a three-day visit in March 2016. While there, Obama also met with dissidents—Cubans who wished to replace the Castro regime with a more democratic government.

Cuban President Raúl Castro

Immigration

America was founded on immigration, but it became a controversial subject in the 21st century as demographics changed. Increasing numbers of illegal immigrants led to a complex debate centered on what America should do with them—whether to absorb them legally into American society, or return them to their place of origin. The recession heightened tensions as unemployment rose.

BILINGUAL SIGNS encouraged people to vote in the midterm elections in New Mexico. It was predicted that more Americans would speak Spanish than English by 2050.

WOMEN IN POLITICS

Women continued to make gains in the boardroom and in politics. In 2007, Nancy Pelosi became the first woman to serve as Speaker of the House. In 2008, Senator Hillary Rodham Clinton narrowly lost the nomination of the Democratic Party to be its presidential candidate, while Alaska's governor, Sarah Palin, became the first woman to be chosen as the Republican Party's Vice Presidential candidate. In 2014, Janet Yellen became the first female chairperson of the Federal Reserve Bank.

BETWEEN 1997 AND 2010, there were three female Secretaries of State, including Condoleezza Rice (above).

Donald Trump

Although Democrat Hillary Clinton was heavily favored to win the 2016 U.S. presidential election, and did win the popular vote, Republican Donald Trump and his running mate Mike Pence won in the Electoral College. Prior to the election, Trump was best known as a reality TV star, hosting the show "The Apprentice." Though his exact net worth is unclear, Trump has built his public persona on the claim that he is a billionaire. Since the 2016 election, US politics have further fractured, and the ideological differences between those on the left and those on the right have increased.

Winning America

Trump's presidential campaign was largely aimed at white, working-class voters. He promised to revive fading industries, such as the coal, steel, and auto industries, as well as reduce the number of immigrants in the country. Those who wanted to ensure that a Republican president chose the next Supreme Court justices also came out in his support. His criticism of Hillary Clinton's use of private email servers while serving in the government bolstered his campaign.

TRUMP AND MEDIA

Trump has often clashed with the media over their reporting of his actions. Reminiscent of Richard Nixon's conflicts with the press before and during his presidency, Trump and his press secretaries have called critical reports "fake news" and have even referred to journalists as "the enemy of the American people." He has often taken to social media platforms, such as Twitter, to voice his side of the story without the filter of the press, frequently bypassing traditional briefings by the press secretary.

SARAH HUCKABEE SANDERS is Trump's second press secretary.

TRUMP PENCE
New York, New York
MAKE AMERICA GREAT AGAIN!

HILLARY CLINTON

Trump's opponent, former Secretary of State Hillary Clinton, made history as the first female candidate to be nominated for president in the U.S. by a major political party. Clinton wore white to accept the nomination, in honor of the suffragists who chose to wear the color as they fought for women's right to vote. However, her bid to become president was ultimately unsuccessful due to many complex factors, including social media campaigns, as well as narrow but strategic defeats in key states that tipped the Electoral College in her opponent's favor.

HILLARY CLINTON was formerly the First Lady. She is married to the 42nd president, Bill Clinton.

DONALD TRUMP at an Election Night event in his hometown of New York City

Foreign Relations

Despite several controversies, relations between the U.S. and other countries have varied throughout Trump's presidency. In 2018, the U.S. imposed economic sanctions on Iran while maintaining a close friendship with Saudi Arabia, despite the murder of *Washington Post* journalist Jamal Khashoggi in that country. Relations with Russia have been mixed since the Director of National Intelligence and Homeland Security officials confirmed that the Russian government interfered in the 2016 elections to destabilize democracy in the U.S. This included hacking into American elected officials' emails. The Trump administration has denied conclusive findings about the interference.

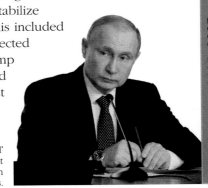

RUSSIAN PRESIDENT VLADIMIR PUTIN has said that his country did not interfere in the American elections.

North Korea

In June 2018, President Trump joined North Korean leader Kim Jong Un at a summit in Singapore. It marked the first-ever meeting between leaders of the two countries. President Trump had earlier made no secret of the U.S.'s strict stance against North Korea's nuclear arsenal. At the summit, both leaders pledged to work toward "complete denuclearization of the Korean peninsula," and Trump promised security guarantees in return.

People Take to the Streets

Trump's victory stimulated a variety of new protests. Beginning with the historic Women's March in January 2017—which drew up to 1 million people to Washington and up to 5 million people to local marches—Americans took to the streets to call attention to many human rights issues. New demonstrations also occurred organized by the Far Right movement, often directed against immigrants and minorities. One incident turned tragic when a white supremacist drove his car into a crowd in Charlottesville, Virginia, killing a woman.

THOUSANDS PROTESTED against the Far Right's sentiments on May 1, 2017, for the nationwide strike termed "Day Without an Immigrant" to show solidarity toward immigrants in the United States.

Guns in America

The U.S. continued to have the world's highest rate of gun ownership. But this came at a price. In 2017, over 15,000 people in America were killed by guns. Since 2000, high-profile shootings, including those at Sandy Hook Elementary School in Newtown, Connecticut, and at Marjorie Stoneman Douglas High School in Parkland, Florida, saw America divided over the rights and wrongs of gun control. Many wondered if the time for reform had come.

Mass Shootings

There were 346 incidents of mass shootings in the U.S. in 2017 alone. The deadliest mass shooting by an individual in America saw 58 people killed at a concert in Las Vegas on October 1, 2017. Previous mass shootings also kept haunting the public consciousness. On July 20, 2012, a gunman wearing protective tactical gear killed 12 people and wounded 58 at a movie theater in Aurora, Colorado. Forty-nine people were shot dead with a legally bought rifle and handgun at the Pulse Nightclub in Orlando, Florida, on September 19, 2016.

Firearms Ownership

Although the U.S. had only five percent of the world's population it had roughly 35 to 50 percent of the world's civilian-owned guns, with 88 firearms per 100 people. That amounted to 270 million guns. The number of guns per household actually declined steadily from the 1970s, yet the number of firearms owned by an individual increased from 4.1 per person in 1994 to 6.9 by 2004.

IN 2013, stricter gun control measures came into force in 15 states. However, other states gave more rights and protection to gun owners.

NEWTOWN REMEMBERS OUR HEROES

ON DECEMBER 14, 2012, at Sandy Hook Elementary School, in Newtown, Connecticut, 20 children between the ages of 6 and 7 and 6 adults were killed.

CONGRESSWOMAN GABRIELLE GIFFORDS was badly wounded in an assassination attempt in Tucson, Arizona, in 2011. Six people were killed and 13 injured during the attack.

Campaign Groups

The Brady Campaign to Prevent Gun Violence, a leading advocate of gun control, argued that as well as the incalculable, tragic human cost of gun violence, there were other costs, such as medical treatment for gunshot wounds and providing rehabilitation, as well as the cost to emergency services. Some estimates put these economic costs at $100 billion a year. However, groups such as the National Rifle Association and the Gun Owners of America argued that the right to bear arms was guaranteed by the Bill of Rights and could not be taken away. Young people who survived the Stoneman Douglas shooting in 2018 formed the Never Again MSD group to push back against the idea that sensible gun legislation would restrict anyone's rights.

Gun Control and the Law

Despite the public outcry that followed each of these tragedies, the federal government failed to pass any new significant gun control laws across the nation. A little over a month after the Sandy Hook massacre, President Obama unveiled a new plan for gun control, including enhanced background checks on people buying guns, and bans on military-style assault weapons. Due to the resistance of pro-gun interest groups and politicians, not one law passed. However, after the high school shooting at Parkland, states took up the cause of gun control and passed 50 new laws. These laws ranged from banning certain types of guns to making it harder for people in mental distress to purchase guns. At the federal level, the Supreme Court is yet to rule on whether automatic weapons can be banned.

GUN ADVOCATES ARGUED that the right to bear arms was as important as protecting free speech and freedom of religion.

GUN VIOLENCE STATISTICS (2017)	
Gun-related deaths	15,643
Gun-related injuries	32,255
Teenage deaths and injuries	3,247
Child deaths and injuries	732
Mass shootings	346
Unintentional shooting	2,036

Self-defense

A common argument made by pro-gun groups was that of self defense, and the belief that guns, in the hands of law-abiding citizens, could help reduce crime. The killing of Trayvon Martin, a 17-year-old African American high school student in February, 2012, exposed the divide on this issue. The shooter, who was the neighborhood watch coordinator for a gated community in Sanford, Florida, shot Martin, who was unarmed, in an altercation. He claimed to have acted in self-defense, and was later found not guilty of murder.

THE JURY'S decision in the Trayvon Martin case split public opinion, with almost 90 percent of African Americans calling the shooting unjustified, compared to a third of whites.

Medicine

Medical care took great steps forward at the start of the 21st century. The federal government controversially sought to expand health insurance to uninsured Americans, while U.S.-funded research mapped the building blocks of life and investigated new treatments for illnesses. Science, it appeared, had entered a golden age of discovery.

The fear of pandemics

Many Americans were concerned that a new pandemic was imminent. The last pandemic, Spanish flu, killed more than 20 million people a century earlier. Health specialists tracked potentially dangerous diseases, such as Severe Acute Respiratory Syndrome (SARS) and avian influenza, commonly called bird flu, to help contain them. Bans were introduced on poultry imported from countries where bird flu existed.

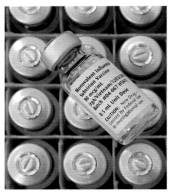

GOVERNMENT SCIENTISTS worked hard to develop vaccines that were then stockpiled in case of an outbreak of dangerous diseases.

Prosthetics

Advances in medical science on the battlefield saw an increase in the number of soldiers surviving traumatic injuries, whether physical or mental. Where once a soldier losing a limb might be confined to a wheelchair or crutches, and most likely retired from service, advancements in prosthetic technology meant that some amputee service members were even able to remain on active duty.

MICROPROCESSOR LEGS significantly improved the quality of life and speed of recovery for amputees. Known as bionic legs, they offered impressive stability and mobility.

Human Genome Project

The Human Genome Project was one of the most groundbreaking pieces of scientific research ever carried out. Completed in 2003, and funded by the United States, a team of international researchers set out with the aim of sequencing all three billion base pairs in the human genome, which is the complete set of DNA in the human body. The project enabled researchers to understand the genetic factors in human diseases, allowing them to develop new methods of diagnosis, treatment, and prevention.

THE COMPLETION of the Human Genome Project was announced exactly 50 years after the discovery of the DNA double helix.

Stem Cell Research

One promising medical development was stem cell research. This involved taking cells from a human being, such as from adult organs or an umbilical cord after a baby is born, that could then be grown into any type of cell found in the body. These stem cells could be used to treat a whole series of currently incurable diseases, such as Parkinson's or Alzheimer's and certain cancers, as well as rebuilding bones and repairing damaged nervous systems.

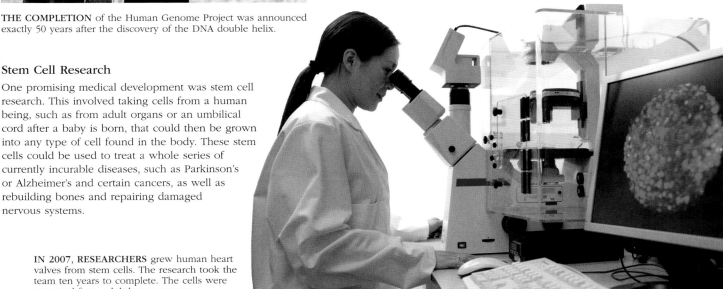

IN 2007, RESEARCHERS grew human heart valves from stem cells. The research took the team ten years to complete. The cells were extracted from adult bone marrow.

OBAMACARE

The Patient Protection and Affordable Care Act of 2010, known as Obamacare, was a policy of the Obama administration. This $938 billion program was designed to extend affordable, quality health care to 32 million uninsured Americans. It was the most significant overhaul of the medical system since the introduction of Medicaid and Medicare in 1965. Many opposed its introduction, fearing it was an unnecessary expansion of federal government power. Not one Republican in Congress voted for Obamacare and it was also challenged, unsuccessfully, in the U.S. Supreme Court.

BY 2014, it was estimated that more than eight million Americans had enrolled for health care under Obamacare.

Encouraging healthy living

The new century saw the U.S. become the most obese nation in the world, with one-third of the population classified as seriously overweight. Obesity-related conditions included some of the leading causes of preventable deaths, such as heart disease, stroke, type 2 diabetes, and certain types of cancer. State and federal governments sought to tackle this worrying epidemic, with First Lady Michelle Obama launching the "Let's Move!" campaign to get people fit, while calorie counts were introduced to menus. Even *Sesame Street*'s Cookie Monster switched to eating more fruit and vegetables.

FIRST LADY MICHELLE OBAMA plays flag football with children in New Orleans as part of her "Let's Move!" campaign to challenge childhood obesity. In 2014, one-quarter of all children in the U.S. were obese.

Appendix

Readers can consult the reference material in this section of the book to check specific facts, or to read original documents that are discussed in the main text. A list of U.S. presidents tells when they served, where they were from, and the party they represented. A chart of the 50 states shows key facts about each one. The appendix also includes original documents that are of great importance to American history: the Declaration of Independence, the Constitution and its amendments, and the Gettysburg Address.

The Presidents of the United States

1. George Washington
Virginia, Federalist
Years in office:
1789–1797

2. John Adams
Massachusetts, Federalist
Years in office:
1797–1801

3. Thomas Jefferson
Virginia, Democrat-
Republican or Republican
Years in office:
1801–1809

4. James Madison
Virginia, Democrat-
Republican or Republican
Years in office:
1809–1817

5. James Monroe
Virginia, Democrat-
Republican or Republican
Years in office:
1817–1825

6. John Q. Adams
Massachusetts, Democrat-
Republican or National
Republican
Years in office:
1825–1829

7. Andrew Jackson
Tennessee, Democrat
Years in office:
1829–1837

8. Martin Van Buren
New York, Democrat
Years in office:
1837–1841

9. William H. Harrison
Virginia, Whig
Year in office:
1841

10. John Tyler
Virginia, Whig or
Whig & Democrat
Years in office:
1841–1845

11. James K. Polk
Tennessee, Democrat
Years in office:
1845–1849

12. Zachary Taylor
North Carolina, Whig
Years in office:
1849–1850

13. Millard Fillmore
New York, Whig
Years in office:
1850–1853

14. Franklin Pierce
New Hampshire,
Democrat
Years in office:
1853–1857

15. James Buchanan
Pennsylvania, Democrat
Years in office:
1857–1861

16. Abraham Lincoln
Illinois, Republican
Years in office:
1861–1865

17. Andrew Johnson
Tennessee, Republican
or Unionist
Years in office:
1865–1869

18. Ulysses S. Grant
Ohio, Republican
Years in office:
1869–1877

19. Rutherford B. Hayes
Ohio, Republican
Years in office:
1877–1881

20. James A. Garfield
Ohio, Republican
Year in office:
1881

21. Chester A. Arthur
New York, Republican
Years in office:
1881–1885

22. Grover Cleveland
New York, Democrat
Years in office:
1885–1889

23. Benjamin Harrison
Indiana, Republican
Years in office:
1889–1893

24. Grover Cleveland
New York, Democrat
Years in office:
1893–1897

25. William McKinley
Ohio, Republican
Years in office:
1897–1901

26. Theodore Roosevelt
New York, Republican
Years in office:
1901–1909

27. William H. Taft
Ohio, Republican
Years in office:
1909–1913

28. Woodrow Wilson
New Jersey, Democrat
Years in office:
1913–1921

29. Warren G. Harding
Ohio, Republican
Years in office:
1921–1923

30. Calvin Coolidge
Massachusetts, Republican
Years in office:
1923–1929

31. Herbert C. Hoover
California, Republican
Years in office:
1929–1933

32. Franklin D. Roosevelt
New York, Democrat
Years in office:
1933–1945

33. Harry S. Truman
Missouri, Democrat
Years in office:
1945–1953

34. Dwight D. Eisenhower
New York, Republican
Years in office:
1953–1961

35. John F. Kennedy
Massachusetts, Democrat
Years in office:
1961–1963

36. Lyndon B. Johnson
Texas, Democrat
Years in office:
1963–1969

37. Richard M. Nixon
California, Republican
Years in office:
1969–1974

38. Gerald R. Ford
Michigan, Republican
Years in office:
1974–1977

39. James E. Carter
Georgia, Democrat
Years in office:
1977–1981

40. Ronald Reagan
California, Republican
Years in office:
1981–1989

41. George H. W. Bush
Texas, Republican
Years in office:
1989–1993

42. William J. Clinton
Arkansas, Democrat
Years in office:
1993–2001

43. George W. Bush
Texas, Republican
Years in office:
2001–2009

44. Barack Obama
Illinois, Democrat
Years in office:
2009–2017

45. Donald Trump
New York, Republican
Years in office:
2017–Present

State	Date of Statehood	Capital	State Tree	State Bird	State Flower	Nickname
ALABAMA	1819	Montgomery	Southern Longleaf Pine	Yellowhammer	Camellia	Yellowhammer State or Cotton State or The Heart of Dixie
ALASKA	1959	Juneau	Sitka Spruce	Willow Ptarmigan	Forget-Me-Not	The Last Frontier
ARIZONA	1912	Phoenix	Palo verde	Cactus Wren	Saguaro Cactus Blossom	Grand Canyon State
ARKANSAS	1836	Little Rock	Pine	Mockingbird	Apple Blossom	The Natural State
CALIFORNIA	1850	Sacramento	California Redwood	California Valley Quail	Golden Poppy	Golden State
COLORADO	1876	Denver	Blue Spruce	Lark Bunting	(Rocky Mountain) Columbine	Centennial State
CONNECTICUT	1788	Hartford	White Oak	Robin	Mountain Laurel	Constitution State
DELAWARE	1787	Dover	American Holly	Blue Hen Chicken	Peach Blossom	First State
FLORIDA	1845	Tallahassee	Sabal Palm	Mockingbird	Orange Blossom	Sunshine State
GEORGIA	1788	Atlanta	Live Oak	Brown Thrasher	Cherokee Rose	Peach State or Empire State of the South
HAWAII	1959	Honolulu	Kukui (Candlenut)	Nene (Hawaiian Goose)	Hibiscus	Aloha State
IDAHO	1890	Boise	Western White Pine	Mountain Bluebird	Syringa	Gem State
ILLINOIS	1818	Springfield	White Oak	Cardinal	Native Violet	Prairie State or Land of Lincoln
INDIANA	1816	Indianapolis	Tulip Tree	Cardinal	Peony	Hoosier State
IOWA	1846	Des Moines	Oak	Eastern Goldfinch	Wild Rose	Hawkeye State
KANSAS	1861	Topeka	Cottonwood	Western Meadowlark	Sunflower	Sunflower State
KENTUCKY	1792	Frankfort	Tulip Tree	Kentucky Cardinal	Goldenrod	Bluegrass State
LOUISIANA	1812	Baton Rouge	Bald Cypress	Pelican	Magnolia	Pelican State
MAINE	1820	Augusta	Eastern White Pine	Chickadee	White Pine Cone and Tassel	Pine Tree State
MARYLAND	1788	Annapolis	White Oak	Baltimore Oriole	Black-eyed Susan	Old Line State
MASSACHUSETTS	1788	Boston	American Elm	Chickadee	Mayflower	Bay State
MICHIGAN	1837	Lansing	White Pine	Robin	Apple Blossom	Wolverine State
MINNESOTA	1858	St. Paul	Red (Norway) Pine	Common Loon	Pink-and-White Lady's Slipper	North Star State or Gopher State or Land of 10,000 Lakes
MISSISSIPPI	1817	Jackson	Magnolia	Mockingbird	Magnolia	Magnolia State
MISSOURI	1821	Jefferson City	Flowering Dogwood	Bluebird	Hawthorn	Show Me State

State	Date of Statehood	Capital	State Tree	State Bird	State Flower	Nickname
MONTANA	1889	Helena	Ponderosa Pine	Western Meadowlark	Bitterroot	Treasure State
NEBRASKA	1867	Lincoln	Cottonwood	Western Meadowlark	Goldenrod	Cornhusker State
NEVADA	1864	Carson City	Single-leaf Piñon & Bristlecone Pine	Mountain Bluebird	Sagebrush	Sagebrush State or Silver State or Battle-born State
NEW HAMPSHIRE	1788	Concord	White Birch	Purple Finch	Purple Lilac	Granite State
NEW JERSEY	1787	Trenton	Red Oak	Eastern Goldfinch	Purple Violet	Garden State
NEW MEXICO	1912	Santa Fe	Piñon	Roadrunner	Yucca Flower	Land of Enchantment
NEW YORK	1788	Albany	Sugar Maple	Bluebird	Rose	Empire State
NORTH CAROLINA	1789	Raleigh	Longleaf Pine	Cardinal	(Flowering) Dogwood	Tar Heel State
NORTH DAKOTA	1889	Bismarck	American Elm	Western Meadowlark	Wild Prairie Rose	Flickertail State
OHIO	1803	Columbus	Buckeye	Cardinal	Scarlet Carnation	Buckeye State
OKLAHOMA	1907	Oklahoma City	Redbud	Scissor-tailed Flycatcher	Mistletoe	Sooner State
OREGON	1859	Salem	Douglas Fir	Western Meadowlark	Oregon Grape	Beaver State
PENNSYLVANIA	1787	Harrisburg	Hemlock	Ruffed Grouse	Mountain Laurel	Keystone State
RHODE ISLAND	1790	Providence	Red Maple	Rhode Island Red Chicken	Violet	Ocean State
SOUTH CAROLINA	1788	Columbia	Palmetto	Carolina Wren	Carolina Jessamine	Palmetto State
SOUTH DAKOTA	1889	Pierre	Black Hills Spruce	Ring-Necked Pheasant	American Pasqueflower	Coyote State or Mount Rushmore State
TENNESSEE	1796	Nashville	Tulip Poplar	Mockingbird	Iris	Volunteer State
TEXAS	1845	Austin	Pecan	Mockingbird	Bluebonnet	Lone Star State
UTAH	1896	Salt Lake City	Blue Spruce	(California) Seagull	Sego Lily	Beehive State
VERMONT	1791	Montpelier	Sugar Maple	Hermit Thrush	Red Clover	Green Mountain State
VIRGINIA	1788	Richmond	Dogwood	Cardinal	Dogwood	Old Dominion
WASHINGTON	1889	Olympia	Western Hemlock	Willow Goldfinch	Coast Rhododendron	Evergreen State
WEST VIRGINIA	1863	Charleston	Sugar Maple	Cardinal	Rhododendron	Mountain State
WISCONSIN	1848	Madison	Sugar Maple	Robin	Wood Violet	Badger State
WYOMING	1890	Cheyenne	Cottonwood	Western Meadowlark	Indian Paintbrush	Equality State

The Declaration of Independence

In Congress, July 4, 1776.

The unanimous declaration of the thirteen United States of America.

When, in the course of human events, it becomes necessary for one people to dissolve the political bands which have connected them with another, and to assume, among the powers of the earth, the separate and equal station to which the laws of nature and of nature's God entitle them, a decent respect to the opinions of mankind requires that they should declare the causes which impel them to the separation.

We hold these truths to be self-evident, that all men are created equal, that they are endowed by their Creator with certain unalienable rights, that among these are life, liberty, and the pursuit of happiness. That, to secure these rights, governments are instituted among men, deriving their just powers from the consent of the governed. That, whenever any form of government becomes destructive of these ends, it is the right of the people to alter or to abolish it, and to institute new government, laying its foundation on such principles, and organizing its powers in such form, as to them shall seem most likely to effect their safety and happiness.

Prudence, indeed, will dictate that governments long established should not be changed for light and transient causes; and accordingly, all experience has shown that mankind are more disposed to suffer, while evils are sufferable, than to right themselves by abolishing the forms to which they are accustomed.

But when a long train of abuses and usurpations, pursuing invariably the same object, evinces a design to reduce them under absolute despotism, it is their right, it is their duty, to throw off such government, and to provide new guards for their future security. Such has been the patient sufferance of these colonies; and such is now the necessity which constrains them to alter their former systems of government. The history of the present King of Great Britain is a history of repeated injuries and usurpations, all having in direct object the establishment of an absolute tyranny over these states. To prove this, let facts be submitted to a candid world.

He has refused his assent to laws, the most wholesome and necessary for the public good.

He has forbidden his governors to pass laws of immediate and pressing importance, unless suspended in their operation till his assent should be obtained; and when so suspended, he has utterly neglected to attend to them.

He has refused to pass other laws for the accommodation of large districts of people, unless those people would relinquish the right of representation in the legislature, a right inestimable to them and formidable to tyrants only.

He has called together legislative bodies at places unusual, uncomfortable, and distant from the depository of their public records, for the sole purpose of fatiguing them into compliance with his measures.

He has dissolved representative houses repeatedly, for opposing with manly firmness his invasions on the rights of the people.

He has refused for a long time, after such dissolutions, to cause others to be elected; whereby the legislative powers, incapable of annihilation, have returned to the people at large for their exercise; the state remaining in the meantime exposed to all the dangers of invasion from without, and convulsions within.

He has endeavored to prevent the population of these states; for that purpose obstructing the laws for naturalization of foreigners; refusing to pass others to encourage their migrations hither, and raising the conditions of new appropriations of lands.

He has obstructed the administration of justice, by refusing his assent to laws for establishing judiciary powers.

He has made judges dependent on his will alone, for the tenure of their offices, and the amount and payment of their salaries.

He has erected a multitude of new offices, and sent hither swarms of officers to harass our people, and eat out their substance.

He has kept among us, in times of peace, standing armies, without the consent of our legislatures.

He has affected to render the military independent of and superior to the civil power.

He has combined with others to subject us to a jurisdiction foreign to our constitution, and unacknowledged by our laws; giving his assent to their acts of pretended legislation:

For quartering large bodies of armed troops among us;

For protecting them, by a mock trial, from punishment for any murders which they should commit on the inhabitants of these states;

For cutting off our trade with all parts of the world;

For imposing taxes on us without our consent;

For depriving us, in many cases, of the benefits of trial by jury;

For transporting us beyond seas to be tried for pretended offenses;

For abolishing the free system of English laws in a neighboring province, establishing therein an arbitrary government, and enlarging its boundaries so as to render it at once an example and fit instrument for introducing the same absolute rule into these colonies;

For taking away our charters, abolishing our most valuable laws, and altering fundamentally the forms of our governments;

For suspending our own legislatures, and declaring themselves invested with power to legislate for us in all cases whatsoever.

He has abdicated government here, by declaring us out of his protection and waging war against us.

He has plundered our seas, ravaged our coasts, burnt our towns, and destroyed the lives of our people.

He is at this time transporting large armies of foreign mercenaries to complete the works of death, desolation, and tyranny already begun with circumstances of cruelty and perfidy scarcely paralleled in the most barbarous ages, and totally unworthy the head of a civilized nation.

He has constrained our fellow citizens, taken captive on the high seas, to bear arms against their country, to become the executioners of their friends and brethren, or to fall themselves by their hands.

He has excited domestic insurrections amongst us, and has endeavored to bring on the inhabitants of our frontiers, the merciless Indian savages, whose known rule of warfare is an undistinguished destruction of all ages, sexes, and conditions.

In every stage of these oppressions, we have petitioned for redress in the most humble terms: Our repeated petitions have been answered only by repeated injury. A prince whose character is thus marked by every act which may define a tyrant, is unfit to be the ruler of a free people.

Nor have we been wanting in attentions to our British brethren. We have warned them from time to time of attempts by their legislature to extend an unwarrantable jurisdiction over us. We have reminded them of the circumstances of our emigration and settlement here. We have appealed to their native justice and magnanimity, and we have conjured them by the ties of our common kindred to disavow these usurpations, which would inevitably interrupt our connections and correspondence. They too have been deaf to the voice of justice and of consanguinity. We must, therefore, acquiesce in the necessity, which denounces our separation, and hold them, as we hold the rest of mankind, enemies in war, in peace, friends.

We, therefore, the representatives of the United States of America, in General Congress assembled, appealing to the Supreme Judge of the world for the rectitude of our intentions, do, in the name and by authority of the good people of these colonies, solemnly publish and declare, that these United Colonies are and of right ought to be free and independent states; that they are absolved from all allegiance to the British Crown, and that all political connection between them and the state of Great Britain is and ought to be totally dissolved; and that, as free and independent states, they have full power to levy war, conclude peace, contract alliances, establish commerce, and to do all other acts and things which independent states may of right do. And for the support of this declaration, with a firm reliance on the protection of Divine Providence, we mutually pledge to each other our lives, our fortunes, and our sacred honor.

GEORGIA, Button Gwinnett, Lyman Hall, George Walton
NORTH CAROLINA, William Hooper, Joseph Hewes, John Penn
SOUTH CAROLINA, Edward Rutledge, Thomas Heyward, Jr., Thomas Lynch, Jr., Arthur Middleton
MASSACHUSETTS, John Hancock, Samuel Adams, John Adams, Robert Treat Paine, Elbridge Gerry
MARYLAND, Samuel Chase, William Paca, Thomas Stone, Charles Carroll of Carrollton
VIRGINIA, George Wythe, Richard Henry Lee, Thomas Jefferson, Benjamin Harrison, Thomas Nelson, Jr., Francis Lightfoot Lee, Carter Braxton
PENNSYLVANIA, Robert Morris, Benjamin Rush, Benjamin Franklin, John Morton, George Clymer, James Smith, George Taylor, James Wilson, George Ross
DELAWARE, Caesar Rodney, George Read, Thomas McKean
NEW YORK, William Floyd, Philip Livingston, Francis Lewis, Lewis Morris
NEW JERSEY, Richard Stockton, John Witherspoon, Francis Hopkinson, John Hart, Abraham Clark
NEW HAMPSHIRE, Josiah Bartlett, William Whipple, Matthew Thornton
RHODE ISLAND, Stephen Hopkins, William Ellery
CONNECTICUT, Roger Sherman, Samuel Huntington, William Williams, Oliver Wolcott

The Constitution of the United States of America

We the people of the United States, in order to form a more perfect Union, establish justice, insure domestic tranquillity, provide for the common defense, promote the general welfare, and secure the blessings of liberty to ourselves and our posterity, do ordain and establish this Constitution for the United States of America.

Article I
Section 1

All legislative powers herein granted shall be vested in a Congress of the United States, which shall consist of a Senate and House of Representatives.

Section 2

The House of Representatives shall be composed of members chosen every second year by the people of the several states, and the electors in each state shall have the qualifications requisite for electors of the most numerous branch of the state legislature.

No person shall be a representative who shall not have attained to the age of twenty-five years, and been seven years a citizen of the United States, and who shall not, when elected, be an inhabitant of that state in which he shall be chosen.

Representatives and direct taxes shall be apportioned among the several states which may be included within this Union, according to their respective numbers, which shall be determined by adding to the whole number of free persons, including those bound to service for a term of years, and excluding Indians not taxed, three-fifths of all other persons. The actual enumeration shall be made within three years after the first meeting of the Congress of the United States, and within every subsequent term of ten years, in such

manner as they shall by law direct. The number of representatives shall not exceed one for every thirty thousand, but each state shall have at least one representative; and until such enumeration shall be made, the state of New Hampshire shall be entitled to choose three, Massachusetts eight, Rhode Island and Providence Plantations one, Connecticut five, New York six, New Jersey four, Pennsylvania eight, Delaware one, Maryland six, Virginia ten, North Carolina five, South Carolina five, and Georgia three.

When vacancies happen in the representation from any state, the executive authority thereof shall issue writs of election to fill such vacancies.

The House of Representatives shall choose their Speaker and other officers, and shall have the sole power of impeachment.

Section 3

The Senate of the United States shall be composed of two senators from each state, chosen by the legislature thereof, for six years; and each senator shall have one vote.

Immediately after they shall be assembled in consequence of the first election, they shall be divided as equally as may be into three classes. The seats of the senators of the first class shall be vacated at the expiration of the second year, of the second class at the expiration of the fourth year, and of the third class at the expiration of the sixth year, so that one-third may be chosen every second year; and if vacancies happen by resignation, or otherwise, during the recess of the legislature of any state, the executive thereof may make temporary appointments until the next meeting of the legislature, which shall then fill such vacancies.

No person shall be a senator who shall not have attained to the age of thirty years, and been nine years a citizen of the United States, and who shall not, when elected, be an inhabitant of that state for which he shall be chosen.

The Vice President of the United States shall be president of the Senate, but shall have no vote, unless they be equally divided.

The Senate shall choose their other officers and also a President pro tempore, in the absence of the Vice President, or when he shall exercise the office of President of the United States.

The Senate shall have the sole power to try all impeachments. When sitting for that purpose, they shall be on oath or affirmation. When the President of the United States is tried, the Chief Justice shall preside. And no person shall be convicted without the concurrence of two-thirds of the members present.

Judgment in cases of impeachment shall not extend further than to removal from office, and disqualification to hold and enjoy any office of honor, trust, or profit under the United States; but the party convicted shall nevertheless be liable and subject to indictment, trial, judgment, and punishment, according to law.

THE FRAMERS
of the Constitution

Section 4

The times, places, and manner of holding elections for senators and representatives shall be prescribed in each state by the legislature thereof; but the Congress may at any time by law make or alter such regulations, except as to the places of choosing senators.

The Congress shall assemble at least once in every year, and such meeting shall be on the first Monday in December, unless they shall by law appoint a different day.

Section 5

Each house shall be the judge of the elections, returns, and qualifications of its own members, and a majority of each shall constitute a quorum to do business; but a smaller number may adjourn from day to day, and may be authorized to compel the attendance of absent members, in such manner and under such penalties as each house may provide.

Each house may determine the rules of its proceedings, punish its members for disorderly behavior, and, with the concurrence of two-thirds, expel a member.

Each house shall keep a journal of its proceedings and from time to time publish the same, excepting such parts as may in their judgment require secrecy; and the yeas and nays of the members of either house on any question, shall, at the desire of one-fifth of those present, be entered on the journal.

Neither house, during the session of Congress, shall, without the consent of the other, adjourn for more than three days, nor to any other place than that in which the two houses shall be sitting.

Section 6

The senators and representatives shall receive a compensation for their services, to be ascertained by law, and paid out of the Treasury of the United States. They shall in all cases, except treason, felony, and breach of the peace, be privileged from arrest during their attendance at the session of their respective houses, and in going to and returning from the same; and for any speech or debate in either house, they shall not be questioned in any other place.

No senator or representative shall, during the time for which he was elected, be appointed to any civil office under the authority of the United States, which shall have been created, or the emoluments whereof shall have been increased, during such time; and no person holding any office under the United States, shall be a member of either house during his continuance in office.

Section 7

All bills for raising revenue shall originate in the House of Representatives; but the Senate may propose or concur with amendments as on other bills.

Every bill which shall have passed the House of Representatives and the Senate shall, before it become a law, be presented to the President of the United States. If he approve he shall sign it, but if not, he shall return it, with his objections, to that house in which it shall have originated, who shall enter the objections at large on their journal and proceed to reconsider it. If, after such reconsideration, two-thirds of that house shall agree to pass the bill, it shall be sent, together with the objections, to the other house, by which it shall likewise be reconsidered, and if approved by two-thirds of that house, it shall become a law. But in all such cases the votes of both houses shall be determined by yeas and nays, and the names of the persons voting for and against the bill shall be entered on the journal of each house respectively. If any bill shall not be returned by the President within ten days (Sundays excepted) after it shall have been presented to him, the same shall be a law, in like manner as if he had signed it, unless the Congress by their adjournment prevent its return, in which case it shall not be a law.

Every order, resolution, or vote to which the concurrence of the Senate and House of Representatives may be necessary (except on a question of adjournment) shall be presented to the President of the United States; and before the same shall take effect, shall be approved by him, or being disapproved by him, shall be repassed by two-thirds of the Senate and House of Representatives, according to the rules and limitations prescribed in the case of a bill.

Section 8

The Congress shall have power:

To lay and collect taxes, duties, imposts, and excises, to pay the debts and provide for the common defense and general welfare of the United States; but all duties, imposts, and excises shall be uniform throughout the United States;

To borrow money on the credit of the United States;

To regulate commerce with foreign nations, and among the several states, and with the Indian tribes;

To establish an uniform rule of naturalization and uniform laws on the subject of bankruptcies throughout the United States;

To coin money, regulate the value thereof, and of foreign coin, and fix the standard of weights and measures;

To provide for the punishment of counterfeiting the securities and current coin of the United States;

To establish post offices and post roads;

To promote the progress of science and useful arts, by securing for limited times to authors and inventors the exclusive right to their respective writings and discoveries;

To constitute tribunals inferior to the Supreme Court;

To define and punish piracies and felonies committed on the high seas and offenses against the law of nations;

To declare war, grant letters of marque and reprisal, and make rules concerning captures on land and water;

To raise and support armies, but no appropriation of money to that use shall be for a longer term than two years;

To provide and maintain a navy;

To make rules for the government and regulation of the land and naval forces;

To provide for calling forth the militia to execute the laws of the Union, suppress insurrections, and repel invasions;

To provide for organizing, arming, and disciplining the militia, and for governing such part of them as may be employed in the service of the United States, reserving to the states respectively the appointment of the officers and the authority of training the militia according to the discipline prescribed by Congress;

To exercise exclusive legislation in all cases whatsoever over such district (not exceeding ten miles square) as may, by cession of particular states and the acceptance of Congress, become the seat of the government of the United States, and to exercise like authority over all places purchased by the consent of the legislature of the state in which the same shall be for the erection of forts, magazines, arsenals, dockyards, and other needful buildings; and

To make all laws which shall be necessary and proper for carrying into execution the foregoing powers and all other powers vested by this Constitution in the government of the United States, or in any department or officer thereof.

Section 9

The migration or importation of such persons as any of the states now existing shall think proper to admit shall not be prohibited by the Congress prior to the year one thousand eight hundred and eight, but a tax or duty may be imposed on such importation, not exceeding ten dollars for each person.

The privilege of the writ of habeas corpus shall not be suspended unless, when in cases of rebellion or invasion, the public safety may require it.

No bill of attainder or ex post facto law shall be passed.

No capitation or other direct tax shall be laid, unless in proportion to the census or enumeration herein before directed to be taken.

No tax or duty shall be laid on articles exported from any state.

No preference shall be given by any regulation of commerce or revenue to the ports of one state over those of another; nor shall vessels bound to or from one state be obliged to enter, clear, or pay duties in another.

No money shall be drawn from the Treasury but in consequence of appropriations made by law; and a regular statement and account of receipts and expenditures of all public money shall be published from time to time.

No title of nobility shall be granted by the United States. And no person holding any office of profit or trust under them shall, without the consent of the Congress, accept of any present, emolument, office, or title of any kind whatever from any king, prince, or foreign state.

Section 10

No state shall enter into any treaty, alliance, or confederation; grant letters of marque and reprisal; coin money; emit bills of credit; make anything but gold and silver coin a tender in payment of debts; pass any bill of attainder, ex post facto law, or law impairing the obligation of contracts, or grant any title of nobility.

No state shall, without the consent of the Congress, lay any imposts or duties on imports or exports, except what may be absolutely necessary for executing its inspection laws: and the net produce of all duties and imposts laid by any state on imports or exports shall be for the use of the Treasury of the United States; and all such laws shall be subject to the revision and control of the Congress.

No state shall, without the consent of Congress, lay any duty of tonnage; keep troops or ships of war in time of peace; enter into any agreement or compact with another state or with a foreign power; or engage in war, unless actually invaded, or in such imminent danger as will not admit of delay.

Article II
Section 1

The executive power shall be vested in a President of the United States of America. He shall hold his office during the term of four years, and, together with the Vice President, chosen for the same term, be elected as follows:

Each state shall appoint, in such manner as the legislature thereof may direct, a number of electors, equal to the whole number of senators and representatives to which the state may be entitled in the Congress: but no senator or representative, or person holding an office of trust or profit under the United States, shall be appointed an elector.

The electors shall meet in their respective states and vote by ballot for two persons, of whom one at least shall not be an inhabitant of the same state with themselves. And they shall make a list of all the persons voted for, and of the number of votes for each; which list they shall sign and certify, and transmit sealed to the seat of the government of the United States, directed to the President of the Senate. The President of the Senate shall, in the presence of the Senate and House of Representatives, open all the certificates, and the votes shall then be counted. The person having the greatest number of votes shall be the President, if such number be a majority of the whole number of electors appointed; and if there be more than one who have such majority, and have an equal number of votes, then the House of Representatives shall immediately choose by ballot one of them for President; and if no person have a majority, then from the five highest on the list the said house shall in like manner choose the President. But in choosing the President, the votes shall be taken by states, the representation from each state having one vote; a quorum for this purpose shall consist of a member or members from two-thirds of the states, and a majority of all the states shall be necessary to a choice. In every case, after the choice of the President, the person having the greatest number of votes of the electors shall be the Vice President. But if there should remain two or more who have equal votes, the Senate shall choose from them by ballot the Vice President.

The Congress may determine the time of choosing the electors and the day on which they shall give their votes, which day shall be the same throughout the United States.

THE CONSTITUTION of the United States of America

No person except a natural-born citizen, or a citizen of the United States at the time of the adoption of this Constitution, shall be eligible to the office of President; neither shall any person be eligible to that office who shall not have attained to the age of thirty-five years and been fourteen years a resident within the United States.

In case of the removal of the President from office, or of his death, resignation, or inability to discharge the powers and duties of the said office, the same shall devolve on the Vice President, and the Congress may by law provide for the case of removal, death, resignation, or inability, both of the President and Vice President, declaring what officer shall then act as President, and such officer shall act accordingly until the disability be removed or a President shall be elected.

The President shall, at stated times, receive for his services a compensation, which shall neither be increased nor diminished during the period for which he shall have been elected, and he shall not receive within that period any other emolument from the United States or any of them.

Before he enter on the execution of his office, he shall take the following oath or affirmation: "I do solemnly swear (or affirm) that I will faithfully execute the office of President of the United States, and will, to the best of my ability, preserve, protect, and defend the Constitution of the United States."

Section 2

The President shall be commander in chief of the army and navy of the United States, and of the militia of the several states when called into the actual service of the United States. He may require the opinion, in writing, of the principal officer in each of the executive departments upon any subject relating to the duties of their respective offices. And he shall have power to grant reprieves and pardons for offenses against the United States, except in cases of impeachment.

He shall have power, by and with the advice and consent of the Senate, to make treaties, provided two-thirds of the senators present concur; and he shall nominate, and by and with the advice and consent of the Senate, shall appoint ambassadors, other public ministers and consuls, judges of the Supreme Court, and all other officers of the United States whose appointments

James Madison

are not herein otherwise provided for, and which shall be established by law; but the Congress may by law vest the appointment of such inferior officers as they think proper in the President alone, in the courts of law, or in the heads of departments.

The President shall have power to fill up all vacancies that may happen during the recess of the Senate, by granting commissions which shall expire at the end of their next session.

Section 3

He shall from time to time give to the Congress information of the state of the Union, and recommend to their consideration such measures as he shall judge necessary and expedient; he may, on extraordinary occasions, convene both houses, or either of them, and in case of disagreement between them with respect to the time of adjournment, he may adjourn them to such time as he shall think proper; he shall receive ambassadors and other public ministers; he shall take care that the laws be faithfully executed, and shall commission all the officers of the United States.

Section 4

The President, Vice President, and all civil officers of the United States shall be removed from office on impeachment for, and conviction of, treason, bribery, or other high crimes and misdemeanors.

Article III
Section 1

The judicial power of the United States shall be vested in one Supreme Court, and in such inferior courts as the Congress may from time to time ordain and establish. The judges, both of the Supreme and inferior courts, shall hold their offices during good behavior, and shall, at stated times, receive for their services a compensation, which shall not be diminished during their continuance in office.

Section 2

The judicial power shall extend to all cases, in law and equity, arising under this Constitution,

the laws of the United States, and treaties made, or which shall be made, under their authority; to all cases affecting ambassadors, other public ministers and consuls; to all cases of admiralty and maritime jurisdiction; to controversies to which the United States shall be a party; to controversies between two or more states; between a state and citizens of another state; between citizens of different states; between citizens of the same state claiming lands under grants of different states; and between a state, or the citizens thereof, and foreign states, citizens, or subjects.

In all cases affecting ambassadors, other public ministers and consuls, and those in which a state shall be party, the Supreme Court shall have original jurisdiction. In all the other cases before mentioned, the Supreme Court shall have appellate jurisdiction, both as to law and fact, with such exceptions and under such regulations as the Congress shall make.

The trial of all crimes, except in cases of impeachment, shall be by jury; and such trial shall be held in the state where the said crimes shall have been committed; but when not committed within any state, the trial shall be at such place or places as the Congress may by law have directed.

Section 3

Treason against the United States shall consist only in levying war against them

George Washington

or in adhering to their enemies, giving them aid and comfort. No person shall be convicted of treason unless on the testimony of two witnesses to the same overt act, or on confession in open court.

The Congress shall have power to declare the punishment of treason, but no attainder of treason shall work corruption of blood or forfeiture except during the life of the person attainted.

Article IV
Section 1

Full faith and credit shall be given in each state to the public acts, records, and judicial proceedings of every other state. And the Congress may by general laws prescribe the manner in which such acts, records, and proceedings shall be proved, and the effect thereof.

Section 2

The citizens of each state shall be entitled to all privileges and immunities of citizens in the several states.

A person charged in any state with treason, felony, or other crime, who shall flee from justice and be found in another state, shall on demand of the executive authority of the state from which he fled, be delivered up to be removed to the state having jurisdiction of the crime.

No person held to service or labor in one state under the laws thereof, escaping into another, shall, in consequence of any law or regulation therein, be discharged from such service or labor, but shall be delivered up on claim of the party to whom such service or labor may be due.

Section 3

New states may be admitted by the Congress into this Union; but no new state shall be formed or erected within the jurisdiction of any other state; nor any state be formed by the junction of two or more states, or parts of states, without the consent of the legislatures of the states concerned as well as of the Congress.

The Congress shall have power to dispose of and make all needful rules and regulations respecting the territory or other property belonging to the United States; and nothing in this Constitution shall be so construed as to prejudice any claims of the United States, or of any particular state.

Section 4

The United States shall guarantee to every state in this Union a republican form of government, and shall protect each of them against invasion, and on application of the legislature or of the executive (when the legislature cannot be convened), against domestic violence.

Article V

The Congress, whenever two-thirds of both houses shall deem it necessary, shall propose amendments to this Constitution or, on the application of the legislatures of two-thirds of the several states, shall call a convention for proposing amendments, which, in either case, shall be valid, to all intents and purposes, as part of this Constitution when ratified by the legislatures of three-fourths of the several states, or by conventions in three-fourths thereof, as the one or the other mode of ratification may be proposed by the Congress; provided that no amendment which may be made prior to the year one thousand eight hundred and eight shall in any manner affect the first and fourth clauses in the ninth section of the first article; and that no state, without its consent, shall be deprived of its equal suffrage in the Senate.

Article VI

All debts contracted and engagements entered into before the adoption of this Constitution shall be as valid against the United States under this Constitution as under the Confederation.

This Constitution and the laws of the United States which shall be made in pursuance thereof, and all treaties made, or which shall be made, under the authority of the United States, shall be the supreme law of the land; and the judges in every state shall be bound thereby, anything in the Constitution or laws of any state to the contrary notwithstanding.

The senators and representatives before mentioned, and the members of the several state legislatures, and all executive and judicial officers, both of the United States and of the several states, shall be bound by oath or affirmation to support this Constitution; but no religious test shall ever be required as a qualification to any office or public trust under the United States.

Article VII

The ratification of the conventions of nine states shall be sufficient for the establishment of this Constitution between the states so ratifying the same.

Done in convention by the unanimous consent of the states present the seventeenth day of September in the year of our Lord one thousand seven hundred and eighty-seven, and of the independence of the United States of America the twelfth. In witness whereof we have hereunto subscribed our names,

George Washington
President and deputy from Virginia

DELAWARE, George Read, Gunning Bedford, Jr., John Dickinson, Richard Bassett, Jacob Broom
MARYLAND, James McHenry, Dan of St. Thomas Jenifer, Daniel Carroll
VIRGINIA, John Blair, James Madison, Jr.
NORTH CAROLINA, William Blount, Richard Dobbs Spaight, Hugh Williamson
SOUTH CAROLINA, John Rutledge, Charles Cotesworth Pinckney, Charles Pinckney, Pierce Butler
GEORGIA, William Few, Abraham Baldwin
NEW HAMPSHIRE, John Langdon, Nicholas Gilman
MASSACHUSETTS, Nathanial Gorham, Rufus King
CONNECTICUT, William Samuel Johnson, Roger Sherman
NEW YORK, Alexander Hamilton
NEW JERSEY, William Livingston, David Brearley, William Paterson, Jonathan Dayton
PENNSYLVANIA, Benjamin Franklin, Thomas Mifflin, Robert Morris, George Clymer, Thomas FitzSimons, Jared Ingersoll, James Wilson, Gouverneur Morris

Benjamin Franklin

The Amendments to the Constitution of the United States

The Bill of Rights

Congress of the United States begun and held at the city of New York, on Wednesday the fourth of March, one thousand seven hundred and eighty-nine.

THE conventions of a number of the states, having at the time of their adopting the Constitution, expressed a desire, in order to prevent misconstruction or abuse of its powers, that further declaratory and restrictive clauses should be added; and as extending the ground of public confidence in the government, will best ensure the beneficent ends of its institution.

RESOLVED by the Senate and House of Representatives of the United States of America, in Congress assembled, two-thirds of both houses concurring, that the following articles be proposed to the legislatures of the several states as amendments to the Constitution of the United States, all or any of which articles, when ratified by three fourths of the said legislatures, to be valid to all intents and purposes as part of the said Constitution; viz.

ARTICLES in addition to and amendment of the Constitution of the United States of America, proposed by Congress and ratified by the legislatures of the several states, pursuant to the fifth article of the original Constitution.

Amendment I

Congress shall make no law respecting an establishment of religion or prohibiting the free exercise thereof, or abridging the freedom of speech or of the press, or the right of the people peaceably to assemble and to petition the government for a redress of grievances.

Amendment II

A well-regulated militia being necessary to the security of a free state, the right of the people to keep and bear arms shall not be infringed.

Amendment III

No soldier shall, in time of peace, be quartered in any house without the consent of the owner, nor in time of war but in a manner to be prescribed by law.

Amendment IV

The right of the people to be secure in their persons, houses, papers, and effects against unreasonable searches and seizures shall not be violated, and no warrants shall issue, but upon probable cause, supported by oath or affirmation, and particularly describing the place to be searched and the persons or things to be seized.

Amendment V

No person shall be held to answer for a capital or otherwise infamous crime unless on a presentment or indictment of a grand jury, except in cases arising in the land or naval forces, or in the militia, when in actual service in time of war or public danger; nor shall any person be subject for the same offense to be twice put in jeopardy of life or limb; nor shall be compelled in any criminal case to be a witness against himself, nor be deprived of life, liberty, or property without due process of law; nor shall private property be taken for public use without just compensation.

Amendment VI

In all criminal prosecutions, the accused shall enjoy the right to a speedy and public trial by an impartial jury of the state and district wherein the crime shall have been committed, which district shall have been previously ascertained by law, and to be informed of the nature and cause of the accusation; to be confronted with the witnesses against him; to have compulsory process for obtaining witnesses in his favor, and to have the assistance of counsel for his defense.

Amendment VII

In suits at common law, where the value in controversy shall exceed twenty dollars, the right of trial by jury shall be preserved, and no fact tried by a jury shall be otherwise reexamined in any court of the United States than according to the rules of the common law.

Amendment VIII

Excessive bail shall not be required, nor excessive fines imposed, nor cruel and unusual punishments inflicted.

Amendment IX

The enumeration in the Constitution of certain rights shall not be construed to deny or disparage others retained by the people.

Amendment X

The powers not delegated to the United States by the Constitution, nor prohibited by it to the states, are reserved to the states respectively, or to the people.

Additional Amendments

Amendment XI

Passed by Congress March 4, 1794.
Ratified February 7, 1795.

The judicial power of the United States shall not be construed to extend to any suit in law or equity commenced or prosecuted against one of the United States by citizens of another state, or by citizens or subjects of any foreign state.

Amendment XII

Passed by Congress December 9, 1803. Ratified June 15, 1804.

The electors shall meet in their respective states and vote by ballot for President and Vice President, one of whom at least shall not be an inhabitant of the same state with themselves; they shall name in their ballots the person voted for as President, and in distinct ballots the person voted for as Vice President, and they shall make distinct lists of all persons voted for as President and of all persons voted for as Vice President and of the number of votes for each, which lists they shall sign and certify and transmit sealed to the seat of the government of the United States, directed to the president of the Senate. The president of the Senate shall, in the presence of the Senate and House of Representatives, open all the certificates and the votes shall then be counted. The person having the greatest number of votes for President shall be the President, if such number be a majority of the whole number of electors appointed; and if no person have such majority, then from the persons having the highest numbers not exceeding three on the list of those voted for as President, the House of Representatives shall choose immediately, by ballot, the President. But in choosing the President the votes shall be taken by states, the representation from each state having one vote; a quorum for this purpose shall consist of a member or members from two-thirds of the states, and a majority of all the states shall be necessary to a choice. And if the House of Representatives shall not choose a President whenever the right of choice shall devolve upon them, before the fourth day of March next following, then the Vice President shall act as President, as in the case of the death or other constitutional disability of the President. The person having the greatest number of votes as Vice President shall be the Vice President, if such number be a majority of the whole number of electors appointed, and if no person have a majority, then from the two highest numbers on the list the Senate shall choose the Vice President; a quorum for the purpose shall consist of two-thirds of the whole number of senators, and a majority of the whole number shall be necessary to a choice. But no person

constitutionally ineligible to the office of President shall be eligible to that of Vice President of the United States.

Amendment XIII

Passed by Congress January 31, 1865. Ratified December 6, 1865.

Section 1

Neither slavery nor involuntary servitude, except as a punishment for crime whereof the party shall have been duly convicted, shall exist within the United States or any place subject to their jurisdiction.

Section 2

Congress shall have power to enforce this article by appropriate legislation.

Amendment XIV

Passed by Congress June 13, 1866. Ratified July 9, 1868.

Section 1

All persons born or naturalized in the United States and subject to the jurisdiction thereof are citizens of the United States and of the state wherein they reside. No state shall make or enforce any law which shall abridge the privileges or immunities of citizens of the United States; nor shall any state deprive any person of life, liberty, or property without due process of law; nor deny to any person within its jurisdiction the equal protection of the laws.

Section 2

Representatives shall be apportioned among the several states according to their respective numbers, counting the whole number of persons in each state, excluding Indians not taxed. But when the right to vote at any election for the choice of electors for President and Vice President of the United States, representatives in Congress, the executive and judicial officers of a state, or the members of the legislature thereof is denied to any of the male inhabitants of such state, being twenty-one years of age and citizens of the United States, or in any way abridged, except for participation in rebellion or other crime, the basis of representation therein shall be reduced in the proportion which the number of such male citizens shall bear to the whole number of male citizens twenty-one years of age in such state.

Section 3

No person shall be a senator or representative in Congress, or elector of President and Vice President, or hold any office, civil or military, under the United States, or under any state, who, having previously taken an oath as a member of Congress or as an officer of the United States or as a member of any state legislature or as an executive or judicial officer of any state to support the Constitution of the United States, shall have engaged in insurrection or rebellion against the same, or given aid or comfort to the enemies thereof. But Congress may by a vote of two-thirds of each house remove such disability.

Section 4

The validity of the public debt of the United States, authorized by law, including debts incurred for payment of pensions and bounties for services in suppressing insurrection or rebellion, shall not be questioned. But neither the United States nor any state shall assume or pay any debt or obligation incurred in aid of insurrection or rebellion against the United

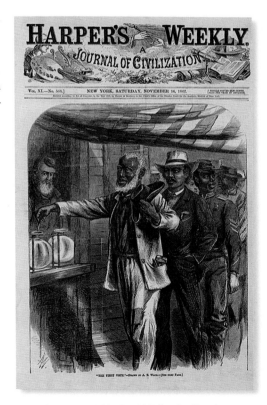

AFRICAN AMERICANS VOTE for the first time, per the rights granted by the Fifteenth Amendment

States or any claim for the loss or emancipation of any slave; but all such debts, obligations, and claims shall be held illegal and void.

Section 5

The Congress shall have power to enforce, by appropriate legislation, the provisions of this article.

Amendment XV

Passed by Congress February 26, 1869.
Ratified February 3, 1870.

Section 1

The right of citizens of the United States to vote shall not be denied or abridged by the United States or by any state on account of race, color, or previous condition of servitude.

Section 2

The Congress shall have power to enforce this article by appropriate legislation.

Amendment XVI

Passed by Congress July 2, 1909.
Ratified February 3, 1913.

The Congress shall have power to lay and collect taxes on incomes, from whatever source derived, without apportionment among the several states, and without regard to any census or enumeration.

SUFFRAGETTES RALLIED for the right to vote. Their efforts were rewarded when the Nineteenth Amendment passed.

Amendment XVII

Passed by Congress May 13, 1912.
Ratified April 8, 1913.

The Senate of the United States shall be composed of two senators from each state, elected by the people thereof, for six years; and each senator shall have one vote. The electors in each state shall have the qualifications requisite for electors of the most numerous branch of the state legislatures.

When vacancies happen in the representation of any state in the Senate, the executive authority of such state shall issue writs of election to fill such vacancies, provided that the legislature of any state may empower the executive thereof to make temporary appointments until the people fill the vacancies by election as the legislature may direct.

This amendment shall not be so construed as to affect the election or term of any senator chosen before it becomes valid as part of the Constitution.

Amendment XVIII

Passed by Congress December 18, 1917.
Ratified January 16, 1919.
Repealed by amendment 21.

Section 1

After one year from the ratification of this article, the manufacture, sale, or transportation of intoxicating liquors within, the importation thereof into, or the exportation thereof from the United States and all territory subject to the jurisdiction thereof for beverage purposes is hereby prohibited.

Section 2

The Congress and the several states shall have concurrent power to enforce this article by appropriate legislation.

Section 3

This article shall be inoperative unless it shall have been ratified as an amendment to the Constitution by the legislatures of the several states, as provided in the Constitution, within seven years from the date of the submission hereof to the states by the Congress.

Amendment XIX

Passed by Congress June 4, 1919.
Ratified August 18, 1920.

The right of citizens of the United States to vote shall not be denied or abridged by the United States or by any state on account of sex.

Congress shall have power to enforce this article by appropriate legislation.

Amendment XX

Passed by Congress March 2, 1932.
Ratified January 23, 1933.

Section 1

The terms of the President and Vice President shall end at noon on the 20th day of January, and the terms of senators and representatives at noon on the 3rd day of January, of the years in which such terms would have ended if this article had not been ratified; and the terms of their successors shall then begin.

Section 2

The Congress shall assemble at least once in every year, and such meeting shall begin at noon on the 3rd day of January, unless they shall by law appoint a different day.

Section 3

If, at the time fixed for the beginning of the term of the President, the President-elect shall have died, the Vice President-elect shall become President. If a President shall not have been chosen before the time fixed for the beginning of his term, or if the President-elect shall have failed to qualify, then the Vice President-elect shall act as President until a President shall have qualified; and the Congress may by law provide for the case wherein neither a President-elect nor a Vice President shall have qualified, declaring who shall then act as President, or the manner in which one who is to act shall be selected, and such person shall act accordingly until a President or Vice President shall have qualified.

Section 4

The Congress may by law provide for the case of the death of any of the persons from whom the House of Representatives may choose a President whenever the right of choice shall have devolved upon them, and for the case of the death of any of the persons from whom the Senate may choose a Vice President whenever the right of choice shall have devolved upon them.

Section 5

Sections 1 and 2 shall take effect on the 15th day of October following the ratification of this article.

Section 6

This article shall be inoperative unless it shall have been ratified as an amendment to the Constitution by the legislatures of three-fourths of the several states within seven years from the date of its submission.

Amendment XXI

Passed by Congress February 20, 1933. Ratified December 5, 1933.

Section 1

The eighteenth article of amendment to the Constitution of the United States is hereby repealed.

Section 2

The transportation or importation into any state, territory, or possession of the United States for delivery or use therein of intoxicating liquors, in violation of the laws thereof, is hereby prohibited.

Section 3

This article shall be inoperative unless it shall have been ratified as an amendment to the Constitution by conventions in the several states, as provided in the Constitution, within seven years from the date of the submission hereof to the states by the Congress.

Amendment XXII

Passed by Congress March 21, 1947. Ratified February 27, 1951.

Section 1

No person shall be elected to the office of the President more than twice, and no person who has held the office of President or acted as President for more than two years of a term to which some other person was elected President shall be elected to the office of the President more than once. But this article shall not apply to any person holding the office of President when this article was proposed by the Congress, and shall not prevent any person who may be holding the office of President or acting as President during the term within which this article becomes operative from holding the office of President or acting as President during the remainder of such term.

Section 2

This article shall be inoperative unless it shall have been ratified as an amendment to the Constitution by the legislatures of three-fourths of the several states within seven years from the date of its submission to the states by the Congress.

Amendment XXIII

Passed by Congress June 16, 1960. Ratified March 29, 1961.

Section 1

The district constituting the seat of government of the United States shall appoint in such manner as Congress may direct:

A number of electors of President and Vice President equal to the whole number of senators and representatives in Congress to which the district would be entitled if it were a state, but in no event more than the least populous state; they shall be in addition to those appointed by the states, but they shall be considered, for the purposes of the election of President and Vice President, to be electors appointed by a state; and they shall meet in the district and perform such duties as provided by the twelfth article of amendment.

Section 2

The Congress shall have power to enforce this article by appropriate legislation.

Amendment XXIV

Passed by Congress August 27, 1962. Ratified January 23, 1964.

Section 1

The right of citizens of the United States to vote in any primary or other election for President or Vice President, for electors for President or Vice President, or for senator or representative in Congress, shall not be denied or abridged by the United States or any state by reason of failure to pay any poll tax or other tax.

Section 2

The Congress shall have power to enforce this article by appropriate legislation.

Amendment XXV

Passed by Congress July 6, 1965. Ratified February 10, 1967.

Section 1

In case of the removal of the President from office or of his death or resignation, the Vice President shall become President.

Section 2

Whenever there is a vacancy in the office of the Vice President, the President shall nominate a Vice President who shall take office upon confirmation by a majority vote of both houses of Congress.

Section 3

Whenever the President transmits to the president pro tempore of the Senate and the Speaker of the House of Representatives his written declaration that he is unable to discharge the powers and duties of his office, and until he transmits to them a written declaration to the contrary, such powers and duties shall be discharged by the Vice President as Acting President.

Section 4

Whenever the Vice President and a majority of either the principal officers of the executive departments or of such other body as Congress may by law provide, transmit to the president pro tempore of the Senate and the Speaker of the House of Representatives their written declaration that the President is unable to discharge the powers and duties of his office, the Vice President shall immediately assume the powers and duties of the office as Acting President.

Thereafter, when the President transmits to the President pro tempore of the Senate and the Speaker of the House of Representatives his written declaration that no inability exists, he shall resume the powers and duties of his office unless the Vice President and a majority of either the principal officers of the executive department or of such other body as Congress may by law provide, transmit within four days to the president pro tempore of the Senate and the Speaker of the House of Representatives their written declaration that the President is unable to discharge the powers and duties of his office. Thereupon Congress shall decide the issue, assembling within forty-eight hours for that purpose if not in session. If the Congress,

within twenty-one days after receipt of the latter written declaration, or, if Congress is not in session, within twenty-one days after Congress is required to assemble, determines by two-thirds vote of both Houses that the President is unable to discharge the powers and duties of his office, the Vice President shall continue to discharge the same as Acting President; otherwise, the President shall resume the powers and duties of his office.

Amendment XXVI

Passed by Congress March 23, 1971.
Ratified July 1, 1971.

Section 1

The right of citizens of the United States, who are eighteen years of age or older, to vote shall not be denied or abridged by the United States or any state on account of age.

Section 2

The Congress shall have power to enforce this article by appropriate legislation.

Amendment XXVII

Originally proposed September 25, 1789.
Ratified May 7, 1992.

No law, varying the compensation for the services of the senators and representatives, shall take effect, until an election of representatives shall have intervened.

A PROHIBITION ENFORCER empties beer kegs into the street in line with the Eighteenth Amendment, which was repealed by the Twenty-first Amendment.

The Gettysburg Address

Four score and seven years ago our fathers brought forth on this continent, a new nation, conceived in Liberty, and dedicated to the proposition that all men are created equal.

Now we are engaged in a great civil war, testing whether that nation, or any nation so conceived and so dedicated, can long endure. We are met on a great battlefield of that war. We have come to dedicate a portion of that field, as a final resting place for those who here gave their lives that that nation might live. It is altogether fitting and proper that we should do this.

But, in a larger sense, we cannot dedicate—we cannot consecrate—we cannot hallow, this ground. The brave men, living and dead, who struggled here, have consecrated it, far above our poor power to add or detract. The world will little note, nor long remember, what we say here, but it can never forget what they did here. It is rather for us, the living, to be dedicated here to the unfinished work which they who fought here have thus far so nobly advanced. It is rather for us to be here dedicated to the great task remaining before us—that from these honored dead we take increased devotion to that cause for which they gave the last full measure of devotion—that we here highly resolve that these dead shall not have died in vain—that this nation, under God, shall have a new birth of freedom—and that government of the people, by the people, for the people, shall not perish from the earth.

LINCOLN WROTE THE SPEECH on White House stationery during the train ride to Gettysburg.

Index

Acknowledgments

The author and Dorling Kindersley would like to thank the divisions of Smithsonian's National Museum of American History: Archives Center, Cultural and Community Life, Education and Public Programs, Medicine and Science, Political and Military History, Work and Industry, and Robert van der Linden, Aeronautics division, Smithsonian's National Air and Space Museum.

Smithsonian Enterprises:
Kealy Gordon, Product Development Manager
Ellen Nanney, Senior Manager Licensed
  Publishing
Jill Corcoran, Director, Licensed Publishing
Brigid Ferraro, Vice President, Consumer and
  Education Products
Carol LeBlanc, President

Thanks also to: Laura Buller for additional editorial work; Andrew Berkhut, a key figure in the conception of the project; Elizabeth Hester for helping to hold it together; and Jill Hamilton for proofreading.

The publisher would like to thank the following for their kind permission to reproduce their photographs:

Key: a=above; t=top; c=center; b=bottom; l=left; r=right; bi=background image; mi=main image

1 Archives of American Art, Smithsonian Institution. 2–3 Library of Congress. 4–5 Nevada Historical Society, Reno: 4tr; National Museum of American History, Behring Center, Smithsonian Institution: 5cr; Library of Congress: 5bl. 6–7: David J. &Janice L. Frent Collection/CORBIS: 6tl; Bettmann/CORBIS: 6bl, 6cr; Hulton-Deutsch Collection/CORBIS: 7tl; DK Picture Library, Monique le Luhandre: 7bl; CORBIS/Pool/Chuck Kennedy: 7crb; 8–9 National Museum of the American Indian, Smithsonian Institution: 8tl; The Metropolitan Museum of Art, Gift of John Stewart Kennedy, 1897. (97.34) Photograph ©1992 The Metropolitan Museum of Art: 8–9b; DK Picture Library, Geoff Brightling: 9tr. 10–11 Underwood & Underwood/CORBIS: 10l; Library of Congress: 10tr; National Museum of American History, Behring Center, Smithsonian Institution: 11bl; National Portrait Gallery, Smithsonian Institution: 10r. 12–13 Bettmann/CORBIS: mi. 14–15 American Museum of Natural History: 14–15t, 15c, 15br; Smithsonian American Art Museum: 14–15b. 16–17 National Museum of the American Indian, Smithsonian Institution: 16tl, 16tr, 16b, 17cl, 17tc; Nevada Historical Society, Reno: 17tr; American Museum of

Natural History: 17cr, 17br. 18–19 National Museum of American History, Behring Center, Smithsonian Institution: 18cl, 18bc, 18tr; Library of Congress: 18–19. 20–21 Dave G. Houser/CORBIS: 20br; Bettmann/CORBIS: 21. 22–23 National Museum of American History, Behring Center, Smithsonian Institution: mi. 24–25 Bettmann/CORBIS: 24tr; Lee Snider/CORBIS: 24br; Library of Congress: 25tr; National Park Service, Colonial National Historical Park: 25b. 26–27 Florida Department of State, Division of Historical Resources (photo by Ray Stanyard): 26bl; Louisiana State Museum: 26–27b, 27cr (Gift of the Friends of the Cabildo). 28–29 Richard J. Berenson: 28bl; National Museum of American History, Behring Center, Smithsonian Institution: 28tr; Bettmann/CORBIS: 29tl, 29r. 30–31 National Numismatics Collection, Smithsonian Institution: 30tr; Bettmann/CORBIS: 30l, 31cr; National Anthropological Archives, Smithsonian Institution: 31tl. 32–33 Library of Congress: 32cl; National Portrait Gallery, Smithsonian Institution: 32tr; National Museum of American History, Behring Center, Smithsonian Institution: 33tl; Charleston Library Society, Charleston, S.C.: 33cl, 32–33b. 34–35: Library of Congress: 34l; National Museum of American History, Behring Center, Smithsonian Institution: 34bc; National Portrait Gallery, Smithsonian Institution. 36–37 National Museum of American History, Behring Center, Smithsonian Institution: 37cl, 37b; Bettmann/CORBIS: 37tr. 38–39 National Portrait Gallery, Smithsonian Institution: mi. 40–41 Bettmann/CORBIS: 40cl; National Portrait Gallery, Smithsonian Institution: 41tr; Library of Congress: 40–41b. 42–43 Smithsonian American Art Museum: 42bl; Dover Pictorial Archives: 42tr; Royal Artillery Institute, Museum of Artillery: 43tr; 95th Rifels Private Collection Mr. A.D. Theobald of the Royal Signals Museum: 43t; National Postal Museum, Smithsonian Institution: 43bc; Library of Congress: mi. 44–45 National Portrait Gallery, Smithsonian Institution: mi; Corbis: 45cr; Scott T. Smith/CORBIS: 45br. 46–47 The Metropolitan Museum of Art, Gift of John Stewart Kennedy, 1897. (97.34) Photograph ©1992 The Metropolitan Museum of Art: 46b; Library of Congress: 46t. 48–49 Bettmann/CORBIS: 48tl; Corbis: 49t; Library of Congress: 48–49. 50–51 National Numismatic Collection, Smithsonian Institution: 50tl, 50tc, 50cl; Corbis: 50bl, 50tr; Bettmann/CORBIS: 51. 52–53 National Archives: 52tr; Bettmann/CORBIS: 52–53. 54–55 National Portrait Gallery, Smithsonian Institution: 54cla, 54cl, 54tr; Navy Department Library, Naval Historical Center, Washington,

D.C.: 54bc; National Museum of American History, Behring Center, Smithsonian Institution: 55. 56–57 Woolaroc Museum, Bartlesville, Oklahoma: mi. 58–59 National Portrait Gallery, Smithsonian Institution: 58tr; Library of Congress: 58c; Bettmann/CORBIS: 58bl, 59tl, 59br. 60–61 Library of Congress: 60bl; National Museum of American History, Behring Center, Smithsonian Institution: 60cr, 61tc, 60–61b. 62–63 National Museum of American History, Behring Center, Smithsonian Institution: 62bl, mi. Bettmann/CORBIS: 62tr, 63tr. 64–65 National Portrait Gallery, Smithsonian Institution: 64cl, 64bl, 64bc; Bettmann/CORBIS: 64cr, 65. 66–67 Museum of the Mountain Man: 66cl; Utah State Historical Society: 67tl; Woolaroc Museum, Bartlesville, Oklahoma: 67cr; Library of Congress: 67bc. 68–69 Library of Congress: 68tr, 68–69, 69tr; National Numismatics Collection, Smithsonian Institution: 69br. 70–71 Library of Congress, Washington, D.C.: mi. 72–73 Bettmann/CORBIS: 72bl; Library of Congress: 73t; South Carolina Historical Society: 73b; 74–75 Library of Congress: 74t, 75br; Corbis ©Joseph Sohm; ChromoSohm Inc./CORBIS: 74cl; Louisiana State Museum, Gift of Mrs. J. Davidson: 74bc; Christie's Images/CORBIS: 75tl; Bettmann/CORBIS: 75tr; Richard Hamilton Smith/CORBIS: bi. 76–77 National Portrait Gallery, Smithsonian Institution: 76tr; Richard J. Berenson: 76c; National Museum of American History, Behring Center, Smithsonian Institution: 76bl; Corbis: 77t; Bettmann/CORBIS: 77b. 78–79 Bettmann/CORBIS: 78cl; Library of Congress: 78–79b. 80–81 Library of Congress: 80tl, 81tc; National Portrait Gallery, Smithsonian Institution: 80cr, 81tl, 81cr, 81br, 81bc, 81bl; National Museum of American History, Behring Center, Smithsonian Institution: 81tr; Francis G. Mayer/CORBIS: 80bl; Medford Historical Society Collection/CORBIS: bi. 82–83 Library of Congress: 83bc; Corbis: 83cr. 84–85 Gettysburg National Military Park: 84cl; Library of Congress: 84tr, 85tr; National Museum of American History, Behring Center, Smithsonian Institution: 85tl; Bettmann/CORBIS: mi. 86–87 Bettmann/CORBIS: 86tl; Library of Congress: 86bl; National Portrait Gallery, Smithsonian Institution: 86–87. 88–89 National Portrait Gallery, Smithsonian Institution: 88cl, 88tr; Library of Congress: 88bl, 89cr; National Museum of American History, Behring Center, Smithsonian Institution: mi, 89tr. 90–91 Library of Congress: 90bl; Bettmann/CORBIS: 90–91; National Portrait Gallery, Smithsonian Institution: 91tr. 92–93 Solomon D. Butcher Collection, Nebraska State Historical Society: mi. 94–95 Library of Congress: 94tr, 94cl; Bettmann/CORBIS: mi, 95cr; National

Museum of American History, Behring Center, Smithsonian Institution: 95tc. 96–97 National Museum of American History, Behring Center, Smithsonian Institution: 96tr; Library of Congress: 96–97b; National Portrait Gallery, Smithsonian Institution: 97tl, 97cr, 97b; DK Picture Library, Geoff Brightling: 97tr. 98–99 National Portrait Gallery, Smithsonian Institution: 98tr, 99tr; Bettmann/CORBIS: 98–99b; National Anthropological Archives, Smithsonian Institution: 99cl; Corbis: 99br. 100–101 Library of Congress: 100bc; Solomon D. Butcher Collection, Nebraska State Historical Society: 100–101c; Bettmann/CORBIS: 101tr; Smithsonian Institution Libraries: 101bra; National Museum of American History, Behring Center, Smithsonian Institution: 101br. 102–103 Library of Congress: mi. 104–105 Library of Congress: 104l, 104c; National Museum of American History, Behring Center, Smithsonian Institution: 104br, 105tl; Bettmann/CORBIS: 105br. 106–107 Library of Congress: 106tr, 107b; Corbis: 106b; Underwood & Underwood/CORBIS: 107tl. 108–109 National Museum of American History, Behring Center, Smithsonian Institution: 108l, 109bl, 109cr; Bettmann/CORBIS: 108–109; National Portrait Gallery, Smithsonian Institution: 109tr. 110–111 Bettmann/CORBIS: 110tl; National Portrait Gallery, Smithsonian Institution: 110tr; Francis G. Mayer/CORBIS: 110bl; Christie's Images/CORBIS: mi; Library of Congress: 111cla; National Museum of American History, Behring Center, Smithsonian Institution: 111cl; Smithsonian Institution Libraries: 111tr. 112–113 Bettmann/CORBIS: 112tr; Library of Congress: mi; Archives of American Art, Smithsonian Institution: 113tr; Union Pacific Railroad Museum: 113bc. 114–115 National Museum of American History, Behring Center, Smithsonian Institution: 114cl; Bettmann/CORBIS: mi, 115br; Library of Congress: 115tc, 115cr. 116–117 National Museum of American History, Behring Center, Smithsonian Institution: 116tr; Library of Congress: 116b, 117tl; National Postal Museum, Smithsonian Institution: 117bl; Corbis: 117br. 118–119 National Air and Space Museum, Smithsonian Institution: mi. 120–121 National Museum of American History, Behring Center, Smithsonian Institution: 120tr, 120bl, 120–121b; National Portrait Gallery, Smithsonian Institution: 121tl; Corbis: 121c; National Museum of American History, Behring Center, Smithsonian Institution: 121bc. 122–123 Library of Congress: mi, 123cr; Corbis: 123tl. 124–125 Library of Congress: 124tl, 124bc; National Portrait Gallery, Smithsonian Institution: 124tr; National Museum of American History, Behring Center, Smithsonian Institution: 125tr; Bettmann/CORBIS: 125b. 126–127 Library of Congress: 126cl; Sagamore Hill National Historic Site: 126bl; Corbis: 126br, 127cl; Underwood & Underwood/CORBIS: 127r.

128–129 Bettmann/CORBIS: 128tr, 129tl; 128bc, 129tr; National Air and Space Museum, Smithsonian Institution: mi, 129br. 130–131 Mary Evans Picture Library: mi. 132–133 Library of Congress: 132t, 132b, 133tr; Getty Images: Time Life Pictures / The LIFE Picture Collection: 132cra; National Museum of American History, Behring Center, Smithsonian Institution: 133b; Medialibrary: 133c. 134–135 Theodore Roosevelt Collection, Harvard College Library: 134cl; Bettmann/CORBIS: 134tr, 135cr; Library of Congress: 134–135b; National Museum of American History, Behring Center, Smithsonian Institution: 135c. 136–137 Bettmann/CORBIS: 136cl; Corbis: 137tl; Mary Evans Picture Library: mi; 138–139 National Museum of American History, Behring Center, Smithsonian Institution: 138bl, 138–139t, 139cr. 140–141 Bettmann/CORBIS: 140–141, 140tr, 141br; National Museum of American History, Behring Center, Smithsonian Institution: 140bc; National Air and Space Museum, Smithsonian Institution: 141tl; National Archives: 141tr. 142–143 National Portrait Gallery, Smithsonian Institution: 142cl; Bettmann/CORBIS: mi. 144–145 Library of Congress: 144cl, 144tr; Bettmann/CORBIS: 145tr; National Portrait Gallery, Smithsonian Institution: 145mi. 146–147 Bettmann/CORBIS: mi. 148–149 Bettmann/CORBIS: 148tr, mi, 149br; National Museum of American History, Behring Center, Smithsonian Institution: 149tr. 150–151 Library of Congress: 150tr; Bettmann/CORBIS: mi; David J. &Janice L. Frent Collection/CORBIS: 150cr. 152–153 Underwood & Underwood/CORBIS: 152l; Bettmann/CORBIS: 152–153, 153cr; National Portrait Gallery, Smithsonian Institution: 153tc, 153tr, 153bl. 154–155 National Museum of American History, Behring Center, Smithsonian Institution: 154cl, 154tr; Bettmann/CORBIS: 154bl, 154br, 155tr, mi; CORBIS: 155bc; National Portrait Gallery, Smithsonian Institution: 155cr; National Air and Space Museum, Smithsonian Institution: 155bra. 156–157 Library of Congress: 156b, 157b; Bettmann/CORBIS: 156c; National Museum of American History, Behring Center, Smithsonian Institution: 156tr, 157c. 158–159 Smithsonian American Art Museum: mi. 160–161 Bettmann/CORBIS: 160bl, mi; Library of Congress: 161tr; National Portrait Gallery, Smithsonian Institution: 161cr. 162–163 National Portrait Gallery, Smithsonian Institution: 162cl; National Museum of American History, Behring Center, Smithsonian Institution: 162br; Bettmann/CORBIS: 163bl, 163t. 164–165 Bettmann/CORBIS: 164b; Franklin D. Roosevelt Presidential Library: 165tl; National Museum of American History, Behring Center, Smithsonian Institution: 165c. 166–167 Corbis: 166tr; Library of Congress: mi; Bettmann/CORBIS: 167tr. 168–169 Bettmann/CORBIS:

168cl, 168tr, bi, 169cl, 169cr, 169br. Forrest J. Ackerman Collection/CORBIS: 168cr; Lake County Museum/CORBIS: 168br; John Springer Collection/CORBIS: 169tr. 170–171 Smithsonian American Art Museum: 170cl; Library of Congress: 170tr; Bettmann/CORBIS: 170–171b; National Portrait Gallery, Smithsonian Institution: 171tl, 171tr. 172–173 Corbis Royalty-Free: mi. 174–175 Library of Congress: 174cl; Imperial War Museum: 174tr, 175cr; National Archives: 154–155c; Peter Newark's Military Pictures: 174bc; Topham Picturepoint: 175tr; National Portrait Gallery, Smithsonian Institution: 175br. 176–177 Mary Evans Picture Library: 176bl; Corbis Royalty-Free: 176tr, 176–177b; Corbis: 177tr. 178–179 National Archives: 178bl; Franklin D. Roosevelt Library: 178tr; National Portrait Gallery, Smithsonian Institution, ©Yousuf Karsh: 179tr; Corbis Royalty-Free: mi; Corbis: 179bl. 180–181 Library of Congress: 180cl; Bettmann/CORBIS: mi; National Archives: 181br. 182–183 National Archives: 182bl; Franklin D. Roosevelt Library: mi; National Museum of American History, Behring Center, Smithsonian Institution: 183br. 184–185 Library of Congress: 184bl; Corbis: 184c; Corbis Royalty-Free: 185br; Imperial War Museum: 184tr; Spink and Son, Ltd.: 185tr. 186–187 National Museum of American History, Behring Center, Smithsonian Institution: 186trc, 186tra, 186trb; Library of Congress: 186b, 187br; Corbis Royalty-Free: 187bl; Peter Newark's American Pictures: 187tr. 188–189 Corbis: 188tr; Bettmann/CORBIS: mi; Imperial War Museum: 189t. 190–191 Imperial War Museum: 190tr; Bettmann/CORBIS: mi, 191tr, 191br; Library of Congress: 191tc. 192–193 Getty Images—Hulton Archive: 192cl; Bettmann/CORBIS: mi, 193br; Corbis: 193bc. 194–195 Bettmann/CORBIS: mi. 196–197 Franklin D. Roosevelt Library: 196cl, 196tr; Hulton-Deutsch Collection/CORBIS: 196–197b; Bettmann/CORBIS: 197tl, 197cr; Library of Congress: 197br. 198–199 National Postal Museum, Smithsonian Institution: 198bl; National Portrait Gallery, Smithsonian Institution: mi, 199tr; National Museum of American History, Behring Center, Smithsonian Institution: 199c; Bettmann/CORBIS: 199br. 200–201 National Archives: 200; Bettmann/CORBIS: 201tr; DK Picture Library, Kim Sayer: 201b. 202–203 National Air and Space Museum, Smithsonian Institution: 202bl, 203br; Library of Congress: mi, 203tr. 204–205 National Archives: 204tl; Bettmann/CORBIS: 204bl; Harry S. Truman Library: 205tc; National Portrait Gallery, Smithsonian Institution: mi. 206–207 Bradley Smith/CORBIS: 206bl; National Museum of American History, Behring Center, Smithsonian Institution: 206–207, 207c; Bettmann/CORBIS: 207tr, 207br. 208–209 Library of Congress: mi. 210–211 National Museum of American History, Behring Center, Smithsonian Institution: 210c;

John F. Kennedy Library: mi, 211tr; DK Picture Library, Stephen Oliver: 211bl; Library of Congress: 211br. 212–213 National Museum of American History, Behring Center, Smithsonian Institution: 212tl, 212br; National Portrait Gallery, Smithsonian Institution, © Ida Berman, courtesy Steven Kasher Gallery, NY: 212bl; Bettmann/CORBIS: 212tr; Library of Congress: 213cl; Flip Schulke/CORBIS: mi. 214–215 National Museum of American History, Behring Center, Smithsonian Institution: 214bl, 215tr; John F. Kennedy Library: 214r; Bettmann/CORBIS: 215b. 216–217 Bettmann/CORBIS: 216cl, mi, 217cl; Owen Franken/CORBIS: 216tr; Library of Congress: 217tl, 217tr; Hulton-Deutsch Collection/CORBIS: 217br. 218–219 Bettmann/CORBIS: 218cl; National Archives: 218cr; Library of Congress: 218br, 219cl; National Portrait Gallery, Smithsonian Institution: mi. 220–221 Advertising Archive: 220cl; Library of Congress: 220tr; National Aeronautics and Space Administration: mi, 221br. 222–223 Nik Wheeler/CORBIS: mi. 224–225 Bettmann/CORBIS: 224; Library of Congress: 225tl, 225tr, 225bc. 226–227 National Archives: 226bl, 227br; Hulton-Deutsch Collection/CORBIS: 226c; National Museum of American History, Behring Center, Smithsonian Institution: 227tr, 227c; Library of Congress: 227bl. 228–229 AFP/CORBIS: 228cl; Cecil Stoughton, White House/John F. Kennedy Library: 228tr; National Museum of American History, Behring Center, Smithsonian Institution: 228bl; National Archives: 229tr; Nik Wheeler/CORBIS: 229b. 230–231 Bettmann/CORBIS: 230bl, 230tr, mi, 231tl; Henry Ditz/CORBIS: 231tr; Roger Ressmeyer/CORBIS: 231cr. 232–233 National Museum of American History, Behring Center, Smithsonian Institution: 232bl, 232tr; Corbis: mi; Bettmann/CORBIS: 233tr; Wally McNamee/CORBIS: 233br. 234–235 National Archives, 234bl; National Museum of American History, Behring Center, Smithsonian Institution: 234tr; Bettmann/CORBIS: 234r; Jimmy Carter Library: 235tl; Rex Features/Sipa Press: 235br. 236–237 ©Lee Snider; Lee Snider/CORBIS: mi. 238–239 James Leynse/CORBIS SABA: 238cl; Ronald Reagan Presidential Library: mi; Bettmann/CORBIS: 239tl, 239cr; Robert Maass/CORBIS: 239br. 240–241 Ronald Reagan Presidential Library: 240tc; ©Lee Snider; Lee Snider/CORBIS: mi; DK Picture Library: 241tl; DK Picture Library, Monique le Luhandre: 241tc; DK Picture Library, Matthew Ward: 241tr. 242–243 Richard Hamilton Smith/CORBIS: 242cl; DK Picture Library, Matthew Ward: 242tr; Neal Preston/CORBIS: 242br; Jacques M. Chenet/CORBIS: mi; Robert Maass/CORBIS: 243tr;

Bettmann/CORBIS: 243bl. 244–245 Wally McNamee/CORBIS: 244bl, 245tr; Bill Pierce/Corbis Sygma: 244tr; Roger Ressmeyer/CORBIS: 244c; Ronald Reagan Presidential Library: 245b. 246–247 Peter Turnley/CORBIS: 246–247b; Rex Features: 246tr; Susan Biddle, The White House: 247t; National Air and Space Museum, Smithsonian Institution: 247br. 248–249 Reuters NewMedia Inc/CORBIS: mi. 250–251 ©Joseph Sohm; ChromoSohm Inc/CORBIS: 250tr; National Portrait Gallery, Smithsonian Institution: 250–251, 251cl; AFP/CORBIS: 251tr; Rex Features: 251br. 252–253 Reuters NewMedia Inc/CORBIS: 252–253; AFP/CORBIS: 253tr; Frederic Neema/Corbis Sygma: 253br. 254–255 Morton Beebe/CORBIS: 254bl; ©Joseph Sohm; ChromoSohm Inc/CORBIS: mi; Adam Mastoon/CORBIS: 255bc; Rex Features: 255tl. 256–257 Rod Aydelotte/Corbis Sygma: 256cl; Rex Features: 256r; Reuters NewMedia Inc/CORBIS: 257tr, 257br, 257bl. 258–259 Les Stone/Corbis Sygma: 258b; John H. White/Corbis Sygma: 258tr; David Turnley/CORBIS: 259tl; Reuters NewMedia Inc/CORBIS: 259br. 260–261 Masatumo Kuriya/Corbis Sygma. 262–263 Reuters NewMedia Inc/CORBIS: 262b, 262tr, 263br; AFP/CORBIS: 263tl. 264–265 Reuters NewMedia Inc/CORBIS: 264bl; Masatumo Kuriya/Corbis Sygma: mi. AFP/CORBIS: 265tr.; Reuters/Dan Lampariello/CORBIS 265cr. 266–267 Epa/Angelia Warmuth/CORBIS 266c; CORBIS/Science Faction/Ed Darack: mi; CORBIS/Christophe Calais: 267tr; CORBIS/CNP/Ron Sachs: 267tc; CORBIS/Peter Souza/White House/Handout/The White House: 267cr. 268–269 Alamy Images/Ian Dagnall: 268clb; CORBIS/Reuters/Aly Song: mi; Alamy Images/lovethephoto: 269cra; CORBIS/Reuters/Shannon Stapleton: 269bc; Getty Images/Stringer/Ben Hider: 269tl. 270–271 CORBIS/Newsport/Mifune Takamitsu: 270cra; CORBIS/Newsport/Paul Kitagaki Jr. 270b; CORBIS/David Bergman 271cr; 123RF.com/Leonard Zhukovsky 271tr; CORBIS/Reuters/Francois Lenoir: 271bc; Getty Images: 271bl; FIFA via Getty Images: 271cla. 272–273 CORBIS/Science Faction/U.S. Coast Guard – digital ve: 272b; CORBIS/Aurora Photos/Svetlana Bachevanova: 273tc; CORBIS/Mike Hollingshead: 273br; Getty Images/AFP/Nicholas Kamm: 273cl, 273cra. 274–275 National Aeronautics and Space Administration: 274bl. CORBIS/epa/Paul Buck: mi; CORBIS/Reuters/Sean Gardner: 275tr; Getty Images/AFP/Stan Honda: 275br; Dreamstime.com: Sergey Uryadnikov / Surz01: 275ca. 276–277 CORBIS/Star Ledger/Bob Sciarrino: 276bl; Getty Images: 276cl; CORBIS/Pool/Chuck Kennedy: mi; CORBIS/Reuters/

Noah Berger: 277tl; CORBIS/Reuters/Harrison Mcclary: 277tr; CORBIS/Steven Clevenger: 277bl; Getty Images: 277br; Alamy Stock Photo: White House Photo: 277c. 278–279 Getty Images: Neilson Barnard/WireImage: mi; Getty Images: Bloomberg: 278bl; Alamy Stock Photo: Shelly Rivoli: 279br; Dreamstime.com: Vladgalenko: 279cra; Getty Images: David Hume Kennerly/Archive Photos: 279cla. 280–281 CORBIS/ZUMA Press/Pat Vasquez-Cunningham: 280cra; Getty Images/Barcroft Media via Getty Images: 280b; CORBIS/Demotix/Yunus Emre Caylak: 281br; CORBIS/T.J. Kirkpatrick: 281tl; CORBIS/Reuters/Daniel Acker: 281cr. 282–283 CORBIS/National Geographic Society/Mark Thiessen: 282r; Getty Images/Alex Wong: 282cl; CORBIS/cultura/Monty Rakusen: 283cr; CORBIS/Reuters/Mike Segar: 283bl; CORBIS/Reuters/Cheryl Gerber: 283br; Getty Images/AFP/Robyn Beck: 283tl. 284–285 Jacques M. Chenet/CORBIS: mi. 286–287 Dreamstime.com: Natallia Hudyma / euro_ace: bi; all other images National Portrait Gallery, Smithsonian Institution except the following: John F. Kennedy Library: #35; Reuters NewMedia Inc/CORBIS: #43; Dreamstime.com/Featureflash: #44; Dreamstime.com: Claudio Lee Smith: #45. 288–289 Todd Gipstein/CORBIS: bi. 290–291 Bettmann/CORBIS: mi. 292–293 National Archives: 293br. 294–295 National Museum of American History, Behring Center, Smithsonian Institution: 294tc; National Portrait Gallery, Smithsonian Institution: 294br, 285br. 296–297 Library of Congress: 297br. 298–299 National Museum of American History, Behring Center, Smithsonian Institution: 298b. 300–301 Bettmann/CORBIS: 300b; Library of Congress: 301bi, 301mi.

Illustration: Dan Green

All other images © Dorling Kindersley

For further information see:
www.dkimages.com